KUNG-FU MONTHLY

THE ARCHIVE SERIES

THE POSTER MAGAZINES
VOLUME TWO

COMPILED AND EDITED BY
CARL FOX

PIT WHEEL PRESS
BARNSLEY

THE KUNG FU CODE!

KUNG FU IS NOT A GAME. KUNG FU IS A HIGHLY SKILLED ART WHICH, IF MISUSED BY THE UNTRAINED, CAN BE DEADLY!

IT TOOK BRUCE LEE MANY YEARS OF BACK-BREAKING TRAINING TO MASTER THE ART OF KUNG FU, AND WHEN HE DIED, HE WAS STILL LEARNING. BRUCE NEVER USED KUNG FU AGAINST ANYONE IN ANGER IN HIS LIFE. HE KNEW ONLY TOO WELL ITS DANGEROUS POWER; THE SAME POWER THAT THE FIGHTING SHAOLIN MONKS SWORE NEVER TO USE TO DELIBERATELY KILL OR INJURE ANY OPPONENT.

SO IF YOU ARE THINKING OF TAKING UP THE MARTIAL ARTS, AND WHO ISN'T AFTER A GLIMPSE OF THE LITTLE DRAGON'S EXPLOITS ON THE SILVER SCREEN, BE PREPARED TO DEVOTE A LARGE PART OF YOUR DAILY LIFE TO ITS STUDY AND PRACTICE. ALSO, MAKE SURE YOU JOIN A REPUTABLE CLUB RUN BY SOMEONE WHO KNOWS WHAT THEY'RE TALKING ABOUT.

AND IF YOU'RE NOT PREPARED TO BECOME A KUNG FU DISCIPLE, THEN LEAVE THE FIGHTING TO THE EXPERTS!

Published by
PIT WHEEL PRESS LIMITED
www.pitwheelpress.com

Copyright © 2024 Carl Fox.
All Right Reserved. No part of this book may be reproduced, scanned or distributed in any printed or electronic form without permission.

KUNG-FU MONTHLY

Copyright © 1974-1984 by H. Bunch Associates Ltd. (except where copyright on certain photographic material already exists). This publication or any parts thereof may not be reproduced in any form whatsoever without permission in writing from the copyright proprietor.

A Pit Wheel Press edition, published by special arrangement with Dennis Publishing, London.

Printed in the United Kingdom
ISBN 978-1-915414-09-0

BRUCE LEE is a trademark of Bruce Lee Enterprises, LLC.

Dedicated to everyone involved in the creation and cultivation of Kung-Fu Monthly

ACKNOWLEDGEMENTS

I would like to thank the following people for their help
and participation in the making of this book:

Richard Adams
Don Atyeo
Ricky Baker
James Bishop
Fergus Byrne
Kieran Clarkin
Jeff Cummins
Jonathon Green
Peter Jagger
Colin James
David Jenkins

John Little
Bey Logan
Tony Lundberg
Michael Nesbitt
John Overall
Dick Pountain
Matthew Robins
Bruce Sawford
Carlotta Serantoni
Paul Simmons
Andrew Staton

CREDITS

Original Poster Magazine Staff

Richard Adams, Don Atyeo, Felix Dennis, Jonathon Green,
Colin James, Bey Logan, Perry Neville, Dick Pountain,
Mikki Rain, Chris Rowley, Bruce Sawford & Paul Simmons

The Kung-Fu Monthly Archive Series

Research, Editing, Layout & Design
Carl Fox

Editorial Assistance
George Fox

Photograph Acknowlegements
**Kung-Fu Monthly, Carl Fox, Michael Nesbitt
& Dennis Publishing**

Kung-Fu Monthly Collage Image
Copyright © 2024 Carl Fox

KUNG-FU MONTHLY

THE ARCHIVE SERIES
CONTENTS

ISSUE	27
ISSUE	28
ISSUE	29
ISSUE	30
ISSUE	31
ISSUE	32
ISSUE	33
ISSUE	34
ISSUE	35
ISSUE	36
ISSUE	37
ISSUE	38
ISSUE	39
ISSUE	40
ISSUE	41
ISSUE	42
ISSUE	43
ISSUE	44
ISSUE	45
ISSUE	46
ISSUE	48
ISSUE	49
ISSUE	50
ISSUE	51
ISSUE	52
ISSUE	53
ISSUE	54
ISSUE	55

039
055
069
083
099
111
125
139
153
167
179
193
207
221
235
249
263
277
291
305
333
345
359
375
391
407
421
437

KUNG-FU MONTHLY

THE ARCHIVE SERIES
ABOUT THE SERIES

Kung-Fu Monthly is a name synonymous with Bruce Lee, not only in the United Kingdom but throughout the world. It is a legend in its own right and a brand immediately recognisable by not only the font but also the famous 'flying man' logo.

The popularity of the magazine at the peak of the Kung Fu Craze in the 1970s was unrivalled and its success was almost entirely down to pure luck.

Legend has it that *Kung-Fu Monthly* began life as a gamble by underground comic book publisher Felix Dennis after questioning a queue of kids outside a Soho cinema, waiting to see *Enter the Dragon* in early 1974. On paper, the idea seemed to serve the then-current trend of Bruce Lee and was deemed to have a shelf life of three to six months but a year after its launch, *Kung-Fu Monthly* had become the biggest-selling Bruce Lee magazine in the world.

After the demise of the Official Bruce Lee Fan Club in 1976, *Kung-Fu Monthly* launched their own. The KFM Bruce Lee Society ran for thirty quarterly newsletters from 1976 to 1983 and at the time of closing, had seen over five thousand eager Bruce Lee fans become members throughout its tenure, with the formidable Pam Hadden at the forefront throughout its seven active years.

Kung-Fu Monthly and The Bruce Lee Society were jointly responsible for the UK's first Bruce Lee Convention held on May 19th 1979 and the first Bruce Lee Film Festival held on December 1st 1979.

Kung-Fu Monthly and later *Personal Computer World*, had turned H. Bunch Associates from an underground publisher on the verge of bankruptcy to a publishing powerhouse, eventually becoming Dennis Publishing, named after its founder, Felix Dennis.

That leads us to today.

In February 2021, I approached Dennis Publishing with an idea for a project that I'd considered for many years - scan, convert, edit and compile all seventy-nine issues of the iconic *Kung-Fu Monthly* magazine into book form, in order to present it to a new audience, as well as preserve its place in history.

It was the longest-running dedicated Bruce Lee magazine of its kind anywhere in the world (by frequency and circulation) and I wanted to pay homage to that. Such was its success and popularity that it was licensed throughout the world; in fourteen countries and in eleven languages. That doesn't even take into account the non-official bootlegs which appeared in China and Turkey. Nothing has matched it before or since. It truly has stood the test of time and having done so, has reached legendary status.

Kung-Fu Monthly is a snapshot of a time long gone; a time which the original fans remember with fondness and a time which new fans will hopefully discover.

The *Kung-Fu Monthly Archive Series* is dedicated to Felix Dennis and everyone associated with the magazine; not just the staff but also the fans, who would buy copies of the magazines in their millions over its lifetime and help cement the publication's place in British Pop Culture history.

Special thanks must also go to Carlotta Serantoni at Dennis Publishing for her assistance in allowing this project to go ahead.

Carl Fox
February 2022

KUNG-FU MONTHLY

THE POSTER MAGAZINES
INTRODUCTION

THE POSTER MAGAZINES - VOLUME TWO

For me, *Kung-Fu Monthly* is a British institution, just like Fish and Chips, Beans on Toast or the humble Sausage Roll. Even though it was published in other parts of the world, it was in Britain - its home - where it was the most popular and is most fondly remembered. It was one of the first of its kind; its folded poster magazine format being cutting edge for the time.

History has always been important and of great interest to me. Being born halfway through Bruce Lee Mania meant that my introduction and education of it came much later. *Kung-Fu Monthly* is representative of the start of the Kung Fu Craze in 1974, through its peak at the end of the 70s with the release of Lee's final film *Game of Death*, to its demise in 1984, a decade after it all began.

Everyone has a story of how they discovered *Kung-Fu Monthly*. As a six-year-old around 1984, I discovered an older cousin watching *Enter the Dragon* on home video, after which he gave me some of his spare *Kung-Fu Monthly* posters. Like a lot of fans at that time, his interest dwindled, and I copped for his 'hand me down' collection of Bruce Lee memorabilia; not that I complained though. It was also a time when I would go with my late Dad to the local video store - The Chantry above the Chinese restaurant on Peel Parade in Barnsley - and sit on the floor at the top of the stairs looking at the Kung Fu video covers, pestering the poor bugger to rent *The Chinese Boxer*, *The Dynamite Brothers*, *Dragon Claw*s or whatever else they had. The funny thing is, he did. He'd happily rent whatever X-Rated Kung Fu video for the eight-year-old me; how cool (and irresponsible) was that?! But that was how my love of Kung Fu movies started. Seeing the *Kung-Fu Monthly* font and logo takes me back to that time. I can almost smell the Chinese food that wafted through the open window of the restaurant kitchen as I climbed the stairs of The Chantry or see the dirty grey carpet I'd sit cross-legged on when I got up those stairs.

A few years after that time, at the age of ten, I began training at the Barnsley Shotokan Karate Club with Mick and Lynn Padgett. The club was located above Mick's Zanshin Martial Arts shop located just two doors up from the old Chantry video shop I had frequented several years earlier. As well as being great ambassadors for Shotokan Karate and the Karate Union of Great Britain, Mick and Lynn have become good friends over the years and in 2021 taught the second generation of my family when my son began training under their wonderful and respected tutelage.

A lot of *Kung-Fu Monthly* collectors regard opening the old poster magazines as something of a special treat. Due to the age and the paper they were printed on, repeated opening and closing weakened the folds and risked permanent damage to their beloved collection. Due to that risk, very few collectors and fans bother to read the magazines anymore which is such a shame, as the articles and letters contained within are a rare snapshot of the material that the first generation of Bruce Lee fans enjoyed.

In February 2021, I tentatively approached the copyright owners of *Kung-Fu Monthly*, Dennis Publishing, to enquire about reprinting the material in a volume of books. After holding an internal meeting and to my astonishment, their Head of Licensing informed me that they had given me permission to go ahead with the project with their blessing. With Dennis Publishing's permission, I began the mammoth task of scanning each magazine, converting the images to text with optical character recognition software and correcting each one manually before reassembling it with a new layout.

While working on editing the magazines, I had the opportunity to speak with *Kung-Fu*

THE KUNG-FU MONTHLY ARCHIVE SERIES

Monthly contributors Don Atyeo, Richard Adams, Bruce Sawford, Jonathon Green, Paul Simmons, Dick Pountain, Jeff Cummins and Felix Dennis biographer Fergus Byrne to ask them about their experiences of working on the magazine and/or with Felix Dennis. After completing the first twenty-six issues at over four-hundred pages, it was apparent that the books containing the poster magazines would have to be split into three separate volumes due to concerns that too many pages would put too much strain on the spine. With that in mind, I decided to write a history of *Kung-Fu Monthly*, to be split into two parts; Part One would cover the first half of the publication's life from 1973-1979 and Part Two would cover the second half from 1980-1984.

From reading the articles as I edited them, I found a new love and appreciation for the material of the time. Some of the articles were extremely informative and looking back at them, its amazing how accurate they were at a time when there was no internet. There are first-hand accounts and reactions to key milestones in the Kung Fu Craze such as the anticipation and then disappointment to the release of Lee's final unfinished film *Game of Death* in 1978 and the organisation of the First Official Bruce Lee Convention in 1979. By reading the magazine articles, you really get a feel of what it must have been like for the fans in those early years. Their overwhelming excitement for one last chance to see their idol on screen in *Game of Death*, turned to bitter disappointment at what they actually saw when the time came; a mish-mash of a plot with a whole now-classic fight scene removed by the British Board of Film Censors. You feel their excitement and hope and then their pain and disappointment; every single last bit of it.

The staff at *Kung-Fu Monthly* realised very early on that if they put in the work, the fans would keep coming back for more, which they did. Their investigative journalism at the time was second to none in terms of Kung Fu magazines, which is hardly surprising considering their pedigree.

Other key features in the magazine include interviews with long-forgotten people of the time as well as full write-ups regarding Linda's forgotten ill-fated attempt to make a Bruce Lee biopic in partnership with Jon Peters and Barbra Streisand, a decade-and-a-half before she finally got *Dragon: The Bruce Lee Story* made with Universal Pictures in 1993.

I have tried to reproduce the magazine articles as closely as possible to the originals but I changed certain things if I felt the need to such as rearranging the order of the Kickback letters page to better utilise space or to correct spelling and grammatical errors. Most of the images were left as they were, with slight amendments to remove lines where the paper folds were. I did have the opportunity to replace some of the images with ones of better quality but if I did that, it wouldn't have been *Kung-Fu Monthly* and therefore I decided against doing so.

I have chopped and changed designs so many times in the past twelve months until I finally felt that I stumbled upon something that I felt truly represented the look and feel of *Kung-Fu Monthly* and here is the result of that work. It is something I am immensely proud to be associated with and I hope that you enjoy reading it - it really has been a labour of love for me.

'Til next time...

Carl Fox
February 2022

KUNG-FU MONTHLY

A HISTORY
THE BEGINNING OF THE END
1980-1984

THE POSTER MAGAZINES - VOLUME TWO

By 1980, the Kung Fu Craze was still going strong in the UK and so were *Kung-Fu Monthly*. The 1979 Convention had gone down a storm, as did the film festival in the same year. After the 1979 Convention, such was the success of the pre-recorded James Coburn tribute, that *Kung-Fu Monthly* did something unusual - they put it on a flexible vinyl disc to give away with *KFM* No.50, though they made a pre-warned one-off price increase to cover the production cost.

With the popularity of *Kung-Fu Monthly* spreading all over the world, foreign fans began attending the UK conventions. One such fan was Tony Lundberg, a 17 year old from Denmark, who travelled the 2000 miles over 24 hours on a bus to the 1980 Convention at the request of Bruce Lee Society president Pam Hadden to assist the *KFM* team at the event. The excitement of the fans was ecstatic as fans eagerly waited to get through the doors, including those who didn't have tickets to the already sold out event. Tony recalls, "I saw this huge line in front of the theatre and knew that I had to skip the line so I could be on time because a lot of people were waiting for me inside. So I had to push myself forward through the line towards the theatre as fast as possible but whilst doing so, people were getting angry at me, and started shouting at me to go back to the end of the line. So I had to tell them that I was there to help out at the convention. Some people started shouting and booing me. Some other people tried getting friendly with me, and thought they could show me the way in and come in for free. Funnily enough, they couldn't but I found my way in by myself eventually."

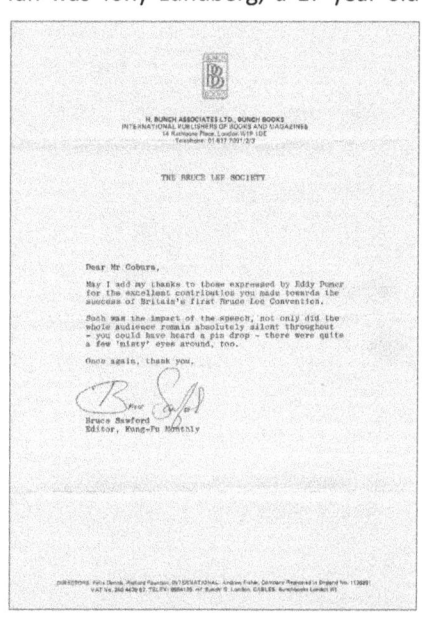

When there's money to be made, people notice and some began to stage their own conventions. Some of these conventions were blatant scams by taking people's money only to have fans turn up on the day to empty venues. Some events were genuine but were not without other controversies.

Such was the success of the *KFM* Conventions that other organisations began staging their own events, often gazumping the "official" ones by staging them slightly earlier.

The Bruce Lee Society's Pam Hadden was especially irked by a certain tactic. Pam spent countless hours creating lists of members' addresses - sorted by area - to send to members

so that they could write to and/or meet up with like-minded fans in their locale. Much to Pam's dismay, someone involved in one of the rival conventions obtained those lists and used them for marketing purposes by writing to Society members to publicise their event. In Issue 16, the June 1980 issue of the Society newsletter, Pam wrote, "Many members

have written to me as it seems confusion was rife on the date of the forthcoming Convention. It seems that, after the announcement of our July 19th event (YES, it is still on!) many members started to receive advertisements for another Convention, held in June. I'll leave you to draw your own conclusions as to the morals of the people concerned and would just add that quite a number of fans have said that they thought it unethical and certainly not something that a true Bruce Lee devotee would even consider doing. I also happen to know that a good number of the fans who were sent this material had NEVER knowingly given their addresses to the businessmen concerned. I can only assume, therefore, that our Area Lists have somehow fallen into their hands. It really hurts to think that one of our members has deliberately helped these people."

The tactics of these organisations wouldn't keep her down though and in a letter to Bruce Lee Society member Tony Lund-

Above: Promotional flyer for one of KFM's rival conventions, organised by SIP on Saturday June 14th 1980.
Below: The foyer and merchandise stand *at* KFM's first Bruce Lee convention in 1979. Photo courtesy of Michael Nesbitt.

berg in August 1981, Pam wrote, "Well, I'm not so angry anymore, only their behaviour in the past, using their proper name of SIP, and trying to ruin our Convention."

The 1980 convention was the last one held by *Kung-Fu Monthly*. The planned 1981 convention was cancelled at very short notice and the reason for the cancellation has never really been known but future editor Colin James was able to shed some light on it. "We had the venue booked but it was 'postponed.' The reason it was postponed was because you needed a name to be there and I can't remember who it was that was advertised but they kept putting off and we couldn't tie them down. The convention date was fast approaching and we still had no confirmation that person would turn up so basically it got pulled or 'postponed' as we said. That was a shame because even though the sales had obviously gone down from the peak of the magazine's success, it was still selling."

Colin James had started out at Bunch Books in the Mail Order Department. James recalled, "I moved from Liverpool to London for a two-week holiday and my sister was working at Bunch Books at the time. I didn't know anyone in London, so she said, 'Well, why don't you stuff some envelopes for us in the Back Issue Department?' which was mainly, *Which Bike?* and *Kung-Fu Monthly*. I just didn't go back to Liverpool after the two weeks."

At the end of the Seventies and the beginning of the Eighties, the original *Kung-Fu Monthly* team had pretty much taken a back seat in the magazine's publication. Bruce Sawford had taken over the role of Editor since *KFM* No.13, however continued to edit the magazine under the Felix Yen guise, before finally putting his name to the Editorial section of *KFM* No.56. A writer who played an integral part in the second half of *Kung-Fu Monthly*'s life was Eddy Pumer, a musician-turned-radio presenter for Capital Radio in London.

In the early 1970s, Pumer was a guitarist in the band Kaleidoscope - later Fairfield Parlour - and after the band folded, he began working at Capital Radio, where he produced radio shows for various presenters including Michael Aspel and Kenny Everett.

Another presenter Pumer would produce at Capital was Tony Myatt. In 1977, Myatt,

From The Archives!!

Two fabulous DOUBLE OFFERS.

BRUCE LEE, KING OF KUNG-FU

PLUS

BRUCE LEE'S GAME OF DEATH COLLECTOR'S EDITION

FOR ONLY £1.55 (Society Member's price, £1.40)

The Book of Kung-Fu

PLUS

Kung-Fu Monthly No. 4

FOR ONLY £1.20 (Society Member's price, £1.00)

All these historic publications are rare — and getting rarer! Don't miss this opportunity to update your kung-fu collection. Rush your order(s) to:

KFM Double Offer
14 Rathbone Place
London W1P 1DE

Cheques and postal orders made out to Kung-Fu Monthly — please allow at least 4 weeks for delivery.

Bruce Lee fans queue round the block at London's Rialto cinema to watch *The Way of the Dragon* during its opening week in April 1974. *Photograph © Cinema TV Today 1974.*

after being persuaded to do so by Pumer, played the song *Wuthering Heights* by the then-unknown teenage singer Kate Bush on his show, which became the most requested song on the station at the end of the year. Both Pumer and Myatt were Bruce Lee fans and that worked in *Kung-Fu Monthly*'s favour. On the airwaves, Myatt would often mention *Kung-Fu Monthly*, The Bruce Lee Society and the Conventions for extra publicity. The duo also formed a friendship with the Society's Pam Hadden, often inviting her to the

Tony Myatt and Bruce Lee's Way of the Dragon co-star Chuck Norris during the latter's visit to London in 1980. *Photograph Courtesy of Michael Nesbitt.*

radio station, where she would sometimes be accompanied by her son Andrew. "The Bruce Lee Society was always my mum's hobby - her thing," remembered Andrew. "But there were certain things I liked doing with her, such as going to see film screenings, going up to Capital Radio, which was good for a while. For a kid, obviously, going up to Capital Radio was like the greatest thing on earth and especially in London in the 1970s."

As the Seventies held the term 'Kung Fu' as one of the hot topics, the Eighties would hold another term as a hot topic - *Censorship*.

As the Kung Fu Craze took hold in the late 1970s, the British Board of Film Censors (BBFC) began to recall Bruce Lee and Kung Fu films in general, in order to reclassify them. Due to the increasing copycat violence exhibited in public and from public pressure, the BBFC took it upon themselves to cut various scenes from various martial arts movies, especially ones involving the famous nunchakus. The fans were in uproar and wrote into *Kung-Fu Monthly* and the BBFC in their droves. Though the reclassification was supposed to across the board, some cinemas - especially the Chinese ones - were still showing uncut versions of the films. Eventually though, the uncut cinema prints died out and the only the cut versions would be shown. In order to avoid complaints from the paying public who may have expected the uncut version of *Enter the Dragon*, Warner Bros. would advertise cut showing of the film as the 'Abridged Version.'

At the end of the Seventies, the only way to obtain movies to watch at home would be on imported film such as 8mm on a projector, though the quality would vary widely and the format would not be financially viable for everyone. That all changed in 1980 with the advent of not one but two home video formats - VHS and Betamax. Though still not necessarily cheap, movies on VHS and Betamax would be around 20-25% of the cost of their 8mm film equivalents and that made them much more affordable for the average Bruce Lee fan. It wasn't just the cost that made the home videos appealing to Bruce Lee fans. The BBFC's censorship rules which had required Bruce Lee's films to be reclassified and cut at the end of the 1970s, didn't actually apply to the new formats of home video - not at that time anyway. Enter the Dragon was the first Bruce Lee movie to make its way to home video uncut in December 1980 from Warner Bros. Rank opened up their Bruce Lee home video account with the release of The Big Boss and Fist of Fury in April 1982, both of which were also put out uncut. When Rank released Way of the Dragon in November 1982 however, they released a cut version, much to the anger of Kung-Fu Monthly's readers. Not as cut as later versions of the film, it still was missing the 'double-nunchaku' scene. It wasn't Rank's choice to release the cut version of the film but they were legally obligated to release whatever version had been officially classified by the BBFC when the films had their original run. Fist of Fury was the first to be classified in November 1972, followed by Enter the Dragon in October 1973, then The Big Boss in February 1974 and concluded by Way of the Dragon in July 1974. Only after the UK release of Enter the Dragon on 13th January 1974 did the Kung Fu Craze begin, therefore that film and Fist of Fury were both released uncut as they preceded that date. With the Kung Fu

Bruce Lee claims his revenge through death and beyond.

Bruce Lee challenges the underworld to a "Game of Death".

Craze, came the censorship and the reclassification in the late 1970s. With the advent of home video, distributors were obligated to release the last officially classified version of the film and as the classification for *Enter the Dragon* and *Fist of Fury* preceded the Kung Fu Craze, they made their debut onto home video fully uncut. *The Big Boss* never really suffered major cuts at the hand of the censors, apart from a small eight seconds. By the time *Way of the Dragon* was classified in July 1974, the BBFC were much more aware of the violence and weapons in martial arts films and Lee's trip to Rome bore the brunt of that awareness. So Rank only released what they were allowed to release. In the years that followed, home video rules changed and distributers could only release material that had exclusively been classified for release on video so for distributors to release a film on home video, they would have to let it work it's way through the BBFC's system first.

Game of Death was the only Bruce Lee to seriously suffer from the censors on its original release in 1978. As the film was released after the BBFC required them to be submitted for re-classification, *Game of Death* had a whole fight scene removed - one featuring Bruce Lee against his friend and student, Dan Inosanto. The BBFC would not have required all of the fight scene to be removed but as the part featuring weapons made up for 95% of the scene, leaving in the 5% would made the scene completely unintelligible. What the UK lost however, they gained with the inclusion of the Ji Han Jae fight scene, which was missing from other versions of the film which had the Inosanto fight intact.

For a VHS re-release in 1986, Rank would re-submit the films to the BBFC for VHS classification who would remove even more footage and that's how it would stay until 2001.

As the films would be cut for their cinema screenings from the early 1980s, many new fans of Bruce Lee would have been unable to see them in their full uncut glory. The same would go for Lee's younger fans, who after finally being legally old enough to watch their idol, were faced with butchered versions of his films. With this in mind, Eddy Pumer would often write lengthy articles describing footage that was cut.

Eddy Pumer's articles were always the ones that really went into great depth regarding the latest news too. As the early 1980s progressed, other writers also began writing for *Kung-Fu Monthly* including Will Johnston - affectionately referred to as The Prof by his fellow Bruce Lee fans - one of the regular contributors to The Bruce Lee Society and once regarded as one of Britain's leading Bruce Lee historians.

KFM No.68 in 1982 would herald a new era in the history of *Kung-Fu Monthly* as editor Bruce Sawford, who was "furthering his knowledge of the martial arts," was officially replaced by Colin James, who, at the age of just twenty-two, had been offered the role directly from Felix Dennis. He remembered, "I think the previous editor Bruce Sawford, who was full time at Bunch Books, didn't have time for that project anymore, because he was working on other Bunch Books projects which had more importance and also *Kung-Fu Monthly* had well passed its peak at that point. It was becoming an irregular magazine as it wasn't monthly anymore. When a monthly magazine becomes irregular, the wholesale trade doesn't like it, because people get used to buying a magazine, book or whatever at a regular interval. I remember me buying Marvel comics when I was a teen and walking three or four miles to the shop that would sell the *Silver Surfer* when it was out and you expect that. When *KFM* became irregularly published, it could be six weeks or it could be three months before the next one was out. That hit sales because the wholesalers didn't have slots for it to get it into the retailers, etc. I remember having a few pints with Felix Dennis and he was talking about how the sales were going on various magazines, etc. And then he came to *KFM* and he says, 'Bruce doesn't want to do it anymore. He hasn't got the time so we're going to close it.' I said, 'That's a shame,' because I got commission on back issue sales. So he said, 'Well, do you want it?' I said, 'Well, yeah, okay.' I hadn't done anything like that before as I was always sales orientated. So it was basically over a few pints with Felix, and telling me, he was gonna close it and I thought it going to hit my bottom line and my weekly income. So I said, 'Yeah, okay. I'll do it.' I didn't realise what I'd taken on until I started trying to do an issue because there was nothing ready for the next issue."

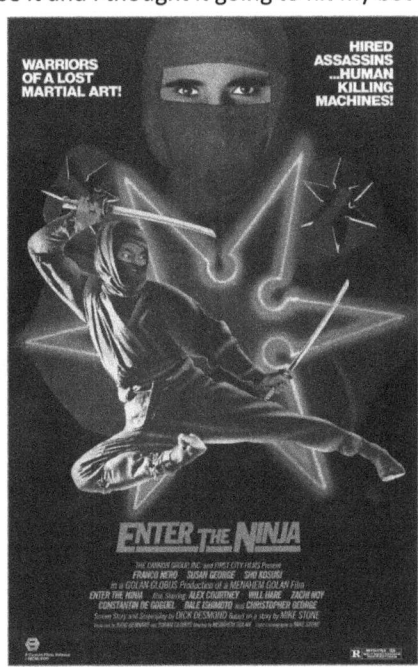

Under James' editorship and due to changing attitudes to other Kung Fu stars and films of the time, the magazine shifted focus and began to feature articles about future stars such as Jackie Chan and due to the success of films like Cannon's *Enter the Ninja*, many Ninja orientated articles began appearing. It was Colin James who would offer an opportunity to a young writer by the name of Bey Logan, then writing under the name Simon Bulley. Logan recalled, "I took a trip to Hong Kong in 1981, really to walk in Bruce's shadow. I ended up meeting Jackie Chan, Sammo Hung, Yuen Biao and all those guys. When I came back from Hong Kong, I was so excited, I sent a long letter detailing my adventures to Colin James, who I think was then newly installed as editor. He found it so interesting that he ran the letter as an article. I guess it was well received, as Colin later asked me to contribute on a regular basis. That was the start of my career in martial arts and movie journalism." James also remembered his young writer, "Back when Bey was writing for *Kung-Fu Monthly*, he was strapped for cash because in those days, you were paid by cheque. He would turn up on a train from Norfolk or somewhere near that neck of the woods to collect his cheque. He would ask, 'Can you go to the bank and get it cashed for me?' so in my lunch hour, we'd have to wander up to Natwest on Tottenham Court Road because he couldn't cash it himself. They wouldn't cash it unless someone from Dennis Publishing - or Bunch Books as it was then - was there to give him his paltry twenty quid or whatever it was. It is heart-warming that to know that someone who knocked on your door, came into the office and said, 'Blah, blah, blah.' I thought, 'Yeah, why not? Give him a go.' I didn't know him from Adam but it's really good to see that he went on to some greatness."

As the magazine entered 1983, the way the magazine was folded changed to accommodate the changed layout of the magazine. This was needed due to the different content featured, written by Logan from James' encouragement. Logan remembered, "Colin was not really into martial arts per se, so he gave me a lot of leeway to pursue different articles and information. I thought we should branch out into other Kung Fu movie stars, but the fans really wanted all Bruce Lee, all the time!"

At the end of 1983, The Bruce Lee Society would publish its thirtieth and final newsletter. Pam Hadden's stewardship of the Bruce Lee Society took a significant toll on her, and she was quite ill by the time the Society shuttered. "Pam was so dedicated to running the Bruce Lee Society that she suffered badly," said former member Andrew Staton. "Most fans are happy with whatever a club offers by way of information and events. However, there is a small minority that have so little in life that their need for knowledge on Bruce Lee (or any of their other interests) - it becomes an obsession for them. If you do not feed that obsession, you become a target. Pam warned me about these fans. She regretted giving her home phone number out to some of them as they would ring her home at all hours and, if she didn't give them the answers they wanted, they'd give her a load of abuse down the phone! You could see she was tired, and her nerves were really bad. When I spoke to Pam, she said it was hard to get money out of Bunch books to pay for sundries i.e., new badges and general materials to run the club. She was using her own money to run the Society which, even though she was generous, there had to be a limit." Sadly, Pam Hadden passed away from breast cancer in 1991 at the age of 49.

In 1984, the year after The Bruce Lee Society folded, *Kung-Fu Monthly* put out issue 79, which despite its re-designed logo (its third since is conception) and new look, would bring about the end of an era. There has never been a completely clear explanation of why *Kung-Fu Monthly* ended, but Andrew Staton offered some insight into the financial and editorial factors that may have contributed to its dissolution. "I am not really sure of the complete reasons, but I did meet former editor Bruce Sawford, editor of *Kung-Fu Monthly*, at Bunch Books in London shortly before it ceased publication. He said that the owners felt that the maga-

zine had done it's run and wanted to concentrate on new more popular and fashionable magazines." This was backed up by Sawford himself, "I wasn't involved by then but it was most probably because (a) it wasn't making money, (b) we'd run out of pictures and things to say, and (c) we had other things to do."

With dwindling sales, using their old printers was no longer financially viable. Just like the beginning of the Kung Fu Boom, where smaller printers could not cope with the increasing volumes of the magazine, the opposite would be true at the end of the magazine's run. As Dick Pountain explained, "So when the peak was being passed a few years later, you had the reverse process of bringing the circulation down and still keeping it economical because at a certain point, you didn't have us printing enough to be with these big heat set people anymore."

A decade after launching *Kung-Fu Monthly*, sales suffered and it seemed that Felix wasn't happy to shut up shop. At meetings, it was increasing apparent that the ship was quickly approaching the iceberg. Roger Hutchinson recalled, "Felix kept *Kung-Fu Monthly* going from sentimental attachment for longer than was economically sensible, but once it began posting irreversible losses due to collapsing sales, he let it go."

Writer Bey Logan felt the same. "My understanding is that it wasn't really making any money for the company. A new management regime took over, looked at the books and decided to axe it. I think they saw it as a holdover from the 1970s. In fact, the whole postermag concept was very much of that era. I think it was purely a business decision. In terms of content, I felt *Kung-Fu Monthly* was still going strong."

Kung-Fu Monthly's final editor Colin James somewhat shared Logan's sentiment, believing that a combination of declining sales and interest in new hobbies such as the home computer market, were to blame for the magazine's demise. James said, "I left Bunch Books sometime in mid 1984 or something like that. I can't remember exactly when but we were still selling *Kung-Fu Monthly*, but maybe, once I'd gone, they decided to close it. All the focus at that point was on computer magazines and that was what was driving the whole company. There was a magazine called *Hi-Fi Choice* which came out five times a year. And there was a monthly magazine called *Which Bike?* and that used to sell 30,000 to 40,000 copies or whatever. Those were established publications when the first home computers like the ZX Spectrum and all the other new stuff was coming out. We were working on that and then there was *Personal Computer World* so *Kung-Fu Monthly* didn't even take a backseat - it was kind of outside the car being driven and running after it. So probably when I left well, they thought they hadn't gotten the resources put into the sales at the time and that's probably when they decided to put the plug on it. At the end of *Kung-Fu Monthly*, the circulation rate of an issue was about 15,000 to 20,000 tops and that was on the decline, largely because of the supply issues to the wholesalers and retailers. If regular buyers can't get it at a regular date, they tend not to go back for it. What we found was that people would write in and say, "Well, my newsagent treats it as a kind of a subscription. I order it from them but it's never on display," and a lot of the copies were sold like that. So without having the copies displayed on counters at WHSmith's etc., it was never going to increase sales again because most of them never touch the shelves for people to see. It was a sad end to it all and I think the death knell was the 1981 convention being postponed for what should have been a year or two. It was the kind of thing, that if it had happened when it should have, it would have given *Kung-Fu Monthly* a minor kick-start."

The timing of *Kung-Fu Monthly* was extremely important. It was the right product at the right time. Bruce Lee had the ability appeal to everyone, regardless of age, colour or size. Working class kids loved him. Black kids loved him. Don Atyeo had a theory why Bruce Lee appealed to British fans in the 1970s. "I think it was because he wasn't manufactured. I don't know how but the word of mouth was amazing because there was very little publicity. It was a real fan phenomenon. They discovered this guy themselves and I think it was real. Bruce Lee was the first phenomenon like that I think, for young people, who discovered, demanded, and got their own choice. The movie houses were even surprised. He hit a chord. His movies are very traditional and I'm not sure why they should work, really. Those early movies are very, very Hong Kong-centric and really have no nod to the West at all. The charm of those early movies is really what kicked it all off - I found them charming, but then again, I hung out in the Far East and Hong Kong for a long period. Why something as esoteric as that touched a chord with British kids? I've no idea at all. They were all different shapes, sizes, races and social classes; it was really right across the board. He was a real deal and very fun to have that period of my life. I think it was something quite revolutionary and it's good to see that people still appreciate it. Perhaps the time was right, I don't know. He was a hell of a good character but he could also fight like a motherfucker!"

After the demise of *Kung-Fu Monthly*, H. Bunch Associates eventually became Dennis Publishing, one of the biggest magazine publishing companies in the world.

Some of *Kung-Fu Monthly*'s original team still work on some magazines published by Dennis Publishing. *KFM* printing master Dick Pountain said, "I was a director of Bunch Books but I also worked on a motorbike magazine that we did called *Which Bike?* I was involved in the editorial and I wrote stuff for it including reviewing bikes. That was the only thing I was involved in the editorial of until we bought *Personal Computer World* and then I disappeared to become a computer journalist which I still am. I still have a column in *PC Pro* which is another Dennis magazine. I'm sort of more or less retired, but I still do my column."

After *Bruce Lee King of Kung Fu*, Don Atyeo penned several more books including *Muhammad Ali: The Holy Warrior* (Bunch Books 1975) a co-write with his former *KFM* buddy Felix Dennis, *Blood and Guts: Violence in Sports* (Penguin Books 1979) and *Muhammad Ali: The Glory Years* (Ebury Press 2002), an update to his original 1975 book. When asked if *Bruce Lee King of Kung Fu* was his work rather than a collaboration between Felix and himself, Don replied, "I used to say, I wrote the book, and he wrote the cheques. But that wasn't true at all. I did the research and I went out to a house belonging to an artist called Joe Petagno. Felix had been publishing *Cozmic Comics* before he did *Kung-Fu Monthly* and Joe was one of the comic illustrators. He had a house somewhere at the end of one of the Tube lines. It was out in the middle of nowhere and he had a room so I went out there and wrote up a first draft of *Bruce Lee King of Kung Fu*. I couldn't really stay in town because there was too much distraction so I went out there and basically wrote the first draft of the book. After I brought it back, Felix then took it away and squirreled away on it and did a good job on it. He didn't do anything original, but he changed a lot of it around and brought some good ideas to it. So the next book that we did, which was about Muhammad Ali, we actually wrote together. I did one chapter and he did another one and then we'd switch and so on. But the first one, I did that; it was very much a case of I write the first draft of it and he polishes that up. He did more than polishing up - he did a lot of good creative stuff on it and made it a lot better." Don currently resides in the South of France.

Bey Logan went on to have a journalism and film career. After *Kung-Fu Monthly*, he worked for the British magazines *Combat* and *Impact*, before embarking on a film production career in Hong Kong, working for Media Asia and The Weinstein Company. "*Kung-Fu Monthly* was the first phase of my professional life; from *Kung-Fu Monthly* to *Combat* to *Impact*. Pretty much as soon as I finished editing *Impact*, I moved into film production, which was the second stage of my career! I just produced a new Bruce Lee documentary, *The Death of Bruce Lee* for History Channel. Having made movies for about thirty years now, I'm onto the third stage of my professional career, as an author and Kung Fu school owner. Its been a wild ride, and I can say it definitely began with that letter to Colin James at *Kung-Fu Monthly*, all those years ago"

As for Felix Dennis himself; he continued his publishing journey with Dennis Publishing and in later life, became a successful poet, publishing many poetry books and touring the world on the back of their success. Unfortunately he passed away on 22nd June 2014, aged 67, after a long battle with throat cancer, but through *Kung-Fu Monthly*, he left behind a legacy that is loved the world over. Whenever you think of Bruce Lee fandom in the United Kingdom, you immediately think of *Kung-Fu Monthly* and Felix Dennis.

In Memory of
Felix Dennis
1947-2014

Photograph Copyright © Dennis Publishing 2011

KUNG-FU
MONTHLY
THE ARCHIVE SERIES

THE POSTER MAGAZINES - VOLUME TWO

27

1977

EDITORIAL

Welcome to the twenty-seventh edition of *Kung-Fu Monthly*! And what a star-studded bill we have waiting in the wings for you this month. A quick glance at the cover will reveal its time for part one of the finale of the Bruce Lee film and TV round-up. There's a whole bundle of new goodies on the late master - enough to satisfy the most voracious Little Dragon information seeker - and next issue, in part two, at last you'll discover the truth about *The Man and the Legend*. That's the film Golden Harvest put together on the life of Bruce Lee just after he died. For years fans have been asking the question, "What happened to it - why has it never been shown here?" Tune in next month to part two of our Film Feature Finale for all the answers.

Next in line, is the much requested feature on Chinese astrology and how in particular, Bruce Lee fitted into it. The systems used in that part of the world contain fascinating differences to our own Zodiac based horoscope and at no extra charge we include a brief look at all their signs and characteristics. With very little difficulty, *KFM* readers will be able to search out their own personalities - Chinese style! One thing that will startle you is just how accurately Bruce Lee fits into his own 'Dragon' sign. The description handed down to us by the ancients of our 20th Century martial master is uncannily close and *KFM* wonders, is there more to it than meets the eye?

Finally, I asked two issues back whether anyone was interested in buying genuine Bruce Lee *Game of Death* suits - I needn't have bothered! Please don't write in any more. I get the message - a very resounding 'Yes!' Wheels are being set in motion and just as soon as any news arrives that they're on their way, be sure you're going to know about it! Be with you again soon...

Felix Yen

Felix Yen
Editor-in-Chief

BRUCE LEE FEATURE FILM FINALE: PART ONE

The amazingly talented Bruce Lee captured the attention of millions of people all over the world with a superb demonstration of fitness and skill. He died at the age of just 32 in July 1973 after completing the action sequences in what was to have been his fifth major film production. During the afternoon of the day he died, he had signed a contract with George Lazenby to co-star in the picture he was working on and in the late evening, he was admitted to hospital, unconscious. Most people know about his five big productions - *The Big Boss*, *Fist of Fury*, *The Way of the Dragon*, *Enter the Dragon* and *Game of Death* - but very little is said on some of his other work. The first film he made was in 1946 and it was called *The Birth of Mankind*. No one knew at the time where Bruce's career was eventually to lead and few could have guessed of the stardom that lay waiting at his door.

There were many other minor productions to follow up the Little Dragon's opening foray into the world of film entertainment - titles such as *Beginning of a Boy*, *My Son A-Chang*, *Kid Chung*, *The Orphan* and they were all very much of the same mould. In fact, it's been said that you only had to watch one of them to have a pretty good idea of what was going to happen in the others and if truth be told, they were almost indistinguishable from one another! Bruce always played the little boy who was always mischievous but somehow or other always ended up good. Some Mickey Rooney films would perhaps bear similar comparison. The young dragon simply couldn't do a thing wrong.

Bruce kept up the pace until he was about seven or eight years old, carrying on his role in the tear-jerker sausage machine. Then, suddenly, he gave it all up. Even at that early age, he had become aware that the road led nowhere and he resolved to forget the whole thing. And he very nearly did! Not until around the age of eighteen did he reconsider that fateful decision and how lucky it was for us that he did. Of that earlier batch, the most popular picture was without doubt *My Son A-Chang*, a film made by the Elephantine Film Company. Now, it will probably come as a surprise to you to learn that, a couple of years

ago (just after Bruce died) Raymond Chow bought the rights for *My Son A-Chang* and re-filmed it in cinemascope (the original was in widescreen). Technically speaking, the result (still in black and white, of course) was in the words of somebody who witnessed a performance of the newly processed *My Son A-Chang*, 'Diabolical!' However, despite the terrible picture quality, Chow made a considerable amount of money out of the idea and perhaps it would be only fair to give him seven out of ten for trying!

The next milestone in the history of Bruce's other productions has to be the famous and fabulous Long Beach Tournament clip. Regular readers will know well, the near fairytale story of Ed Parker's film of Bruce performing at the event and how, ultimately, it led to a brief but glittering TV career. It is probably no overstatement to say that, without that film, the Little Dragon might never have been re-discovered. Everyone needs a break and Bruce got his at Long Beach. Within a few months, it had all started to happen and of course *The Green Hornet* was the very first link in the chain of success that was to lead to ultimate stardom.

A question: Why has the Long Beach film never been released on the cinema circuits? It would make one of the most sensational shorts and wouldn't there be a queue in a million to see that piece of history to end all history? Sad to say, *Kung-Fu Monthly* at this moment, is unable to trace the owner of this remarkable clip, but rest assured, just as soon as we are able to dig up any information, well be letting you know. This particular reel was of course the very same one that TV producer, William Dozier, saw. It hardly took him a second to realise the latent talent in that good-looking martial athlete who was displaying his Kung Fu wares to a stunned audience. Dozier at once lined Bruce up for the *Charlie Chan's Number One Son* part but, unfortunately, due to opposition from the

sponsors (who felt that the series wasn't yet ready for a remake) the idea was dropped. However, this potential disaster was averted when *The Green Hornet* appeared on the horizon. Dozier recalled the Long Beach clip and the rest is history.

Stirling Silliphant, one of America's great screen writers, penned Marlowe, starring James Garner and thus he assured Bruce's first ever Hollywood screen appearance. Stirling specially wrote Bruce Lee into the plot of the film - he hadn't been there at all originally - and although the picture wasn't acclaimed as one of Garner's best, it was certainly more than enhanced by the Little Dragon's dynamic introductory performance. Stirling, by then himself a great fan of Bruce, no doubt had it in the back of his mind that here was a man destined for the top and the only upsetting part of the whole business was Bruce's all-too-brief appearance. In fact, had the Little Dragon been featured more heavily, many would argue that the film could have really gone places. Had the opportunity been taken, the box-office receipts might have told a different tale.

But then, maybe it was a blessing in disguise, for had Bruce made it, in what amounted to a straight acting role, the chances are that he would have placed far less emphasis on the martial arts. One of the more memorable scenes from *Marlowe* has the Little Dragon jumping about from side to side on the top of a building and James Garner asking if there is anything abnormal about him! At one point Bruce also demonstrates the art of leaping over the side of a building - a wasted role if ever there was one. It all starts off well enough in scene one with the Little Dragon kicking all manner of hell out of an office - then suddenly the role fades out and the excitement goes. What could have been a good first try, turned out in the end to be a disappointment.

Some time ago, the original Bruce Lee Fan Club virtually forced the re-release of *Marlowe* through sheer weight of demand. The result was astounding. Cinema managers were amazed to see their packed houses simply walk out after the first two scenes (where Bruce's appearance ended). As the film was supporting a main feature there was frequently nobody there at all to see the so-called number one attraction!

Stirling Silliphant's next production was a love story entitled *A Walk in the Spring Rain*. What many people don't know, is that as there were fight scenes in it, Stirling decided to call Bruce all the way over to Tennessee to choreograph them. Now for the sad part of the story. Although the people who have seen the 'rushes' of these action clips all agree that they were very cleverly done, the censors (in their wisdom) in most countries have cut them out! Although Bruce himself doesn't fight in the sequences, apparently the Little Dragon's influence comes over very strongly and anyone having an opportunity to watch these forbidden feet is well advised to do so.

Despite the fact that around this time Bruce wasn't doing a lot of acting, he did very much keep his hand in with choreography work and other bits and pieces. Also he attended many charity events and TV guest shows, not to mention bit parts in *Ironside*, *Blondie*, *Here Comes the Brides* and of course, *Batman*. In the latter, again Bruce had to suffer a wasted role and probably the only reason he took it was to keep himself in the public eye. Of the rest, information is scarce. *Blondie* was a comedy series but nobody seems inclined to discuss it at any length. The only conclusion to be made is that it was not a success. In Ironside and *Here Comes the Brides*, he took on his usual kind of 'battling' role.

OK, that's about it for the first half of our Little Dragon's 'other work' extravaganza. Next month, tune into part two and learn the truth about *Longstreet*, what actually hap-

pened to change Warner's *The Warrior* into *Kung Fu* starring David Carradine, Bruce's brush with Unicorn Chan and finally, the latest up-to-the-minute news on Golden Harvest's final epitaph to the Little Dragon - *Bruce Lee The Man and the Legend*. See you then!

CHINESE ASTROLOGY: YEAR OF THE SNAKE

1976 was Bruce Lee's year - it was the Year of the Dragon. Now it's 1977 and from around the beginning of February, it is the Year of the Snake. To everyone in the western world, the normal sun-based zodiac astrology system is fairly well understood. You are either Capricorn, Gemini, etc, etc (12 signs in all) and theory has it that many of the planets around us, too, exert a considerable influence over our lives. Some eastern countries, however, have totally different systems to help decide on character assessments, predictions and so on. They consider the moon rather than the sun, to be the dominating influence. There is another difference - in the west, the 'newspaper-type' horoscope is read rather indulgently and with a good deal of scepticism. Out east - for instance in China - people set their lives by it.

Bruce Lee, along with most Chinese people, was a superstitious man. Well, he knew about good and bad omens and well, he understood the fearsome consequences of ignoring such signs. Marriage partners are often chosen by it, business deals can be made or delayed depending on what the signs have to say. Even seemingly trivial daily decisions (like what to have for lunch) can be affected by what the charts are indicating.

So, how does it all work? Well, to start with, every year is given one of the following twelve signs: Dragon, Snake, Horse, Goat, Monkey, Rooster, Dog, Pig, Rat, Buffalo, Tiger and Cat. Now, there's a slight problem here. Chinese astrological years are a little different from the ones you and I are used to - they don't start on January 1st and come to that, they aren't at all consistent about the dates they do begin and end. For instance, 1960's year of the Rat began on January 28th and ended on February 15th 1961. If your birthday falls in January of February, then to find the Chinese sign under which you were born, you'll probably have to do a little research in the library.

For others, however, finding your sign is quite simple. Here is a list of sample years that one each of the twelve signs fell on: Dragon 1940 - Snake 1941 - Horse 1942 - Goat 1943 - Monkey 1944 - Rooster 1945 - Dog 1946 - Pig 1947 - Rat 1948 - Buffalo 1949 - Tiger 1950 - Cat 1951. Now, if your birthday was on one of those years, you'll know immediately what your sign is. If, however, you were born later, find which year from the list that you can add 12 to in order to get the year in which I you were born. For instance, if your birthday was in 1961, then you are a Buffalo because 1949 plus 12 years equals 1961.

OK, by now most of you should have worked out your Chinese astrological sign. The next move is to go briefly through each, outlining any particularly strong characteristics and how 1977, the year of the Snake, is likely to affect you. This time around, the sign of the Dragon is to be left until last because obviously, concerning as it does the Little Dragon, there's far more to be said.

THE SNAKE

Snake people are good humoured and inclined towards being romantics. They think deeply and dispense wisdom and intuition in an almost spiritual way. Though generous to others almost to a fault, the Snake will hang on to his money, which also goes to explain probably why he has so few financial worries! Decision making comes easily. Faults - well, the only failing worth talking about is a tendency to carry just about everything to excess.
Prediction for 1977: A once-in-a-lifetime year with misfortune almost out of the question.

THE HORSE

A bit of a big-head, so far as the horse is concerned, for all practical purposes, he is the centre of his own universe. Mind you, there's plenty there to bring the others around him. Physically attractive, sparkling and quick-witted, the horse simply reeks of animal cunning and the only sad part out it is that all this is simply covering up a rather weak character!
Prediction for 1977: Not a happy year romantically. The temptation to go overboard in the cause of love must be strongly resisted.

THE GOAT

Essentially, people born under this sign are followers rather than leaders. They seek security in others and make rotten fighters when it comes to serious war. So good are they, however, at living off friends, often their parasitic nature can barely be noticed. The goat lacks any sort of self control over his life, but generally he falls on his feet through this good-heartedness and charm. As far as professions go, the world of art is a fairly safe bet.
Prediction for 1977: There's a good time year ahead of you - plenty of things to enjoy doing and plenty of people's backs behind which to talk!

THE MONKEY

Is the fun-loving comedian of the charts. He is, however, marred by his belief of superiority over all others. He can be vain, conceited, sly and overbearing, but by the same token, his clear thinking and cleverness in getting people to do what he wants carries him through. Wise in matters of money, he has the intellect to deceive just about anybody he wishes.
Prediction for 1977: Plenty of opportunity for the Monkey to exercise his diplomatic skills and the rewards are just waiting round the corner to be reaped.

THE ROOSTER

Can be very rude - even to the point of pure selfishness. As callous as the Monkey is diplomatic, the Rooster needs no one to support him as he builds his armchair pies in the skies. He can, however, work hard and he constantly attempts to do more than he is capable of realistically achieving. He is the loner who needs to be noticed.

Prediction for 1977: Watch out for problems at home this year. Otherwise a good outlook ahead.

THE DOG

Honest, dependable and at times, petty-minded perhaps sums up man's best friend. Wherever he looks, he sees gloom on the horizon, but for all that, he is intelligent and totally dedicated to the task athand. Often that task is fighting injustice and happily his straightforward approach almost guarantees he gets what he wants.
Prediction for 1977: plenty of occasions for involvement will present themselves, but choose your path carefully.

THE PIG

If you want to take somebody for a ride, try a Pig! You can bet he'll fall for just about anything hook, line and sinker and the funny thing is, he doesn't really seem to mind. Trusting, gullible, but at the same time, intellectual, he hides a kind of decisiveness under an easy going facade. Sincerity and strength of ambition add to the character of this likeable sign.
Prediction for 1977: After a slow start, things will begin moving smoothly into top gear later this year.

THE RAT

Plays games, but he plays them for high stakes! Sometimes calm, sometimes aggressive, he finds it almost impossible to gain real friendship. Because of the barrier he builds around himself, few if any can ever hope to meet the real Rat and anyway, he's too busy making his fortune off the efforts of all those around him to worry about that. Honest, intelligent, critical, generous to a few, and mean to most, his laziness can sometimes be his downfall.
Prediction for 1977: Boom year for business - your troubles are over.

THE BUFFALO

Has rather similar traits in many ways to that of the sun sign Capricorn in the western zodiac. Flag-wavers - 'king and my country' - 'if it was good enough for my father, its good enough for me.' His role in chief is to act as the 'safe as houses' man behind the scenes. Working with clockwork precision, the Buffalo will stick to his chosen course right through to the bitter end - often with a determination amounting to fanaticism.
Prediction for 1977: Marriage is not advised this year and look out for the possibility of problems at home.

THE TIGER

Is James Dean and John Wayne all rolled into one. He plays the hero it isn't always prudent to follow - often his decisions lack good judgement. Nevertheless, he'll fight to the end for the battle of what he believes is right. Risk-taker, leader, stubborn at times and often surprisingly hesitant at just the wrong moment, the Tiger exudes an air of confidence that trusts not a little to Lady Luck.

Prediction for 1977: No time for sitting around - it's all out action as usual.

THE CAT

At first glance appears to be ideal - almost too ideal! For the fact of the matter is that these charming, restrained, pleasant and happy people can easily lean towards the superficial. Unmoved by any but the greatest of catastrophes, all they seek is peace and quiet and to be left alone. In financial matters, however, the Cat's cunning comes into play and although he will seek to earn his living doing something that pleases him, that doesn't make him any the less of a businessman.

Prediction for 1977: A comfortable year when much will be gained from hard thinking.

THE DRAGON

OK, here it is, Bruce Lee's own sign and take a look at the remarkable accuracy of the rundown. He's full of beans, straight dealing and happy to stay healthy. He also is a perfectionist and constantly demands that same perfection from the others around him. The only trouble is he sometimes lacks the tact to ask people in the right way. Occasionally his enthusiasm simply boils over and he becomes accused of conceit. Whatever he puts his mind to, the Dragon will see it done - nothing is too difficult or dangerous and he is a natural winner all down the line. He tends to be a loner, however, and true friends will be few and far between. In his chosen profession, the Dragon's talent will rise above all others.

Predictions for 1977: a fantastic year - the Dragon shines on.

So there we are! I have to admit my amazement on seeing such an apt description of the Little Dragon - in fact I'd say it was uncanny. As a suggestion, how about you readers of *KFM* letting me know how YOU figured in the character predictions. If on balance, the majority of you write in saying that there is just a grain of truth in the personality run-down of your particular sign, then I'd say it was time we took an even closer look at the ancient world of Chinese Astrology.

THE BRUCE LEE SECRET SOCIETY

Hello, Pam and Carmella here - welcome to another Secret Society News Page!

There are lots to tell you this month, but first off we want to put in huge, great letters, a very special THANK YOU to all the members who sent in Christmas cards to the two of us. We weren't actually expecting them and some were so ingenious we're thinking that one or two of them should go into the Secret Society magazine that's in the making.

Talking about the Society magazine, the response has been very good and there are lots of entries to choose from. Don't forget though that there's a few more weeks to go yet before we have to raise the 'full-up' sign, so now the Christmas break is well and truly over, it's back on with the thinking caps. Remember, we're after just about anything that can be put into a magazine - things like poems, drawings, short essays and stories – whatever really crosses your mind, PROVIDED of course, it's about the Little Dragon!

News time and we hear from Member No. 1036, Marlene Condy, that she was recently able to buy the *Enter the Dragon* soundtrack through the John Menzies group of shops and newsagents. Their London office is at: 8 St. John's Lane, London EC1 so anyone interested in having a copy is recommended to try that address first. The number of the album is WEA Records Ltd K46275 ES2729 and its best that you quote that when ordering.

OK, this is the part we haven't been looking forward to! Last issue we told you that the Secret Society would be increasing its cost of membership and, sad to say, that will be taking effect as from March 1st 1977. The new price is £3.25 and, fingers crossed, that's where it's going to stay for some time to come. Although costs seem to be rising almost by the week, we're going to try and make sure that Secret Society Members get every single penny's worth of value out of the £3.25 that we can give them.

And now, the results of our first ever Bruce Lee Secret Society Competition. Firstly the answers: 1. Shih Kien, 2. 'My Way', 3. 1973. The first five correct postcards out of the hat were sent in by: Stephen Hatcher (1191), Kay Drummond (1195), Deborah Pledge (1301), James Hynes (1167), Hugh Lagan (1218). Well done! Your signed copies of The Wisdom of Bruce Lee should be reaching you in a few days. Watch out for the next Competition in the March News Sheet!

One final piece of late news. Our friend, Gary Kohatsu in America has written telling us that the international pen pals effort is starting to pay off handsomely. He is so pleased with your response to the names and addresses we printed in the last News Sheet that he's sent in another list of red hot USA Bruce Lee fans - to be printed in our March edition. Stand by for that! See you all again soon - **Pam and Carmella**

KICKBACK: THE LETTERS

Hi... Jenny here again, dipping into top gear and letting out the clutch on another mountain of readers' mail! Right away, I just have to tell you the amazing news about our *Game of Death* poster competition. To start with, as I mentioned last month, Cathay Films very kindly stepped in and agreed to choose not just one but five winning entries and, first off, my thanks go to Art Consultant Jim Launder and Executives Tony Love and Roy Byrne for taking on the task. Well, they came up with the following result: 1. Kelvin Richard of London. 2. A. Briers of St Helens. 3. Neil Baldwin of Hull. 4. Trevor Dower of Bishops Stortford. 5. Andrew Felton of Leeds. Congratulations to all you five and, as promised, there's a free years subscription to you. Jim, Tony and Roy all ask me to say how delighted they were at the very high level of imagination shown by many of the entries and for Kelvin in

No.1 position, there's another surprise coming. Cathay Films may be using a part of your winning design on the actual *Game of Death* cinema poster! What a knock-out and in fact, Kelvin, there's £5.00 from Cathay Films on its way to you as a special reward for your efforts. And now, it must be time for the letters!

DOCUMENTARY IDEA

Dear Jenny,
Here is my theory for a documentary on Bruce Lee's life and films. I think the film should be called *The King and I* (the 'I' being his wife, Linda). At the start of the film I would have Mrs. Lee making speech to the followers of Bruce. After that, I'd show Bruce with his family and then some of the interviews and demonstrations he gave on television. In between all this, I'd want clips of Bruce in action and to end the film another speech from Mrs. Lee.
Colm Quinn, Limerick, Eire

Dear Colm,
Thanks for your fairly straight-forward and sensible ideas on a Bruce Lee Documentary, although I have a feeling if you used the title The King and I, *you might just have Messrs. Rogers and Hammerstein breathing down your neck! Talking of documentaries, I hear that Linda's has in fact been completed, but as yet there is no release date. Also, it seems fairly certain that Robert Lee will indeed soon be making a film tribute to his brother.*

BRUCE'S SWEAT GLANDS

Dear Jenny,
When did Bruce Lee have his sweat glands from under his armpits removed? Also, why was *The Way of the Dragon* stripped of 98% of its nunchaku sequences when *Fist of Fury* was left untouched?
Paul Nayman, Linthorpe, Cleveland

Dear Paul,
Thank you for your letter - I'm sorry I only had the space to answer a part of it! To be absolutely honest, I've never heard of Bruce having had the sweat glands removed from his armpits. In fact, to me, it sounds positively dangerous. If it's true, can anyone tell me about it? As far as the second part of your question goes, well I think I can be a bit more helpful there. It's not in fact true to say that Fist of Fury *was virtually untouched, although I would agree that* The Way of the Dragon's *mutilation was far worse.* The Big Boss *in fact, is the least affected of the three and the reason for this apparent inconsistency is simply this: Public pressure against screen violence was less in the early Lee days but it grew to almost insane proportions around the time* The Way of the Dragon *was being censored. Hence the current ridiculous situation.*

CINEMA POSTER REPRINTS

Dear Jenny,
How about for pin-up posters in *KFM*, doing reprints of the cinema posters of Bruce Lee films and how about some more from *Game of Death*. I would be pleased to see some articles on Bruce Lee outlining how he trained with his nunchakus, as these are my favourite martial arts weapon.
Robert Bear, Charminster, Bournemouth

Dear Robert,
Cinema posters for KFM eh? Well, it's an idea we have though of. The only thing is that to do it, we'd have to get the permission of the film company, and that's not always as easy as it sounds. As far as Game of Death *pictures go, we will be having some more in the magazine soon. Again, they're a little hard to find right now - the film company is jealously guarding them until the picture comes out. If you're interested in Bruce Lee's training methods, then keep your eyes peeled for* The Secret Art of Bruce Lee, *soon to appear in our mail-order list. You probably saw the first chapter in last month's KFM and it really is stacked full with brand new action pictures.*

NOT A REAL MARTIAL ARTIST?

Dear Jenny,
Recently I read a book and it said that Bruce Lee was just good for the box office and that his style of fighting was just flashy and would never be used in real self defence. What do you think about that?
Craig Burgess, Caister-on-Sea, Norfolk

Dear Craig,
Looks like someone's waving a red rag at me again! Every time I hear such arrant nonsense, it makes my blood boil! To start with, the very basis of Bruce's art was that it was practical and could be used in real life. And if whoever wrote that had known what he was talking about, he'd have been aware that Bruce was in fact challenged many times in public and I don't think I ever recall him having come out second best!

KICKBACK QUICKIES

Kevin Foster, Chopwell, Tyne & Wear - Thanks for your congrats! I think you know my opinion of Bruce Li by now.
Donnacha Quinn, Limerick, Ireland - I agree, it would be nice to know about Bruce's parents and a bit more about how they reacted to his fame - One for the editors - So far as I know they never needed police protection.
Gerard Rogers, Edinburgh, Scotland - Thanks for the compliments and I agree, Bruce was indeed years ahead of his time. I'm pleased to hear you joined the club.

Philip Boardman, Manchester - Wu Chi style info? I reckon that's one for the editors. In *Game of Death*, Bruce's yellow nunchakus were in fact similar to the normal ones he used - Except they were covered in yellow leather PS.I've got my face pack on ready for the picture, honest. Stand by for the Official Angela Mao Fan Club - All interested write to: M. Moore, Crook, Co. Durham.

Kevin Brewerton, Newcastle - In *Enter the Dragon*, I'm told that in fact Bruce leapt out of the tree to the ground and the film was then reversed. He wasn't too happy about doing it but the producer insisted.

Linda Tyrrell, Norwich, Norfolk - Regarding Robert Lee. 1. He's not married. 2. He has no fan club in the UK at least. 3. There's no plans for him to visit here at present. 4. I'll try to dig out more on him soon.

THE KFM PEN PALS

Paul Ashton, Dundee, Scotland aged 14 wants female pen friend (own age) preferably living in Great Britain. Please send photo.

PRICE INCREASE!

KFM regrets to announce an increase in cover price to 35 pence. This has been forced upon us by rising prices.

STOP PRESS!

Reports coming in say that Sham Basra from Erdington has been chosen by the BBC to star as the Little Dragon in a new six part programme entitled *The Legend of Bruce Lee*. We're told that shooting for the series is now complete and it's scheduled to be televised around mid-summer. More details soon!

1977

EDITORIAL

Hi there Kung Fu fans. Something tells me we've got a bombshell for you this month! Sorry first of all that Part Two of the Film Finale has had to be postponed to the next issue, but when we saw our first copies of *The Secret Art of Bruce Lee*, the entire office flipped over into an outside loop! Right away we just knew that this issue had to be a special in every sense of the word. Yup, the whole magazine has been turned over to saluting a remarkable new martial arts landmark, and once you've checked out inside this *KFM*, you'll understand why.

The book has got to be the biggest sensation in the history of Kung Fu publishing. Just think about it - where else could you expect to find over a hundred never-before-seen pictures of Bruce Lee, the one and only King of Kung Fu, in full flight? Once again the staff of *KFM* are responsible for bringing you this scoop of the century and, boy, we aren't too modest to admit it! Inside this month's issue, you can discover what the whole sensation's all about - not to mention just how the 'Lost Pictures' actually turned up in the *KFM* office.

The Secret Society's not missing out on the fun either. This time only, they're pushing the news and views back into the file to introduce a great new competition and they've got 20 copies of *The Secret Art of Bruce Lee* to give away to the winners! On top of all that, there's an exclusive mail order offer open only to readers of *KFM* - Oh and some of those are going to be signed and numbered collector's editions - look inside for the low-down on that.

Jenny has taken a month's leave of absence from the Kickback columns to help us get together this momentous edition of *Kung-Fu Monthly*, and if you think we've all gone mad - don't worry - it's back to normal next month!

See you all then!!

Felix Yen
Editor-in-Chief

THE SECRET ART OF BRUCE LEE

Incredible? Amazing? Superb? - just how do you describe a book that has everything? Two issues back, we gave you a sensational first chapter taster of the things to come and now, to mark the historic publishing of this martial master-piece, we are proud to offer through the pages of *Kung-Fu Monthly*, a chapter by chapter and page by page synopsis. Remember, you won't have found any such review elsewhere. This truly is the first time

ever that *The Secret Art of Bruce Lee* has been checked out in its entirety. Soon, the work itself will be available through book and magazine shops all over the world to become a priceless addition to every Bruce Lee admirer's book collection. First though, it is to be offered exclusively to readers of *Kung-Fu Monthly*. Right here in the pages of *KFM* No.28, you'll find you have the chance of a lifetime to buy through our mail order service, a signed and numbered copy of this fabulous book. There will only be a small quantity of these available so the advice is to move fast. Stay with us now and find out what you'll be getting as we leap into the pages of *The Secret Art of Bruce Lee*.

For anyone who missed out on the first chapter sneak preview two issues back, here to kick off is a brief check of the opening pages. Appropriately entitled, The Maydole Photographs, we're taken quickly through the sum total of Bruce's work up to the posthumous publishing of his *Tao of Jeet Kune Do*. Unfortunately, as the author points out, the *Tao of Jeet Kune Do* was sadly incomplete at the time of the Little Dragon's tragic death and despite Linda

Lee's excellent work in correlating and producing the book, the end result fell far short of the mark Bruce Lee would have set himself. What a stroke of luck therefore that the Maydole pictures should have come to light. Taken by Chester Maydole, a freelance Hollywood photographer, around 1966, they represent the outcome of no fewer than four photo sessions. This of course accounts for the very wide area of the Little Dragon's Life that they cover. Some were taken at home in Bruce's West Los Angeles apartment, some at the beautiful Malibu Beach, others at Portuguese Bend in South Los Angeles.

Chester first latched on to the martial wizard when picking up fanzine shots of Bruce starring as Kato in the doomed The Green Hornet series. They hit it off well and Maydole was impressed enough to fix up some private sessions. And he was around too to see the Little Dragon set up those Kung Fu schools - the first in the Los Angeles Chinatown. A famous pupil at the school was Danny Inosanto and he it was, who was chosen to act out the set pieces with Bruce on Malibu Beach. These pictures represent some of the finest action shots of the Little Dragon every seen - the words of the Tao of Jeet Kune Do finally translated into pure action. For over ten years, these momentous pictures have been locked away in the files of Chester Maydole - now they have been set free in the pages of The Secret Art of Bruce Lee.

The book then divides into two distinct halves, the first dealing with Bruce's upbringing on the tough streets of Hong Kong and the second, a record of how he distilled and developed the system we now know of as Jeet Kune Do. In the first action strip sequence, we see the Little Dragon first blocking an attack and then retaliating with a spear thrust to Inosanto's eyes. His early days had taught him many unpleasant (though sometimes necessary) 'tricks of the trade.' As he said, "I was a punk and went looking for fights. We used chains and pens with knives hidden inside!" In fact, as we learn from these pages, there was a very real possibility at one time that Bruce would commit himself to life with the dreaded Triad Society. Thankfully, the Little Dragon had the sense to pull back from the brink and reason out better things.

When you get your copy of the book, be sure to flip through to sequence four, where you'll see a really sensational shot of Bruce executing a powerful sidekick to Inosanto's stomach. The expression on his face is one of his grittiest! Meanwhile, we're taken along to a major point of transition in the Little Dragon's life. Dissatisfied with Hong Kong's underlying violence, he switches his energies to the study of Wing Chun under the guidance of Yip Man. Such is his enthusiasm, Lee rapidly becomes the star pupil and we're treated to many delightful accounts of his early successes. Naturally, as the book indicates, his physical skills developed initially at a far greater pace than the spiritual considerations. Without doubt, he knew of the subtlety that lay beneath the martial art's rough exterior, but capturing it was altogether something else. Yip Man, however, did his job well and we are told how Bruce set sail for America with new and more constructive philosophies on his mind.

Next up, we're treated to some very rare picture sets indeed. Bruce, handling the big sweeper (a staff hinged at two points), is defending himself against a spear attack. Though very familiar with the technique of handling this weapon, for some reason in later years he rarely made use of it. In one particularly brilliant sequence, he is actually synchronising some of his famed kicks with the sweeper. At this point, *The Secret Art of Bruce Lee* has traced his career through to the Los Angeles school he set up and has introduced us to Taky Kimura. Gradually, you can see through the academy's trials and tribulations that something very important is developing and that, of course, is Jeet Kune Do. More clearly than ever, we understand why Bruce refused to open up Jeet Kune Do schools on a purely commercial basis. He hated the whole idea of selling the martial arts as some sort of package and in fact, begged his star pupil, Danny Inosanto, not to do it either.

Picture sequence thirteen features Bruce in action with the nunchakus. Follow the split second timing of his movements as the camera captures him in full flight. It is also particularly interesting in that it depicts the Little Dragon in the classic 'ready' position. Back to the words, however, and Bruce has now become a fitness fanatic and is patiently building his body into the world's finest fighting machine. We hear of how Bruce, on meeting his 'skinny' brother, Robert, at the airport remarked, "Don't tell anyone you're my brother - you'll embarrass me!" Within days, his brother was pushed into early morning runs and a special diet. Poor Robert hardly knew what had hit him and we discover here the gruesome details of the Little Dragon's tailor-made special concoction. Diet in general gets a special mention and we learn of some of Bruce's more bizarre eating habits.

The next step along the path of Jeet Kune Do training to be covered is that of warming up. The Little Dragon was absolutely insistent that all activity should be turned on slowly and we hear many of the techniques that he practiced. Running was a very favourite item on the Lee menu and he was also very attached to isometric exercises and the book gives

many examples. However, much as Bruce tried to ensure that he had just about every piece of useful equipment going, he knew only too well that little would substitute for the real thing. *The Secret Art of Bruce Lee* offers us a word on training with partners - an invaluable section of the book and one which can of course be read in conjunction with the really excellent sparring picture sets. The importance of wearing or carrying protectors is correctly stressed for, as many of the Little Dragon's sparring partners knew to their cost, absent or incorrectly placed safeguards can produce more than just painful results.

The importance of attaining a correct stance is paramount although the difference between this and classical posture is made absolutely clear. The positioning of the body must suit the individual. Sequence nineteen picks out a selection of superb Lee kicks, featuring in particular a great 'flying kick' shot. Back on stances again and how about the opener of sequence twenty for a horse stance. From this you can see him 'snake' into a two finger spear position. Speed of movement gets a good deal of attention around his part of the book plus some helpful tips from the Little Dragon on balance and endurance. The final action sequence, number twenty four, is a masterpiece, containing as it does no fewer than eighteen consecutive pictures of Bruce performing an extremely complex Kung Fu form. The explanatory notes, as always throughout this book, are excellent with Paul Simmons magnificently carrying on from where he left off in *The Beginner's Guide to Kung Fu*.

As a fitting finale to this memorable treatise, we catch a glimpse of the master 'at home.' Firstly we see him using his own home built lifting apparatus and discussing some of his many 'party tricks' - like the one inch punch - and secondly, we catch him relaxing in the library. Bruce was no stranger to his enormous collection of books and in fact Linda frequently remarked that the only time he ever sat still for more than five minutes was to read. The Little Dragon didn't have anything handed him on a plate. Studying was as important to him as any training routine, for what use is skill without the tools to exercise it?

And there we leave *The Secret Art of Bruce Lee*. As a fountain of the Little Dragon's enthusiasm and expertise it is extremely important - as a demonstration of his supreme ability in the martial arts, it is unique and totally invaluable. Probably never again will we have the opportunity to read, understand and own a book of this stature. To the casually interested there is much to whet the appetite and baffle the imagination - to the dedicated student, we present the perfect companion reading to Bruce's own *Tao of Jeet Kune Do*. *The Secret Art of Bruce Lee* is an essential addition to everyone's bookshelf.

THE LOST PICTURES
AS TOLD BY THE EDITOR

The action began nearly eight months ago - back in fact to August 1976 when the almost tropical heat of that scorching summer made producing *Kung-Fu Monthly* the nearest thing I've known to a labour of dispair! No one in that sultry office could have guessed for one minute that a miracle stood hovering in the wings. After all, there was *KFM* No.20 to polish off - lines to correct, pictures to choose, wet, sticky fingers tapped away at typewriters while ever present iced Cokes absolutely refused to remain cold for more than five short minutes. The clock ticked onwards towards the end of another unremarkable *Kung-Fu Monthly* day. We made the deadline and watching issue No.20 vanish out of the door was like having a great weight lifted. "Nothing much to shout about now for a day or two," somebody muttered - at least that's what he thought!

Now, for those of you who don't have much idea how *KFM* comes about, let me explain a thing or two. To start with, we rely to quite a large extent on outside researchers

- both for pictures and information. Most magazines tend to have helpers scouting around for what's needed and *KFM* is no exception. All over the world we have Kung Fu contacts just waiting with one hand on the telephone. Suddenly, the steady drone of the traffic outside the window was interrupted by the clanging of the telephone. "Hi - it's Fred here," said a very familiar voice. "Look, I don't know if it's of any interest to you but I've got a huge collection of martial art pictures that have been hanging around for a while and the boss wants them out of the way. I don't suppose it's anything important, but they may be worth a look." Fred didn't sound too enthusiastic but - well, maybe it was something we could think about for a second feature. "OK," I said, "Why not come by tomorrow and we'll have a look at them." And that's how it was left - one last sip of lukewarm Coke and we all went home!

The next day was Friday and it began normally enough with a quick check through

the freshly written features for *KFM* No.21. The one about nunchakus was particularly interesting and I was musing over what sort of response we'd be getting to it in the mail, when my moment of daydreaming was halted. The door buzzer went - it was Fred. In he came and throwing first a large unopened box on to my desk, he suggested we go out for something to eat.

    We had a bit to talk about - to start with, only a week before, he'd located a batch of really fine Bruce Lee colour pictures that were just out of this world - in fact, so far out of this world, to the best of my knowledge, they hadn't ever been published before. (Two of them were later used as poster sides for *KFM* No.22 and No.23). That deserved a pat on the back if anything did and, chatting about the chances of finding more where they'd come from, we arrived back at the door of the office.

    Fred went his way and I went mine. He had plenty of work to do that day and couldn't hang on. Maybe if he'd known about the sensation hiding round the corner he'd have found a few extra minutes, but the company he worked for supplied pictures to anyone and everyone and other customers were waiting. Back in my room, I noticed that the box of photos was no longer there - obviously the library people had taken them away to be properly checked in. I made a mental note to pop upstairs and flip through them when I had a moment to spare.

Now, I should mention here that the library people in fact take care of the needs of several different magazines and they'd make no claim to be Bruce Lee experts. Their job is to book in and book out photographs and to make sure nothing ever gets lost - an invaluable requirement for any publication. This particular batch must've taken a while though - by three o'clock they were still counting! This puzzled me a little. Normally speaking, when a set of pictures arrives, you can expect there to be a dozen or so photographs to choose from. The impression I got over the phone from a harassed librarian was that there were nearer a thousand! More than a little intrigued, I decided to poke my nose in the door to see what was going on.

Setting off up the stairs, I had no idea that the next few minutes were going to make Kung Fu history - Columbus discovering the New World was to have nothing on this! I walked into the library and although everything looked more or less the same as ever, in retrospect, there was something about the atmosphere that seemed strangely different. I moved over to the huge, unmistakable pile of pictures and not knowing exactly what to expect, I idly flipped through the first three or four. The truth took roughly thirty seconds to hit me! Now, that may seem a long time to you, but sometimes it takes a few seconds

THE POSTER MAGAZINES - VOLUME TWO

Not Since The Death Of The Master Himself Has Such An Important Event Appeared On The Kung-Fu Horizon!

At last Kung-Fu Monthly, the publishers of the world's greatest martial arts magazine, are delighted to have on *exclusive* mail order offer to its readers, the book that everyone's been talking about. Never before has KFM been privileged to offer such a unique and outstanding product. So important is the occasion, we requested the author to sign and number 500 copies — and this he has done. They will become valuable collector's items in the years ahead.

- Over a hundred never-before-seen photos of Bruce Lee in full dynamic action...
- Stacks of invaluable Jeet Kune Do demonstration picture sequences — superb material for the serious student...
- Crystal clear step by step explanatory notes written by Paul Simmons, the man who brought you *The Beginner's Guide to Kung-Fu*...
- Page after page of brilliantly researched and intelligently edited comment on the Little Dragon...
- Quote after quote and instruction after instruction taken direct from the lips of the master himself...

Rush your orders in NOW for *either* the signed and numbered:

Collector's Edition
The Secret Art of Bruce Lee
Kung-Fu Monthly
39 Goodge Street
London W1P 1FD
and enclose a Postal Order/Cheque for £5.00 (made out to Kung-Fu Monthly, please)

or far:

Standard Edition
The Secret Art of Bruce Lee
Kung-Fu Monthly
39 Goodge Street
London W1P 1FD
and enclose a Postal Order/Cheque for £4.00 (made out to Kung-Fu Monthly, please)

IMPORTANT NOTE
Orders for the Collector's Edition arriving too late (remember there are only 500) will receive instead the Standard version plus a refund.

Finally, please allow at least 3 weeks for the delivery of your order.

This Unique Hardbound Volume Is Something To Be Treasured For A Lifetime.

for the mind to accept the impossible. My first inclination was to refute the evidence that sat before my eyes. Surely these photographs are of someone imitating the Little Dragon but doing it well though. And he looks so similar to the master, why on earth hasn't he been chosen to take over Bruce's part in the *Game of Death* - or perhaps even star in Linda Lee's tribute? But then, the truth started to sink in. No, it's not possible! I mean, how could over a thousand pictures of Bruce remain undetected for all these years? Fakes? If they are, they're good ones. Great heavens, can this really be happening? Sweat was breaking out as I feverishly tore at the pile of pictures - to everyone in the room, I must have looked demented! Strangled words caught in my throat. Saints alive, do you know what I think these are? I just don't believe it. This must be the sensation of the century! People appeared out from nowhere to gaze in awe at the making of history. Work everywhere jammed to a standstill as the entire staff of *Kung-Fu Monthly* crowded around to pay homage to the kindest stroke of luck that fate ever delivered. I'm not exaggerating when I say the emotion of those few precious seconds of discovery will stay with me a lifetime.

Gradually, the realisation of what had just dropped into our laps started to sink in and now the moment had come to evaluate the full worth of the awe inspiring collection. Hour after hour we flipped through the treasure trove of Bruce Lee photographs, handling each priceless print as though it were something out of Britain's crown jewels! Obviously their value was beyond measure - not only to the collector, but also to the serious martial arts student. Here finally, was living proof of the Little Dragon's ultimate gift to the fighting world. Move by move action sequences of him demonstrating his own unique style of Jeet Kune Do abounded. No one could ever again doubt the efficiency of Bruce Lee's twentieth century fighting formula. Each picture flowed like liquid from the one before - sheer poetry in motion - and the beauty behind his deadly art was enough to take one's breath away. It was the nearest thing I had ever known to personal instruction from the master.

But revelations were still to come, for on top of all that we'd witnessed already, lower down in this veritable chest of discovery were to be found pictures of Bruce and Linda, at home with a very young looking Brandon. Close, intimate family portraits that said so much more than whole books full of words and shots too of the Little Dragon training in his home made gymnasium. At last we could examine at first hand, the purpose built equipment that every fan has heard so much about but so few have ever seen.

Some time later, having had a chance to reflect on all that had happened, I got to wondering where the 'Lost Pictures' had come from. How could they have remained hidden for so long and what quirk of fate had delivered them into our hands? Inappropriately perhaps, the answer was quite simple. Taken by freelance photographer, Chester Maydole, they had sat in his files for nearly ten years just gathering dust until one day, he handed everything over to a big USA Photo Library. Presumably they were checked in by someone who wasn't really thinking. Not realising that the pictures were of the master, they became filed away under the general heading of 'martial arts,' where in fact they could have been undetected and unused perhaps forever!

Thankfully of course, that wasn't to happen, and immediately the discovery had been made, wheels were set in motion to produce the best and most concise book ever on Bruce Lee and on his Jeet Kune Do. Now, I believe we've done just that! Drawing on the wealth of experience available from the staff of *Kung-Fu Monthly*, I'm pleased to offer to the legions of Little Dragon fans the world over, *The Secret Art of Bruce Lee*. Representing the fruits of nearly a year's labour, this book will be a treasure to possess and I'd guess it to be absolutely essential reading for anyone who has ever cared for, followed after, tried to emulate, or has simply been plain interested in the world's number one martial athlete. Lady Luck played the cards into our hands and I know you're going to love the way we shuffled them!

THE BRUCE LEE SECRET SOCIETY

Hello, it's Pam and Carmella here and they've given us a really exciting job to do this month.

There we were, reading our pre-publication copies of *The Secret Art of Bruce Lee*, when up came the *KFM* Editor to tell us that we had twenty of them to give away! Put like that, how could we refuse? So, anyway, here goes and fingers crossed, we haven't forgotten anything! (Oh, in case you're wondering, there'll be lots of news, views, gossip and scandal again next month - honest!).

That's right, to celebrate this historic moment, the Editor of *KFM* has agreed to donate 20 SIGNED AND NUMBERED copies of this sensational new book. All you have to do is write the answers to the following five questions (labelling them A, B, C, D and E) on a postcard ONLY PLEASE and NOT FORGETTING TO INCLUDE YOUR NAME, ADDRESS AND SECRET SOCIETY NUMBER!

A) MGM approached Bruce to co-star in a film with one of America's most famous pop singers. Who was he?
B) What year did Bruce take part in the famous Long Beach Tournament?
C) Who took the film of Bruce performing at that Tournament?
D) In *Fist of Fury*, what does Bruce disguise himself as to gain entrance into the Japanese club.
E) What was the name of the actor who played the son of the Big Boss?

Send your entries to: The BLSS Secret Art Competition, *Kung-Fu Monthly*, 39 Goodge Street, London, W1P 1FD. Postcards to arrive not later than midday May 31st 1977. Answers arriving in letter form will not be considered. The senders of the first 20 correct entries to be drawn out of the mail sack by an executive of Cathay Films Ltd, are each guaranteed to receive a SIGNED AND NUMBERED COPY of *The Secret Art Of Bruce Lee*. By the way, if you're not a member of the Secret Society but wish to take part in our fabulous competition, this time only, we will be accepting entries from non-members, PROVIDING SUCH ENTRIES ARE ACCOMPANIED BY A REQUEST FOR MEMBERSHIP. You may, in this case, send your postcard INSIDE your application letter to join the Secret Society.

What? You STILL haven't joined the Bruce Lee Secret Society? Well, here's your chance to make amends AND catch up on all that's happening for Little Dragon fans everywhere. No true Bruce Lee fan would want to miss out on the opportunity to become part of the world's fastest growing Secret Society - so get in now!

THOUGH THE MASTER IS GONE

The K.F.M.

BRUCE LEE SECRET SOCIETY

Yes, sad to say the Master has gone but that does not mean he will be forgotten — far from it! *The Bruce Lee Secret Society* is devoted to the memory of the Master. We are governed by his teachings, his sayings, his way of life. Though the Little Dragon himself is no longer here to lead the way, the great gift that he left with us and the example of excellence he set, lives on in our hearts and minds.

And when you become accepted as a member, just take a look at what you're entitled to get:

* A personal *membership card* — to carry with you always!

* The absolutely unique *badge* and *sticker* — available ONLY to members — plus photos, a biography and a fact sheet.

* Your very own *membership scroll*, tastefully designed for mounting and displaying.

* A superb THREE-MONTHLY *News Sheet*... full of gossip, rumours, secrets, fan's comments, pix, pen-pals, competitions, a swop shop and much, much more.

* A regular page in Kung-Fu Monthly, the world's greatest ever martial arts magazine — not to mention great money saving reductions on all the KFM mail order goods.

* A guarantee that ALL your letters will be answered and wherever possible, all your problems solved!

Remember, the only way you can be absolutely certain of having a share in the great movement which the Master has created is to become a part of the *Bruce Lee Secret Society*.

NO OTHER FAN CLUB HAS EVER OFFERED AS MUCH... and yet, unbelievably, all this can be yours for ONLY £3.25. That's right, and new members are ALWAYS welcome, so don't just think about it, MAKE SURE you join right now — you'll never regret it!

Send immediately your £3.25 cheque or postal order to:

The Bruce Lee Secret Society
39 Goodge Street
London W1P 1FD

THE POSTER MAGAZINES - VOLUME TWO

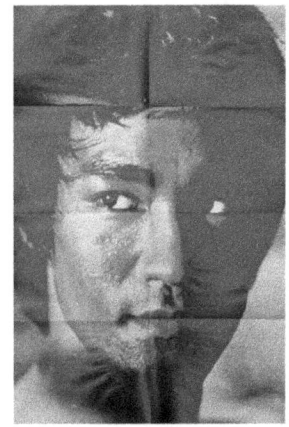

29

1977

EDITORIAL

    Hi there Kung Fu fans. After last month's *Secret Art of Bruce Lee* smash issue, you might have thought that *KFM* No.29 was going to be an anticlimax! Well, that goes to show just how wrong you can be. A blockbuster every time is our motto and here to prove it are two fantastic new features, both chock full of facts and information. For instance, there's the long awaited Bruce Lee Film Finale Part II (postponed from the last issue) and what a bag full of revelations we've got lined up for you there. So you want to know all about *The Man and the Legend* - and how about the low-down on *Longstreet*? Look no further, 'cos it's all there in our unique Film Finale Part II.
    Next in line, we've got a real turn up for the books! How often have you been sitting there in the cinema wondering just how a particular actor is going to live through to his next film with a hatchet buried in his back? And how about the man who has just caught an arrow in the chest? Common sense tells you that it hasn't really happened - otherwise

we'd soon be running short of actors! So what's it all about? *KFM* decided several months ago that the time had come to strip back the blanket of secrecy surrounding this intriguing part of the movie business. Bruce knew the game well - the only difference between him and most everyone else was that he knew how to use it sparingly to maximum effect. The Camera Lies - read on to find out how and why!

After last month's ace issue it hardly needs me to remind you about *The Secret Art of Bruce Lee*. The book's already become a legend and if sales are anything to go by, we'll soon be needing one of the fastest reprints ever for all our legions of loyal readers - and that means you. Okay - that's all I've got to say, except on with the show!

Felix Yen

Felix Yen
Editor-in-Chief

BRUCE LEE FEATURE FILM FINALE: PART TWO

OK, here we are again, back to normal after last month's very special issue and ready to pull the Bruce Lee Film Finale Part 2 out of the *Kung-Fu Monthly* bundle of goodies. We left you last time just as the Little Dragon was about to embark on yet another milestone in his star-studded career - this time, the TV series, Longstreet. After we've picked up on that, the magic moment will have arrived to untie the 'info bag' on *The Man and the Legend* - and boy have we got some facts and figures to let loose on you concerning that little number. Finally, there's a bit more to divulge on Warner Brother's Kung Fu TV series and *KFM* poses the question, maybe Bruce had a good reason for not wanting to do the series anyway. With a line up like that ahead of us, there can be absolutely no excuse for a moment's delay! The time has well and truly come to get stuck into the Bruce Lee Film Finale Part II.

It took nearly ten years of downright hard work for him to reach the heights he finally attained. It's true that many fans only climbed aboard the bandwagon once he'd got there and to them of course, it was something new. To the Little Dragon, however, it was simply the culmination of a natural sequence of events.

Next along the line was *Longstreet*, written by - you've guessed it - Stirling Silliphant. The series starred James Franciscus and together with Stirling, Bruce worked on the first story, finally named - wait for it - *The Way of the Intercepting Fist*. Nobody really knew what to expect when they turned on their sets to see that first episode and what a surprise was in store for them. Viewers were glued to their TV's. Franciscus was playing a blind detective who had lost his eyesight in a bomb blast and who tries to get back at the gangsters who did it. He decides to learn the martial arts and this is where Bruce comes in. Straight away, the Lee philosophy is spelt out. He tells the detective that no one can fight properly when there is anger in the heart and he tries to teach him control over his emotions.

In fact, watching the program, it becomes obvious that Stirling Silliphant took the Little Dragon's outlook on life very seriously indeed and by no means did he, like so many others, underestimate Bruce's abilities. The most important aspect of that first momentous episode of Longstreet was that it showed Bruce Lee the man, rather than Bruce Lee the actor and that was a very important step forward. Time and time again, he was asked to appear later in the series but after two or three episodes he called it a day. Things were hotting up for him in Hong Kong and time was getting to be at a premium. The series folded only a short time after Bruce's departure, which many feel to be no coincidence.

No mention of Bruce's other work would be complete without reference to Warner's TV spectacular, *The Warrior*. Ted Ashley had contacted Bruce about the idea and, finding time where he could, the Little Dragon completed the pilot. As most fans now know, that series became *Kung Fu* and Bruce Lee was dropped in favour of David Carradine. The original pilot was actually shown, however, and many viewers were amazed to hear that Carradine had been chosen to replace Bruce. Warner's attitude seems to have been that Bruce was 'too Chinese!' It's hard to see how a Chinese man can be too Chinese to play a Chinese character. Be that as it may, it's a fact that had Bruce landed the part, and had he stayed with it for the same length of time that Carradine did, he would never have had the opportunity to make any of his film classics. In fact, one theory I've heard is that Bruce, knowing he was dying and wanting to make the biggest impact possible in the shortest space of time, threw up the series in favour of feature films. That kind of fantastic theory is hard to prove - but then again, you never know...

As a result of Bruce's American TV success, over in Hong Kong, Raymond Chow approached Bruce with a proposition for a contract. There is some new evidence about this meeting that's recently come to light. To start with, it's said Bruce completely ignored Chow and in fact returned to the States without even seeing him! Strong rumours have

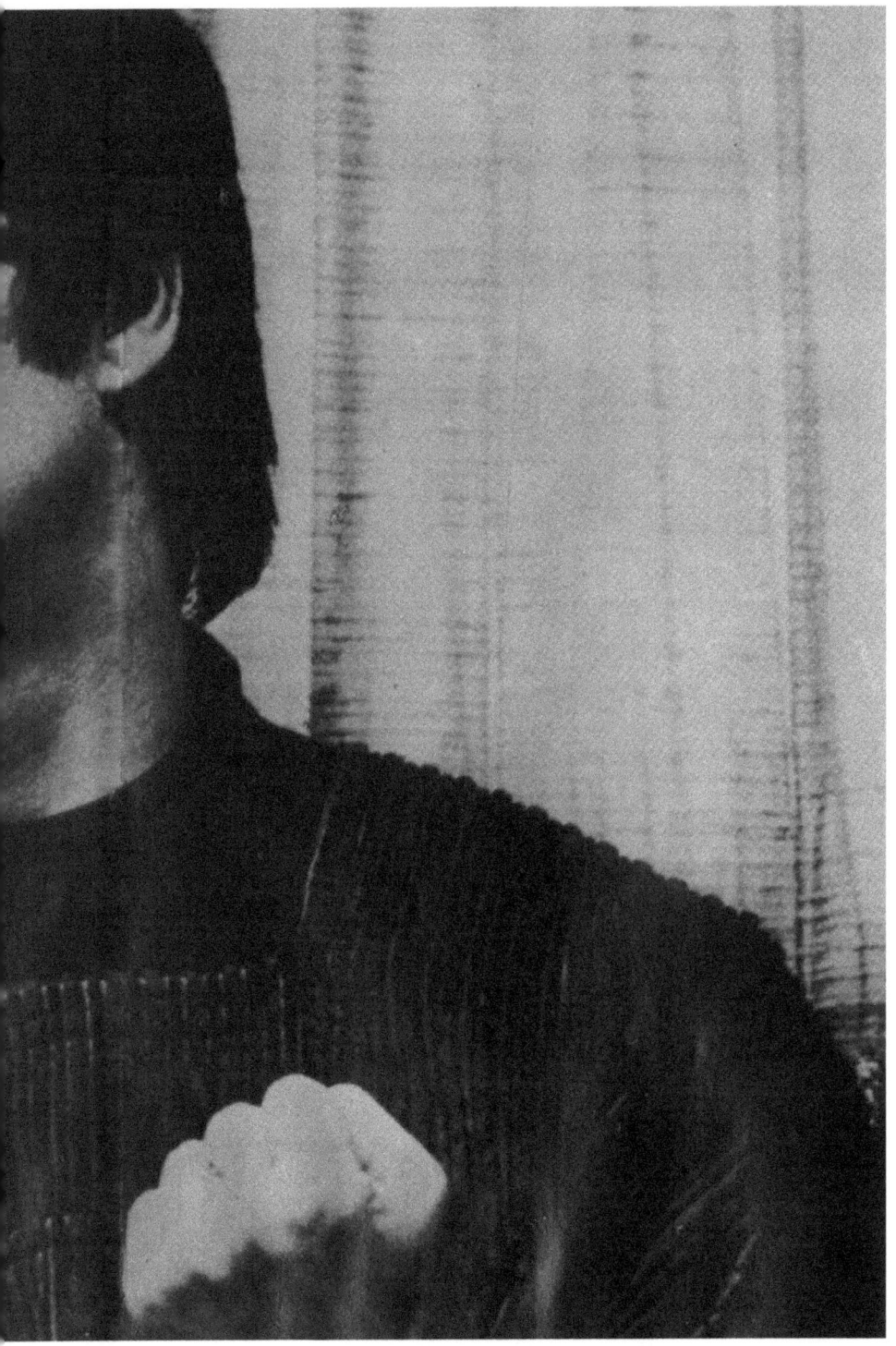

it that the wife of Lo Wei (a top Chow producer) was sent in pursuit of Bruce. She met up with him in America and somehow persuaded him to return to Hong Kong and that's where it all began. Naturally, accusations were made that Bruce was having an affair with her but these were never substantiated.

While Bruce was making *The Big Boss* and *Fist of Fury* he was also doing some technical direction on the side. One of his private jobs was a production called *Fist of Unicorn*. It was about a fisherman called Loon Chi Chu who lived with his wife and son in a coastal village in San Tung. One day, while fishing, they stumble upon a murder. The culprit, being discovered, kills everyone there except Loon Fai who is saved by a monk. The fights are all directed by Bruce and anyone having the opportunity, should not miss seeing what otherwise is a fairly ordinary Chinese film. The star of the film was Unicorn Chan who many fans will remember as the waiter, Tony, in *The Way of the Dragon*.

And that leaves just one more stone to be turned - that of *The Man and the Legend*. Next to *Game of Death*, this has to be the most talked about Bruce Lee film ever and the following contains extracts from a rare Chinese synopsis of the film.

There were in fact two films made - one was a twenty minute short called *Tribute to a Superstar* which was entirely in Cantonese and was shown around the Bijou clubs in the UK. Golden Harvest executive, Andre Morgan handled the production. The full size version, *The Man and the Legend* has never (to our knowledge) been on general release in the western world and fans in Britain are invited to write to Cathay Films Ltd in London to demand its release. The picture according to an early information sheet, was made to help devotees gain a fuller insight into Bruce Lee the man and Bruce Lee the star. The original title was *Bruce Lee - His Life and Death*. This was subsequently changed to *Bruce Lee - The Man and the Legend*. The film consists of hundreds of valuable scenes showing Bruce practicing his Jeet Kune Do and it also catalogues his many achievements in the martial arts and film worlds. It spotlights some of his famous kicks and of course there are excerps from the funeral. The American portion alone is about 3,000 feet long and it again was produced by Andre Morgan. Andre, accompanied by cameramen and technicians, spent some weeks in the USA shooting the memorial and burial services held in Seattle. The film includes interviews with Bruce Lee disciples, Steve McQueen, James Coburn and Robert Wu. The cameras also visit Bruce Lee's school and feature an interview with the principal. They also photograph his martial arts school.

Another portion of the film was shot in Hong Kong and it again shows the Little Dragon practicing his art. There's the three fast kicks that appeared in *The Big Boss*, now shown in slow motion plus the eight lightning kicks from *Fist of Fury*. There is also the famous sequence of two hundred chain kicks from *Game of Death*. The slowing down really allows everybody for the first time to see just how accurate Bruce was. The kicks repeatedly arrive within an eighth of an inch of their target! Other scenes from *Game of Death* are shown, including the battle with Kareem Abdul-Jabbar and also the Korean Hapkido master Ji Han Jae. There are many interviews with his friends - pictures of the equipment in his training room - a shot of the inside of his 'Den' and a general view of his house. The final length approaches 8,500 feet and to be honest, anyone calling himself a true fan of the Little Dragon has got to see this film - it's ninety minutes of pure magic!

So, with all this in the can, why, you may well ask, has it not yet been shown? Well, there are several answers to that thorny question. First of all, the film is apparently badly put together and not too well dubbed either. The chances are Golden Harvest would prefer to make a number of improvements before it ever got released. Another stumbling block is naturally the fact that *Game of Death* itself has not as yet seen the light of day. No doubt the company feel it wrong to show excerpts from Bruce's greatest epic before the film itself has been premiered.

So there we are - some more vital pieces of information on the TV and film career of Bruce Lee. But, as the puzzle draws nearer completion, let us not forget Bruce's spirit as he brushed with destiny. Adulated he may well have been, but he was never one to let down a friend. Enormously skilled he may have been at his chosen art but he was never one to scorn a student at the bottom of the ladder. Remember, as long as his life's work endures, so too will the memory of a kind, generous and remarkable man.

THE CAMERA LIES – PART ONE

It's well known that Bruce Lee had seldom to resort to tricking his audience. Being the greatest martial artist of our time, he was well able to handle most of the required action himself, although as we shall see later, there were just one or two instances when, for artistic effect, he did indeed pull the wool over our eyes! Generally speaking, he liked to 'play it as it was' - his avowed intention in fact was to make his films believable. However, as is usual in the film industry, the decision wasn't always his to make. Early on in particular there were times when 'cinema tricks' were added to the production - often very much to the Little Dragon's displeasure. There are arguments in its favour - after all, where would James Bond be now without the help of a special effects department? If an audience were to insist on complete realism from its film makers, much of what we see on our cinema screens would be all the less interesting for it. The deciding factor is of course the use to which a 'trick' is put. Has it or has it not enhanced your enjoyment of the film? Read on and see what you think!

The special effects that appear on cinema screens are either physical or optical so let's distinguish between the two. An example of the physical trick is the use of a trampoline by an actor to jump higher than he is normally capable of doing. In this case, physical apparatus is being used to improve his performance (naturally the trampoline itself is kept well out of sight of the camera!). The optical effect is quite a different bag of tricks. One simple example of this kind of illusion is to be found in many a Kung Fu film. Ever recall seeing a fighter jump up on to a high wall with apparently hardly any effort at all? Of course you do and believe me, the actor wasn't acting the ease with which he carried out the leap. In fact he jumped off the wall and what you're seeing is the film going backwards!!

Perhaps one of the most used effects these days is the bullet-hole technique. For the really gruesome close-up clips, the potential victim has a metal plate strapped to him and above it, a bag containing animal blood and meat or a blood substitute. On the word go, a small explosive detonator goes off on the plate, causing his clothes to split and the blood to run through. Done properly, the effect is totally realistic and quite shattering. The only slight difficulty is that the actor frequently suffers rather painful bruising. It's worth noting by the way that in the early days, no one would have dared to actually show blood oozing from a wound. Later, it became acceptable, but only recently has the gore been included!

But back to Bruce Lee and let's take a look at one of the Little Dragon's absolutely valid camera stunts. Remember in *The Big Boss* where Bruce is being attacked by dogs? Right, now the scene was in fact shot in several parts and then put together later. The close-up of him dealing personally with a maddened canine was faked - and not surprisingly! The animal, at this particular point, is stuffed! However, so well shot is the sequence, it really is hard to spot where the switch has been made.

A Kung Fu action favourite has got to be the 'hatchet in the back' routine. Here the actor straps a wooden box across his back (it's filled with blood of course!) and, on impact, the hatchet buries itself in the wood, thereby releasing lots of red stuff! This same technique applies equally well to 'death' by arrows or spears although some feel they rely rather too much on the skill of the marksman who's handling the weapon. Any directional error on his part could easily have fatal consequences. Back in *The Big Boss* and a snip you won't have seen here in the UK, is the part where somebody gets hit on the head with a knife (censored, naturally!). In this particular instance, because of the difficulty of having nowhere to hide the blood where it won't immediately be spotted by the camera, here the red liquid is actually stored in the knife blade itself. As the blunt edge makes impact with the scalp, the pressure on the blade operates a simple switch and out it all comes.

Simulating head injuries poses a great number of problems for the film director. Hiding places for tricks and gadgets are almost non-existent on this part of the body and generally he resorts to the 'camera stop' technique. In essence the idea is very simple - in practice, it's sometimes hard to produce convincing results. Let's say, for instance, that the person concerned is about to be shot through the forehead. Just on the time of impact, the camera is stopped and kept absolutely still. The actor then has to remain as immobile as possible while a bullet hole is 'made up' on his forehead with cosmetics. So skilled is the average make-up team, this operation may take only a few seconds. Immediately after the job has been completed, the camera starts up again and the victim falls down and 'dies.' Unfortunately it's almost impossible for anyone to sit stock still without moving for even a few seconds and the more sharp sighted among a cinema audience may often detect where the 'stop and start' has been made.

The illusion of a dagger being plunged into a body is achieved in a fairly painless way, so far as the actor is concerned! The weapon will usually have a trick blade that, on im-

pact, retracts immediately into the handle. As it does, it punctures a small sack of 'blood' which then realistically flows out from around the hilt. An example of this technique appears in *Fist of Fury*, only on this occasion the instrument of death is in fact a Samurai sword. Another production using this type of trick is *Dracula*!

Gunfire and explosions appear in many a modern day cinema film or TV action spectacular and the desired effects may be manufactured in one of several different ways. Firstly, in the case of gunfire, blanks can be used. This is fine in the case of a normal pistol or rifle but where something more exotic is appearing, say a ray gun in a show like *Star Trek*, then a light bulb is fitted into to the nozzle of the weapon, illuminating the whole thing in convincing fashion. The actual 'death ray' that you see leaving the gun would be added to the film sometime later by a special effects team. Other explosive type effects - flashing lights and so on - are usually supplied by the very expert lighting men at the time of filming. Generally, the sounds needed to accompany the chosen visual effect - guns going off, bombs exploding - are added sometime later. In fact, there are libraries around for just this sort of problem. They contain virtually every sort of noise you can imagine and playing through a few of them makes pretty comical listening!

Crashes and burnings are obviously very important items on the film maker's agenda and a fair degree of ingenuity is needed to produce the right effect. Let's take a burning building as an example. Even bearing in mind the sometimes huge budgets laid out on modern day spectaculars, genuine fires can be just too expensive to contemplate. It's not simply a case of applying the match and turning on the cameras! Fire regulations are tight - and rightly so. A top actor tends to be insured against accidents for millions of pounds so you can bet the insurance companies will want to make sure he's not in any danger! The way out of this problem is to build and then set fire to specially made models. The cost of doing it this way is only a fraction of what the real thing could run to but, once again, some of the realism may easily be lost.

Car crashes look even less likely when models are used and these days, companies try if they can to afford the real thing. Again, there is a collection of ready filmed crashes available, so if for instance the producer intends the villain's car to drive off the top of a cliff, to save money, he may well pay a visit to the library to choose a suitable stock shot. Naturally the wise man will take care to ensure that the car as it appears in the rest of his film bears at least a passing resemblance to the one crashing off the cliff! Even so, eagle-eyed watchers often spot the difference. One exception to a lot of this is James Bond. Most of the trick driving, crashes and so on are very real and done by highly paid stuntmen. In the new *The Spy Who Loved Me* epic, watch out for the car that drives around underwater. Although really best described as a glorified model, it really is doing just that.

Staying with 007 for a moment; do you remember an occasion when Bond's car drove down an alley on two wheels (the only way it would fit) while the police car behind overturned? Here's how it was done. The car was driven off a special ramp which put it over on to two wheels - the camera was then cut. A 'pulley ramp' was then attached, holding the car at roughly the same angle and the whole thing was propelled down the alley way. The police car crashing behind was genuine and carried out by a very brave stuntman!

And here we draw the line for this time. Next issue, in part two, we'll be thinking about some more of the problems that beset the filmmaker. How do you conjure up an Arctic landscape without actually travelling to the North Pole? What about driving a motorbike over a chasm? And how actually did Bruce Lee manage to pick up Mr Wu in his rickshaw in *Fist of Fury*, surely a feat beyond even the immense capabilities of the Little Dragon? Tune in next month for the answers - some you will hardly believe!

THE BRUCE LEE SECRET SOCIETY

Hello again, Pam here, and if you've read your News Sheets, you'll know by now that Carmella has been forced to give up her joint presidency of the Secret Society due to the pressure of her daytime work. As I said in News Sheet 3, it's very sad that she's had to make this decision but she does hope to be popping by now and again to help out when time permits. On behalf of all the members; thanks Carmella for all the invaluable work you've put in - we'll miss you.

Now, hands up all of you who answered the questions in last month's special Society Competition No.2? You know; the one with the 20 copies of *The Secret Art of Bruce Lee* books to be given away? Hmm, it really wasn't too difficult. By the way, don't get confused between that and the News Sheet No.3 Competition - they ARE completely different! Actually, the No.3 Competition is much the harder of the two so I don't really expect to receive very many correct entries - but I'd love you all to prove me wrong!

Next up, quite a number of members have written in to me asking why *Kung-Fu*

Monthly doesn't print more posters from *The Big Boss*. Well firstly, let me assure you that your favourite martial arts magazine in no way thinks any the less of Bruce's first major film success. In fact the answer to your question is quite simple. For some reason, very few good quality 'stills' were taken on the set while the film was originally being shot. Those that were have all been seen many times before and only very occasionally does something new come along. Perhaps rather than moan about it, we should instead, just be thankful that his other masterpieces received better coverage!

I've had a really exciting letter from members Martin Hughes (1695) and Mark Burns (1687). Lord knows the amount of work they've put into it but how about this for a labour of love. The two of them have collected a huge list of names and addresses of places where you can send off for Bruce Lee posters. What a great idea - it must have taken months of research to accomplish such a worthwhile task. Obviously this is something that just has to be shared with everyone else, so here's what I propose to do. Anyone wanting a copy of this list (and let's face it, who doesn't) just write in to me, enclosing a stamped and self addressed envelope please, and I'll see that one is popped in the post for you. By the way, many of the sources are in the States, so I strongly suggest that first of all, you just write asking for catalogues and prices. I wouldn't send money off straight away - unless you feel absolutely sure.

You'll all be glad to hear that I've made a start on separating members into areas. As you'll probably remember, the idea is for Secret Society people to be able to contact others who are living not too far away. I've often noticed while browsing through member's letters that two have come from the same town. I wouldn't mind betting though that neither knows of the other's existence! Well, here's everyone's chance to find out where their nearest Secret Society neighbour is. Once again I must insist that anyone writing in for information must include a stamped/addressed envelope, oh, and by the way, don't expect a really quick reply. It's going to take a little while yet to fully complete the lists. Send your request to: BLSS Area Lists, 14 Rathbone Place, London W1.

See you all soon - **Pam**

SECRET SOCIETY SWOP SHOP

And now it's time to open up the door of The Swop Shop.

Andrew Timber land (1251) of Shawford, nr Winchester has *Dragon* Vol. 1 No. 2,7,8,10,11,12,13,14 and Vol. 2 No. 1,4,6,7,8 and *Popster* Bruce Lee poster (opens into a Kung Fu poster) in fair condition. Wants *KFM* No. 2 and 3.

Martin Frampton (1712) of Petit Sentier, Jersey, requires *KFM* No. 1,2,3 and *KFM Book of Kung Fu* and any pictures or photos of Angela Mao - good price paid.

David Fieldhouse (1238) of Halton, Leeds offers *KFM* No. 8,9,11,16,17. He wants *KFM* No.1 and any other Bruce Lee posters/books.

Keith Milner (1541) of Mastin Moor, Chesterfield, has *KFM* No. 6-11, 13-16, 18-22 (2 of No.8). Offers please.

KICKBACK: THE LETTERS

Hi there, Jenny here again and I'm just raring to dip into this month's double sized sack of mail and get going on the last two month's letters! First up though, I've just had news from Cathay Films that *Game of Death* looks like being postponed yet again! No reasons have been given, but the proposed autumn premiere is now almost certainly off. I think I speak for most of you when I say that disappointment is hardly the word. This further delay is absolutely scandalous and I, for one, intend to try and do something about it. At the moment, I'm thinking along the lines of a petition to be sent to Raymond Chow at Golden Harvest and if that looks possible, I'll be letting you know more details next time. One other problem which I must mention is the lack of stamped and addressed envelopes I'm getting in with the mail these days. Anyone writing to Kickback and expecting a reply must include a SAE. And now, the letters!

PROUD CHINESE LADY

Dear Jenny,
I have been reading *KFM* ever since the first issue and feel a little disappointed to find that there seem to be hardly any Chinese readers writing in. After all, Lee Siu Lung is Chinese and being the same nationality as him, I am very proud. I once caught a glimpse of Bruce (about six years ago) at Kai Tak Airport. Of course he wasn't as famous then, though it was still a struggle trying to get close to him. One more thing, Jenny, is it just a coincidence that your surname is Lee?
Anita Choi, Wallasey, Merseyside

Dear Anita,
Many thanks for your kind words. What can I say to someone who has actually seen Bruce than, "I wish I were you!" So far as letters from Chinese readers go, I must say I don't get that many and it's puzzled me a little too. Okay all you brothers and sisters of Bruce Lee - let's be hearing from you. Finally, it grieves me to say my surname is indeed a coincidence.

NO KIDS ALLOWED

Dear Jenny,
In most of your *KFM*'s, you receive letters from people under 18 who cannot get in to Bruce Lee films. They feel they're being discriminated against because they are too young to see the King. But have they ever looked at it from this angle? If youngsters were allowed in to see him in action, a majority of them would go home and cut up a broom handle, get some string and start swinging and the chances of them avoiding serious injury is very slight. Probably the most adventurous youngsters would go to school and start cutting throwing stars out of metal and they'd hurt someone. No matter from which angle you look at it, the censors are definitely right.
Parmjit Singh Kang, Forest Gate, London

Dear Parmjit,
Your letter looks like stoking up a few fires. I wonder how many readers will agree with you? Actually, the thought occurs to me that many of the irresponsible people I've met in my life have looked well over 18. Anyway, clear the decks for a tidal wave of protest.

EARLY ISSUE REPRINTS?

Dear Jenny,
I am sure that I am one of many *KFM* fans who is not in possession of some of the earlier issues. Personally, it only involves issue No.1 but from reading the letters in Kickback, I gather that there are those who are missing issues up to No.5. Would it be possible to make these early editions available again with reprinting?
Lee Percy, Hainault, Essex

Dear Lee,
Actually, I've had many similar requests in from other readers over the last year so, to put you all in the picture, here is the situation with early issue reprints. One of the facts of life about magazine publishing is that small quantities (say 1,000 copies) are simply not economical. Each magazine would probably cost more than ten times the usual price to print and then we'd have no guarantee we'd be able to sell them all. Although there are readers who would dearly love to get hold of, say, issue one, remember that thousands actually do have it already and they wouldn't want another. It really is difficult, but believe me if I ever find a solution, I'll be the first to let you know.

SHAM BASRA SHAM

Dear Jenny,
I was reading your *KFM* No.27 and I saw something about Sham Basra from Erdington being chosen by the BBC to star as the Little Dragon. Does he bear much resemblance to Bruce?
John Lee

Dear John,
I'm afraid that the Sham Basra business has in fact, turned out to be a bit of a sham! After exhaustive enquiries via many departments in the BBC (who all steadfastly denied the whole thing) the truth finally emerged. There is a Kung Fu series for children that they are planning to show this summer. In one of the programmes, the 'Kung Fu Kid' dreams he is the Little Dragon and Sham, so I'm told, acts out the part of Bruce in the dream. A far cry from the documentary we were promised and, no, so far as I can see from the picture I have, he doesn't look much like the master.

QUICKIES CORNER

Paul Taylor, Dundonald, Northern Ireland - This information about the sweat glands looks pretty dodgy to me. *Game of Death* won't have an English soundtrack. *The Wisdom of Bruce Lee* is late, but coming soon.

James Ruddy, Greenock, Scotland - There is sadly no legal way that 8mm versions of Bruce's films can be manufactured and sold in the UK.

K. Steel, Battersea, London - Bruce certainly did have trouble with his sight - How bad, I don't know.

Dieter Crockett, Immingham - Glad the astrology feature had you well taped!

Dean Robinson, Portsmouth, Hants - Yes, Bruce did visit London. There are more 'specials' in the pipe line.

Philip Heath, Edinburgh, Scotland - I can vouch that Inosanto's signature is absolutely genuine in the book from Cimac.

Michael Dunn, Wheatley Hill, County Durham - Yes, we still have B*ruce Lee King of Kung Fu* on sale - £1.30.

Mr. J. Kay, North Humberside - Thanks for Hong Kong information.

Paul Chambers, Shirley, Southampton - Try Cathay Films for a picture of Linda (27 Soho Square, London W.1.).

Barrie Jones, Wolverhampton, Staffs - Bruce's home life would be a good feature - We'll try.

Dave Langley, Runcorn, Halton - Keep up your good work in keeping Bruce's name alive.

Al Briers, St. Helens, Merseyside - Best move is to ring Eccles Police Station and ask them to check the company still exists.

Chris Brett, Sidcup, Kent - Wasn't it great to see Bruce in *Batman*!

David Maguire, Dublin, Eire - Write to Linda, David Chiang, Raymond Chow c/o Cathay Films (address above).

Ricky Baker, Hinckley, Leicester - I've heard bad reports on *The Black Dragon Revenges Bruce Lee's Death*.

Paul Furr, Gedling, Nottingham - Only poor quality *Game of Death* suits available at present - Still trying.

Chris Gannon, Dublin, Eire - Scrapbooks - 45p. Write to Pam regarding joining the club.

John Kemp, Patchway, Bristol - Glad to hear that the *Enter the Dragon* trailer soon available on 8mm.

Patrick Hennesy, Dublin, Eire - I agree, there's more violence on football terraces than in Kung Fu.

S. Senior, Blackpool, Lancashire - Bruce made five major films, plus many early Mandarin ones.

THE POSTER MAGAZINES - VOLUME TWO

1977

EDITORIAL

Hi there Kung Fu fans. Well, what do you know - we've made it to *KFM* No.30! It's a bit early to start celebrating again, but what a thumb on the nose to all the knockers! I've said it before and I'll say it again. So long as there's all you fans out there wanting facts, figures and information on the Little Dragon in particular and the world of Kung Fu in general, we're going to keep on turning out *Kung-Fu Monthly*. And I hope that's gonna be for a long time yet! Believe me, it really it a labour of love and that's on behalf of not only myself, but everybody here at the *KFM* offices.

First up this month we've got part one of a really fantastic feature entitled The Bruce Lee Press File. Yes, Lady Luck came by the door again and delivered into our hands, an enormous scrapbook of Little Dragon press clippings. Naturally, the *KFM* staff turned up trumps yet again and we've produced for you what amounts to an invaluable historic document on the often confused way film reviewers received his cinema work.

Misunderstandings, prejudice, bigotry on one hand and adulation, praise and clarity of thought on the other serve as superb ingredients to yet another *KFM* 'first.'

Number two in line is the second part of our investigation into the film industry's 'tricks of the trade' department. Surprises there are a plenty and some of the revelations about creating the perfect 'cinema illusion' will amaze you. Probably never again will you be able to sit watching the screen without wondering to yourself, 'Now just how did they do that?' Bruce Lee, of course, was no novice when it came to pulling the best out of a situation and he also knew well how to minimise the danger of a difficult routine without stealing away some of the reality - truly an expert at his craft!

That said, on with the show!

Felix Yen
Editor-in-Chief

THE BRUCE LEE PRESS CLIPPINGS

There is probably nothing more revealing than a glance through the press clippings of a world popular figure. This is especially so for a superman like Bruce Lee. His brief but star-studded career has enabled a full and exciting investigation to become possible and the results of what really amounts to just an initial survey are printed right here in *KFM* No.30. The huge content of forgotten comment mixed with wise observation and misguided prejudice serves up a menu both tasty and intriguing. It is the earnest hope of the editors of *KFM* that sometime soon, a fuller and even more revealing check-out may be made possible, perhaps in the form of a 'Special issue' - rather like the *Game of Death Collector's Edition* of around a year ago. The wealth of material available is, in itself, a credit to the man who organised its collection and although he prefers to remain anonymous, the very least *KFM* can do is thank him for making available a vast and previously untapped reservoir of Bruce Lee history.

It maybe goes without saying that press clippings seldom reveal to future generations words of absolute truth. Rather, they serve to capture the flavour of events as they happened at the time. One major event some years ago was the gradual emergence of a man destined to be the 20th Century's master of the martial arts. To flip through the news reports of the Little Dragon's historic rise to fame is to almost relive the birth of the King of Kung Fu all over again! There will be little attempt made here to follow through news reports in date order - that perhaps is a task to be considered in the future. For now, we shall simply pick at random, some of the more illuminating comment on a man who seized success by the throat and who never let go!

Naturally many of the reports dwell on the so called 'violence' of Bruce's early masterpieces. For example, *Fist of Fury* is a film with an impact like a sledgehammer. It relies on its fight scenes for its appeal - and what fight scenes they are. So begins a review dating back to the latter months of 1973. The writer (initially at least) seems to have caught the excitement of the Little Dragon's second full length feature film. He goes on, "The combatants move as if they're in a ballet, but they strike to maim or kill. Fists and feet fly, bodies whirl through the air, and there's no shortage of blood. For sheer skill and raw violence, the fights make the average Western set-to seem pretty tame." Well, he's obviously got something out of the experience, even though he finishes up, "When the fighting has to stop and the fiercely pro-Chinese story (spiced with a little romantic interest) takes over, things become a little tedious."

It's worth remembering of course that around 1973, the western world was by no means ready to accept Kung Fu films on their face value. Reviewers everywhere were still desperately trying to fit Bruce's work into some kind of recognisable slot and finding, as they frequently did, that they were not able to, worried many of them. Another writer almost grasped something when he remarked about the same film, "For its story content, its heavy handed acting and stifled dialogue, *Fist of Fury* might well have been made in the early days of the movies". And later he noted, "... I can recommend a viewing of *Fist of Fury* to all who wish to see something quite unusual in the way of film making..." and then, "In the forefront of the action is the amazingly agile Bruce Lee..." Of course, the give-away on many of these reports is the obvious ignorance of many of the reviewers to the real part Bruce Lee played in things. Let's face it, all in all, *Fist of Fury* was the Little Dragon! And perhaps it's a little unfair that they should feel the need to compare the result with the more normal run-of-the-mill 'cinema fodder.'

Didn't anyone tell them that Bruce's early films were made exclusively for the Asian market and therefore adjustments in critical comparison have to be made?

Late in 1974, Kung Fu cinema was really getting into its stride with the fantastic success of *The Way of the Dragon*. Strangely enough, Nigel Andrews, writing at the time for the UK *Financial Times* remarked, "Bruce Lee's last disappointing film (*Way of the Dragon*) broke all box office records at the Rialto"... and then, "...the genre (of Kung Fu films) has declined since the death of its first superstar, and none of Lee's rivals seems quite ready to assume his mantle." There seem to have been many people at the time who mistakenly believed that *The Way of the Dragon* was Bruce's last film. It wouldn't have taken much research to have discovered *Game of Death*, it was there for all to see! It's a little, peculiar too, to hear on one hand the film dubbed as 'disappointing' and on the other to be told it was breaking all records! Not, in my book, a very constructive review.

Another gentleman, this time back in September '73 wrote, "The dialogue is strictly grade two and the acting primary school pantomime," but went on, "Amazingly in the face of these timber-shivering drawbacks. *Fist of Fury* is one of the most entertaining films I've viewed this year." In fact, throughout many of the early Bruce Lee reviews, this double comparison is strangely evident. "The acting was second rate - but I loved it!" type of comment - it's really all too easy to criticise the Little Dragon's acting ability on sheer technical grounds. After all, he never received any proper training. It could truly be said that Bruce played it for real - he had no other way and he needed no other way!

As most *KFM* readers know, 1973 spawned a huge variety of ideas and theories as to how death could have struck down 'the fittest man in the world.' Many of these stories bordered literally on the fantastic and if truth be known, were almost certainly thought up by people trying to get rich quick! However, Albert Watson, writing in an English evening paper reported one of the favourite explanations of the time, that "He died of internal haemorrhages caused by fight scenes in his films." It must have been a guess by whoever first put forward the statement and time has, in fact, proved the theory to be totally false. Albert, however, believed it and even headed his article, "Bruce - a star who died for his art." He finished up saying, "Bruce Lee, thou shouldst be alive at this hour. Because Hollywood producers are now scouring the Orient for your replacement." This same wish has echoed through the pages of *Kung-Fu Monthly* for several years now - but not surprisingly, the replacement has never been discovered.

Another very common mistake at this time was to confuse the names of Bruce's film smashes. This all came about because of title changes each side of the Atlantic for *The Big Boss*, *Fist of Fury* and *The Way of the Dragon*. Frequently, one would see the Little Dragon's production list grow in length because writers believed, for instance that *Fist of Fury* and *The Chinese Connection* were two different films! Albert

Watson again, "*The Big Boss* (UK title to the USA *Fists of Fury*) broke all box office records in Hong Kong. *Fists of Fury* followed (!), then Lee expanded his talents by writing and directing his third feature film, *The Chinese Connection* (USA title for the UK's *Fist of Fury*)." What a pile of confusion there!!

Not all reviewers fell into the trap of dismissing Bruce's acting appeal for its tack of finesse and training. Many slowly began to understand its more deep-lying attraction, especially coupled with the sheer power of his unique charisma. Gillian Cooper wrote, "Although there are many stylised characterisations such as the long-suffering detective (in *Fist of Fury*) and the thoroughly villainous Japanese interpreter, the acting is first class. Nothing of the high tension drama is lost by the film being dubbed with American accents." Peculiarly, the UK's Financial Times, when checking out *Enter the Dragon* sometime later, suggested that for, "...the superior, genuine article..." one ought to go see *The Big Boss* and *Fist of Fury*, despite the fact that *Enter the Dragon* undeniably contained more of what we in the West like to term 'good acting.' Reviewers just didn't seem to be able to make up their minds.

Charles Maclean, however, took *Enter the Dragon* a little bit more seriously. He wrote, "His (Bruce's) control, his bravery and skill are supreme; what makes him so exciting to watch, is that these heroic qualities are communicated almost entirely by gesture and expression. The way he approaches an adversary, delivers a blow, swivels his body, moves his neck and makes use of his eyes, is worth any amount of dialogue. It's naive and funny but always powerful stuff." Charles completed his wise and pertinent observations on the Little Dragon by concluding, "After the phenomenon of Bruce Lee there can only be imitators. He was unique".

And so we draw a halt for this month on our browse through the Bruce Lee press clippings. Its *KFM*'s hope that you, the readers, have found the same enjoyment we have in sifting through the newspaper world's legacy to the name and history of the Little Dragon. Next issue, we'll be dipping once more into the scrapbook to bring you another bagful of facts, figures and muddled misunderstandings on the man the world grew to know quite simply as Bruce Lee, the King of Kung Fu.

THE CAMERA LIES – PART TWO

It's time once again for another look at the world of camera tricks and special effects. Last month, we took you through just a few of the techniques for, film-wise, making the inconceivable look possible. We said then, that as far as Bruce Lee's films were concerned, such illusions were used sparingly and only where the viewer's enjoyment would not simply be heightened at the expense of reality. The Little Dragon's martial arts expertise was very much for real and only occasionally did the need occur for him to exaggerate anything. Frequently in fact, such distortions were introduced more to increase the 'humour rating' of his films than anything else and who could complain about that? We look here too at some of the more general devices used by cinema directors to overcome either moments of great physical danger for the actors concerned or, just as often, to avoid having to pay out vast sums of money on expensive film sets. Filming costs can be quite prohibitive these days and any attempt by the film maker to cut his costs should eventually be reflected in how much we the public have to pay at the box office.

In many a power-packed action film, we end up having a car chase. And how many times has the hero, seeing his attackers in hot pursuit, chosen to drive over a gaping chasm, or a river to safety on the other side? Bond's done it a few times (e.g. *The Man with a Golden Gun*). There's a picture going around called S.T.A.B. where a motorbiker does it. So what's the trick you may ask? If Evel Knievel can do it, why can't somebody else? Well, the answer is that Evil gets paid for risking his neck - actors aren't allowed to! The secret behind the faking is this: Sure enough, the shot of the car or motorbike approaching the chasm is real enough, and so too is the one of it driving away on the other side. But as for the actual leap, well that's a different story. The trick is to build an almost perfect replica of the location area in the studio itself. The same machine is then filmed making a far less dangerous jump in relative safety. Finally, the before, middle and after are all strung together into what often turns out to be a most realistic and convincing action sequence.

In films built around a wartime setting, models come into their own. Take *Tora Tora Tora* for example where the shoot-out between the Japanese and American fleets was almost exclusively filmed in miniature. So too in the fabulous Battle of Midway where all the ships and planes seen destroying each other were in fact, again, just models: imagine the costs if they hadn't been! Shots of a city burning are produced using the same techniques and in fact, the clever director knows just how to simulate a very realistic blaze using only a dozen or so models! The resulting optical illusion can turn out to be almost perfect.

To can more historic productions, obviously it's imperative that all traces of the modern day are removed from the area. You'd hardly believe in fact just how much does have to be hidden. Cars, parking signs, yellow lines, telephone wires, TV aerials and so on. Paint sprays can iron out some of these difficulties but clearly one of the most pressing problems is having to disguise modern architectural structures. Two solutions are possible. One is to build a huge back drop which is generally painted. However, this is expensive and often impractical. A second scheme is quite ingenious. Sheets of glass can be laid over offending areas and something more authentic painted over. In fact this illusion is used quite extensively in the picture making business. Next time you're seeing a film, look closely at the scenery outside the window of the room where the action's taking place - chances are it's been painted!

BRAND NEW OFFER
BACK ISSUE
BONANZAS
5 & 6!

KFM is delighted to announce the arrival of Back Issue Bonanza No.6. Now at last, readers who missed out on some of the more recent editions have got a chance to 'plug the gaps'!

BONANZA 5. Issues 18, 19, 20, 21 and 22
BONANZA 6. Issues 23, 24, 25, 26 and 27

Each of the above BONANZAS is on offer for £1.20. In the years to come, your back copies of Kung-Fu Monthly will become sought after items and complete sets will be valuable. Don't miss out on this chance to update your collection. Send your cheque or postal order off immediately to:

Back Issue Bonanza 5/6
Kung-Fu Monthly
14 Rathbone Place
London W.1.

CLUB MEMBER'S PRICE, £1.00 ONLY
(Please allow at least 4 weeks for delivery)

Last issue we mentioned how arrows are often shot by marksmen to make sure as much danger as possible is removed from the actors. The contact point has to fall in the protected area! To make this more certain the following cunning little device is often used. A thin wire is connected at one end to the bow and to the intended point of impact at the other. Along this wire is threaded the arrow - yes its centre is hollow! To simplify the contraption, the weapon used is usually a crossbow and a perfect example of this kind of illusion is to be seen in *The Man from Hong Kong*.

Okay, we promised you last time an explanation of how Bruce lifted that rickshaw in *Fist of Fury* and here it is! The rickshaw was real, but Mr Wu wasn't - a light model was used. Finally, the arms of the carriage had been specially extended and just behind Bruce (but out of camera shot) were two helpers. Now you may feel this is a fiddle - the Little Dragon wasn't all that happy at doing the stunt himself - but he figured no one in their right senses would ever seriously believe a mortal man could heave that sort of weight. Bruce may have been a superman, but he wasn't immortal! He decided finally to allow the scene's inclusion because of its undoubted humour. Actually, you may be pleased to hear that in *Game of Death*, very few illusions have been used and for instance. Kareem Abdul-Jabbar actually does lift James Tien up by the neck! Tricks have, however, been used in most of the rip-off Bruce Lee films that have appeared since the King's tragic death. Early on, to take an example, many of Bruce Li's attempts were shot in slow motion and then strung together and speeded up again later! What a startling contrast to the Little Dragon's masterpieces which frequently needed to be slowed down so that everyone could fully appreciate his fantastically skilled action.

Most of Bruce's stunts were very real and generally, only where some outside danger

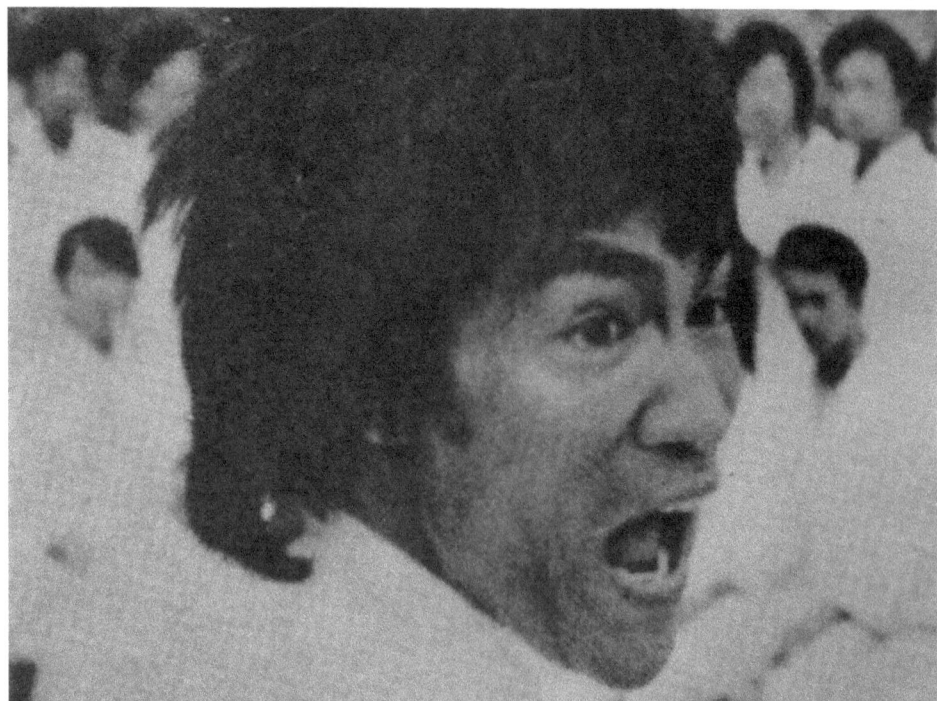

threatened would he consider faking. In *Enter the Dragon*, where the master was actually bitten by a fortunately more or less de-venomised snake, part of the sequence was completed using a rubber version of the brute - a sensible decision. However, no such caution tempered his decision when doing battle with Bob Wall, with the latter wielding genuine broken bottles. On the morning of the shooting, we're told that Bruce and Bob had an argument - almost certainly because of Bruce's insistence that he do battle against lethal jagged glass. Bob had no doubt about Bruce's abilities, he was just worried that one slip from him could permanently damage the Little Dragon. Normally on this sort of occasion, fake bottles would be used - almost unrecognisable from the real thing, but not good enough for Bruce. He was determined to protect the realism of the scene. The result, as most people by now know, was a badly gashed hand for Bruce, although which one of them was responsible for the mis-timing is not positively recorded.

The Little Dragon at times had a great affection for dart throwing and there is no doubt that he was an expert marksman. But, there is always the chance of error - the target may move a little for instance - and no actor can be allowed to take that risk, it's likely therefore that Bruce made use once again of the thin wire technique to ensure the weapon reached its intended point of contact. A possible variation to this that's frequently used for arrows, spears, knives and so on, is this. The camera follows the attacker as he fires or throws the weapon and whips through the air apparently following it in flight. It isn't - it just appears to be. Meanwhile, the film of the man already clutching, say, an arrow to the chest is taken and then later spliced on to the first shot. The final effect is often absolutely realistic. To all intents and purposes, the camera has seen the weapon fired - it's followed it in flight and finally it's seen the arrow hit the chest of the victim.

Kung Fu film makers are very fond of using certain sorts of sound effects. The martial artist flying through the air noise is produced by the flapping of heavy material, for instance, a coat! Fists landing on target are also fairly distinctive and two sorts of 'thump' are used to produce the desired sound. Either a carbine shotgun recording or more often, the sound of two bats, generally covered in some sort of light material. As far as voice dubbing is concerned, it's worth emphasising here that although you don't hear Bruce's voice in any of his feature films except *Enter the Dragon*, his cries are absolutely genuine - which so far as the fans are concerned, has to be a million percent better than nothing! A point worth mentioning too, is that it's said by some people that the Little Dragon only spoke on part of the soundtrack to *Enter the Dragon*. It's rumoured Bruce's English - never really that good - was simply not up to some of the lines and therefore a 'soundalike' was hired later to dub over some of the difficult words. As I say, this hasn't been confirmed by the film company as yet and whether or not it can be proved remains to be seen.

It was not without some heart searching that *KFM* finally decided to publish this two part feature on the tricks and illusions of the film industry in general and Bruce Lee in particular. Some feel that the exposing of such information will ultimately effect the enjoyment of the fans and in some cases I might agree. However, as I remarked some time ago when deciding to feature a particular nunchaku article in *KFM*, I regard the readership to be both mature in mind and discriminating in my estimation, knowing the real truth behind an illusion should in fact, heighten one's appreciation of the ability of artiste(s) concerned and to that end, no harm whatsoever can result from its disclosure. I hope I'm right!

THE BRUCE LEE SECRET SOCIETY

Hello once again, Pam here, with some more titbits of news for all you Secret Society members.

First off, just a couple of reminders to you regarding the club itself. One or two of you seem a little confused about the subscription charge. As much as I'd love to make it £3.25 for life, I'm sorry to say it does have to be renewed annually! Even so, with prices the way they are, we have to keep our belts well buckled in this end. And the other thing is the special BLSS News Sheet. Please don't expect one to arrive every month as it is in fact quarterly; in other words, you'll receive one every three months.

John Kemp (1729) writes to tell us that Jim Kelly appeared in *Shamus* with Burt Reynolds in 1973 and played a 'heavy' called Grifter. Also, Chuck Norris was in *The Student Teacher*, made also in 1973. I've had word from Michael Moore of Co. Durham. He's just started an Angela Mao fan club and anyone wishing to add their support to that lovely lady of the martial arts should contact him. Talking of fan clubs, I've also had word for anyone interested, that the Steve McQueen club is at London SW16.

I'm sorry to hear that some of the problems regarding the non-arrival of club mail around Christmas time and just after, have still not been completely sorted out. If any of you are still awaiting books, etc. PLEASE let me know straight away. We're still not exactly sure what DID go wrong but we're working hard on putting things right. That over, I suggest you all start looking forward right away to the next BLSS News Sheet. I've managed to work in a little extra surprise for everyone but I'm not telling you what it is here. Now that's got you thinking, hasn't it!

I've had a letter from Steven Walpole (1554) of Huddersfield. He'd like anyone who can help him find out the following information so write DIRECT please. He wants to know about Sonny Chiba who played Terry Surugy in *Blood of the Dragon* and *Kung Fu Street Fighter*. What style is he, what other films he's made, where and when born, is there a fan club, and so on. I hope somebody out there will be able to help you Steven.

A rather strange snippet comes in to me from Gary Green (1007). He says he was in London's 'Chinatown' area and heard that *Game of Death* had been made into a documentary with guest stars James Coburn and Muhammad Ali, who talk about Bruce. I'm completely mystified. Does anyone have any idea what's going on? Gary Chedzoy (1032) writes to say that there's a Phillips LP out called *Flashpoint* (No.638211) by the Ray Davies Orchestra. It features *Fist of Fury* and *The Big Boss* theme tunes, although I have a hunch they are the original Chinese versions rather than the ones we're used to in this country.

Sadly, two members have written in to say that the service we advertised in the last News Sheet regarding the blowing up of cuttings into posters by Foto Post is now no longer operating. Does anyone know of a substitute we can advertise instead? Keith Milner (1541) has had a good idea. If you're interested in him making up a collage of some of your pictures and magazines (perhaps using some of the torn or creased material) just send him 60p (inc. handling) plus the pictures and wait around two weeks for the result. His address to write to is: Mastin Moor, Chesterfield.

See you again soon - *Pam*

SECRET SOCIETY SWOP SHOP

Brian Beck (1890) of Co. Armagh, Northern Ireland wants *KFM* No. 1-5, price please.

Mick Bargota (1322) of Tipton, West Midlands has *Game of Death* magazine - offers please? Also wants *KFM* No. 1 & 3 - high price paid.

Richard Miller (1638) of Aberdeen, Scotland has *Legend of Bruce Lee* by Alex Ben Block and wants *The Way of the Dragon* poster.

Anthony Clarke (1715) of Carlisle, Cumbria wants *KFM* No. 1-3. Has *Clash Monthly* No.1 & *Legend of Bruce Lee* & *Bruce Lee King of Kung Fu* magazine, *Kung Fu* and *KFM* No. 6,7,8.

Molly Cullen (1749) of Blackwood, Gwent wants film poster from each of Bruce's films - high prices paid - please contact a.s.a.p.

Guardsman Luke (1478) Waterloo Barracks desperately wants *KFM* No.3.

KICKBACK: THE LETTERS

Hi, Jenny here once again, as ready as ever to pull out the pick of the mail bag for another page of readers' letters! First though, there's the very important matter I brought to your attention last month concerning the further postponement at *Game of Death*. After some discussion with the *KFM* Editors, I've decided that a petition to Raymond Chow could and should be arranged. Here's how I'm going to go about it. I'd like every single reader of *Kung-Fu Monthly* - and that means you - to write the following. "I, the undersigned, wish to put on record my dismay at *Game of Death* being held back from general release yet again. It is inconceivable that, after all this time, the film should not have been completed and I demand that action be taken to remedy this further postponement immediately." Get as many of your friends as possible to sign your petition and then pop it in the post to me, Jenny Lee, as soon as possible. If everybody pitches in, I reckon Golden Harvest will have to sit up and take notice so don't let me down, please!

RECENT PRICE RISE

Dear Jenny,

KFM did not have to apologise for the price rise. To someone not interested in Bruce Lee, *KFM* might be dear, but to us Little Dragon fans, *KFM* is something very special and I personally would be prepared to pay much more for such a fine publication. Long Live *Kung-Fu Monthly*.

Gary Chedgzoy Norris Green, Lancs

Dear Gary,
Very many thanks for your loyal words. When I read letters like this one, suddenly I know it's all worth it. Actually, although in this day and age, 35p is a good deal of money, it's worth remembering that a poster in a shop of Bruce could cost anything up to £1.00 and you won't get a magazine with it either!

BOB WALL - JEALOUS?

Dear Jenny,
I recently bought a magazine and in it was an interview with Bob Wall. My god, some of the things he said about Bruce! He said the Little Dragon had no confidence in himself or his wife. Also Bob said, "When me and Bruce were doing the bottle fight in *Enter the Dragon* and his hands were cut, he told everybody it was my fault and that when his hands were healed he would kill me." Wall also said that Bruce cut chunks out of the original fight because he was scared that Wall was as good as he was. As you'll recall, Bruce got his revenge by killing Oharra with a running sidekick. And what's more, instead of pulling the kick, he really whacked Wall - so hard in fact that the stunt man positioned to catch Oharra got a broken arm for his pains. Bob Wall sure is jealous of Bruce Lee.
Roger Egerton, Wilmslow, Cheshire

Dear Roger,
First of all, sorry I had to cut a few chunks out of your really interesting letter but it was just a little bit too long. I haven't actually seen the offending article as yet, but I dare say I will soon. As you say, it seems to be becoming all the vogue to knock Bruce now that he's dead and can't answer back. It doesn't do me any good at all reading rubbish like this and I don't suppose it did much for you either! The only real conclusion to be reached is that they are the words of a coward.

BEHIND THE SCENES OF *KFM*

Dear Jenny,
How about doing a few articles with these themes? A three part feature entitled, Bruce Lee's Schooldays? Part one would be about his infant school, part two about his teenage education and part three, his days at the Seattle University. Another idea is for a Behind the Scenes at *KFM* feature. I am sure readers would be interested in what goes on before the magazine reaches the shops. We got a bit of insight in *KFM* No.28 in Felix Yen's article about the Secret Art of Bruce Lee pictures, but we want more.
Michael McDonnell, Kilmarnock, Scotland

Dear Michael,
Dealing with the first part, I'd say, yes it is a good idea and in fact it's one we've toyed with for a while now. The only problem is actually digging out the information. The part three Seattle days is quite possible, but as to the Little Dragon's early school years, well, new facts are definitely rather thin on the ground. Your second idea strikes me as really good and it certainly isn't one that's crossed our minds. I've already mentioned it to the Editor and judging by the way his eyes lit up, I'd say there was a real chance we'll be seeing something on it soon.

THE POSTER MAGAZINES - VOLUME TWO

LIFE SIZE BRUCE LEE POSTER

Dear Jenny,
Would it be possible to print a life size picture of Bruce in sections? This would encourage people never to miss the magazine and the final picture would look great.
William Dickson Irvine, Scotland

Dear William,
I've had so many letters mentioning this idea lately, it looks like we really are going to have to do something about it. The first move is to find exactly the right picture. It'll have to be clear enough to still look good when blown up to some immense size. We're working on it!

KICKBACK QUICKIES

Peter Leung, Birkenhead - Several readers have questioned our astrology article - I'm told there are several variations and the ones you mention are equally correct.

No Name, Acocks Green, Birmingham - Fold Out Poster Magazine No. 1-8, *Film Star* Series? Don't know it - Can anyone help?

Philip Page, Cleckheaton - The Bruce Lee sweat gland thing again - Sorry, really think somebody made it up some years ago!

Trevor Weaver, Tuffley - I agree *The Secret Art of Bruce Lee* is something to treasure for a lifetime.

James O'Lea, Kilmarnock, Scotland - How about you joining our fan club?

Alex Pontikopoulos, Athens, Greece - Thanks for your kind words - It's nice to know Greece is on our delivery route.

No Name, Gosport - A scrapbook competition is a great idea - Judging it might prove difficult though.

John Cunningham, Dublin, Ireland - Thanks for the US poster information - I'm checking it out.

Thomas Uprichard, Portadown, Co. Armagh - *KFM* No. 17, 24 & 27 available - Send 30p for each plus 15p p&p.

Colin Walton, Northampton - If you're having problems obtaining *KFM* please do subscribe. It's £4.50 for 12 issues.

Michael Daft, Mansfield, Notts - Looks like more than just the title of *Game of Death* is to be changed - Stand by for more news.

Trevor Richards, Hull Spring Bank - Very many thanks for the pictures of Bruce you sent along - They were great!

Philip Dunn, Washington, Tyne and Wear - Agree, a poster of *KFM* No.26 cover would be great.

Paul Stubley, Hove, Sussex - Please, please do send a copy of your book when it's finished - I'd love to see it.

Sheila Herberts of Hullworth, Humberside is 16 years old and would like a Chinese male pen pal aged 16-18 years old.

Glynn Barker (1567) of Bradway, Sheffield wants good looking Chinese pen pal aged 16-19 (female). Also pen pals in the UK interested in Bruce, Kung Fu and items on Bruce - Photos please.

Tom Surgenor (1662) of Co. Antrim, Northern Ireland is a fan of Bruce of just a year wants male/female pen pal, preferably Chinese, interested in Bruce. Studies Shotokan Karate and needs a little encouragement.

Paul Ruiz (1718) of Hadleigh, Essex wants male/female Chinese pen pal.

THE POSTER MAGAZINES · VOLUME TWO

EDITORIAL

Hi there Kung Fu fans. Another month flips on by on the calendar and I hardly have to remind you that it's time once more to light the fuse to another ace edition of *Kung-Fu Monthly*. First off though, let me remind you of Jenny's *Game of Death* petition (for full details, see Kickback last issue). If like me, you are looking forward to witnessing Bruce Lee's ultimate legacy to the martial arts world - and let's face it, who isn't - then please help us in our quest to get the film onto the cinema circuits by writing to Jenny and saying so. Remember, every letter counts. And talking of Kickback, you'll see there details of a particularly unsavoury incident that took place at a cinema in Birmingham. Anyone who was at that Kung Fu All-Nighter and has any info to offer on the subject, I'd be delighted to hear from them. I don't like too much what I've heard and *KFM* may be in a position to do something about it.

Right away this month, let me say that we've got a real cracker for you, courtesy of the

Hong Kong Jeet Kune Do Club. Stepping back in time to the days just after the Long Beach Tournament, we bring the gist of an interview Bruce attended at the 20th Century Fox Corporation - a discussion that was to lead finally to his making the historic *The Green Hornet* series. The dialogue is superb and the symbolism - the Little Dragon at his most explicit.

Number two, this issue is of course the second part of our Bruce Press Clippings article. Seldom has a feature evoked such interest amongst the *KFM* readership. From bias and bigotry to careful observation and clear-minded thinking is the order of the day and it's all captured right here in our final, sensational trip through the pages of the world's press. That's all from me for this month...

Felix Yen

Felix Yen
Editor-in-Chief

BRUCE LEE MEETS 20TH CENTURY FOX

Let no one believe that stardom came easily to Bruce Lee. On the contrary, like any ambitious man, he had to claw his way up the ladder of success, rung by rung. Nothing was ever handed to him on a plate - never would he consider taking the easy way out. That he believed himself to be on the threshold of a star-studded career there is no doubt. His single-minded attitude towards himself and the life he led implied this. Every move and every decision was geared for that end and no doubt it was this quality of sure-mindedness that was instrumental more than anything else in seeing the Little Dragon settled finally on his Kung Fu throne as the undisputed King of the martial arts world. To see and understand the battles Bruce fought on his way to reaching that elevated goal, is to appreciate the one-track thinking of a man inspired. The story behind just one of those hurdles is related here. It was a familiar enough situation for Bruce to have found himself in. Like anyone else, he was being given a chance to prove himself worthy of moving up a rung. However, unlike many others, the Little Dragon simply didn't know the meaning of the word 'failure!' We take you now to the offices of 20th Century Fox Corporation - the month is August and, the year, 1965.

They say in China, that the birth of the first son brings a family good fortune. Very probably, as Bruce approached his interview at that world famous picture company, the thought crossed his mind that with Brandon having just been born only three days before, Lady Luck must surely be walking at his side. He wasn't wrong - although some would feel he had no need of such luck anyway! At 24, he looked rather unlike the Little Dragon we know of from his later screen smashes. A man as yet to reach his peak of fitness, in some of those earlier pictures he seemed positively chubby! Dressed conservatively in a dark suit and tie he looked every bit the quiet and unassuming young man. Few around him on that day to remember could have guessed the true potential of the Kung Fu dynamo in their midst!

Initially, discussion centred around Bruce Lee the man - name, age, education and so on. Things didn't stay at this formal level for too long however. He was soon asked why he preferred Kung Fu to Karate and Judo. He replied that the essence of Kung Fu lay in its lack of rigidity - its strength was in its softness. "The nature of the art is like a fluid, rich in mobility." It's clear that the concept of Jeet Kune Do was already in the back of his mind as he went on to point out the analogy between Kung Fu and water. Water, he explained, could be beaten and kicked but, because of its all-pervasive qualities, it could never be conquered. That, he felt, was the ultimate quality of his art.

Well, so much for the theory, but what, he was asked, when it came down to the nitty-gritty, is the actual difference between a Karate and a Kung Fu punch? Bruce's illustrative reply was a delight. He likened the Karate punch to a rigid, iron bar - powerful, but lacking in pliability. The Kung Fu punch, on the other hand, was more like a ball and chain - bending and twisting its way to maximum effect.

Probably by way of loosening up, he demonstrated first of all, some of the acting tricks he'd picked up from his days with the Cantonese Opera. Even here, his superb fitness shone out like a beacon and a study of different walking techniques kept everybody enthralled for several minutes. Once again, his childhood acting experience was to come to his aid - because when all said and done, a martial artist can only be of limited value to a film company, but one who can also act has to be quite a different kettle of fish! Bruce needed someone to bounce his ideas off. A display of punching and kicking techniques can only be given the right degree of realism when an opponent is present and luckily, a white-haired and rather elderly gentleman was on hand to offer his courageous services. The martial master didn't bat an eyelid. He knew the old man was safe enough, although at first his 'opponent' seemed less sure!

The Little Dragon chose first of all, to dazzle everybody with a lightning two-finger

eye thrust. Hardly knowing what had almost hit him, Bruce's gallant foil backed nervously away at the sight of the Kung Fu King's first and third fingers of the right hand almost touching his eyeballs! He hadn't seen them coming - they'd arrived as if by magic. To add a little spice to the occasion, Bruce then made it clear that it was just possible that an accident might happen. He, of course, knew it wouldn't, but he knew too that there's nothing

like keeping everybody guessing. Punching came next and the interviewers were educated in the art of synchronised attack. The Little Dragon explained carefully the need to put one's whole body into a punch - not just an arm and fist and the old man reeled back under a hail of near-misses. Variety, of course, is the spice of a Kung Fu attack and Bruce dug deep down into his sack of tricks to produce a wondrous display of punching and kicking techniques.

Although, to be honest, by this time, the worthy members of the 20th Century Fox team must have been well aware of the capabilities of the man before them, such was their captivation, they wanted to see more. Delighted to oblige, the Little Dragon continued his one man display of Kung Fu supremacy. He kicked, punched and danced his way around the office like a man inspired. To the people watching, a very valuable added bonus must have been the beauty of it all.

Bruce's display had, on one hand, the power of a lion, and on the other, the grace of a ballet artist. A superb combination, one must agree, when it comes to considering cinema entertainment. His wry humour certainly wasn't lost on them either and all in all, for the small group of people privileged to be there that day to observe the Little Dragon in full martial flight, it was an occasion to remember for the rest of their days.

Another question. He was asked to explain the essential difference between Kung Fu and the more ritualised examples of the martial arts. Again, the glimmerings of Jeet Kune Do appeared within his answer. He replied that many of the more formalised styles relied far too heavily on rules, regulations and particular stances - fighting by numbers, you could call it. In a real life confrontation, no maddened attacker is going to allow you time to assume the 'correct' position for defence. Kung Fu teaches you to be ready to adapt yourself to cope successfully with the position you're in.

Obviously these sentiments weren't anything like as comprehensive as his final concept of Jeet Kune Do, but as a pointer to the direction in which his thoughts were heading, they are invaluable. He was asked to display some of the more classical Kung Fu stances and first of all he chose to adopt that of the crane. Arms flung out beside him he imitated the actions of that beautiful bird to perfection. His hands were the beak and his wind-milling arms, the wings. Suddenly, the poetry of his imitation was destroyed by a single front kick - deadly in its power. The amazed audience were then treated to a tiger stance. Hooked fingers clawed the air a hairs-breadth away from the face of Bruce's, by now, extremely nervous opponent and then back again to the crane, fingers ready once more to thrust beak-like into the eyes of a confused old man.

And so the display was over. By now, most *KFM* readers should be well acquainted with the story of how the Little Dragon went on to make that sensational *The Green Hornet* series - so let's just say that the interview was indeed a success. Another hurdle jumped and the decks had been cleared for Bruce Lee to move a few steps closer to the making of his first major feature film. The magnetism and power of his amazing personality, plus of course his skill and expertise had combined to prove once more that when it came down to it, nobody around could touch the Little Dragon, martial artist and showman extraordinary!

WHAT THE PAPERS SAID!
THE PRESS FILES – PART TWO

No doubt about it, when it came to provoking pressmen to dust down their pens and get writing, there've been few people in the world of cinema entertainment to touch the abilities of Bruce Lee. Most loved him, some misunderstood him and just a few couldn't make up their minds! Last issue, we browsed our way through some of the more enlightening clips to find, if we could, more dues to account for the Little Dragon's world-shattering success. Since seeing *KFM* No.30, many readers have kindly lent us prize cuttings from their own collections and many of these have played no small part in making this, the second instalment of our Bruce Lee Press File feature, the success it is. Last issue, we mentioned the possibility of perhaps expanding the idea and publishing a *KFM* Special on the subject. With your help, this has now become a distinct possibility. Stand by in future issues for further details. For now though, it's time once more to dip into the pages of press history to find out what the reporters were saying about Bruce Lee - our conquering Kung Fu hero.

Late in 1973, film critic, Peter Mortimer took a long, hard look at the latest 'fad' to hit the cinema screens. He remarked, "Short on character portrayal or plot, their forte is the incredible fighting skills of the East," and then, "The front runner was *King Boxer*. In its first week in London's West End, it grossed almost £9,000 in takings and ran for eight consecutive weeks." However, he was the first to admit that it took a certain genius for the whole

> **THE ROBERT LEE ALBUM!**
> *A Must For Every True Bruce Lee Collector.*
>
> In recording this album, Bruce's brother, Robert, paid the finest compliment he could to the memory of the Master!
>
> His admiration and feeling of loss for the Little Dragon's sad passing have been captured superbly on this fine, top quality LP. Many of the tracks are self-penned, some you may know already. One in fact was co-written by Bruce himself.
>
> The album is not on general release and therefore you're unlikely to find it in many shops. Don't miss out on this unique opportunity – order now while stocks last.
>
> Send £4.35 (includes handling) to:
> Robert Lee Album Offer
> Kung-Fu Monthly
> 14 Rathbone Place
> London W1P 1DE
> (Cheques and postal orders made payable to KFM.)
>
> CLUB MEMBER'S PRICE...£4.10.

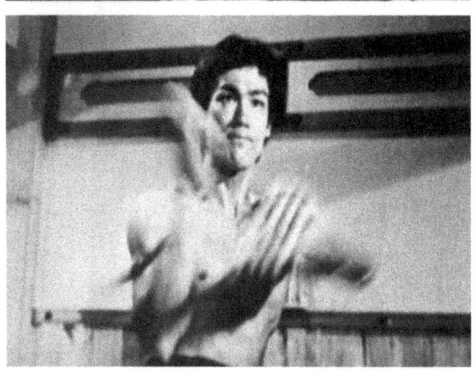

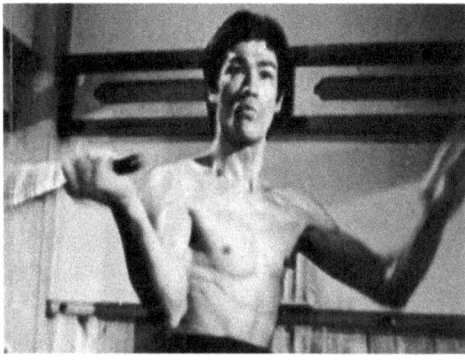

scene to explode. "The boom created a new superstar, Bruce Lee, arch exponent of Kung Fu, cart-wheeling his half naked, lithe body through the angry mobs and scything them down with deadly blows from his lightning-fast fists and feet."

KFM would respectfully like to suggest that rather than the boom creating Bruce Lee, in fact the exact opposite was true. Kung Fu films had by no means been rare in the years before the arrival of the Little Dragon. For some time, they had been immensely popular throughout Asia and for many years too, specimens had been available for inspection at Western Chinese cinema clubs. So does Mr. Mortimer really feel it to be a coincidence that Bruce should have appeared at the start of the Kung Fu boom? Perhaps he'd failed to notice the enormously long queues outside the cinemas where Little Dragon films were on view - as opposed to the relative disinterest shown to more run-of-the-mill Kung Fu productions. One important point in favour of earlier martial arts films, according to Mike Jones, then of Cathay Films was their cheapness. *The Big Boss* and *Fist of Fury* were of course shot on very low budgets in Hong Kong and the English soundtrack was added later. Therefore profits were much higher. Later, when Hollywood decided to get involved (with *Enter the Dragon*, for instance) the situation was to change.

Many a commentator at the time made the mistake of thinking that the Little Dragon was part Western. Roy Litherland wrote, "*Fist of Fury* stars Kung Fu exponent, Bruce Lee, a handsome Chinese-American star who died two months ago at the age of 32." The error is easy to understand. Bruce did after all have something western about his looks and of course, he did speak English fairly well. However, he then goes on to say, "The story, the performances and the production as a whole are laughably naive - just about as sophisticated as beans on toast," and then, "I watched it thinking that I'd got into a children's matinee!" At the end of his article, he rather condescendingly admits that, "I suppose it's possible to forget about the simple story and the abysmal acting and see *Fist of Fury* just for its breathtaking, almost non-stop demonstrations of Kung Fu by Bruce Lee. These are quite balletic on occasions. Karate fans especially, will enjoy it no end."

Naturally, reading a report like the one above would be enough to make any true Little Dragon fan want to throw up! Why, we ask Mr. Litherland, should one necessarily want to forget a simple story? Why does a film require sophistication in order to deserve his seal of approval? And how dare he insinuate that only Karate fans are liable to enjoy what he considers to be rubbish. A critic generally is able to submerge his own likes and dislikes at least to the degree where he is able to appreciate that something is good of its kind. Can all those millions of fans really be wrong?

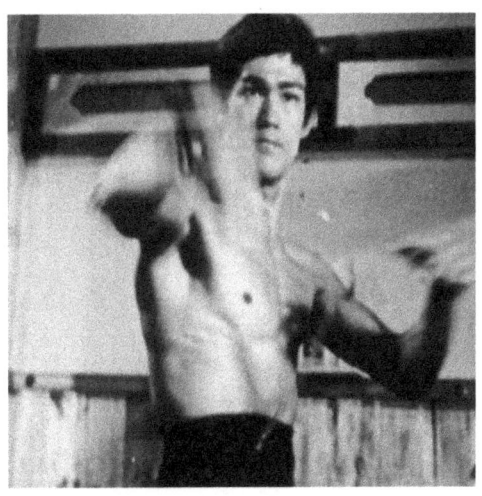

Peter Ward, reviewing *The Way of the Dragon* in September, 1974, had this to say. "Throughout the 91 minutes, Lee dominates the set from first to last and in addition to incredible skill at the martial arts, he also displays a touching flair for an appealing gentle comedy." Oh dear, what happened to the abysmal acting? Mr. Ward also remarks on the amazing fact that not only was Bruce the leading figure, but he also directed it and wrote the screenplay. Colin Davidson, however, writing at about the same time, found the plot to be unlikely and commented too that, "Lee even tries to be humorous in the first part of the film, although his efforts are rather ham fisted." What's that they say, one man's meat is another man's poison. He also got a little worried at some of the violence. Apparently the sound of the Little Dragon crushing Chuck Norris' bones was a little too much for him to take!

Without doubt, the most abusive comments I've ever read on the Little Dragon are those that appeared in a provincial UK paper, dated January 15th 1974. The writer concerned, perhaps understandably, neglected to include his name on the piece but his drift becomes absolutely clear when he writes, "Frankly I am amazed that audiences have become so hooked on this Oriental garbage!" He goes on, "I have already stated in this column that Bruce Lee was a remarkable athlete and no mean ballet dancer. Unfortunately his routine is a drag after 40 seconds because it is unbearably repetitive." It's astonishing that someone in such an apparently responsible position can find his way to utter such bigoted nonsense. The film under review is in fact *Enter the Dragon* and after decrying Hollywood for following the misplaced footsteps of the Orient he remarks, "It is a preposterous hotch-potch, impossible to follow even if one wanted to follow it." Well, well, just a few paragraphs back, we were hearing complaints about the simplicity of the plot. Evidently this poor gentleman still found its complications too much for him.

Okay, it's goofs time once again, and how about this lot for a star collection. Dated December 1973, a staff writer on Films Illustrated wrote, "When Bruce Lee died in Hong Kong earlier this year, he was in the middle of directing his first film, *The Way of the Dragon*, co-starring George Lazenby." Our ill-informed reporter continues, "He was taught the principles of Kung Fu by his father, a star of Chinese opera," and if that wasn't enough, "The martial arts he performed so brilliantly were to cause his death by internal haemorrhage." And there's more to come. "As a teenager he appeared in several Chinese films and made his first screen appearance in San Francisco at the age of three months." We are also told, erroneously, that Bruce received a Masters Degree in Philosophy at Washington University. Sorry, but he dropped out before completing his studies.

Many a would be reviewer of Kung Fu films around the time of Bruce's tragic death refused to take the whole business seriously. Some were unsure that martial arts films would last more than a few more months and most dismissed the idea of the Little Dragon becoming a legend. One who epitomises these two attitudes wrote in April that year, that it was, "A disaster... for all the chubby Chinese cheeks behind that cinema phenomenon, Bruce Lee." And he commented, "It was inevitable that big-hearted Hollywood would jump up on the rickshaw as soon as his patron-pulling powers began to show. Thus came *Enter the Dragon*, a joint effort with a huge cash uplift and a new status for Lee." But would the Little Dragon have held on to all this had he lived? "Probably not, because the craze will pass and will do so fairly quickly."

And so the arguments fly back and forth. Could he? Should he? Did he? Would he? If just one thing has become clear from reading these clippings, it's that most of us will just have to agree to disagree. No two people seem to think alike and if we wanted to be uncharitable, it could be said that some don't appear to think at all! Perhaps the only real conclusion to be drawn from it all is that only a man of the stature and importance of the Little Dragon could have ensured the collection of over 5,000 separate press clipping entries in the short space of two years. Such a man has surely to have something very special - and such a man was Bruce Lee.

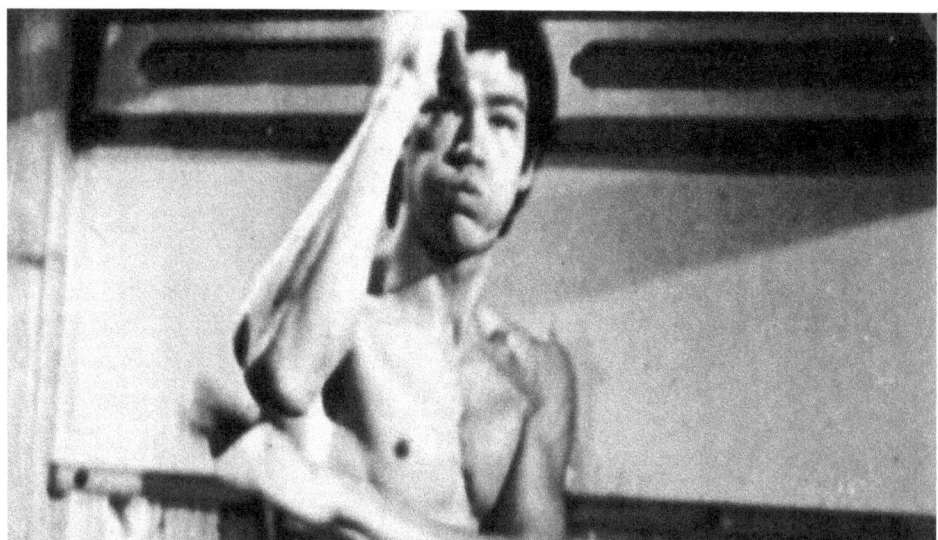

THE BRUCE LEE SECRET SOCIETY

It's Bruce Lee Secret Society time again and a big hello from me, Pam, to all you marvellous members.

Right away, I've got to tell you that the fabulous news is our own Secret Society magazine of pictures and poems will be ready in time for the next News Sheet. Remember, all those of you with contributions included will be entitled to a free copy. All other members will be able to purchase a copy at cost price (sorry, you'll have to wait for News Sheet 4. to find out the exact cost). Work, by the way, is now almost complete on News Sheet 4 and I promise you it's going to be the best yet.

For anyone who is having difficulty obtaining a copy of the original *Enter the Dragon* soundtrack by Lalo Schifrin (Warner Bros. K46275-BS2727), I've managed to locate a shop who seem able to supply it in just a matter of days. I'm quite happy to place orders and mail LP's off to you, so any members interested, just send me £3.60 (to include post and packing) and I'll handle it for you (cheques and postal orders made out to *KFM*, please). Remember this is a very special Society service and for time reasons, I have to insist that it's open to Society members only.

Jerry Green (1007) has written to tell us about a great London shop called P.H. Crompton Ltd at 638 Fulham Road, London SW6. Apparently they stock a very reasonable list of Kung Fu and Bruce Lee books, plus a good selection of Little Dragon posters. And talking of posters; so far as I know I've managed to mail all the 'poster shop name and address' sheets that have been requested. However, I will repeat again that most of the sources are American. Anyone sending off money and then receiving nothing is going to find it very hard to do anything about it. Please, please write only to start with and ask for a brochure and price information. You may feel impatient now, but past experience has taught me the delay is worth it!

The other service I'm looking forward to providing is the area name and address sheets but its taking longer to do than I thought. In fact, it's really hard work so please don't blame me if the info is a bit of a time coming; it really shouldn't be long now. Michael Hodson (1755) has some useful information in particular for our Welsh readers. J. Lee of 52 St. Paul's Avenue, Barry 5, Glamorgan, has for sale some cheap and apparently good quality nunchakus. They measure 13" long and the natural wood finish costs £2.75 and the black finish, £3.00.

One last thing for this month. Over the time that the Society has been running, many members have sent in photographs of themselves to me. Some have been 'action' shots, many have been ordinary portrait pictures. Well, I think it's a lovely idea and one that I'd like to see grow and grow. When I'm reading your letters and writing back to you there's nothing I like better than being able to SEE who I'm talking to, so how about it? As Jenny might say, let's hear those cameras a'clicking!

Best wishes... **Pam**

SECRET SOCIETY SWOP SHOP

Mr. S. Green (1511) of Wrexham wants *My Martial Arts Training Guide to Jeet Kune Do* by James Lee.

Burket Ali (1582) of Coventry has soundtrack of *The Way of the Dragon* with war cries. Wants Kung Fu suit or £4.00.

Setudeh Nejad (1419) of Bembridge, Isle of Wight wants *KFM* No.1 - High price paid.

David Ryder (1069) of Ramsgate, Kent wants *KFM* No. 1, 2 and 3 - Very high price paid.

George Tseu (1905) of Wisbech, Cambridgeshire - wants *KFM* No. 1 to 4 - Price please.

John Aspinal (1527) of Chorley, Lancashire - wants *The Man Only I Knew* by Linda Lee.

KICKBACK: THE LETTERS

Hi there everyone, Jenny Lee here again, opening up the mail sacks for another month's letters. Actually, this time, I really will be very quick with the intro because, not only do we have some very fine letters, there's also one in particular that carries a word of warning for everybody. It's quite long, but please read it. The petition I printed in *KFM* No.30 has brought in several hundred replies already. That's good - but not good enough. We need lots more yet to be able to make Golden Harvest take notice. Honesty, if you want to see *Game of Death* at your local cinema soon, please write in to me saying so. And now, the letters!

TREASURE KIT

Dear Jenny,
First may I congratulate you and the *KFM* team on producing such a great magazine. I think it's worth every penny - right down to the last half pence! Please could you tell me if the Bruce Lee Treasure Kit is still available as I'd like to buy it?
Norman Kavanagh, Kilmarnock, Scotland

Dear Norman,
Thanks for the letter and the compliments. The original Kit is not only unavailable, I should think by now, it's a collector's item. But, plans are afoot this end to produce a Treasure Kit No.2 which, hopefully, will be on offer quite soon. Eyes glued to the Mail Order Pages.

BACK ISSUE BONANZA LIST

Dear Jenny Lee,
I think it would be a great idea if you printed out the whole list of Back Bonanza issues for sale instead of five issues at a time for £1.20. I think this would be a better idea and the reader could choose and pay for the numbers he requires.
Michael Santucci, Clapham, London

Dear Michael,
Although we don't usually advertise the fact too much, back issues, in most cases, are still available at their cover price plus 10p handling. Selling single copies is a time consuming business and I know the Mail Order Department, in general, prefers to deal with larger, bonanza-sized quantities. For the record, by the way, the sold out issues are 1, 2, 3, 4 and 13.

CINEMA RIP-OFF!

Dear Jenny,
Recently I saw an ad in the paper for an all night martial arts spectacular. So I, with two mates, bought tickets at £1.50 each. The night came and we set off, arriving at twenty to eleven. The time passed and the crowd grew bigger. Eventually the police were called in with dogs. After a lot of pushing and shoving, I got separated from my friends and landed inside the cinema. The following day, I phoned my mate who told me he and his cousin had been turned away. In the paper that night, it said 400 had been turned away, including ticket holders. We were pretty disgusted and phoned the cinema and the restaurant who had sold us the tickets. After paying three visits to the restaurant, we found that the man behind it had over-sold the tickets and then skipped off with the money. The restaurant denied any responsibility and said this man was doing the same all over the country. I am writing to you to put a warning in your magazine to other fans, who, like us, may be taken in.
Damien Sullivan, Tyseley, Birmingham

Dear Damien,
Thanks for letting us know the details of an incident that I myself had read about in the national press. I recall that the evening was arranged by Mr. Raymond Wong of the Sunny Film Society and to be fair, I'd like very much to hear his side of the story. Perhaps if he reads this, he'd like to write in outlining how disappointed fans can have their money refunded. Meanwhile all you Kung Fu fans - be warned!

TOURNAMENT TRIBUTE

Dear Jenny,
I have though of an interesting idea. How about a Martial Arts Tournament dedicated to Bruce Lee. I know there would be many problems in doing and arranging it but wouldn't it be spectacular? You'd be sure to make a profit because thousands would flock to see it. What do you think?
Gerard Rogers, Edinburgh, Scotland

Dear Gerard,
Now that sounds an interesting idea. You're not kidding though when you say there'd be many problems! Still, I've passed your letter on to the Editor to see what he thinks about the scheme - so stand by for news.

KFM REPRINTS

Dear Jenny,
After reading about KFM reprints in No.29, you said that thousands of readers already have the first issue and wouldn't want another, so you couldn't be sure of selling all the reprints. Well, I have the first issue but I would still buy another as mine's in bad condition - and then I'd be able to cut the photos out of the older one. I'm sure that there are many other readers who'd do the same.
Alan McDade, Edinburgh, Scotland

Dear Alan,
I'm certainly not going to try and pretend that yours was the only letter I had in on the subject as there were quite a few, actually, who shared your opinion. Again, all I can do is push them all through to the Editor. When it comes down to it, he's the one to finally decide whether or not a reprint is possible.

THE BRUCE LEE SECRET SOCIETY

Darren Souter, Wallsend - Nothing in *Enter the Dragon* was speeded up.
M.C. Oliver, Eastgate, Peterborough - You want the Robert Lee album? Just turn to the Mail Order page!
Glenn Layfield, Greetland, West Yorks - These rip-off Bruce Lee films are made for one reason only - to make more money out of the master's name. Sad but true.
Marcos Kodrigues, London Colney, Herts - Sorry, *Game of Death* is not released - believe me!
Valda Johnson, Heme Hill, London - Pam at the Secret Society is trying to arrange a Hong Kong trip for members. Bruce's home life is an idea we're working on.
John Rogers, London - The Binders idea is being looked into at this very moment. A Bruce Lee's films project is due to begin shortly.
Paul Lee, Manchester - If you have some written info on the subject of Gung Fu, I'd be quite interested in seeing it.
David Morris, Wakefield, Yorkshire - Why doesn't the TV show Bruce's films? The answer is they're still earning lots of money on the cinema circuits.
Derrick Fleming, Wolverhampton, Staffs - The *Bruce Lee Scrapbook* contained many black and white pictures of Bruce and we published it over two years ago. It's sold right out I'm afraid.

THE POSTER MAGAZINES - VOLUME TWO

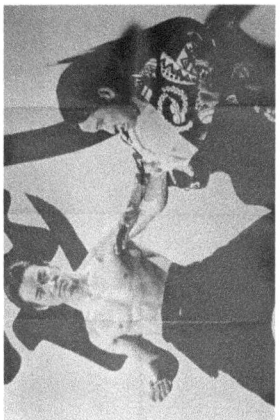

32

1977

EDITORIAL

Hi there Kung Fu fans. Here we go, pulling into orbit with *KFM* No.32 and, though I say it myself, we've got a stunner of an issue for you this month! First up, there's some more red hot news on the state of play of *Game of Death*. The *KFM* investigators have been poking their noses around to reveal momentous happenings behind the scenes. Check out on the Kickback page with Jenny for the latest.

And, talking about momentous happenings - sad news of the month is the reported closure of Cathay Films UK! Apparently, the move has been forced on them by adverse financial circumstances. The good news is that all of Bruce Lee's film product will from now on, be handled by EMI (as far as this country is concerned) - except *Enter the Dragon* which stays with Warner Brothers. I'd like to thank without reserve, Cathay Films and in particular, executives Roy Byrne and Tony Love for their long-lasting and whole hearted support of our magazine. It sounds corny I know, but honestly, without their help, *KFM* just wouldn't have made it in the way it has.

And quickly on to our first feature, What the Stars Said About Bruce Lee! With an address book that read like the who's who of the film industry, it could truly be said that the Little Dragon knew 'em all! But what did they say about him? Tune in this month and the next for some no-punches-pulled revelations - most of the names may be familiar but for a lot of the info, it's the first time published!

Second in line, we ask, "Where's the Magic in Kung Fu?" *KFM* rips into the superstitions and legends of thousands of years - and comes up with some pretty amazing answers. Can faith protect you against bullets? Could Bruce Lee defend himself blindfold? *Kung-Fu Monthly* takes on this mystifying subject in fine style to offer a pile of insights that'll keep you wondering for weeks. Fact or fantasy?... read on!! That's gotta be it for now.

Felix Yen
Felix Yen
Editor-in-Chief

HIS FRIENDS REVEAL THE REAL BRUCE LEE

In last month's issue of *KFM*, we introduced you to the thoughts and feelings of many press reporters throughout the world. Their views and ideas, however prejudiced, misjudged and ill-informed were important for they reflected how the world in general was thinking at the time. This month, we moved one step further on and indeed, one step nearer the Martial Master himself. Bruce had many friends and acquaintances and such was his power and charisma, just about all of them had something to say about him. This time, however, the comments are strictly accurate and for the most part, the facts correct. That's only reasonable when you think that, for many of the Little Dragon's Inner Circle, he was the fulcrum around which they all turned. When Bruce held court, everybody listened! As before, we take the contributions as they come and in no particular order. Though the sources may vary wildly, one thing they all have in common. They all refer to a man mourned these last few years as the deviser and ultimate exponent of Jeet Kune Do, Bruce Lee the Master.

Perhaps it's only right that the first words on the Little Dragon should come from his wife, Linda. Who, after all, could know a man better than his wife? This snip is an interesting one indeed. It dates from an interview she gave in July, 1972 to the Hong Kong New Nation - a time, of course, when the Master was still very much alive and basking in the new-found success of *Fist of Fury*.

She said, "He is not the sort of person who pays a great deal of attention to ceremony and form. For example, he thinks that opening doors or bringing flowers are unimportant things. These are merely actions. It is the thought you have for a person that is important. But he is very considerate - he always remembers birthdays and anniversaries. He has got the knack of getting along with people. He makes friends easily but he can read people

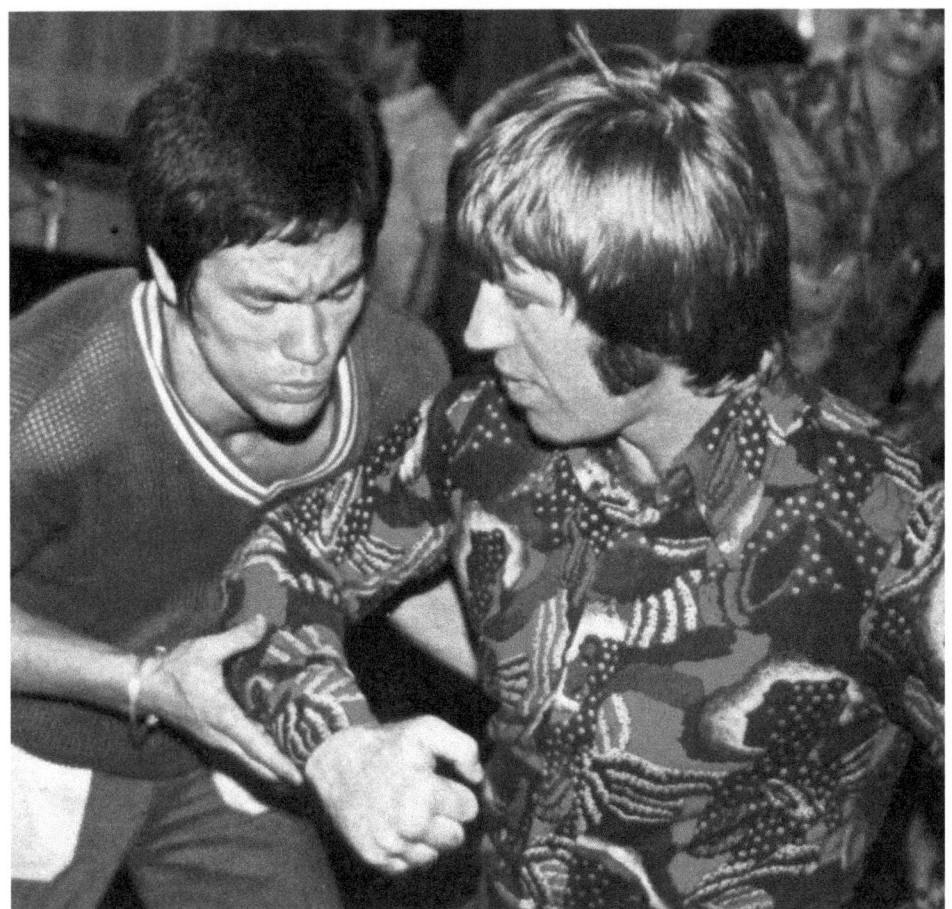

better than I can. I think I am more gullible and tend to take people at their face value, but Bruce can make very accurate assessments of people's characters at first meetings."

This is obviously a very sensible judgement of Bruce Lee as a husband and man. Naturally, somebody with his list of accomplishments must have been very skilful when it came to sorting out his friends from his enemies. An empire not only has to be founded upon a solid base (Bruce's art), it must also be built of well-chosen bricks. That's not to say, of course,, that the Little Dragon lorded it over his compatriots. Far from it - when it came to making those brilliant films, he very much saw it all as a team effort. And talking about the Master's cinema productions, Golden Harvest boss, Raymond Chow, had this to say about Hong Kong's platinum protégé.

"He is a very dedicated man. He concentrates very hard on what he is doing." On Bruce's remarkable success, Chow commented in August of 1972 that, "As for the reasons behind his popularity; partly it is because of his fighting sequences. People know that he is doing the real thing. Another factor is the characters he has played so far. In both films (*The Big Boss* and *Fist of Fury*), he played very likable and admirable men of guts and courage. Finally, I think his personality has something to do with it. His happy-go-lucky attitude appeals to movie-goers." Chow was absolutely right! When it came to appreciating a Little Dragon film, nobody was fooled by what was going on around him. It was Bruce Lee himself, rather than the character he was portraying, that all the fans were queuing up to see and although no one understood this more than the Master himself, he was always quick to point out the invaluable work put in by the team. Paul Wei Ping Au (remember, the fawning interpreter in *Fist of Fury*) - an actor many years in the Hong Kong film industry - spoke these words on a man he saw originally as very much a beginner in the cinema world. "I think he is great. He is a very easy person to work with. Because he is such a frank person, you tend to like him immediately. I first met him when we were shooting *Fist of Fury* and we got on very well, partly because I could speak English with him. His first attempt at directing was beyond my expectations. He is clearly very concerned with his work and takes great care over it. He has also read a lot of American literature and books on movie production and this has helped him succeed in putting beauty into his work." These are fine words from a man who has seen stars come and go and who knows exactly where to look to find true potential. Bruce was no doubt very happy to work with such an accomplished actor and Paul's unique mixture of professionalism and humour must have been a god-send to the Little Dragon's avowed aim to lift the level of the Asian film industry.

Many of the Hollywood heroes learnt a great deal from Bruce and such was their enthusiasm for the Martial Wizard, most of them were not ashamed to admit it either. Steve McQueen for one, not generally a man of many words, had this to say in his appreciation of the Little Dragon's helping hand. "The good head that he acquired was through him knowing himself. He and I used to have great long discussions about that. No matter what

you do in life, if you don't know yourself, you're never going to be able to appreciate anything. That, I think, is today's mark of a good human being - to know yourself." The wisdom in this train of thought is beyond dispute. After all, to not know yourself is to maybe have skill upon skill at your disposal but with no idea of how to put them to good use.

"Bruce and I were due to have dinner together. He didn't turn up so we rang his house several times. I'd been with him earlier in the day and he was fine. Unbelievable, the fittest man I've ever met, suddenly gone like a burnt-out light bulb." Those, by now famous words, were of course spoken by one-time Bond man and latterly Wang-Yu co-star, George Lazenby. George had good reason to be aghast at the incredible news. His whole future was to have hinged around Bruce's upcoming production of *Game of Death*. Not only that, he'd just lost a fine friend and there was little to console him. George's fine sentiments have somehow since, served to sum up the feelings of the cinema world. No one was expecting the death of the King and for a time at least, many of the tans just refused to believe it had even happened!

James Coburn was similarly stunned at the news of the Little Dragon's tragic passing. A one time pupil and still close friend, James chose his words wisely and well when he said, "The last I saw Bruce, just before his death, he was beginning to settle in the atmosphere of fame - which is a hard one to get used to. It wasn't a question of him competing with anybody, it was a question of everybody else competing with him. Because he was like a beacon - the source of energy that everybody got something from." He later added, "He had a great force which he created within himself - the only thing that really scared me was when he started drinking beef blood!" Many people have passed comment on the Little Dragon's sometimes unusual eating and drinking habits but the nub of the matter surely has to be simply this. A great deal of thought, research and experiment went into his dietary theories. His conclusions were never intended for anybody else (each athlete must find his own path) and no medical opinion has ever been offered that in any way linked his death with his protein and vitamin intake,

Bruce Lee had many martial art friends who sometimes turned actor for the sake of achieving maximum cinema realism. Such was the Little Dragon's flexibility of thought, he was only truly happy when he achieved the right mix of movie professionalism and Kung Fu expertise. One very handy ace in Bruce's pack was Danny Inosanto - a man of awe-inspiring talent and a martial master from way before the time he met up with China's number one son! Danny remarked some time after the fateful day, "He was of a calibre far beyond other Kung Fu artists. He's the Edison, Einstein and Leonardo Da Vinci of martial arts. Bruce reminded us of Johnston Livingstone Seagull because he was always striving to be better and better. If he had any shortcoming, he was such a perfectionist, he couldn't stand anything that didn't come up to his own standards." Dan's words certainly have the ring of truth about them. After all, to a man who can beat the world at his chosen profession, it must seem strange when others fail to meet the same high standards!

And that's as far as we go for this month. In Part Two, we'll take the story through to its conclusion with the recorded words of such people as Jim Kelly, Bob Wall, Chuck Norris, Nora Miao - to name but a few. Raymond Chow steps forward again too, this time to tell us a little more of what really happened the day he decided to try signing up Bruce Lee. The *KFM* researchers have really set the trail ablaze for the next issue, so all you Little Dragonologists, get those fact-files ready! See you then.

WHERE IS THE MAGIC IN KUNG FU?

Stories abound in Kung Fu history of what is often considered to be, the well neigh supernatural. But the martial arts, taken by and large, are most certainly not magic in origin. They consist of solid, tried and trusted techniques which, although maybe unusual in form when compared to more well-known western arts, nevertheless do exist in real fact. Remember, to a man living in the 18th Century, the very idea of some invisible electricity running through wires to power anything from a light bulb to a television set would have been laughed at. Anybody able to work such wonders at that time would surely have been called a magician - if not a charlatan! And yet, we now accept such things as commonplace, the same way we now accept that maybe, just maybe, it is possible to box somebody while blindfolded. If radar exists as a mechanical/electrical gadget, can it not therefore exist in man's mind? The answer seems to be yes! *KFM* is taking time this month to probe into a few more impossible feats to check whether perhaps there's a grain or more of truth behind the facade of legend and mystery. Where indeed is the magic in Kung Fu?

In China in the year 1899, Governor Yuan Shik-k'ai of Shantung proved in the crudest, but maybe best way possible, that the Boxers had no supernatural defence against com-

mon or garden bullets. He had some executed by firing squad! And yet, despite evidence to the contrary, still that belief has held fast in many countries of the world, right up to the present day. Thousands of Japanese soldiers believed themselves invulnerable to bullets while fighting in World War Two - and often to their cost. So why should such an idea persist - where, if anywhere, is that grain of truth? One obvious point is that to spread such a rumour would frequently work in favour of the commanding general. His men would be less inclined to hold back with the battle at its height and arguably, although many more would be killed, providing plenty of reinforcements were waiting in the wings, victory would more likely be his.

But is this callous attitude the only answer? *KFM* says maybe not. No warfare technician would doubt the power of the mind working both for and against him. To begin with, how about the army fighting against the men claiming such supernatural powers. One or two setbacks in any walk of life is enough to make people believe that fate is acting against them. Therefore rumours of invulnerability might wreck havoc amongst the opposing forces. Then again, skilful use of the art of not attracting attention can make somebody seem to be invulnerable! Their cunning actions involving perhaps persuasion of the mind, can render them as good as invisible,

though they be as solid as you or I!

    The fabulous Japanese Ninjitsu have been mentioned before in *Kung-Fu Monthly*. Hardened to tough living, trained to perfection in a multitude of fighting arts and in general, sworn to secrecy, the Ninja has remained a shadowy folk figure right through to this day. Reputedly he was able to walk in snow without leaving foot-prints, become invisible at will, walk on water, climb up vertical walls with only his bare hands and feet and perform many other impossible and magical feats too numerous to mention. But did he, or was he, perhaps as good at deceiving the eye as he was a superbly trained athlete? Many would say that the key word here is 'illusion.' You've seen the woman being sawn in half on the television - and yet you know she's not been touched. You've seen a man pulling live rabbits out of a hat, knowing full well they couldn't have been there in the first place.

    But it looks real and so, to the superstitious folk of Japan, did the antics of the Ninja. Clever and ingenious really sums it up. Often the vanishing Ninja was seen to disappear in a cloud of smoke. Well, it just so happened, he'd learned the art of making smoke bombs. When in a tight situation, he'd simply pull one out of his bag of tricks, let it off, arid then escape amid the confusion! Walking on water became similarly possible by the use of specially constructed leg pontoons, strategically hidden at various points along the river

side. How about walking on snow, without leaving footprints? Well, that's an interesting one. One's immediate reaction is to suggest use of trees, hedgerows and so on, or perhaps a small, leafy branch to wipe away the tell-tale prints. On the other hand, there is a legendary Asian skill known as walking light. We are told that with many hours of practice and prodigious exercise of skill, it is, in fact, possible to render the body almost weightless!

Orthodox science says this is not possible but Asian writings say it is. If the latter is correct, then the answer must surely lie with the body's internal energy, that is, ch'i. Western science, however, also cannot explain how a woman can lift a car from a trapped child - a

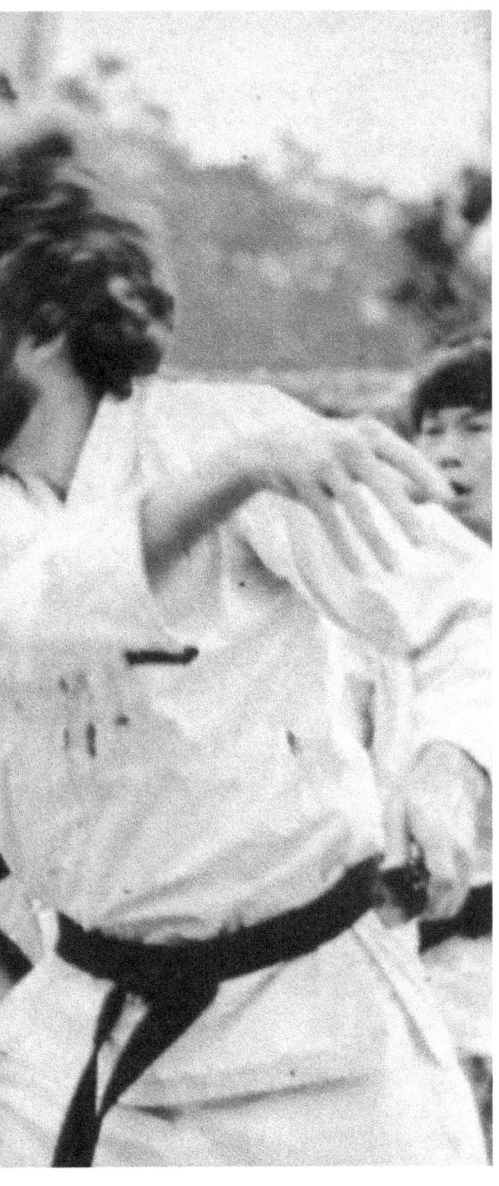

task far beyond her muscular powers. Levitation, the so called spiritual art of lifting heavy weights with the barest amount of energy is now being investigated seriously. Some might in fact say that western science is only now starting to catch up with eastern common sense.

Bruce Lee himself is said to have shown the impossible to be possible. He didn't! He simply removed another layer of our blindfold. He refused to work to the limits accepted by other people and he created his own. Some readers will undoubtedly see the connection between this action and his ultimate concept of Jeet Kune Do.

Many a man with supernatural abilities had his magic touch attribute to his diet. We're told, for instance, that famed Indian wrestling champion, Ghulam Mohammed (known as Gama), while training, consumed two or three gallons of milk a day, five pounds of crushed almonds, plus goodly quantities of soup and vegetables! The Little Dragon followed a food regime that would horrify many a dietician. The problem could be that science thinks very much in terms of vitamins, proteins, carbohydrates and so on. And yet in this country, a very large number of serious minded people cock-a-snoop at all this and eat only pure food, grown under friendly conditions and without the use of artificial fertilisers. They believe that such food has an almost spiritual value and although science can find no improvement in the nutritional content, they could be right! To a believing person, such food has magical qualities. The western world in general laughs at the superstitions surrounding that ancient Indonesian weapon, the kris. Stories of its usefulness and abilities abound as with virtually no other weapon. Appearing in just about all shapes and sizes, without going into enormous detail, it might best be described as a sort of dagger. It's said that water may be drawn from it, that some are able to fight battles on behalf of the owner, that each must be matched perfectly to its respective owner, that a man can be slain by the stabbing of a kris into his shadow, that a fire may be directed by it, and so on. However unlikely these claims may be, it's easy to see how the weapon rapidly assumed the same importance as the horse did to the cowboy. The owner's reliance become almost total, thus greatly increasing his confidence. Again, drawing water from the blade may simply be an illusion, but none the less a powerful one. To the all-believing onlooker, such a weapon clearly has supernatural powers and the owner is certainly not a man to be meddled with!

The story is told of a young man who approached a famed Chinese boxing master with the idea of becoming his pupil. The teacher obliged and for three long years, seven days a week he was made to crush heavy sheets of coarse paper into balls only to then lay them flat again with his palms. After the third year, the master told him to go and, disappointed at his lack of learning and progress, the student went home. That night, he offered to help rub his younger brother's back as the boy was bathing. The ex-pupil was horrified to see his brother's skin peel away beneath his hand!

The legend is useful in that it tells a tale of perseverance, of keeping faith in one who seems worthy of your attention and in thinking, as the young man hadn't, of the probable outcome of all that training. For such things are possible. There is no trick about breaking bricks in two with bare hands. Science will calculate that a certain force, applied at the centre of the brick, will ensure its fracture. A human hand can quite easily attain that force but, if there is doubt in the mind of the practitioner and he holds back, then the pain will be immense. If, however, it is sufficient and the brick breaks cleanly, there will be no damage done to the hand. Even so, this should never be attempted without the guidance of an expert.

To Bruce Lee, much of this fell into the category of party tricks. He knew where his real strengths lay and he knew he had no need to resort to the unreliable world of magic when it came to demonstrating his exceptional martial arts prowess. Of course, to an onlooker, much of what the Little Dragon achieved must look like magic. But Bruce knew he'd just set his own limits!

THE BRUCE LEE SECRET SOCIETY

Hello again, Pam here with another knockout Secret Society page for all you thousand plus members.

Did I say a thousand? YES I DID!! We've made it and if you want to find out who the lucky 1,000th member is, take a look inside your Society News Sheet number 4. Sorry, by the way, that it's been a little later than I was hoping, but you've no idea how much I've had to do lately! There's been this *Kung-Fu Monthly* Secret Society page to write, News Sheet number 4, The Member's Souvenir Magazine to assemble and finally, the area lists I've been promising you. On top of all that, of course, there's been the usual pile of letters to answer too, so if I've been bit slow in replying to yours, now you know why! Don't worry though; I'm catching up slowly.

Member, John Kemp, has informed me that a friend who is in the Elvis Presley Fan Club was with him one day when John bought a copy of *KFM*. The friend remarked, 'I can't see that magazine lasting for much longer' - it was *KFM* No.3! John also tells me that he's got some great posters from 'Dolans' and although he says he's had to wait a long time for them to come, he reckons it's been well worth it. For the address of the company, check out in our News Sheet No.4 as we've got all the details there.

Apparently old monster magazines (such as *Modern Monsters* and *Castle of Frankenstein*) sometimes have articles in them on *Green Hornet* and on Bruce Lee in particular. I suggest everybody roots through old magazine and book shops whenever they get the chance. I expect there's quite a few of these rarities around, if we did but know it!

By the way, a good place to write to for Little Dragon Cinema Posters, stills and press books is the following address: 34 Southwood Avenue, Bournemouth, BH6 3QB.

Here are a few more goodies from members Martin Hughes and Mark Burns. They're the two nice people who gave us our fabulous poster list and to help keep the ball rolling, they've sent in a few more names.

1) A Memorial Poster of Bruce Lee is obtainable from PO Box 54338, Terminal Annexe, Los Angeles, California 90054, USA, for the sum of $2.50

2) A Jeet Kune Do Technique Poster from George Foon of 7011 Sunset Boulevard, Los Angeles, California 90028, USA for $1.00

3) And you can get a Bruce Lee T-Shirt for £1.40 at Conray Publications and Enterprise Co., PO Box 2599, Kowloon Central, Hong Kong. Also, from the same address, there are Bruce Lee Kung Fu Uniforms, small and medium for $19, large and extra large for $20 and *Fist of Fury* rubber nunchakus for $10.60. To be honest, I'd be rather less than enthusiastic about sending large sums of money abroad for the latter items as it really can be so difficult if something goes wrong. I will leave it up to you take whatever precautions you can.

As you'll be able to see from News Sheet No.4, the Society Souvenir magazine of member's own contributions has finally been completed. Well, I won't say it wasn't a struggle. There was a lot to put in and not much space in which to get it all. Still, all's well that ends well! By the by, if in the future we decide to assemble a club souvenir magazine No.2, could you all bear in mind the following points when it comes to submitting drawings and paintings? 1. As the magazine itself will be in black and white, it usually helps a lot if the work you send us is also in black and white. 2. Please try to use plain and not lined paper. 3. For the best possible results, try to use ink rather than pencil. If you really do prefer to use a pencil, please try to make sure it's a dark, that is, a hard one!

This month we've decided to put all the swaps into the News Sheet, so there's none here in *KFM* this time - the same applies to the pen pals. Next issue, it's back to normal again! See you then... **Pam**

BACK ISSUE BONANZAS 5 & 6!

KFM is delighted to announce the arrival of Back Issue Bonanza No.6. Now at last, readers who missed out on some of the more recent editions have got a chance to 'plug the gaps'!

BONANZA 5.   Issues 18, 19, 20, 21 and 22
BONANZA 6.   Issues 23, 24, 25, 26 and 27

Each of the above BONANZAS is on offer for £1.20. In the years to come, your back copies of Kung-Fu Monthly will become sought after items and complete sets will be valuable. Don't miss out on this chance to update your collection – Send your cheque or postal order off immediately to:

Back Issue Bonanza 5/6
Kung-Fu Monthly
14 Rathbone Place
London W.1.
CLUB MEMBER'S PRICE, £1.00 ONLY
(Please allow at least 4 weeks for delivery).

THE BRUCE LEE SECRET SOCIETY

Hi, Jenny here again and how about this for a blockbuster! The scorching news from Hong Kong is that *Game of Death* was, in theory, finished a while back. But, apparently Raymond Chow was unhappy with the result and this, plus all the rip-off versions of the *Game of Death* storyline, has prompted Chow to do a script remake! There's no details of changes as yet and all we've been told, is to stand by for a Christmas release. I've had some really interesting letters this month so I won't hold things up any longer. Here we go!

BRUCE LEE'S GRAVE

Dear Jenny,
KFM stated that the coffin of Bruce Lee had been moved from Seattle to Los Angeles (in rumour). I have received a letter from a Mr R.A. Bladine, who is the Assistant Manager of Lake View Open Cemetery, where the coffin still lies. He confirms that as of 10th May 1977, Bruce Lee is still buried at Lake View. As you will know, it is getting near the time of the 4th anniversary of the Death of our Master the Late Li Yuen Kam. Anybody wishing to send flowers to the graveside should post the money (preferably in US dollars) to Capitol Hill Florist Company, 1534 15th Avenue East, Seattle, Washington, USA. Don't forget to tell the shop what the money is for, and remember all Bruce Lee fans, that Linda Lee will be visiting the grave, so let her see that the true fans of Bruce Lee are from England. By the way, when I read that *Game of Death* had been stopped again, I personally wrote to Raymond Chow at his private office. I'll tell you of my reply.
Dave Langley, Runcorn, Cheshire

Dear Dave,
What a great letter and what good news too about the Master still being in Seattle. May I emphasise that July 20th is the fourth anniversary of Bruce's passing and both KFM and I would like to take this opportunity of honouring his name. Though the Master is gone, the memory of the world's greatest martial artist will continue to live through the pages of Kung-Fu Monthly. *We wish his spirit well.*

PETITION

Dear Jenny,
I enclose a petition which you asked every reader of *KFM* to send. I think it's a bright idea and well done. I'm sorry there's only 15 signatures, but I thought people who really didn't know or care much about Bruce shouldn't sign. As for your message, 'Don't let me down, please,' which you printed in *KFM*, don't worry, I would insist on taking part.
Paul Furr, Gedling, Nottingham

Dear Paul,
Sorry first of all to have to cut your letter which was a little too long for us. You don't have to be sorry about only having 15 signatures. That's 15 more than somebody who hasn't bothered at all and every single one counts. Thanks for your help.

BOB WALL

Dear Jenny,
I find it hard to believe that Bruce's English was not good enough to do the whole of the *Enter the Dragon* soundtrack. I also once read that Bob Wall deliberately cut Bruce that time in *Enter the Dragon*. A few weeks later, I read that Bob was a true friend of Bruce's?
Jason Phillips, Kilburn, London

Dear Jason,
Thanks for your letter. Actually, several people have voiced similar opinions about Bruce's dialogue in *Enter the Dragon*. They too say his English was too good to make this necessary and I must say I tend to believe them. Regarding the Bob Wall incident, I suspect the truth lies somewhere between the two.

ALEXANDER HOW-PONG HO

Dear Jenny,
Recently, I read an article on Alexander Hon-Pong Ho: Kung Fu Rebel. Here are some extracts. 1. Bruce Lee as a movie superstar, was the worst thing that ever happened to the martial arts. Before his triumphs, there was honour among instructors. Now all that is gone. The myth of his life created a monster that may destroy us all! 2. He also said that Bruce's skills were little more than an average martial artist. 3. Finally, that the nunchaku Bruce Lee used in his movies were just hollow plastic.
No Name or Address.

Dear KFM Reader,
Here we go again. Somebody else getting ready to cash in on the Kung Fu market with a great big ker-ching! You see, the trouble is, me saying he is talking poppycock still gives him publicity - which is exactly what he wants! I shall say no more than this. If he cares to bend his head before me to allow me to whack him around the ear with the nunchaku Bruce used when making Fist of Fury, I suspect he might retract his statement about hollow plastic - that's if he can still talk, of course.

FILM STAR MAGAZINE

Dear Jenny,
You asked a while ago about the *Film Star* magazine series. Well, it was a poster magazine and it included stars like Clint Eastwood, Charles Bronson, etc. Issue two was of Bruce Lee. The poster came from *Fist of Fury*, the other pictures from *The Way of the Dragon* and *The Big Boss* (the famous leap). It was published three or four years ago and cost 15 or 20 pence. It's now out of print. PS: Any chance of getting *KFM* No.24?
Paul Marston, Peverell, Plymouth

Dear Paul,
What more need I say? The KFM reader's information service does it again! For such great work, how else can I reward you but with a copy of KFM 24!
Alan McDade, Edinburgh - Thanks for the Bruce Lee 8mm info. Sorry I can't advertise it - sales are illegal in the UK.

QUICKIES CORNER

Owen Lonergan, Co. Durham - I'm afraid the Little Dragon TV thing is still just a rumour.

Marlon Whetton, Streatham, London - We know *Enter the Dragon* should be ahead of *Freebie and the Bean* - try telling the film company!

Ann Perrer, Portsmouth, Hants - Ask your censor to write to EMI. They will confirm *Game of Death* exists.

Pete Barnacle, Battersea, London - Glad you agree with me about this sweat gland thing.

John Kemp, Patchway, Bristol - Sorry but *Game of Death* has been postponed. Our info comes direct from the Hong Kong studios.

Ken Shepherd, Clifton, Notts - Cathay UK's work has been taken over by EMI Ltd.

Kevin Foster, Chopwell - Point taken about all the *Enter the Dragon* posters.

Richard Maldment, Southampton - *The Man and the Legend* will almost certainly be 'X' cert when it comes.

Kenneth Evans, Morden - No *Beginner's Guide to Kung Fu* left here - check your local shop for the newer paperback version.

S. Singh, Huddersfield, Yorkshire - Now Bruce's gone, all the worms are crawling out to knock him. They wouldn't have dared when he was alive.

Paul Waines, Normandy - Bruce's nunchakus were specially made for him.

Steven King, Leeds, Yorks - More fighting posters? - we'll do our best!

David Rapier, South Shields - Issues 5-13 yes, but 1-4, you've got problems

David Evans, Sidcup, Kent - Yes, a less-edited version of *The Big Boss* is going around now.

Peter Davies, Runcorn is looking for female friend interested in Bruce Lee - picture please.

Angela Lee, Bedford is 17 years old and black and she's looking for a Chinese Bruce Lee look-alike aged 17 to 19 years.

Miss C. Reece, Liverpool is 22 years old and looking for a male friend over 16 years from anywhere but England.

Vincent Teo, London is 21 years old, likes Kung Fu, travelling, reading and is Chinese.

THE POSTER MAGAZINES - VOLUME TWO

1977

EDITORIAL

    Hi there Kung Fu fans. Light the blue touch paper, step back off the launching platform and stand by for another explosive edition of *Kung-Fu Monthly*! And first up, I want to congratulate everyone concerned for their response to Jenny's *Game of Death* petition. I don't have the exact and final figure in front of me - check the Kickback page for that - but I do know that it exceeded my wildest expectations. It really gives us some deadly ammunition to aim towards Golden Harvest and you can bet your life, as soon as we get any sort of response from the company, we'll be letting you know about it. So far as I can see, the view of many of you is - don't bother with doubles, new story lines, camera tricks and so on. Just get what Bruce left us on the cinema screens. I'm inclined to agree.
    This month, we click into action with the second half of our 'Superstars Speak Out About Bruce Lee' feature and if I'm any judge, you're going to find it amazing! Some of the sources we had to dig out you just wouldn't believe; rare Hong Kong newspapers weren't

the half of it. It's all been worthwhile though and the result is yet another fitting *KFM* tribute to the master, Bruce Lee.

Second in line, we notch up something of an experiment for you. I've always wanted to put in *KFM*, features that actually help readers as well as entertain them. This month, we start the ball rolling with some handy advice on the great art of concentration. Of enormous value to Kung Fu aspirant and layman alike, inward control over the mind is one of the most important aspects of the spiritual progression of 20th Century Western Man. I know I can count on you all to let Jenny know how you felt about the article. That said, it's on with the show.

Felix Yen

Felix Yen
Editor-in-Chief

THE REAL BRUCE LEE – PART TWO

Like moths around a flame, so Bruce Lee attracted the finest actors, cinema producers and martial artists of the day to his side. They came to bounce off the enthusiasm and to soak up some of the scorching hot energy coming off the world's greatest exponent of Kung Fu. For Lee's talents were multifarious. To be superbly fit physically is one thing, but to turn out films like *The Big Boss*, *Fist of Fury*, *The Way of the Dragon* and *Enter the Dragon* is something else. He was a good talker too. Bruce Lee holding forth at the meal table on some subject or other was an occasion not to be missed. His force of personality, his mesmerising charisma and his very full knowledge on so many things all combined to almost guarantee that any restaurant would grind to a halt within minutes of him entering. Other customers and waiters alike would frequently become transfixed at his very presence. This month in *KFM*, we finish the story we started last issue. Some more of the people and stars he knew, met, worked with or simply just talked to step forward to help us understand just a little more clearly the man who revolutionised the Kung Fu world.

Golden Harvest boss Raymond Chow, describes how he got Bruce to sign a two year company contract. "Actually, I've known Bruce since he was a child actor years ago. I was impressed but he went to the States and we forgot about him. In 1970, he appeared on Hong Kong TV for a demonstration of Jeet Kune Do. I didn't see the show but everyone who did, acclaimed it. Then I heard that Bruce was interested in making a film here. He had asked a friend to approach Shaw Brothers, but the deal fell through, apparently because Shaws wanted to treat him as a completely new actor. So I rang him up in his L.A. home, asked him if it was true that he was interested in doing a film here and he said yes. Bruce suggested I should post him the terms but I decided that if he were serious, I would send Liew Lian Hwa (wife of Lo Wei) to talk with him personally in L.A. The contract was signed in the States."

Golden Harvest executive, Andre Morgan, saw Bruce's fantastic enthusiasm - the way he grabbed life by the throat - in rather a different light. He said, "As a person, he was very intense and deeply into everything. That was part of the problem. He was always going in too many directions at once to find out about everything as quickly as possible - always in a hurry. The May 10th collapse in the heavy dubbing studio of Golden Harvest may have been a warning from a superbly toned, but over-taxed body, that something was wrong. But he didn't take any heed of it. That's probably what killed him."

But is that what killed him? It's very easy to seize on the life he led and claim that it was responsible for his death. The assumption must be sweeping and it's not an opinion ever to be shared by the medical people who attended him during his triumphant life and at his tragic death. However, one aspect of the master has seldom, if ever been noticed or talked about. That is his apparent, steady loss of weight that can be checked with a vengence by examining pictures of him fighting in *Game of Death*. Compare his slight (though still muscular) body appearance and his bony face with the almost chubby looking Little Dragon of several years before. The change, you'll agree, is dramatic and perhaps bears some investigation at a later date.

Chow again, when talking of Bruce's tragic passing to a Hong Kong reporter said, "His death came as a shock to Hong Kong people who had begun to accept him as a symbol of rightfulness as portrayed by him in his movies. Bruce was the king of boxers, a crown no one dared challenge. His sudden death has left an empty throne for Hong Kong, or even the world, to find a man, an actor, a fighter great enough to fill his shoes." Well of course, since the time Chow uttered these words, nothing very much has happened to fill that giant hole. Still Bruce holds the posthumous crown of glory and still nobody has been able to step forward and challenge for it. As world famous scriptwriter and one-time buddy of the Little Dragon, Stirling Silliphant, put it, "No man, no woman was ever as exciting as Bruce Lee. Bruce was more than just a single success story. He represented a whole race finally accepted in films."

During his star-studded career, the Little Dragon was naturally responsible for handing out inspiration to many an aspiring motion picture Kung Fu star. One perhaps Bruce Lee fans have cause to remember more than others, has to be Jim Kelly - renowned for his supporting role in *Enter the Dragon*. Jim made no bones about it; when it came to respect, his friend was top of the league. "Bruce gave me respect as a martial artist to do whatever I wanted to do. He didn't say, 'Jim, this is what you're going to do - that's it.' Before we even got into the fight scenes which he choreographed he said, 'Jim, I want you to do what you want to do. I know that you did your technical advising on Melinda. You know your art and you can do whatever you want to do. I'll give you any help you want.' So I did the fight

scene in the stadium myself. Bruce had something laid out and he said, 'Jim, do you like this?' I said, I may change this and that, but it wasn't, 'Hey Jim, this is it and you've gotta do it cos I'm Bruce Lee... I'm the technical advisor.' It wasn't like that at all."

Even the currently somewhat controversial Bob Wall has been reported as saying, "It was always exciting working with him as he was always teaching something new. Maybe he'd be busy trying to learn how to take a punch or a kick or something and he wouldn't be paying attention to the camera. He'd say, 'Look, there are so many things to observe. Don't just get hung up on one thing.' He was always spouting philosophies and he was very stimulating."

A man of his way to the top of the film business has somebody he must certainly be able to impress - the head of the film company involved. Bruce's relationship with Raymond Chow is legendary, but his association with Ted Ashley, chairman of Warner Brothers, is less well known. Ted knew a good man when he saw him and he had this to say about the Little Dragon. "Bruce was an amalgam. He had a kind of reserve - a very becoming modesty and dignity. Almost a softness of manner. On the other hand, there was the occasional spark of the living room demonstration. During the course of an evening, somebody would want to know what he could do. To be accommodating, he would snatch a fly out of mid-air or do a trick with his hands that was so quick, it would take everyone's breath away. Above all, Bruce's really lovely, bright personality made him a very attractive person." And that, in fact, highlights superbly how Bruce had so surely reined-in his killer instinct to have it work to the best of his advantage. Whatever he did, he did it well and that surely is the mark of the complete human being. His necessary self-assurance was never allowed to turn itself into smugness. One man whose name regular readers will know well, is that of Jhoon Rhee. Jhoon, of course, we hope to be seeing as soon as possible in *Game of Death*. Although he claims to have been close to Bruce, it has been strongly rumoured that, in fact, no love was lost between the two of them. These sort of rumours fly around backstage in show business all the time and although not necessarily to be taken with a pinch of salt, a certain degree of scepticism would probably be in order. Jhoon said of Bruce, "I thought in amazement, that such a young man had read so much. His vocabulary was amazing." The Little Dragon's thirst for knowledge was fantastically helpful when it came to him having to think his way out of a tight situation. No matter what the problem might have been, years of thought and studying enabled him to come up with the right answers. Chuck Norris said, "Bruce was a genius at creating new ideas. This is what amazed me about him. His inventions, the new things he could create and develop. I feel he accomplished more in his lifetime than most people will accomplish in 70 or 80 years." Taky Kimura once commented, "Like an electrifying force that drew you to him he was in outstanding person."

Actress Nora Miao went as far as claiming a family tie-in with Bruce! She said, "It is a rather complicated sort of relationship, but Bruce Lee's sister-in-law is the daughter of my father's classmate, who was very close to my family! And Bruce's brother used to be my boyfriend. He is now studying in the US. Naturally, I used to hear a lot about Bruce Lee so he wasn't really a complete stranger when we began working together."

And Herb Jackson has this tale to tell as a tribute to a facet of Bruce's character that has been barely touched on - his generosity. "Bruce was a true friend. Honest almost to a fault. The few times he used criticism, it was biting because his words had the ring of truth in them. He was also the most generous person I've ever known. Once in Hong Kong, I was admiring a beautiful suede suit of his. He showed me the quality of the material the silk lining, and explained how specially made it was. Then he said, 'See how you look in it Herb,' and then he said, 'It's yours.' Just like that!"

And so the testimonials continue to flood in. Maybe sometime ahead, we'll find the space to say a little more on what the stars said about Bruce Lee. Perhaps the greatest compliment to be paid to him, is that he lived his life according to the precepts of Jeet Kune Do. Whether directing a film, handling a fight sequence, eating at a restaurant or tussling with some personal problem, his course was always clear - bend like a willow, adapt to a situation, for if the truth be told, situations rarely adapt to meet the people involved in them!

The last words go to George Lazenby. On being told in his hotel room of the death of Bruce Lee he said, "I can't believe it - he's such a great guy."

THE INWARD BATTLE

Kung-Fu Monthly has, during its power-packed history, deviated only occasionally from its intention of bringing readers all the latest news about Kung Fu superstars in general - and Bruce Lee in particular. Normally speaking, the magazine has steered clear of actual Kung Fu instruction for two clear reasons. One that the 'how to' type of approach is far better dealt with in books (and better still, by teachers) and secondly, many of *KFM*'s customers are not practicing the fighting arts anyway. They're simply interested in what's going on in the martial arts/Little Dragon world. However, this magazine feels that little is to be lost and perhaps, much is to be gained by offering easy instruction in some more general subjects - age-old secrets that could be of use to anybody from the martial arts expert through to the just plain interested. This month, we kick things off with a feature on concentration. Read on and discover just how precious this powerful commodity is!

Cast your minds back. Do you remember being told sometime or other, that whenever you were having trouble dropping off to sleep, to count imaginary sheep? Well, if you were anything like me, your first reaction was to poo-poo the idea. What have sheep got to do with dozing off, you may well ask? Strangely enough, there is a lot of truth to the old adage and here's why. Sleep, like anything else, can only be accomplished if the hopeful subject is in the right state of mind. So what is the right state of mind? The answer is one that is under the control of the owner! Things that prevent sleep are worry, tension, panic, excitement - all states of mind that we have trouble in consciously controlling. But where do sheep come into it? Simple. By the very act of concentrating on one particular - and in this case, virtually never ending - subject, you'll actually be regaining control of your mind. Relaxation and consequently sleep, stand a pretty good chance of following on soon after.

This is all very well as a rather useful game but the thought occurs, wouldn't it be a much better idea to have control over the mind most, if not all, of the time? Of course it would be. A budding Kung Fu artist can learn all the kicks, chops and punches he wants, but without the right mental condition, success will rarely be his. The better read among you will understand that the basis of this feature lies very much in the mystic and religious philosophies of the East. Why do you think Bruce Lee had his library shelves crammed with such books? Not for him to look learned I assure you! Linda testifies that his nose would be buried in the pages for hours on end and the fruits of his dedicated investigations are there for all to see - a man utterly in control of his own mind and body.

Although the points that have been made so far - and the basic instruction to be touched on shortly - will obviously be aimed towards the aspiring martial artist, there is every reason in the world for other people to get involved too. The average person of untrained mind finds it difficult to think of one thing for more than just a few seconds. Try and see it how you do. Clear your mind as far as possible and think of a suitable subject - say, a tree. How long are you able to consider a tree before your mind takes over again and drifts on to something else such as what's for dinner today or, what's on TV tonight? Not many seconds, I'll be bound. This little trick brings home the unpleasant truth that most of us have little conscious control over our own minds.

But such control is possible, provided the person concerned is willing to work hard

inwardly. In the Eastern world, their culture is very much more in tune with such an idea and as such, results tend to come more easily for them. The Western world on the other hand has long since neglected such essential aims and only through people like the great Bruce Lee has the rebirth in this part of the world began. In the remainder of this feature, *KFM* is going to consider and outline just a few basic first steps in concentration. That is all a magazine can really do - the rest is up to the imagination and dedication of the reader.

Take a sheet of paper - a fairly large one - and write in the centre of it the name of a person or object. For the sake of this example, we will use the one and only Bruce Lee himself! So, on our sheet of paper there is written 'Bruce Lee' in the centre and round the two words we draw a small circle. Now, like the spokes of a wheel, draw lots of lines coming away from the circle. Don't worry if it all starts to sound rather complicated - it isn't really. The name of the game now is to sit down somewhere comfortable with pen in hand. Make sure there are no distractions like a radio, TV or noisy neighbours and so on and you're ready to start.

First of all, clear your mind as far as possible and relax physically. Now begin thinking about Bruce Lee. Every time you think of something connected with the Little Dragon, write it down on the paper at the end of one of the spokes. Typical thoughts might be: martial artist, film star, Hong Kong, Raymond Chow, Chuck Norris, nunchakus and so on. Don't rush the procedure, but on the other hand, don't do it so slowly that you give your mind a chance to slip onto another subject. To begin with, a time limit of just a few minutes will probably be all most people can manage without their concentration drifting away. Later, you'll be easily able to extend this.

The example I've used is a very easy one. Anybody reading this magazine knows plenty about Bruce Lee and probably, such is their enthusiasm about the man, they'll have no difficulty in concentrating on the king for minutes at a time. But, suppose I'd given the subject as 'a candle flame' or more difficult still, 'beauty' - try thinking of new things to say about those subjects for minutes on end! Obviously, the end result of the whole exercise is that the person trying out this routine is learning, in a not at all unpleasant way, to concentrate the mind at will. Naturally, positive results take time to come out and particularly after many years of mental inactivity. Nevertheless, after a while, very welcome improvements will appear. Working out solutions to problems in everyday life should get quicker and become easier. You'll be less inclined to worry and to panic - simply because you'll be able literally to tell yourself not to and your mind will take notice.

Furthermore, the Kung Fu artist will achieve new levels of coolness and calmness. As Bruce Lee so often pointed out, the opponent who loses his cool almost by definition becomes the loser. Of course there are many, many other routines designed to produce similar results and to get stuck into the subject thoroughly, readers are recommended to go to their local libraries and bookshops to see what's available. There are some everyday routines which, In a way, stick with these guidelines and which we follow without even realizing it. Working on crossword puzzles is an excellent mind occupier - with a fair amount of education thrown in for good measure!

Another aid to relaxation and hopefully greater concentration is what I like to call, the 'water method.' Take a look at a cat as it sits dozing by the fire. Chances are you think to yourself, what a lazy brute, just lying around all day. And yet you'd be wrong. Like most of the members of the cat family, that furry creature sat curled up in front of you, on sensing a danger signal, will wake up and disappear from view in just about no time at all.

The ability to be relaxed while still alert and on guard to the slightest sign of warning, is one that most Kung Fu artists will look on with envious eyes. Most of them go around in a tensed up state that does nobody any good at all. I bet right at this moment, that ninety-five per cent of *KFM* readers are looking at this with their teeth clenched together! What a complete waste of the body's energy.

The 'water method' of relaxation is just one of possibly hundreds of routines, but I favour it for its very simplicity. Select an area of floor - preferably lightly carpeted - and lie on it with your arms slightly out from your sides and legs a little apart. Imagine you're floating in the sea with the sun shining from above and the warm water lapping gently around you. It takes time for the illusion to become strong, but as it does, your body will appear to weigh less and less.

As you approach the weightless state, true relaxation will be your reward.

Having problems getting there? Well, a useful little addition is another piece of mind trickery. While you're floating there, imagine that your body is gradually disappearing! Yup, starting with the feet, then ankles, legs and so on until finally just the top of your head's showing. Lose that too and you should be well on the way to your goal.

Not only the martial artist, but everyone stands to gain from increased powers of relaxation and concentration. A fitter mind is a fitter body and why shouldn't the brain be exercised as much as anything else. Jeet Kune Do philosophy takes its lead from this very point. In order to know what suits you best and in order to read a difficult situation carefully and to apply the correct defensive measures, the mind must be in first class order. What use is a club without an arm to swing it?

THE BRUCE LEE SECRET SOCIETY

Once more, it's a big hello from me, Pam, to all you members of the Bruce Lee Secret Society.

It makes me really proud to think that every single one of you is dedicated to helping keep the name of the Little Dragon alive. And much more than that, don't forget the aim of this club is to see his ideas and his valuable philosophies on living are literally spread to the four corners of the globe. Let's have the memory of the master influencing the running of nations! It may sound over-hopeful of me to say that, but looking at the state of things right now, I reckon the world can do with all the help it can get.

As many of you may know, we have a sister Secret Society in the United States now and so far as I can make out, they're going great guns over there too! I've arranged for State-side members to write and tell me if they want to correspond with their UK counterparts and I'm pretty sure many of them will want to do just that! So, what I'd like members this end to do, is write and tell me whether YOU want your name and address to be included on the list I'll be sending to all the USA enquirers. It's a great opportunity to get to know what's happening across the water and so far as I'm concerned, it's the first link in a chain I'd like to sec stretch right round the globe. UK members who want to be included on that list, please send me a postcard saying so. Don't forget to include your name, address and Society number and mail the card to: The Bruce Lee Secret Society, USA Pen Pals List, 14 Rathbone Place, London W1P IDE.

Member, M. Lockwood (2040) says that Magpie Records of Hop Market, Worcester, Worcs. WR1 1UR have in stock an impressive collection of hard-to-get-hold-of LPs. For 15p they'll send you their complete brochure – featuring largely American, British and Italian product. Although we're not told for sure, it seems to me that the shop must be worth trying for Bruce Lee soundtrack material.

M. Hobson tells me about The Martial Arts Centre, 81 Broad Lane, Tottenham, London N15. Apparently they stock a number of Bruce Lee items including a T-Shirt and photos so I'd say they are well worth checking out. Their terms are a full refund if not satisfied and they claim a 'same day' despatch system.

I haven't had much response as yet on the Bruce Lee Mirrors idea I mentioned in the last News Sheet. As I said then, provided a good number of you write in and say you're interested, I'll go ahead with an order. If enquiries don't improve from the smallish number we've had so far, I'll have to knock the idea on the head. You have been warned!! And speaking of warnings; Following on what I said a few months ago, I am NOT replying to letters that arrive for me that DON'T include a stamped and addressed envelope. If you've written to me and as yet have had no reply, that may well be the reason why. I'm being really firm about this. Costs for everything are rising astronomically these days, so please help me in this small way.

See you again soon - **Pam**

KICKBACK: THE LETTERS

Hi, Jenny here again with this month's pick of the post bag! And right off, let me repeat what a fantastic response we've had to the *Game of Death* petition. I'm calling a halt to contributions now and I'll be sending the letters off in about a week. The final tally of signatures came to nearly 5,000! If that doesn't make Golden Harvest sit up and take notice, I reckon nothing will. Something I'm a little disturbed about, maybe needlessly, is news I hear that punk or new wave bands and their fans are starting to associate themselves with the name of Bruce Lee. It seems ridiculous I know, for a man who was dedicated to peace and self control, to be taken as a figurehead for a movement that, as I understand it, thrives on fear and violence. I really don't know what to make of it all. If any of you have anything to add to the subject, I'd be delighted to hear from you. On now with the letters!

KFM ANNUAL

Dear Jenny,
I have been buying *KFM* since the first issue now and I think it's great. How about doing a special issue to include the best articles and pictures that have appeared to date? And how about a *KFM* annual which could include the best of *KFM* for the year.
Ian Hamilton, Sunderland, Tyne & Wear

Dear Ian,
Regarding your first idea, well, funny you should say that! Even at this moment, pens are being raised in preparation of putting together a sort of 'Best of Kung-Fu Monthly.' *Your second idea, we hadn't considered. I like it except I think I'd be inclined to add new things to the annual as well. What do you other readers think?*

GAME OF DEATH PETITION

Dear Jenny,
Firstly, let me say that if *KFM* keeps going as well as it is, it will almost certainly become, as Bruce the Master, a legend. I agree totally with your *Game of Death* petition. By now, I should think that Bruce Lee and *KFM* fans don't give a hoot as to how the film is finished off, as long as we see it. It's a pity Bruce isn't here to give them a kick where it hurts most and make them move!
D. Ashby, Bury St. Edmunds, Suffolk

Dear D. Ashby,
First, thank you for your very kind words. Secondly, well you've seen how successful the petition has been response-wise so let's just hope it does as well, results-wise. Actually, I'm sure you're right. Were Bruce here today, I don't think he'd stand for one second the continuing saga of delay associated with Game of Death. *I'd go further and say it was a scandal.*

BRUCE LEE AND APOPLEXY

Dear Jenny,
After reading through a home medical book, I came to an important conclusion. I think that Bruce Lee died of something called 'Apoplexy.' Here are some of the symptoms: "There is great congestion of the blood vessels in the brain, with sudden rupture of one or more. The cause may be through, immoderate eating, abuse of alcohol and prolonged muscular exertion. The patient is liable to prolonged coma, even death." Most of Bruce's symptoms point to apoplexy. For example, immoderate eating - the time no meat could be found when location shooting. Then, most important, prolonged muscular exertion - Bruce certainly did a lot of that!
Al Briers, St. Helens, Merseyside

Dear Al,
It looks like you've really been doing your homework. Actually, I spot a flaw or two. To begin with, Bruce's diet was, by and large, quite safe medically speaking. There was only the odd occasion when he had to go without some of the essentials. I agree though, the prolonged exertion bit is interesting and many other people have voiced similar theories.

FILM CENSORSHIP PETITION

Dear Jenny,
I have come up with an idea to have a petition for the BBC to buy a Bruce Lee film and show it. I think there would be a big response from little Dragon fans, all over the country. Just like it says in KFM No.19 in the feature about film censorship: "Then again, possibly the BBC will decide to buy a Bruce Lee film." What do you think?
Andrew Tattersall, Lane, Preston

Dear Andrew,
Yes, you might be on to a good plan there. Certainly the BBC are very sensitive to demands from their viewing public and providing they were able to buy one of his films, I suspect such a petition might have some effect. However, I'd say now was just a bit too early to run a second petition. It takes a lot of effort and time for fans to collect such huge quantities of signatures and surely everyone could do with a rest for a while. Perhaps in a few months time we'll give it a try.

QUICKIES CORNER

Jim Vernon, Stoke on Trent, Staffs - Thanks for the enormous scroll - I enjoyed every inch of it.
A. Akred, Barrow-in-Furness, Cumbria - The best place to try for martial art books is Cimac Ltd of 606 Stratford Road, Sparkhill, Birmingham.
Paul Kelly, Whitleigh, Plymouth - Sometimes there are legal reasons why we can't use a picture for a poster.
Mr U.P. Gross, Aylesbury, Bucks - Many thanks for the article on Bruce - we

may be able to use it soon.

Mrs M. Jasinski, Cheltenham, Glos - The Robert Lee Album - yes, there is a printing mistake on the sleeve.

Bradley Morris, Pretoria, South Africa - So, a picture of Bruce Lee used to advertise Bruce Li? Will the rip-offs never end?

Michael Durrant, Plymouth, Devon - I suspect *Game of Death*'s completion has been slowed for reasons we may never really discover.

Chris Tapp, Trowbridge, Wilts - Still no *Game of Death* suits that we consider worth buying.

David Chatworthy, Bristol - Somebody else on the poster side? I asked for opinions on that some time ago - 95% of the replies said no.

Kraige Lee, Halifax, W. Yorks - A Bruce Lee Picture Album has to be a good idea - let's see if the editor can work out a way of doing it.

Brian Berk, Co. Armagh, Northern Ireland - A film hiring club may become possible next year.

J. Smyth, Accrington, Lancs - We scour the world for action pictures but they're thin on the ground.

John Duthie, Ayr, Scotland - Thanks for the clips - good luck in your Jeet Kune Do training.

Barry Munns, W. Yorks - According to Warner Bros., *Enter the Dragon* is not now due for general release for some while so try persuading your local cinema manager on a one-off basis.

NEWS EXTRA

Finally, not a letter, but a hot little piece of news for which we are indebted to Colm Quinn. David Carradine, when asked about his new film, replied, "It's called *The Silent Flute*. I regard it as good a project as *Bound For Glory*. It deals with the martial arts and the late Bruce Lee. Jeff Cooper, who is the leading martial arts star in South Africa, will have a key role and I will portray the part originally written for Bruce Lee. Frankly, I think it will be the hottest thing I've ever done." Hmm, it might get hot in more ways than he thinks!

KFM PEN PALS

David A. Jones, Llan Ffestiniog, N. Wales would like a pen pal from either UK or America, female if possible, 14/15 years old - picture please.

Lorraine & Linda Robinson, Northwick, Cheshire would like two Chinese male pen pals, aged 19-21 years old.

Mark Sun, Pretoria, South Africa - hobbies Bruce Lee and Kung Fu - would like male/female pen pals, 13-15 years old.

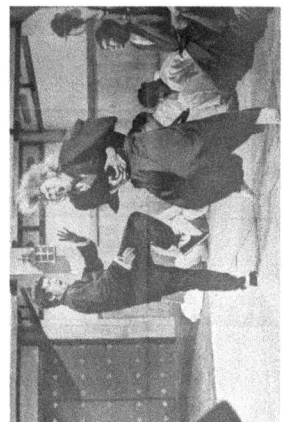

34

1977

EDITORIAL

Hi there Kung Fu fans. Welcome to this landmark edition of *Kung-Fu Monthly*! And landmark it is, for seldom do I have the opportunity of announcing a feature with an interview of such profound interest. The Golden Harvest company it is who are on the receiving end of the many penetrating questions and few punches have been pulled in their frank and illuminating replies. Such details as the production costs of Bruce's cinema classics, his earnings and the bounteous offers that came his way after the obvious success of *Fist of Fury* and *The Big Boss* are all noted and described. And then there's the old chestnut of the Little Dragon's rumoured retirement. Did he really have such an idea in mind or was it just talk? For the latest on all these questions, and lots more, turn to the Golden Harvest interview.

Number two in line, as a result of the many, many letters we've had in over the years, here at last is the low-down on Shih (Mr. Han) Kien. A veteran star of literally hundreds of

Mandarin Kung Fu movies, Shih provided exactly the sort of charismatic and evil opposition Bruce Lee needed in his mammoth Concord/Warner Brothers production, *Enter the Dragon*. All agree that the final confrontation in the mirrored room is virtually without equal in its breathtaking suspense and super-skilled action. An age difference between the two of nearly a third of a century seems barely possible, yet it's true. Read on and discover the real Shih Kien.

Lastly, this issue can hardly pass by without our saluting the first year in action of our fabulous Bruce Lee Society. The approval of the fans, so far, has been virtually unanimous and to celebrate this moment, there are a few momentous plans afoot - not the least of which is a slight change of name! I'm not going to steal Pam's thunder, so flip through to the club page for a surprise or two.

That's it from me - with you again next issue...

Felix Yen
Editor-in-Chief

THE GOLDEN HARVEST INTERVIEW

Throughout its long history of thirty-three power-packed editions, *Kung-Fu Monthly* has regularly been bringing its readers all the news, views, pictures and vital information available on the world's finest Kung Fu exponent, Bruce Lee. Naturally, much of the word we receive on the Master comes to us very much second hand - culled from other reports and writings, and so on. It's a pleasure therefore, to announce the discovery of a rare interview made with the heads of Golden Harvest. Few can claim to have known Bruce's public career as intimately as Raymond Chow's Hong Kong based film production company. There, was where the Little Dragon's glamorous screen life truly caught a'fire and there, too, was where it all ended - the bright light so cruelty extinguished. The scope of this question and answer debate is huge and although a little of the fact contained has since become common knowledge, much is new. For the sake of completeness, all has been left in. An interview scoop such as this cannot be relied on to appear too frequently - let us savour this important moment.

Question: To what do you attribute the success of the martial arts movies around the world and in particular that of Bruce Lee?

Golden Harvest: Mr. Chow, Golden Harvest's boss, believes the world likes to see action in a beautifully simple plot in which good is contrasted against bad. His Kung Fu movies are the answer. Bruce Lee radiates an intense personality, beautiful action and an all-conquering charisma. These made him the only Kung Fu star worshipped by the world.

Question: How would you describe Bruce?

Golden Harvest: Bruce Lee was a perfectionist. He read and practiced intensively. He had very little use for indolent relaxation. He did not go to parties. He did not gamble. He

liked his house to be big and tastefully decorated. He liked good cars, fast cars especially. He read all kinds of books, philosophy being his favourite. He trained very hard in his own gymnasium and jogged at least one hour around daybreak. His life was the same wherever he happened to be.

Question: Could you tell us how much it cost to produce *Fist of Fury* and *The Big Boss*.

Golden Harvest: *The cost of production for* The Big Boss, *before overhead publicity and all other production expenses, was a quarter of a million US dollars.* Fist of Fury *was produced at a higher cost, about 25 per cent over that of* The Big Boss.

Question: How did you become interested in Bruce?

Golden Harvest: *Mr. Chow was impressed by Bruce Lee's performance in the television serials* The Green Hornet *and* Longstreet. *He therefore approached Mr. Lee as soon as he learned Bruce was available.*

Question: Could you tell us what sort of contract Bruce had with you?

Golden Harvest: *Bruce Lee signed a contract with Golden Harvest to make two pictures. After that, Golden Harvest distributed his Concord productions.*

Question: Is it really true that Bruce was going to retire after making only about three or four more films?

Golden Harvest: No, Bruce never thought seriously about retirement. But it's almost a convention for an actor to say that he will retire after a few more good pictures.

Question: Going back for a few moments to Bruce's Concord productions, does Mr. Chow or Golden Harvest have any interest or control in Concord.

Golden Harvest: Immediately after the success of The Big Boss, Bruce Lee set up Concord Productions to plan for his future films. Mr. Chow had a hand in its creation, but he does not run it. Concord is still in operation because The Way of the Dragon and Enter the Dragon are still in distribution and Game of Death is to be completed. Our understanding is that Concord is not currently planning to make new pictures.

Question: As Enter the Dragon was a Concord co-production, could you tell us how much it cost to produce?

Golden Harvest: With all the expenses incurred in the United States, so far no final accounting has been made.

Question: Well then, could you tell us how much the film made in Hong Kong?

Golden Harvest: HK $3,307,620.40.

Question: Do you have any idea how much money Bruce made during his lifetime?

Golden Harvest: We could only guess. A few million dollars, maybe.

Question: What was Bruce Lee like in the last few weeks of his life?

Golden Harvest: Bruce Lee was very tense because of his concentration on plans to complete Game of Death and because of his loss .0of weight. He had a complete medical check-up in Los Angeles in June and was declared as good as a 21-year-old. Still he looked lean and intense.

Question: Does Mr. Chow have any personal theory of how and why Bruce died?

Golden Harvest: Mr. Chow supports the coroner's finding that Bruce Lee died of hyper-sensitivity to a certain ingredient contained in a pain-soothing pill.

Question: I believe that Bruce had been offered a large amount of money before he died by an independent producer - do you know anything about this at all?

Golden Harvest: Bruce was approached by a producer but he did not pick it up.

Question: Do you have any idea of how much he was offered?

Golden Harvest: US $1,000,000 upon signing and another US $1,000,000 in percentages guaranteed.

Question: Do you at Golden Harvest and indeed Mr. Chow, have a favourite film in which Bruce starred?

Golden Harvest: No producer ever compares his own pictures. Please excuse us for not answering your question.

Question: Are Kung Fu movies still popular and are you still going to produce more of them in the future?

Golden Harvest: Golden Harvest will continue to produce and distribute good, saleable films in the future. Kung Fu movies shall continue to be part of Golden Harvest's products as they were in the past, but variety will be emphasised. We shall keep a sensitive finger on the movie-goer's pulse.

Question: What area does the film studio cover, and how many staff do you have at Golden Harvest?

Golden Harvest: Our studios cover about 100,000 square feet with a staff of over 120.

Question: What kind of salaries do your actors, writers and directors get? Could you tell us approximately?

Golden Harvest: *Our top director gets over US $10,000 a month in salary, plus bonus. A scriptwriter is paid between US $1,800 and US $7,000 per scenario.*

Question: And the actors?

Golden Harvest: *In the motion picture business, it's difficult to determine the average pay.*

Question: Is it true that you do all your own film processing?

Golden Harvest: *Yes, we do process and print our own films. The Cine Art Laboratory with a full line in colour film processing and printing is our associate company.*

Question: How do you distribute your films throughout the world?

Golden Harvest: *Through cinemas and contracts, Golden Harvest controls chains of cinemas in Hong Kong, Taiwan and Chinatown. Through co-operation with the mighty Cathay organisation headquartered in Singapore, our films are exhibited in the 100 Cathay cinemas in Singapore and Malaysia. The Cathay organisation and Golden Harvest also co-operate in the formation of worldwide distribution networks. For instance, Cathay Films Limited in London distributes for us throughout Europe, Africa and the Middle East. EMI handle our product in the U.K.*

Question: What was the company's biggest hit?

Golden Harvest: *So far,* Fist of Fury *(renamed* The Chinese Connection *in the United States) starring Bruce Lee has been chalking up the highest box office record.*

Question: Earlier you mentioned that Raymond Chow was impressed by Bruce's performances in the television serials *The Green Hornet* and *Longstreet*. Are you suggesting that Mr. Chow discovered Bruce Lee?

Golden Harvest: *Raymond is modest about the role he played in the Bruce Lee success story. He says he did not discover Bruce Lee. He says he merely provided the facilities for Bruce to set free his genius at the right time.*

Question: I believe that Mr. Chow shares Bruce's passion of driving fast cars?

Golden Harvest: *Yes, Mr. Chow has a passion for fast cars, golf and bridge. He drives a Porsche 911 these days to the golf course if he is not working or playing bridge.*

Question: Can you tell us a little about Mr. Chow? For instance, is he married and does he have any children?

Golden Harvest: *Mr. Chow is married to Miss Felicia Yuan. They have a daughter and a son.*

Question: I have been told that he speaks very good English. Is that true?

Golden Harvest: *He speaks excellent English, Mandarin and three Chinese dialects. Mr. Chow is a hard worker but he takes a philosophical view about his employee's failings.*

Very popular among friends, he is also gentle and considerate. He also has a keen sense of humour.

Question: I believe Mr. Chow studied abroad. Could you tell us where?

Golden Harvest: In the University of New Mexico in Alberquerque.

Question: Could you give us a brief history of Mr. Chow up to the time he founded Golden Harvest - how Golden Harvest was financed and what its capital position is now?

Golden Harvest: In 1949, as a very young reporter, he came to Hong Kong from Shanghai. Raymond, born in Hong Kong but educated most of the time in Shanghai, joined Shaw Brothers later in 1956. He helped establish Shaw's movietown and make it the largest in Southeast Asia. He also cultivated and made a host of stars. In short, Raymond was the incubator of the Mandarin film industry in Hong Kong. Mr. Chow decided to strike out on his own. In 1970, he founded his Golden Harvest production company. His reputation as the top flight movie producer made his venture a success. Since its inception, Golden Harvest has been adequately financed by its investors. Not a public company, its capital position is extremely strong as most of the profits have been ploughed back into production.

And there we conclude *KFM*'s report on the Golden Harvest Interview. The latter part - devoted mainly to Raymond Chow - we feel is quite a scoop in itself. Very little has previously been known about the thoughts, feelings and ambitions that drove the master of the Mandarin film industry right to the top of the tree. This omission has now been put to rights. The current success of the Asian movie business is a two-sided coin. It took Chow to spot the true value of the talent available to him and it took a man like Bruce Lee to seize these opportunities and exploit them to the full.

THE TWO SIDES OF SHIH KIEN

Consider the film *Enter the Dragon* and which Chinese actor do you think of? A silly question, of course, for the answer has to be Bruce Lee. Alright, think again - what name springs to mind after that of the Little Dragon? For most people, I suspect the answer would again be obvious, the arch villain, Mr. Han, played by veteran Kung Fu actor, Shih Kien. In the Mandarin film industry, Shih Kien is invariably the number one choice when it comes to casting the role of evil. Once aptly described as the Peter Cushing of the Orient, few Kung Fu actors have enjoyed such long term success and adulation as Mr. Kien. And yet, strangely, his introduction to the world of martial arts bore some resemblance at least to that of the Little Dragon. Now in his mid-sixties, Shih Kien - looking half his age - is still making superb action films in the great tradition of the Asian movie market and hopefully, will continue to do so for many years to come. Who is this man who, although long famous in the East, was grateful enough to accept the assistance of Bruce Lee to help spread his fame to the Western world? *KFM* investigates...

Comparisons between Shih Kien and Bruce Lee have been many. The rare combination of great Kung Fu ability, good acting and distinctive appearance is an elusive one and other than Lee, the Master, the number of candidates able to lay claim to these attributes could probably be counted on the fingers of one hand.

It's hard to imagine a more prolific film actor than Shih Kien. Now approaching the golden achievement of forty years in the business, his tally of roles has been reported to be approaching three figures! This is easier to understand when one considers how prolific the Eastern film business is as a whole and also how fast the movies are canned. Remember, that although by Western standards, Bruce Lee's *Enter the Dragon* was a quickie, out East, it was undoubtedly considered something of a mammoth production. The Little Dragon may have only completed four major productions at the time of his tragic death, but he'd also starred in a score or more quickie productions during his childhood and teenage years.

Though long an exponent of Kung Fu, Shih didn't in fact really get going in the film business until after the last world war. He'd filled in a few times for an acting troupe but always behind the scenes. That, however, was enough to create a thirst for the business that could only grow and grow. Outside of his *Enter the Dragon* fame, probably his greatest moments came in what were known as Wong Fei Hung films. In epic after epic in this extended series, he assumed the role of the arch villain and time after time poor Shih Kien found himself ingloriously dispatched by Wong, the hero, to some unsavoury fate.

To see Shih Kien in action, is to see a half-way vision of how the Little Dragon might have looked, many years on, had the Master survived that final bout of illness. Radiating fitness, gained from countless hours of training in his youth, Shih is a living example of results borne of healthy living. Once, like Bruce, a sickly and delicate child, he too found the reserves necessary to fight his way back, not just to health, but to supreme fitness. An uncle, Shih Tse Kee, we are told, was responsible for setting the young boy on the path to recovery and whereas Bruce entered the martial arts world in order to defend himself against the rough and tumble of street life in Hong Kong, still both saw beyond their immediate needs into a world of physical perfection.

Though in no confessed expert on the training and philosophies behind Jeet Kune Do, still Shih feels he has always agreed, though unconsciously, with its basic precepts. Defend in whatever way is handy, in whichever style suits the occasion the best. Throughout his long and happy life, Shih Kien has found the time to study many different styles, including Chinese wrestling, Eagle Claw and Shaolin (Siu Lam) and his inclination not to adhere completely to basic forms of Kung Fu came through his association with a certain master, Chui Kwai Lam.

Chui should certainly be acknowledged for having formulated a prototype form of Bruce Lee's final illuminating concept of Jeet Kune Do. He called for imagination, variation and experimentation from his students and not so much the regimentation and strict adherence to routine that in Shih Kien's early days. And from that solid background of learning and good advice, Shih forged ahead to construct a movie future for himself, the envy of most Kung Fu film actors. For Shih, as for Bruce, however, the essence of his fighting method has never been allowed to become distilled through his association with the glittering world of the cinema industry.

And for him, life's greatest thrill is the sight of people of all creeds, colour and race joining forces to promote the health, exercise and happiness of Kung Fu. In the pursuit of this pleasure, much of Shih's time is in fact spent travelling the world, meeting people and giving martial arts demonstrations. A high spot was his appearance at Kuala Lumpur's National Stadium in 1969. The audience responded with tremendous warmth to his personal display of Kung Fu and few that night left the great Shih Kien with any doubts as to his martial abilities.

Of course, to partly repeat what was said earlier, Shih's other great card was his acting ability. A man may appear in movies for a lifetime and still not have that strange magic touch so jealously guarded by the big stars. Mr. Han provided the finest foil imaginable to the Little Dragon in *Enter the Dragon*. After all, how can the forces of good triumph without there being a thoroughly nasty evil? Shih took to the role as if it were written for him alone. The marvellous final confrontation in the mirrored room which left Mr. Han fatally impaled has successfully kept enthusiastic audiences on the edges of their seats ever since the days of *Enter the Dragon*'s premiere and no wonder! The build up to the last scene is superb, with Han flexing his diabolical muscles in truly sinister style.

Only an actor and fighter of Shih Kien's stature could have carried off the role with

such total conviction and, there again, we hit on another facet of Bruce Lee's near limitless abilities - that of his being able to select from a world full of people, exactly the right candidates for the most important jobs. Well Bruce realised that, however proficient he may be and however good his ideas, still a movie to a great extent stands or falls on the suitability of everyone concerned.

The Little Dragon knew how to pick his crew and in Shih Kien he made the perfect choice for the diabolical, scheming figure of Mr Han. And yet, in real life, Han is considerably less diabolical than his character in *Enter the Dragon* would suppose! He is content to be a relaxed, family man. He neither smokes nor drinks and there's nothing he likes better than just chewing over everyday matters with friends. Much of his day is still spent in keeping in fighting trim. To compare this figure with the notorious Mr. Han is to compare chalk with cheese. Yet, strangely, history can tell of many such personifiers of the devil who were the complete antithesis in their daily life - Peter Cushing again, to name but one. Perhaps it takes a particularly good man to truly understand the character of evil.

It's said that Shih had met Bruce some years before their *Enter the Dragon* collaboration - probably during the time that the Little Dragon-to-be was painstakingly putting together his childhood films. Whether he felt at the time that he had come across something special goes unrecorded - all we do know is that Shih got to know Bruce well, only during the *Enter the Dragon* filming and that they both developed an enormous amount of respect for one another. No doubt Shih's polish and looseness of technique would have appealed to the Little Dragon and there's little doubt either that Bruce's freshness and vital new approach to the worlds of Kung Fu and the cinema would have caught the eye of *Enter the Dragon*'s Mr. Han!

It must be obvious to everyone that for the Little Dragon's ultimate foe to have been anything less than ultra proficient would certainly have destroyed the credibility of *Enter the Dragon* as surely as Shih's total suitability to the role in fact greatly enhanced the production. Time, and the critic's near unanimous approval justified ultimately all of Bruce's faith in a man nearly a third of a century older than himself!

Though, tragically, the Little Dragon will make no more films, let us hope that Shih Kien will continue, for many years to come, to produce sparkling characterisations such as that of Mr. Han - a more than worthy opponent for Bruce Lee, the all-conquering hero of *Enter the Dragon*.

THE BRUCE LEE SECRET SOCIETY

One year on and what a great event for the Society that's sweeping the world! And in line with our new-found maturity (as you can see above) I've decided now to call the club simply, The Bruce Lee Society.

Over the last year, the achievements of the Bruce Lee Society have been considerable. Who'd have believed to start with, that such a young club would be so soon, welcoming its 1,000th member! In addition, a sister Society has already been formed in the United States and many more are planned for the future. It really does look as though our dream of linking the countries of the world is starting to come true.

Another feather in our cap is the getting together of the club's first souvenir magazine. This, to me, has been very important, for it shows beyond any doubt, that the Society is acting as a society in the truest sense of the word. By that I mean it consists of members who LIKE and WANT to participate. The souvenir magazine is NOT mine; it belongs to everyone who took part in its making. I congratulate all of you.

For my part, I don't think there's a member who could claim that a letter to me hasn't been answered, where, of course, a stamped and addressed envelope has been enclosed! And while on that subject, I feel I must say, that although I love hearing from you, it would be really helpful if you restricted yourselves to asking just the main questions you want answered. I only have a certain amount of spare time in which to run the Society and everyone, after all, deserves a fair crack of the whip.

Another important thing I've been meaning to mention is if you have any queries on mail order goods, could you please address your letters direct to the *KFM* mail order department. I don't deal with that side of things and writing to me only delays solving your problem. For all you members about to send in your £3.25's to join up for another year in the Bruce Lee Society, I've got great news for you. After much hard thinking at this end, here's what the 2nd year members will receive: 1. More new and really great action photos of Bruce Lee; 2. A new membership card and scroll, both coloured red to signify your second year membership; 3. One free-standing, mounted action picture of Bruce Lee; 4. A superb, solid metal brooch/badge showing the Master's Yin/Yang sign and bearing the words, "Bruce Lee Society - 2nd Year." The badge will be unique to 2nd year members only and, subject to confirmation, the colours will be gold on black.

Back again next month - **Pam Hadden - President of the Bruce Lee Society**

SECRET SOCIETY SWOP SHOP

Michael Butler (1963), Uckington, Nr Shrewsbury has to swap, *KFM* No. 11, 12, 13, 14, 22. Wants *KFM* No. 16, 20, 21 and 25. Also requires urgently, *KFM* No. 1, 2 & 3 - Prices please.
Orijsia Zwiryk (1709), Hull has *Tao of Jeet Kune Do* by Bruce Lee in great condition for £4.00.
Kathryn Wray (2033) Codnor, Derbyshire wants *Kung Fu Cinema of Vengeance* - State price please.
Rojenetra Chandarana (1927), Hemel Hempstead has two *Top of the Pops* LPs. Wants *Fist of Fury* LP (original) or two books - *The Legend of Bruce Lee* by Alex Ben Block and *The Man Only I Knew* by Linda Lee.

KICKBACK: THE LETTERS

Hi, Jenny here again with another bumper bundle of readers' mail pulled from this month's sack! And right off, a reminder. If you are one of the two hundred plus people who wrote in to me and haven't received a reply - the most likely reason is you didn't enclose a stamped and addressed envelope. Say no more! Please, please, no more *Game of Death* petitions. The huge pile of signatures has gone off now and anything else that arrives will be too late. Thanks again for a tremendous response. And talking about *Game of Death*, thanks, too, to everyone who sent in to me details of Robert Clouse's recent newspaper interview. It's marvellous; the signs actually are that something's happening at last. And good news too that apparently, Clouse considers the remaining Bruce Lee fighting footage to be among the best the Little Dragon has ever made. On that up-note, the letters!

GAME OF DEATH PETITION

Dear Jenny,
In *KFM* No.30 you started the *Game of Death* petition. Do you think if we did a similar thing to the British Board of Censorship, we could get them to release Bruce Lee's films again with less cuts? After all, there are a damned sight more useless, storyless films going around with a lot more violence and blood in them. The news these days is more violent than Bruce's films and that is for everybody to see, three to four times a day on TV.
Terry Barrett, Bradmore, West Midlands

Dear Terry,
I like the way you put it! I agree, it would certainly be one way of making the film censors stand up and take notice. In fact, a stiff letter or two might be a help. The thing is though, I'm not actually sure what action the censors are strictly allowed to take when it comes to reversing previous decisions. I suspect a certain amount of time has to elapse first. I'm going to check all this out - would anyone who can help like to write in?

ANOTHER HAPPY READER

Dear Jenny,
I would like to take this opportunity to say a big thank you to all those concerned with the magazine. All the issues that I have ordered through the post have reached me in perfect condition and safety, as well as being at least a week in advance of all the shops in Leeds. Please keep up the tremendous work.
Kenneth Tagg, Leeds, Yorkshire

Dear Kenneth,
What can I say? As nice a testimonial as I've received in a long time and, believe me, it's very pleasant to hear such kind and appreciative words.

BRUCE'S SWEAT GLANDS

Dear Jenny,
The Bruce Lee sweat gland information was published in an edition of one of the old Bruce Lee Fan Club magazine. It read as follows: "When Bruce Lee came to making *Fist of Fury*, he found he was sweating too much and had an operation to remove the glands. The aftermath of this was that he became short tempered."
D. Thomas, No Address Supplied

Dear D. Thomas,
Thanks to you and also to Mark Taylor of North Humberside, Colin Smith of Newcastle and Gail Arnold of Cardiff for taking the trouble to write in about the sweat gland thing. I agree, the information appears all over the place and specifically in Rhona McVay's original fan club papers and Dennis and Ateyo's Bruce Lee: King of Kung Fu book. The problem is I simply cannot find any confirmation from Hong Kong or America and I honestly do find it hard to believe! My investigations are continuing however.

BRUCE LEE ON TV

Dear Jenny,
First let me say what a wonderful job *KFM* is doing. You are the only consistent, reliable source on Bruce Lee. Now to my question. Robert Clouse, the director of *Enter the Dragon*, was quoted as saying that he would advise *Enter the Dragon* not to be shown on TV. But do you think *The Big Boss*, *Fist of Fury* or *The Way of the Dragon* might be shown?
Mark Freeth, Birmingham

Dear Mark,
As usual, many thanks for the much appreciated comments. I can't say I'm completely sure why Clouse should recommend Enter the Dragon *not to appear on TV. To my mind, the real reason why none of Bruce's films have come on television simply boils down to this. While a movie can still go around the picture circuits making money, there is not much reason for selling it to the TV companies. It's felt that once a film has been on TV, it loses much of its drawing power in cinemas. In this case, I'm not too sure I go along with the theory.*

A POSTAL SCAM?

Dear Jenny,
A month or two back you advertised for a Mr. Lai Ah Choy. He said if you send 40p, he would send hundreds of names and addresses back so I wrote up to him, enclosing a postal order. I received a letter back saying my postal order had got mutilated in the post and asking me to send another - 50p this time instead of 40p. If you didn't know what to make of it then, do you know now? I wonder if any other *KFM* reader's postal orders have been mutilated in the post or have any other readers received anything which they found of value? By the way, I'm still waiting for my mutilated postal order to be returned from Lai Ah Choy.
C. Reece Waterloo, Liverpool

Dear C. Reece,

That's just what I was hoping not to hear. I sincerely hope this is just an isolated incident and not something more dubious. In the meantime, I suggest that nobody else uses Mr Lai Ah Choy's service until I confirm this is all cleared up. To check whether the mutilated postal order story is correct, take the counterfoil to the post office where you bought it and ask them to check whether it's been cashed or not. Explain exactly what has happened. Will anyone who has received satisfaction - or otherwise - from Mr Lai Ah Choy, please write and tell me.

QUICKIES CORNER

Duncan Andrews, Rockbeare, Exeter - Thanks for a great letter. *KFM* No.12 available - 35p.

Tony Moore, Oldham, Lancs - Thanks for reporting the Clouse interview to me.

John Harrison, Frecheville - Try imported magazines mail order sections for 8mm Lee films.

Lawrence Senior, Blackpool, Lancs - Angela Mao posters? Can anyone help?

Peter Ward, Leicester - A petition for the BBC to revive the Bruce Lee Documentary? Might be a good idea.

Paul Smith, Telford - Binders news coming soon - promise!

Subash Sadas, Poplar, London - If you join the Society, Pam will have a list of Bruce Lee supply shops for you.

William Garland, Belfast, Northern Ireland - Sorry, the swap/buy facility is only available to Society members - have you joined yet?

Ray ???, Plumstead, London - We shall be running a *Game of Death* poster sometime soon.

Carl Humpage, Newcastle, Staffs - Bruce studied many forms of Kung Fu.

Kevin McCardie, Cambridge - Bruce's pulse rate? That's a new one - can anyone help?

Chris ??? - I suggest you start shouting for *The Green Hornet* on TV after *Game of Death*.

David Giles, Erdington, Birmingham - There has been a delay in *The Secret Art of Bruce Lee* books - now it's OK.

Richard McColl, East Kilbridge, Scotland - There's no record of Bruce having killed anyone! Send 40p for *KFM* No.30.

Gregory Bland, Capetown, South Africa - Sorry, I've never heard of any Raymond Lee.

Andrew Robinson, Leeds, Yorks - Bolo scene is censored - Sorry, no *KFM* No.2 left.

Kim McCallum, Chichester, Sussex - Approach your local cinema manager direct for Bruce's films - It CAN work!

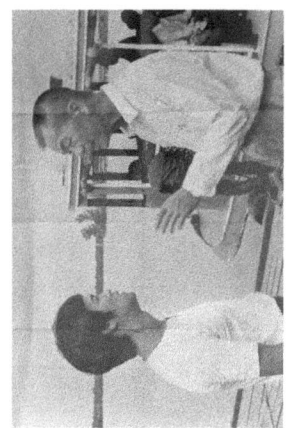

1977

EDITORIAL

    Hi there Kung Fu fans. It's time to turn on and tune in to another milestone in the history of *Kung-Fu Monthly*. A short while ago, I introduced you to a major new book breakthrough on the Little Dragon horizon. Of course, that was *The Secret Art of Bruce Lee*. Now it's time for the sequel! Packed once against with many previously unseen photographs, we present, *Bruce Lee in Action*. As the title suggests, the direction in which this masterpiece looks is very much that of Bruce in full, fighting fury. Whether filming, or battling for real, there's never been anyone able to touch the excitement of the Master.
    As before, there are more superb full colour pictures of the Little Dragon, plus some sparkling explanatory captions by *KFM*'s own Paul Simmons, to go with the full-action photo sequences. Considering the reception accorded to *The Secret Art of Bruce Lee*, I can imagine that the demand for *Bruce Lee in Action* will be enormous. This issue, our number one feature is devoted to this new, smash publication. Hopefully, next month, the book

itself will become available exclusively in the UK through our mail order department!

This issue, *KFM* No.35, I'm proud to present for the second feature, an investigation into the wisdom of the ancient Chinese culture and in particular, that of Lao Tzu. The name may not, I perhaps, be too familiar but his truths and ideas most certainly will be. Much of Bruce's great concept of Jeet Kune Do is based upon the centuries-old philosophies of this one great man. We put under the *KFM* microscope, many of Lao's wise words and look, too, at why the Little Dragon interpreted them as he did. Lao Tzu has guided an entire race of people for over 2,500 years. Read on and find out how and why.

Felix Yen
Editor-in-Chief

BRUCE LEE IN ACTION

Only a short while ago, the world welcomed the arrival of a Bruce Lee book with a difference. Much more than just another brief look at the Master, *The Secret Art of Bruce Lee* took us right into the fabulous world of Jeet Kune Do, to explain the whys and wherefores of a system that was not a system - a style without a style! We were helped during the journey by some of the finest sets of action photos, of Bruce Lee ever discovered. Taken many years before the Little Dragon's death by Chester Maydole, they symbolised and encapsulated Jeet Kune Do in its very infancy. Now, once again, history has been repeated in a sequel to that great book, entitled, *Bruce Lee in Action*. Many more pictures from that fine collection appear yet again, plus the usual flowing caption explanations, penned for us by our own Paul Simmons. And as for the text, well as the title suggests, the finger points firmly in the direction of that part of the Little Dragon legend we know and love the best - his fighting art. Step with us now as we take you through the chapters.

The gentle-faced teenager wheeled quickly round, crouched before the two youths, opened his mouth, and at ear-splitting volume began to screech every obscenity that came into his mind. Set back by the unexpected sight of this swearing, screaming quarry, it took the larger of the two a moment to compose himself and lumber unsurely towards him. The second troublemaker, disconcerted, remained some yards away. He turned out to be the wiser. As the larger youth approached his raucous victim, the boy stopped shouting, fell to the ground and whack, a shiny patent leather shoe crashed into his attacker's shin-bone, sending him reeling headlong onto the pavement, where he lay, clutching his leg and moaning.

His friend's disconcertment grew, but any ideas he might have entertained about lending a hand were quickly dispelled as the teenager leapt to his feet, recommenced screeching, and hurled himself in the direction of the second youth's waist. Just in time, the thug turned and ran. The teenager stopped, grinned happily, brushed himself down, and continued his walk home with a jaunty step.

The young Bruce Lee wasn't looking for the fight but on the other hand, he wasn't looking to have himself beaten up either! At this early stage he wasn't the invincible fighting machine he was later to become and it was very much a case of some you win and some you lose. As a training ground for the development of his later skills, however, the experience he gained was beyond value.

Bruce Lee in Action examines the period carefully. His association with the venerable old teacher, Yip Man, and his frequent brushes with members of opposition Kung Fu schools (including, of course, the infamous Wong Man Jack confrontation) all make instructive and exciting reading. In fact, Yip Man it is, who takes the tail-end of the chapter with new, and startling revelations as to their eventual relationship. Nothing's being given away here, though so you'll have to read about that for yourselves!

The second chapter is superbly entitled, 'So I Said The Hell With It!' and it takes us right through the whole gamut of his screen fighting career. His attitude to it all is perhaps best summed up by an interview he gave to the *Hong Kong Standard*. He said, "I'm dissatisfied with the expression of the cinematic art here in Hong Kong. It's time somebody did something about the films here. There are simply not enough soulful characters here who are committed, dedicated, and are at the same time professionals.

"I didn't create this monster - all this gore in the Mandarin films. It was there before I came. At least I don't like violence. I don't call the fighting in my films violence. I call it action. An action film borders somewhere between reality and fantasy. If it were completely realistic, you would call me a bloody, violent man. I would simply destroy my opponent by tearing him apart or ripping his guts out. I wouldn't do it so artistically. I have this intensity in me, the audience believes in what I do. But I act in such a way as to border my action somewhere between reality and fantasy.

"I can't express myself fully on film here, or the audiences wouldn't understand what I was talking about half the time. That's why I can't stay in Southeast Asia all the time. I am improving and making new discoveries every day. If you don't, you are already crystallised and that's it."

Nothing is omitted in this powerful section of *Bruce Lee in Action*. Censorship, the transferring of his great skill onto the silver screen, and his unique adaptation of the age-old cinema tricks of the trade all get a thorough going-over. His determination to be master of all he got involved in, "I was burned once, and didn't like it," points more surely than anything to the Little Dragon's no-nonsense attitude to stardom and film making.

We hear of new opinions being expressed on the Master by more of the great names he worked with, and they tell us how their careers were helped along by the skills of the Little Dragon. Although Chinese films have always been over-the-top in terms of fighting violence when compared to the West's more conservative feelings on the subject, Bruce somehow managed to link the two. As the book relates, often the only people he managed to offend were, predictable, the film censors.

Well, perhaps not only the censors, for in Chapter Three, we read more details of the sloppy and sanctimonious attitude taken towards his genius by various misguided members of the world press.

"What is obvious to simple-minded souls such as me about the popularity of such films is their appeal to audiences via the belief that you can have your cake and eat it. Indignation is all right so long as it is righteous. Killing is fine if the slaughter is committed in the name of honour. Death can be excused if the people upon whom it is perpetrated are seen to be as plastic as any puppet in TV's *Thunderbirds*. Everything is always skin deep. Black or white. And the blurring of moral distinctions that, paradoxically, it implies is a smudging of values which I find most unpleasant; a witness to the cynical way in which the producers of these movies believe that audiences can be manipulated."

Regular readers of *Kung-Fu Monthly* will recall the two features we ran on this very subject and the necessary examination this side of the coin is given, benefits us by giving a balanced view of world opinion around the time of his early productions. Another reporter remarks, "The hero, like a diminutive Samson with the jawbone of an ass, mows his way through countless identical opponents, using a mixture of Judo, Karate chops, Jujitsu and strange salutatory feats which involve somersaulting in mid-air and kicking the victim in the groin with the sole of the foot, all to the accompaniment of sudden sharp cries like a violated parrot, which is apparently to do with correct breathing techniques. Leaving grunting, squirming and expiring novitiates of

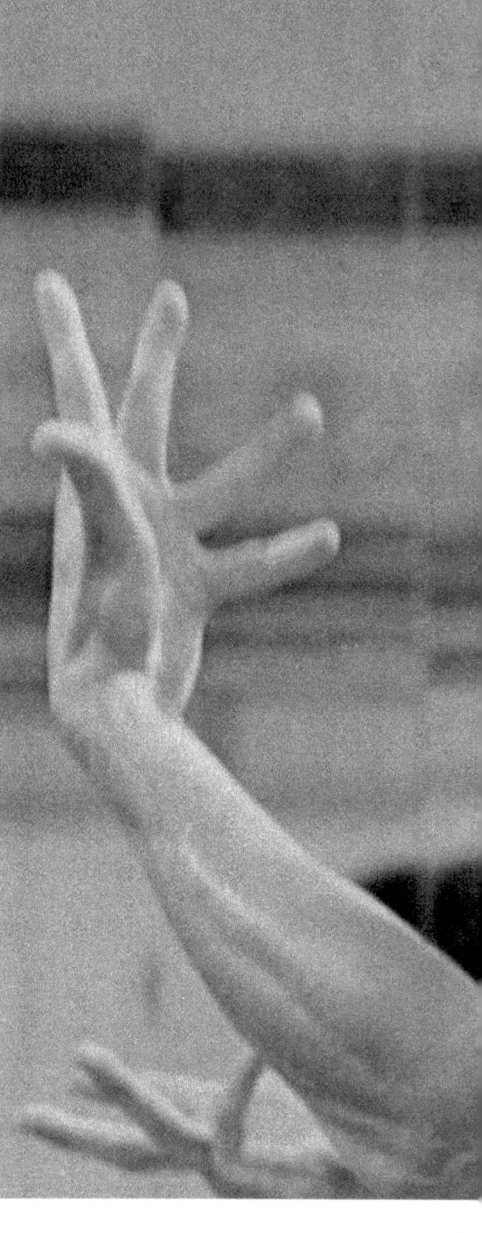

the martial arts in his wake, the hero eventually comes eyebrow to eyebrow with the Master, upon whom he has several good reasons for revenge. There begins a protean struggle with hands, legs and bamboo sticks, until the Master, battered and broken, blood pouring from his nose and mouth, sinks to his knees, and the hero administers the coup de grace."

Reluctant as he is to admit it, that writer has certainly got the message!

And so to the last chapter, 'The Lessons Of Jeet Kune Do' and here, *Bruce Lee in Action* pulls not a punch. What's in it for the serious practitioner? What are the goals? "Look on any tool as an art," Bruce Lee is quoted as saying and surely a book could be written on that sentence alone! The steps he took to prevent the usual lame rigidity sneaking into his Jeet Kune Do legacy are counted out and the Little Dragon's feelings on the Taoist origins of it all are fully discussed.

"Bruce Lee lives! In the months following his terrible, untimely death in Hong Kong, this was the cry that echoed round the world. From the Hollywood stars who had befriended and learnt from the Master, to the martial artists from China to California who had accepted him in his own time as the greatest of their kind; from his humblest fan in downtown Kowloon to the biggest studio executive at Warner Brothers - people who had seen or known Bruce Lee were aware that his legacy would never die."

And what better quotation on which to end our review of *Bruce Lee in Action*. To repeat what we said in the beginning, what has been looked at here is the text alone! Running alongside are, of course, the marvellous action sequences displaying the Little Dragon at his breathtaking best. Once more, there's a wealth of material to keep the serious Jeet Kune Do student busy for a long time to come - and for everybody's enjoyment, there are no fewer than sixteen pages of full colour pictures of the Master. Which ever way you look at it, *Bruce Lee in Action* is far more than just a sequel to *The Secret Art of Bruce Lee*. It's a power-house of information in its own right!

THE ROOTS OF JEET KUNE DO

Often it has been said that Bruce Lee was the proud enormous library of books. Shelf upon shelf of rare volumes lined a room of his house - sufficient indeed to keep the Master browsing busily for many a long morning or afternoon. The range of subjects was vast, as many have discovered after examining the famous autographed photo of Bruce sitting by his books that was given out to first year members of the Bruce Lee Society. His interests ranged from fighting techniques of the world to the history of Asia in particular and the world in general, plus philosophy. China has a rich heritage of poets and philosophers and the starting point for Bruce's ultimate concept of Jeet Kune Do lies buried deep within these priceless pages. In this feature, we examine in particular the great truths of Lao Tzu. His words - the very essence of Taoism - were responsible probably more than any other for fashioning the Little Dragon's path to glory. It is right that we should look closely at the 2,500 year old thoughts and ideas of this wise and enlightened man.

Lao remarked that: "Having and not having are born together. The hard cannot exist without the easy. The long and the short are close companions. High and low rely upon each other."

There can be no black without white and there can be no right without wrong. This important truth is one often not discovered by the average man. Bruce Lee, though he strove for perfection, had first to experience the shortcomings of his then untapped abilities.

Early on in his life, he had to contend first with sickness and then, physical inferiority. Both these two he conquered, using nothing other than that which is available to all of us.

His mind told him that physical fitness can be no god-given gift. Quite the reverse, such a worthwhile body condition had, by its very nature, to be the result of rigorous training and a sensible lifestyle. Hence we see the intrinsic truth in Lao's wise observation that: "The hard cannot exist without the easy." Bruce Lee the world's number one martial artist, could not have existed without first there having been Bruce Lee the beginner.

Lao Tzu also said: "Give way - to overcome, bend - to be straight. Empty - and be overflowing, grow old yet be as new. Possess little - and you will gain. Possess much, and you will be troubled."

Here, in this exciting translation, it's possible to see an early inkling of the Little Dragon's way of thinking - an approach which could not have failed to have made itself felt in his supreme fighting technique. Without saying so in as many words, Bruce would undoubtedly have echoed the sentiments behind these fine lines. "Give way - to overcome," could almost be a subtitle to Jeet Kune Do. Understand your opponent, and more important still, understand yourself.

The next time you're having a discussion with somebody - and find yourself in disagreement with them, try this old trick. Just as things are starting to get heated, say something like, "You know, I think you are probably quite right. I'm wrong and I apologise." An interesting thing may well happen here. Your companion will quite likely reply, "Well now, hold on, there could well be some truth in what you are saying, too," In fact there's no surer way of stopping dead in his tracks the person with whom you're arguing, than by suddenly apparently coming around to his way of thinking. It's a sort of verbal judo and many an argument has been won in this fashion.

But, you will appreciate, this is simply a trick. The real truth of the matter is that the worthy opponent will be studying very carefully indeed, all that his opponent has to offer

anyway! Part of the Jeet Kune Do concept relies upon this simple fact. How properly can one defend without having first studied carefully, the other fighter's tactics of attack?

"Possess much - and you will be troubled." How true these words. The man of material wealth has plenty to worry about. A wrong turn of the card of fate and without warning and all may be lost.

"In life, stay close to nature. In thought, consider every detail. To others, be kind and thoughtful. Speak what you feel. Be just to those beneath you. When working, be con-

scientious. In action, use good timing."

Lao certainly hit the Jeet Kune Do nail on the head with the final line! In its original form, the great philosopher was almost certainly referring to the general actions of life. The making of decisions, arrangements to be made during the working day. And yet, these same sentiments hold true in the context of a battle, just the same as in other situations. Bruce, in his *Tao of Jeet Kune Do*, was at great pains to point out that all the footwork, strength, weight, height and speed advantage in the world can likely come to nothing without the correct timing.

"To others, be kind and thoughtful," is again, a lesson the Little Dragon had hardly any need to learn! "It is better to give than to receive," could well have been the martial master's watchword as many a surprised acquaintance will still testify. He expected no more of anyone than they would have expected of him and such acts of overflowing generosity as the giving away of expensive suits and his frequent insistence on allotting bit parts in his films to the people he knew bear testimony to a well-developed character. "Speak what you feel," is the point of overwhelming importance. The man who is afraid to stand his ground must surely have his feet upon shifting sands. No one, least of all themselves, will take much heed of a word said - and hardly surprisingly! Often there is an urge to say something just to fill a moment's silence. Ignore it, for the result will be of little consequence. Worse still, the deliberate lie. It is the last resort of a weakened man. The ignominy when the untruth is discovered, is generally a bitter experience. Far better, like Bruce Lee when decrying the limited use of traditional forms of Kung Fu, to stick with one's beliefs - however unpopular they may be.

Lao Tzu said, "That which grows smaller must first be larger. Whatever breaks down has once to be strong. That which is cast aside must first have been gathered. Without giving, there can he no receiving."

Nothing should be cast aside without a good deal of thought, for as Lao points out, it must once have been strong. Why was it strong? Nothing is strong without reason and that is why Bruce Lee was so loathe to neglect any part of the fighting arts, be it Kung Fu, boxing, or whatever. Remember, Jeet Kune Do isn't knowing which particular stance to make use of in one particular situation. Rather it's one's total reaction to a given set of circumstances. Each individual person must discover what line of action is best for them.

Therefore, the Little Dragon was at great pains to ensure that every single scrap of knowledge he'd ever learned, remained constantly available to be used wherever needed. One particular style, in itself, may have been useless to him. As one of many, however, it may have been of enormous benefit. Bruce Lee's greatest triumph - and perhaps one for which we all ought to strive, was to marry his trade and his style of living to the ultimate Asian concept of life. None before had ever done it so successfully.

Lao also noted that, "A well-made door requires no lock." By this he means that the real stepping stones in life need not be concealed from others for they can only truly be found by one who is ready to make that discovery. This is exactly why Bruce Lee was so exasperated at his compatriots attempting to conceal the mysteries of the East.

He knew that, such mysteries as there were, could only be stumbled upon by those who were ready for them. What use is a computer in the hands of a gorilla!

Throughout this feature, the aim has been to illustrate how closely Bruce's concept of Jeet Kune Do followed the time-honoured principles of Taoism. That he followed this path is hardly surprising. Many believe the Eastern World to be far more evolved spiritually than the West, and if such is the case, it could only have been right for the Little Dragon to have taken hold of the great truths.

Finally, there is just one more quotation which, I'm sure, Bruce would have wanted to be included: "Gain results but don't bathe yourself in glory. Gain results but don't show-off. Gain results but remain humble. Gain results because it is the way of things. Gain results but only through peaceful ways."

If ever there were an epitaph for the Little Dragon, then this has to be it! It summarises just about everything he stood and worked for, and moreover, it points the way for others to achieve the same sort of goal. Any man or woman who bases his or her life on these precepts will have all, although they will expect little. Bruce Lee understood the power of these words, and there is little doubt that he read them as avidly as you or I. The one thing that stands him out from most others is that he acted upon them which is perhaps, the most difficult task of all.

THE BRUCE LEE SECRET SOCIETY

A great big hello from me, Pam, to all you members of the *KFM* Bruce Lee Society.

First off, to celebrate the start of the second year of the club, I'm going to announce a similar offer to the one we ran last year around this time. Up to this Christmas, anybody joining the Bruce Lee Society for the first time can do so at the reduced rate of £3.00!! Remember, this bargain reduction can only last until December 31st so get your membership applications in quickly. Naturally, I can't reserve the special offers to new members alone so for renewing members only, on January 1st I shall be pulling one of your names from the hat. The lucky person will receive a set of *KFM*'s (issues 5 to 35).

As December draws nearer, what I'm thinking about is not so much Christmas but the confirmation of the release date for *Game of Death*. At the time of going to press, the film company is still not letting on about anything, perhaps because they're organising a big advertising campaign. Anyway, I myself (plus the entire staff of *KFM*), will continue to keep hammering away at them to try and find out when the great day is going to be. Keep watching these pages! By the way, nothing back yet from Raymond Chow regarding the *KFM* petition, but Jenny's pretty confident we'll be hearing something soon!

As you'll see when you read the fifth News Sheet, it looks like there's a growing number of Rip-off mail order merchants around, many of whom (I'm sorry to say) seem to be in the States. Obviously it's much easier to deal with people who cheat you out of your money in this country than it is when the villain is somewhere abroad! There is no real hard and fast solution, other than to say just try to be cautious. That means sending for a brochure or price list BEFORE parting with the cash. Not many crooks will be bothered to go to the trouble of printing up lists (although I can think of one or two who HAVE!) so, generally, all you'll have lost is the price of a stamp. Normally speaking, try and base your decision on whether or not to part with money on the QUALITY of service apparently being offered. Tried and tested sources are, of course, the best.

Now this month, a great big reminder that for many of you, IT'S TIME TO RENEW YOUR SUBSCRIPTION. I've had a sneak preview of the great '2nd Year' brooch we've had designed to celebrate a full years membership to all renewing members and it's absolutely amazing. It's totally in keeping with the 'maturing image' of the Bruce Lee Society. If you've got any doubt at all about what's in it for YOU to join up with the world's most exclusive Society, then turn to the advertisement you'll find elsewhere in this *KFM*. The strength of the Bruce Lee Society rests with YOU the members. We count upon your dedication.

Finally, how about that News Sheet number 5?! I think I can honestly say we've never packed so much in before. A really GREAT new competition, lots more swaps, news to keep you drooling for hours, and what's more (at long last) a picture of yours truly! Yup, the camera finally caught up with me.

Back with you again next month. **Pam**

NOTICE

Would readers please remember that, at present, *KFM* is NOT running a Swop Shop. That particular service is run by the Bruce Lee Society for members only. That means, if you've got something to buy, sell or swap, then join the club! Do it quickly and you can take advantage of their special reduced subscription offer.

Over the years, many readers have complained that they have difficulty sometimes in obtaining current copies of *KFM*. There are two ways around the problem. One is to take out a subscription at £4.50 for 12 issues. The other is this: If you'd like to supply your friends and make a little money for your trouble, we will supply the magazine at the following prices: 10 copies at 28p each, 25 copies at 26p each and 50 copies (maximum) at 24p each. The cost includes all handling charges. We must emphasise that this service is intended only for areas where *KFM* is difficult to locate. Also, cash must accompany all orders and no returns please! Send orders to *KFM* Bulk Buy Offer, 14 Rathbone Place, London W1P 1DE.

KICKBACK: THE LETTERS

Hi, Jenny Lee here with another fine stack of letters sent to me by you, the readers. And right away, may I repeat what I said last month: Please, no more petitions! The package containing all your hard work went off some time ago and as much as I appreciate the enthusiasm, new arrivals are a bit too late! Many of you have written in singling out *KFM* No.33 as one of the finest issues ever and how I do agree. The features and pictures really are exceptional. I must say, I don't know how our editors do it, but it seems to me *KFM* just continues to get better. Kicking off this month is part of the letter I sent to Raymond Chow, along with the *Game of Death* petition. Fingers crossed and next month we'll be able to print his reply. It really does begin to look as though Bruce's masterpiece will soon be here at the cinemas - but after the last few hiccups, I'll believe it when I see it! Time now to open up the letters...

The final part of the *KFM* letter to Raymond Chow...

Dear Mr Chow,
The number of replies to the petition surprised all of us. I'm sure it will give you an idea of the kind of enthusiastic following Bruce Lee still retains in this country. Please accept the response and the feelings of our readers to the continued cancellation of Game of Death. *We hope for better news soon.*
Kung-Fu Monthly Magazine, London

THE ALL-NIGHT KUNG FU SHOW

Dear Jenny,
I have read Damien Sullivan's letter regarding the All Night Kung Fu Show in Birmingham. I just had to write and explain what really happened, otherwise people will think that I am a con man and give Sunny (Martial Arts) Film Society a bad name. It was because of the bad behaviour of Kung Fu fans that police assistance was required. We asked all fans to queue up and wait quietly outside the cinema, but no one co-operated. Instead, they used great force to get in. Hundreds got in through the emergency exit without paying. The main door was at the point of collapsing because everyone was pushing so hard. Eventually it got so bad, the police had to guard the door and put a ban on entry for the sake of public safety. The cinema was not even full, but of those unlucky ones who did not get in and who were told by the police to clear off, some were ticket holders. All their money has been refunded. Advanced tickets had not been oversold.
Raymond Wong, (Chairman), Bristol

Dear Raymond (and Damien),
As both of you know, this carries on the story begun in KFM No.31. Raymond's side of it sounds quite reasonable to me. The only question I have to ask is: Has everybody's money been refunded? I sincerely hope this is the case, as an enterprise like the Sunny Film Society is, to my mind, very much needed.

3D BRUCE LEE PICTURES

Dear Jenny,
I just received the latest copy of *KFM* No.33 and at first glance, I though I was seeing things - but no! *KFM* is getting better each month! I ask myself - how do you do it? The pictures in this issue are all knockouts! Keep it up! Oh yes! Has anybody down there at *KFM* ever thought about doing Bruce Lee 3D pictures or postcards?
Mike Devereux (1061), Orford, Cheshire

Dear Mike,
Now that's the kind of enthusiasm I like to see in a letter! Actually, talking about what goes into the magazine, you've probably noticed that we've started introducing some more serious features, like the second one in this issue. Personally I find it great getting my teeth into something like this, but perhaps you could let me know how you feel. Regarding 3D pictures of the Little Dragon, funnily enough I did see one several years ago. I think it came from Germany. I've passed the idea onto the mail order department to see what they can dig up.

HONG KONG RECORDINGS

Dear Jenny,
Regarding the petition to Golden Harvest, I must agree the footage already shot could and should be used as a climax to a film about Bruce and his life, his friends, pupils and even Linda Lee could contribute narrative/interviews. Also there must be recordings in Hong Kong of his many TV spots. By the way, a Bruce Lee picture album is an absolute must, as are the other two ideas of a Best of *KFM* and a *KFM* Annual.
Mr. J.G. Worthing, Shrewsbury, Salop

Dear Mr. Worthing,
I must say I agree with your first point. Even though Game of Death *should soon be emerging, there must be many feet of unused material that should be slotted into such a production. As far as KFM specials go, after the launch of* Bruce Lee in Action, *I suspect that next on the stocks, will be a comprehensive and up-to-date book on* Game of Death.

QUICKIES CORNER

Joseph Hamington, Swanscombe, Kent - Bruce didn't become a movie actor for the money! Also he did at times use weights.

Stephen Hill, Birkenhead, Merseyside - *KFM* No. 6, 7 & 8 available from the mail order dept - £1.00.

R. Bell, Cramlington New Town, Northumberland - Thanks for a great letter - I only wish his death were just a stunt for *Game of Death*.

C. Smythe, Accrington, Lancs - *Game of Death* censored? - it gives me the shudders just to think about it!

Donnacha Quinn, Singland, Limerick - Thanks for the feature suggestions - some are impossible, some we'll work on.

P. Ashford, Mile End, London - A certain Birmingham shop selling *KFM* No.1 at £5.00? I think I'd complain.

Mr. A. Watts, Exmouth, Devon - Where to buy a kimono like Bruce had in *The Way of the Dragon* - can anyone help?

Anthony Wilson, Armagh, Northern Ireland - Mr. Yen turned down the part-poster idea, I'm afraid.

Leslie Fox, Mirehouse, Whitehaven - Bruce Lee wallpaper - I don't know about that one - I'll check it out.

Johnny Tandon, Omagh, Co. Tyrone, Northern Ireland - Thanks for telling us that the back issue of *Film Review* magazine featuring Bruce Lee is available for 26p from Old Court House, Old Court Place, Kensington High St, London W.8.

J. Thomas, Aberkerfig, Glamorgan - Thanks for the cutting on Clouse - I hope he's right and *Game of Death* is finished this time.

Godfrey Wynne, Northfield, Birmingham - Sorry but swaps are available only through the Society.

Muhammad Husain, Bretton, Peterborough - A funeral poster? A little depressing although it might please some.

Ronnie Walker, Glasgow, Scotland - *KFM* devastating - I can but agree.

M.S. Lowe &. C. Harris - Bruce did, at times, use rubber nunchakus when he couldn't totally rely on his opponent keeping out of the way.

Ronald Ramsay, West Calder, West Lothian - If you've lots of Bruce Lee stuff to sell, contact Pam and join the Society.

D.S. Bharj, West Croydon, Surrey - Thanks for the news that Bruce Lee boxing gloves are at AtoZ Centre, 3 Macclesfield St, London W1 and priced at £38.85

KFM PEN PALS CORNER

Daniel Tracy, Havant, Hants is looking for an American or Chinese male pen pal around 12 years old.

Miss Ann Kyle, Londonderry, Northern Ireland is 17 and would like a male pen pal around 17-21 years old. Hobbies are Karate and Chinese art.

Finally, a message: Would John Duthie of Ayr in Scotland get in touch with Satpal Willon of Swindon in Wiltshire.

36

1977

EDITORIAL

    Hi there Kung Fu fans. We've another of our extra-special issues for you this month! To begin with though, I've just got to tell you all about my once-in-a-lifetime trip to California, USA. After years of trying, I finally found time to visit the birthplace of Bruce Lee's TV and feature film career, to see for myself the famous arena where they staged the Long Beach Tournament. Although at the time, a skateboarding contest was being held there, somehow it all seemed so familiar. From the photo I took with me of Bruce performing at the event, it was easy to pick my way over to the exact spot where he stood in the picture - believe me, it was an eerie feeling!
    But that's enough of visits, time now to get into the first feature for this month. Adapt or Be Destroyed is an investigation into the Little Dragon's super-theory of bending like a willow in the wind. In other words, how and why he learnt so well to adapt to changing circumstances. It's an important idea that underlines the whole basis of Jeet Kune Do.

There are no rules - in everything, simply select what seems the best solution to a given problem. In part one this month, we hear how *Game of Death* symbolised this approach more than any other of his films - each floor of the pagoda featuring different fighters with different styles. The philosophy behind it makes fantastic reading!

Secondly, I'm delighted to present the natural follow-up to our recent feature on concentration - entitled Fitness and Health - The Bruce Lee Way. Though few of us are likely to become Kung Fu superstars, the Little Dragon's kind of fitness has got to be good for everybody. It all makes tremendous sense to the casual reader and expert alike. The Master combined fitness with determination to produce the finest human fighting machine the world has ever seen. Everyone in their own way can benefit from his advice so read on and discover how! Back with you again soon...

Felix Yen

Felix Yen
Editor-in-Chief

ADAPT OR BE DESTROYED

Mankind, they say, has been in existence for a comparatively few million years, Many of the early reptiles whose skeletal remains line the interiors of the world's natural history museums held on for maybe fifty million. With luck, we may last a while longer too! But is it luck? Circumstances change and over huge periods of time, the weather, the land, the sea and the air we breathe all alter - slowly and almost imperceptably. Some part of the change was obviously too much for animals like the dinosaur; they simply vanished from the face of the earth. Man, with his ego and consciousness, rarely considers that such a thing could happen to him. Only farsighted thinkers like Bruce Lee understand the importance of bending like a willow. Nobody is indestructible and history proves that those who cannot adapt will surely be destroyed.

It took *The Way of the Dragon* to show the drift of the Master's way of thinking. In his classic finale clash with Chuck Norris in the Colosseum, things to begin with, weren't going too well for the Little Dragon. His early fighting, though brilliant, was predictable and the inspirational Chuck was catching him all too often. Obviously some quick thinking was necessary and Bruce lost no time switching tactics to a more broken rhythm. Chuck carries on the story, "He was doing nothing more than attacking me. That was all - attack. He was trying to wear me down and it was all a slow-motion thing. I remember him moving around in those beautiful fluid movements of his, trying to attack. He was ducking and weaving all the time." The broken rhythm started to affect Chuck's punching power. His blows began to miss and he grew tired. The Little Dragon moved in to finish it, carefully selecting his contact areas with the ease of a butcher carving out Sunday joints. Chuck went down - he had to! One last attempt at retrieving a hopeless situation ended with Chuck being hurled against the wall, an elbow, a wrist and a knee all completely shattered.

The general course of this great battle illustrated with superb martial imagery, how the Little Dragon adapted his fighting method to overcome a powerful and dangerous opponent. Had he continued in the routine of his initial attack, the chances are that Chuck would have won. This unthinkable result was averted by Bruce's great skill and high speed thinking.

The fight was not quite over. Tradition demanded that the winner must be the only one of the two combatants left alive (in the film world only these days, thankfully!). Regretfully, the Little Dragon completes the job with, principally, a flying headlock. Chuck's fight has ended, but Bruce symbolises the honour he feels for his defeated opponent by almost religiously laying the cloak of the vanquished fighter over his lifeless body - it's a touching moment. This scene from *The Way of the Dragon* is important in more ways than one. Though on one hand, it demonstrates the supremacy of Bruce's quickness and individuality, it shows too the importance of honouring one's opponent. In battle, the rules are few and only the fittest will survive. In death or defeat, a man must be respected.

In *Game of Death*, as we will soon see, the Little Dragon carries the story a few chapters further forward. He continues his now established practice of bringing in the top martial artists of the world for the battle in the famous pagoda. Between them, they offer many different styles - Karate, Hapkido, Escrima, and so on - and Bruce's powers of adaption serve him here as never before. No one style could have pulled him through to the top floor. Only the Master, with his punch bag of tricks and wizardry could have selected exactly the right tool to counter each attack at exactly the right moment.

Things get even worse for him on the top floor, where there are no rules, no guidelines and, above all, no second chances. As most readers know, his formidable opponent is basketball giant, Kareem Abdul-Jabbar, formerly known as Lew Alcindor, before his conversion to the Islamic faith. Kareem, described variously by the US press as 'unfriendly,' 'uncooperative,' 'un-American' and 'unjust switching everything else,' presented Bruce with some nail-biting problems. To start with, at 7' 4", he stood nearly one foot taller than the Little Dragon. What kind of adaption could Bruce conjure up to overcome such a colossal handicap?

The Master's lightning mind grasped at least part of a solution. He was hopelessly outreached so obviously he had to rely on speed. The huge Kareem could never move as fast as the Little Dragon. In this respect, Jabbar's sheer size was to count against him - fatally! Bruce darted in and out like a wasp, stinging his opponent with energy-sapping blows about the body and head. The big man, for all his height, weight and reach advantage, simply couldn't match the compact power and super-skilled thinking of the world's finest martial artist.

Kareem first met Bruce after going one day to the office of *Black Belt* magazine. Mito Uyehara, *Black Belt*'s President talked to him and soon realised that the basketball king was no mean slouch when it came to Kung Fu. Jabbar had studied aikido in New York but now he wanted to expand his horizons. Mito pushed him towards Bruce Lee and the result Kareem described to a reporter some time later.

"He set up a meeting for me to go and see Bruce. When I went by and talked with him, I found that we shared a lot of the same ideas. I think Bruce was kind of intrigued by the fact that I was an athlete. I had good size and I was in good condition. I could be more than just big and it was kind of a challenge for him to train someone like that. I started training that winter."

This happy meeting offered Bruce a real 'adapt and bend' situation. While Kareem had much to learn of the ideals, the philosophies and the training routines of the Little Dragon, for Bruce himself, the confrontation was fruitful. It was the first time he had had the opportunity of battling against a man of such huge proportions and the challenge was immense.

Kareem started on the Kung Fu trail after seeing one of the Japanese *Zatoichi* film series, starring Shintaro Katsu. Kareem said, "I was quite impressed to see something like that. To be raised in New York, you have to know how to fight as a matter of survival - egotistical survival, not really physical survival. You have to fight just to keep face." It was during their close, winter-long relationship that Kareem discovered Bruce's interest in mysticism - an interest they shared. They would talk for hours on end about Oriental, African and Asian history and the rights of the common man and gradually, though Kareem Abdul-Jabbar hardly noticed it, he was getting to grips with one of the most basic concepts of Jeet Kune Do - bend to adapt.

Through their discussions, he learnt that the general maxims underlying Bruce's ultimate art could be translated into principles of life. For many years, the Little Dragon had realized the need to adjust to circumstances. To be dogmatic is often to close the door to reasoned argument. Slowly, as Kareem learnt his martial art, he got to realise too, how the philosophy of adaption fitted so neatly into it.

Living in America had the effect of broadening Bruce's horizons to a quite considerable degree. He found himself face to face with boxing exponents (western style), wrestling and just about every other known fighting art. The USA, with its vast cultural wealth, offered the young Bruce Lee enormous scope. He saw, he read, he learnt and finally, having assimilated all he could, he put it all together and succeeded in upsetting just about everyone!

The various experts hated seeing their prized professions put in the melting pot along with all the others as to them, it was total sacrilege. Bruce didn't care. Essentially, he was a practical man and to his eyes, something that worked was useful. Everybody knows the trouble he got in to doing just that and it says something for his indominitable character that he stood firm against the accusations and warlike rumblings to uphold his beliefs.

Next month, *KFM* investigates further Bruce's policy of adaption. We discover how and why he smashed the single-minded schools of secrecy, plundered their valuables and dismissed the dogma. The Little Dragon's over-riding urge to have every fighting fact at his fingertips was to lead him into all sorts of avenues - some he'd probably have preferred to have passed by. And could he have missed one fatal clue that was ultimately to have led to his death? Read on next issue...

FITNESS AND DETERMINATION

The key to the success of Bruce Lee can be summed up at least in part as the result of fitness and determination. His positive thinking, his killer instinct, if you like, and his Kung Fu powers, owed much to these two vital considerations. Plenty has been said about his, at times, rather strange diets. Were they really of any use, or were they merely fads? It's a question that no one can really answer for sure. One thing for certain, is that the Little Dragon displayed almost super-human qualities and surely, diet must have played a part. His martial excellence was the result of many things; great skill, superb timing and power, a tremendous sense of balance and an ability to absorb and utilise much of what he read and saw. Can we, his followers, achieve any of these qualities? Up to a point, the answer has to be yes! Our bodies and minds are much the same as his, the possibilities open to us much the same as those that, early on, faced the young Dragon. Therefore, the clue lies in what we make of these possibilities and that is what will be discussed here. *KFM* asks, "Are you fit for success?"

To become a Kung Fu expert, you will have a life time of dedication in front of you. And just to be good at anything you're attempting, you need mind and body fitness. The accountant who spends hours studying books and figures and who rarely ventures outside of the front door, will quickly become inefficient and stale. Often it will be outsiders who first notice the deterioration. A slow mind will naturally be slow to notice the problem.

So what is the solution? Few of us are in the position (unfortunately) to devote many hours to the pursuit of fitness as our work demands just won't allow it. The basic ingredient in the Little Dragon's fitness formula was running. He saw it as tremendous exercise for mind and body alike - and he was right. When the body is being driven hard, the mind magically becomes sharpened. Great concentration is literally forced upon it in the person's determination to keep going. Remember though, to build up slowly. Years of staleness must not be followed immediately by a five mile run!

Try starting by jogging - around the streets if necessary. Just a few hundred yards will be enough to start with. You'll soon get an idea of how fit you are by the puffing and panting. Smokers will be in the worst trouble - cigarettes and fitness can be incompatible, to say the least!

Gradually the distance should be increased and the jogging into running. Remember, it's far better not to overdo it to start with - severe stiffness the following day will be the reward for the over-keen. And talking of stiffness; if this should occur, it's a good rule not to run again until the feeling has completely gone. The muscles which cause this trouble have been stretched way beyond their normal limits and they need to recover fully before being used in such a way again.

Bruce Lee usually found time to put in two miles of hard running a day, even when involved in the time consuming business of filming. At a reasonable pace, the distance should only take twenty minutes to half an hour and what valuable minutes they are. It can't be pretended that running offers the body everything it needs in the way of exercise, but it certainly goes a long way towards it.

The first few days of a new exercise routine are the hardest. The self-discipline is hard to muster up and it seems much easier to just go in the other room and watch TV. Don't give up! The way over this is to set targets. Check the clock when you start. Seven Thirty? Okay, whatever you're about to do you're not going to stop until eight. That's all right for now, but will you be doing it again tomorrow? Tell yourself you'll be getting into the training routine every day this week - and you're going to hate yourself if you miss out.

Believe it or not, after a while, the problem just won't be there and the difference between feeling fit and unfit is impossible to put into words. You can help yourself in other ways too. Who needs lifts? Use the stairs if it's only a few flights. If you live near an underground rail system, walk up the moving escalators, don't just stand there!

Many will complain that they're too tired after a long day. Nonsense. That sort of feeling is borne of tedium. Push yourself into action and you'll soon wake up again. Many a wise businessman has developed the art of working in intense bursts - and then relaxing for a few moments before starting again. With a bit of practice, the body can be kept in a fairly charged condition - almost continuously. For the real enthusiast, say an exponent of Kung Fu like Bruce Lee, such delights as speed of movement (can you snatch a fly out of the air?) and concentration will naturally follow, though practice of certain exercises will

certainly assist you even further.

For most *KFM* readers, this is probably as far as you will wish to go. The rewards, in terms of health, will be felt almost immediately. Fewer colds and flu's and the almost total disappearance of that 'I'm just not feeling too good today' complaint. It would be foolish to claim that good health equals a longer life - although it may well. But it certainly offers a happier one!

How often have you heard it said that Bruce Lee packed more into his short life than most of us fit into seventy odd years? Often enough and that's because it's true! His rigorous fitness sessions gave him an enthusiasm and a love of living that most of us can only dream of. The day didn't end for him after a hard day's work when at Six Thirty, the TV got switched on. His work was his life and his life was his work - the two were inseparable and he delighted in both.

It would be impossible right here to go into specific exercises to further encourage a healthy body. The variety is limitless and their type depends so much upon what the person has it in mind to achieve. There are of course general ones that fit into most practise routines such as press-ups, sit-ups and so on, and all are more than adequately covered and described in the many books available.

It's best to remember though, that whatever exercises you do choose to practice, it's vital that the body - much like the engine of a car - is given time to warm up. Muscles will offer nothing near their best when used cold. If pushed too far, too early they will simply break down, resulting in what is known as torn muscles. The pain is unpleasant to say the least and the time it can take for them to repair themselves can run into days of even weeks. The fit person is just as concerned with food as with exercise. Naturally, the overweight have some dieting to do before getting down to working out regular eating habits. Both, however, will do well to keep away as far as possible from highly processed and artificial foods. The best things are lean meat, dairy produce and fresh vegetables. As a rule, steer clear of too many sweets, cakes and biscuits. Avoid stodge as it slows the body down. Huge quantities of potatoes may look appetising but they don't do much to keep you live and alert.

In fact it's important not to over-eat. The wise person leaves the table still feeling a little hungry. And many believe too, that the idea of three big meals a day is incorrect and outdated. One, plus occasional snacks, should provide all that's physically needed to keep the body in good trim. It's often said too, to eat only when you feel hungry and in some ways, it's a fair enough statement. Unfortunately, boredom tends to bring on hunger so it's not a totally reliable yardstick by any means!

Most doctors and dieticians agree that drinking a good amount of liquid every day is essential. They do tend, however, to come up with pet theories on how many pints that should be. It stands to reason that needs vary from person to person and from day to day. As to what you should drink, well most things are okay, although it's best if water type drinks make up the bulk of it.

Self-discipline is a very important part of getting and keeping fit. It's hard work doing exercises - especially to begin with. A good amount of self control is necessary to keep going when it matters most. The funny thing is, after a while, the whole process gets to be enjoyable. As the body and mind get fitter, so do one's alertness and enthusiasm increases. In fact, getting fitter is just as much a vicious circle as getting unfit. Once either is begun, it's hard to break it!

And there's no point in going looking to find the formula of Bruce's special energy-giving concoction, simply to copy it. To begin with, he didn't just have one, but many. As in everything else, he was constantly chopping and changing and experimenting. That is exactly what everyone should do. Discover what suits you the best - then see if you can't improve on it. Again, for starters, many books have been written on the subject of special foods and diets so why not check out some of them?

Nobody - least of all *KFM* is suggesting that all readers should try and become super-athletes - far from it. What we do suggest though is that as many of you as possible grab just a part of what the Little Dragon had going for him. To repeat what was said at the beginning, there's little that most of us could not reasonably achieve given fitness plus determination.

THE BRUCE LEE SECRET SOCIETY

Hello, it's your very own Society president, Pam Hadden here once again with a really hot bit of news concerning film censorship.

Just before that though, word from Alan Mount (1109) on Bruce's appearances in the *Batman* series. Apparently many of the regions are showing episodes and Alan thought everyone would like to know which particular ones the Little Dragon appeared in. They are A Piece of the Action and Batman's Satisfaction. As anyone who has caught these two will testify, it's fantastic seeing Bruce on TV. It's just a pity it's not more often, or come to that, not one of his feature films. Oh well, I suppose it will happen sometime. Meanwhile, all of you who haven't seen these particular *Batman* shows, now you've got the titles, how about writing to your local TV stations and asking when they're coming on?

Back on to the old question of censorship and how about this for a stupendous piece of news, sent in to us by John Rogers (1009)? I'm told that the Home Office has appointed a committee to look into the laws concerning violence, indecency and obscenity. Part of their work is to check up on how film censorship is arranged in the UK and the word is, the committee welcomes everybody's views. Well - do they now? I hardly think I need to spell out just exactly what I'd like to see you do sometime during the next few days. The address to send your comments is: Jon Davey, Committee on Obscenity and Film Censorship, Department 17, Home Office, Queen Anne's Gate, London SW1H 9AT. The sort of questions you might like to direct to Mr Davey are ones such as: What excuse can possibly be given for scissor-happy censors mutilating film footage of the world's finest latter-day Kung Fu expert? Would they perhaps consider also banning film shots of Muhammad Ali actually knocking out his opponent? Why not just leave in the bits between rounds?!? When you consider the sheer, savage brutality - very often characterised by dreadful acting - that actually IS shown in cinemas these days, to me it is astounding that Little Dragon fans continue to be deprived of this rare Bruce Lee footage. Other countries, for example France, have left much of the Master's material untouched and I can't say I noticed any rioting in the streets when I was last there. So come on all you Society members - this is the moment we've all been waiting for. Mr Davey wants to know our feelings on film censorship so let's tell him about Bruce Lee! **Pam Hadden - President of the Bruce Lee Society.**

NOTICE

Would readers please remember that, at present, *KFM* is not running a Swop Shop. That particular service is run by the Bruce Lee Society for members only. That means, if you've got something to buy, sell or swap, then join the club! Do it quickly and you can take advantage of their special reduced price subscription offer.

Over the years, many readers have complained that they have difficulty sometimes in obtaining current copies of *KFM*. There are two ways around the problem. One is to take out a subscription at £4.50 for 12 issues. The other is this: If you'd like to supply your friends and make a little money for your trouble, we will supply the magazine at the following prices - 10 copies at 28p each, 25 copies at 26p each and 50 copies (maximum) at 24p each. The cost includes all handling charges. We must emphasise that this service is intended only for areas where *KFM* is difficult to locate. Also, cash must accompany all orders and no returns please! Send orders to *KFM* Bulk Buy Offer, 14 Rathbone Place, London, W1P 1DE.

KICKBACK: THE LETTERS

Hi, Jenny here again with one of the finest sets of letters I've ever had the pleasure to put into print. I know I don't have to start plugging it, but this month I particularly want everyone to read the Society Page and to take notice of Pam's piece on censorship. It looks like she's found somebody worth writing to! And on that subject, just take a look at our first letter from Challis Liang of Hong Kong. If ever we needed confirmation of the hackwork that's been carried out on Bruce's films, then this is it. While speaking to a friendly film censor the other day, I took the opportunity of raising this thorny subject. Apparently it's not unknown for a film to be re-judged, although it is fairly rare. That's good enough for me - let's all get the pens out and start writing to this new committee - address on the Society Page. Time now to hit the letters trail!

CUT BRUCE MOVIES

Dear Jenny,
Hello! I'm here on holiday in London. I'm from Hong Kong and I must say I like it here very much. The other day, some friends and I went along to see *The Big Boss* and we were quite surprised to see a large proportion of the film missing. In Hong Kong, you see all of Bruce's films to the full length. I read that the reason for so many cuts, especially in the fight scenes, was because of the violence. Well I suppose they have a point there. The magazine went on to describe another scene where Bruce, who is faced with confronting the villains, instead goes back to a certain lady and makes love with her. Apparently that particular scene was too explicit so it had to be trimmed. Well as I see it, he had a very great decision ahead of him which could not be avoided. He is only human and so, feeling the need for another human being, did what comes naturally.
Challis Liang, Herne Hill, London

Dear Challis,
Really marvellous to hear the opinions of a fan from Bruce's own part of the world. Naturally, the biggest gripe this end is the removal of the action sequences - far less is said about the chopped up love scenes. Having never seen the one in question, I must say I'm not too qualified to judge on it. However, from what I've heard about some other films these days, it's hard to see how anything can be too explicit!

THE BRUCE LEE STORY

Dear Jenny,
As my wife and I are fans of the late Bruce Lee, we went to see the film, *The Bruce Lee Story*. I must say I have never seen anything like it. The film completely dissolved any memory of the great man that we had. All it did was make a mockery of him. I don't think we will be the only people to complain to you as many of his fans in the cinema walked out before the end of the film. I only hope his wife didn't see it. I don't think anyone in their right mind would let such an absolute load of rubbish be seen by his millions of fans. I am sure that if and when you see this film, you will feel the same as we do - very upset.
Mr A. Harrington, Ely, Cardiff

Dear Mr Harrington,
I have to be completely honest and say that I haven't yet seen The Bruce Lee Story, although I really should. The reason is I've heard so many similar reports from people feeling like you do about it, I can hardly bear to. At least the fans are doing the right thing and showing their displeasure by walking out! Why oh why can't somebody come up with a good film on Bruce's life? Actually, there is one showing in the States about which I hear far better reports. More on that soon.

WAY OF THE DRAGON PAINTING?

Dear Jenny,
I thought you said you were running out of pictures? If coming up with posters like No.33 and No.34 means running out then please keep on running out or are you saving the best for last? Anyway, if you can get guys to paint like that *The Way of the Dragon* picture in No.34, then I figure there's years of life left in you!
Philip Marcum, Doncaster, Yorkshire

Dear Philip,
Many thanks for your congratulations. I think you're right - those two issues were real bombshells. It does get harder all the time to find good, unseen colour pictures of the Master, although occasionally we strike lucky and our patient researchers dig up another bundle. Actually, the artist of that The Way of the Dragon *picture in No.34 has come in for a whole lot of praise so I think we'll definitely be using him again. Would you believe that was his first published work!!

QUICKIES CORNER

Ivan von Czapiewski, Picketberg, South Africa - It's easy to say somebody could have beaten Bruce, now the Master is gone - Just ignore them.
Philip Ferris, Helston, Cornwall - sorry to hear so little is happening in Cornwall, martial arts-wise - How about starting up something yourself?
Ian Hamilton, Sunderland, Tyne & Wear - Same old story and I personally

don't believe Chuck Norris would have beaten the Little Dragon in open contest.

Nigel Hall, Warley, West Midlands - If you're after information on Bruce, why not check out our back issues though I suggest you write to the mail order department to see what's in stock these days.

Paul Dean, Macclesfield, Cheshire - I shouldn't try to copy Bruce too much - just be yourself. Regarding exercises, there are many books around on the subject so try the library.

K. Lam, Bedford, Beds - I'm worried, too, about what might happen, censorship-wise, when Bruce's films get on TV. *The Secret Art of Bruce Lee* has been in and out of stock lately so write to our mail order department for the latest availability.

D & A Palmer, Laceby, S. Humberside - Glad you liked No.34 so much - We do try!

David Milburn, Sale Moor, Cheshire - Thanks for a long and interesting letter. If there ever could have been an Ali vs Lee contest, to make it fair, it would have had to have been no hold barred.

J. Stockford, Bristol - *KFM* No.14 is available from our mail order department.

Paul Kyffin, Wrexham, Clwyd - Yes, Cimac in Birmingham do have a fantastic range of books and equipment.

David Wright, Glasgow, Scotland - Kick & Dragon posters sold out years ago. *KFM* No. 7 & 14 are available.

C. Domville, 051-489 XXXX has a load of Bruce Lee stuff for sale.

EDITORIAL

Hi there Kung Fu fans. How do we do it! Once more, *Kung-Fu Monthly* hits the streets with another really impressive bundle of Bruce Lee pictures, plus two more fabulous features. First off though, some hot news regarding *Game of Death*. The information we've got, I must first emphasise, does come from unofficial sources, so don't complain too loudly if time proves some of it to be a little inaccurate. Word is, that US actors Hugh O'Brien and Gig Young have both been given parts in the revised version of the film. Hugh, in fact, you may recall played a sort of early bionic man on TV.

The plot, we're told, has been injected with an *Enter the Dragon* type of atmosphere (not surprising when you consider that Robert Clouse directed both films) and it seems that the problem of a Lee double has been overcome in some scenes by the use of a helmeted, motorcycling lookalike! Release date has still not been confirmed as we go to press, but it looks like a January or February premiere.

This month's dramatic first feature is part two of the explosive Adapt or Die article that began last issue. The message is truly amazing. As we pinpoint some of the major cornerstones of Bruce's career. so too we see the gradual evolving of his Jeet Kune Do Super-Theory. The message is clear and concise. Success for anyone is simply the understanding and adaption to circumstances. Read on!

Secondly, we've got a real bombshell. At least we bring you the low-down on Bruce Lee's *The Silent Flute*. David Carradine is certain he will be able to take over where the Little Dragon left off, but can he? *Kung-Fu Monthly* looks at the situation and comes up with some unexpected conclusions!

Felix Yen
Editor-in-Chief

ADAPT OR BE DESTROYED – PART TWO

Years of tradition had seen the chief exponents of the various Kung Fu styles retreat into their school strong-holds and it had taken a man like Bruce to see through the hypocrisy of it all. Many an attempt was made to dissuade him from his chosen path - some physical, some argumentative, but all to no avail. He knew what he was doing. The Little Dragon was in business to win fights and to be the best. To keep that cherished position secure, he knew he had to keep on learning, finding new moves to add to his repertoire, finding new ways of putting it all together.

He had to keep bending with the wind, otherwise his art, his philosophy and his future could never be secure. It's been suggested that he missed just one thing - that his body could not be driven past its physical limits. Ignoring this, people say, ultimately caused his death. It's more likely that Bruce did understand and take account of this. Perhaps the trouble is that he was let down by one unreliable factor - he was only a human being!

Last issue, we introduced you to the basis of what will surely become known as the 20th Century's most important philosophy - Adapt or Die! Only the fittest can survive and that lesson holds true whether in the human or animal kingdom. Bruce Lee, the self-elected keeper of this essential truth became the exception that proved the point.

Game of Death star, Abdul Kareem Jabbar, said once, "The way of the warrior is that he accepts the fact he is a warrior, he lives it. I have been living it. I guess maybe it's just being what I'm about, how I see myself and how I see my people. Most Africans who were sent over (to America) were captured warriors sold into slavery. Afro-Americans, in this country have long martial traditions, it's kind of getting back to it, in a sense."

Kareem's unswerving modesty gives proof, if proof be needed, of his total conversion to Bruce's famous philosophy of life. And in the words above, his awareness of the need to adapt one's aims and inclinations to suit the individual is pure Little Dragon. His attitude is not so much one of anger at his forefathers having been forcibly taken from their

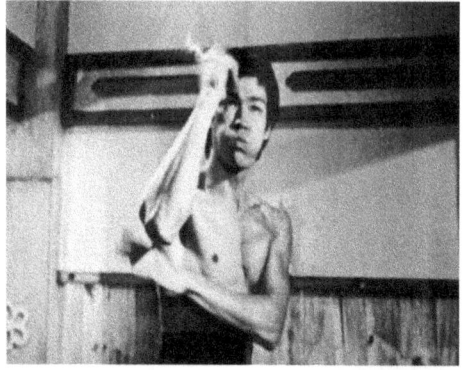

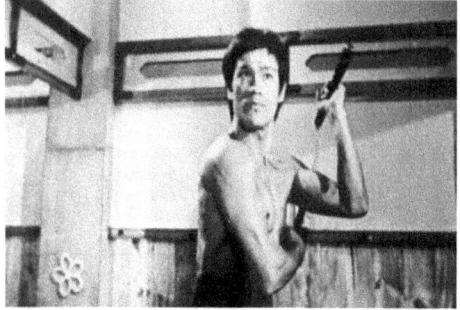

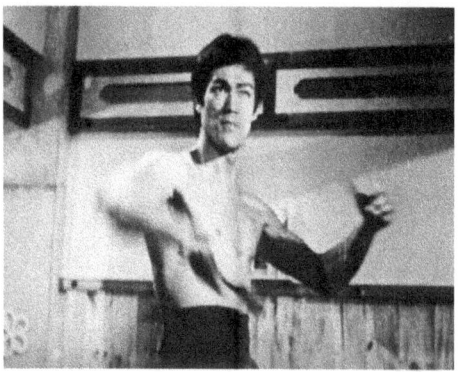

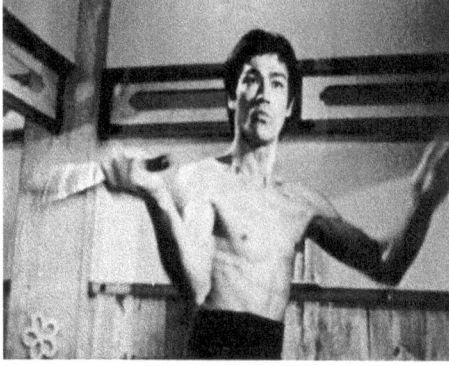

lands - more one of concern that for the good of all he should take steps to become aware of, and closer to, his past. The giant basketball player belittles himself - characteristically when he remarks on his 'insignificant' role in Bruce's ultimate film legacy. It takes two to produce the fight scene of the century and though one may be the martial Master of the world, his opponent must be no slouch either! Those fortunate enough to have seen the *Game of Death* clip in *The Man and the Legend* will know exactly what I mean. As a battle, it is tremendous - as an action film finale, it must be the number one. At the start of that collossal clash, the odds seemed well and truly stacked against the Little Dragon. Naturally, Bruce planned it that way. He wanted to demonstrate coolly and calmly just how clear thinking and supreme attention to detail could help turn the tide. The problem he set himself was extreme! A super-fit giant of a man who, like himself, saw the wisdom of taking the best of all styles.

It's a problem the Little Dragon had been tussling with for some considerable time and during the months he had been training Jabbar up to perfection, he'd learnt the answers well. In a flash it had come to him. *Game of Death* was to be his masterpiece. It was to show to everyone in a symbolic way, that Jeet Kune Do could conquer the world. What better obstacle for the Little Dragon to overcome than Kareem Abdul-Jabbar. It was a stroke of genius as the great can always be tamed, so the humble may become mighty.

Spontaneity was the keynote of Bruce's film success. As another 'bend and adapt' man, Danny Inosanto, put it, "He didn't know what he was going to do the night before so he made up the details as he went along." And Jim Kelly, of *Enter the Dragon* fame, once remarked that, "Lee even had his own stuntmen who knew exactly what to do when he threw a punch. Lee had an ego as big as Muhammad Ali's. Most people couldn't dig it, but I could appreciate what he was doing for himself, his family and his people. Those Chinese (Kung Fu) movies have done more (for the Chinese) than Henry Kissinger could ever do."

Jim is perhaps being unfair when he insists that most people couldn't take Bruce's ego. For many other actors and film people lucky enough to have been on the set of one of his films, this simply didn't ring true. Maybe Jim is still a little sour at being killed-off so early in *Enter the Dragon*.

Bruce often did in fact have his own stuntmen standing by on the set. He needed people there who would react in the best possible way to his martial skill - and that meant fighters trained for the job. Though always totally able to cope with a sudden surprise attack, the Little Dragon needed trained opponents to turn the action into a good battle rather than a one-sided rout. Jim Kelly's attitude stems maybe from Bruce's decision to do away with him rather than John Saxon (the original plan was the other way around). He feels his 1971 International Middleweight Karate Champion title should have enabled him to head off John who holds a brown belt in Karate and Tai Chi Chuan.

In the end though, the latter's screen credits list turned the tide his way. It's interesting to take note of Jim's final remarks on the subject, "It was Bruce's movie, and he's going to look the best because he's the star. After this year, I will be the number one black star, and in three years, I'll be the number one worldwide box office champion - black or white." What happened, Jim?

Kelly's claim that he was using Karate simply as a stepping stone to get on the screen - presumably to win himself glory - was so unlike Bruce's premiere interest. That was to provide the world with a better understanding of the arts so that everyone could, if they wished, practice them without feeling the need to show off at every chance their physical prowess. Jeet Kune Do teaches completeness and modesty; qualities that are hard to find in many another Kung Fu star or film actor.

Bruce didn't pull his punches when it came to passing opinion on other forms of martial arts. "Judo is the most realistic self defence art. Karate, Aikido - they are not practical. If you don't hit or get yourself hit, how do you know if your technique will work? It is like teaching a person to swim. You can teach him day by day how to do kicks and strokes on dry land, but until he gets into the water, he doesn't really know if he's going to sink or swim."

This superb argument is but one step away from his 'adapt or die' master theory. The Kung Fu exponent who plays at fighting will never be able to take his art seriously. His technique is unlikely to easily translate to real-life situations. It will be difficult for him to adapt! As Bruce once said, "If you haven't been hit, how do you know if you can take a blow? If you haven't hit someone, how do you know if you're going to stop him?"

Naturally, the Little Dragon was fully prepared to adapt his all-out approach when it came to matters of training. Much as he preferred to mix it with real live opposition, still he recognised the difficulty of always having suitable candidates to hand. Frequently, the punch bag or something similar had to substitute. Bruce remarked, "Wearing gloves and protective gear and going all out is not the same as real fighting, but it's the closest thing."

The whole of Bruce's life and fighting was geared to adaption. To overcome his earlier setbacks on the streets of Hong Kong, he'd had to adapt. In order to formulate new concepts of Kung Fu, he had to adapt the ones that already existed. In order to achieve total screen realism, once more his techniques needed adaption. The idea is, in theory, a simple one. Decide where you're going, then arrange circumstances to make it possible. The Little Dragon did it - could you?

THE SILENT FLUTE

Since those early days of *Kung-Fu Monthly* when the world's finest martial arts magazine was but in its infancy, little has been mentioned of that star of TV's *Kung Fu*, David Carradine. Little Dragon fans have for many years been less then enthusiastic about the man who pipped Bruce to the starring role and insult was only added to injury when word got out that many of his fighting scenes were just fakes, or at best, slow motion sometimes speeded up. David, to his credit, made no great claims to being a Kung Fu star. He was simply a good actor with a passing knowledge of Oriental fighting techniques. And again, it would be unfair to blame him for pulling the rug from under Bruce's feet, however sick about it Little Dragon fans were over the incident at the time. And that might have been where the Carradine/Bruce Lee controversy would have ended had it not been for a recent, dramatic announcement. Suddenly, the word was that TV's Mr Kung Fu was to pick up the threads of Bruce's most famous 'shelf-bound' project - *The Silent Flute*.

Is Carradine doing it in the attitude of just another film or is there something more? David would certainly point to the latter. His well reported remark that he "feels almost possessed by the spirit of Bruce" certainly seems to bear it out. In *Fighting Times*, he described recently some details of the plot.

"The action takes place over a century ago in a desert type land (no name is given to it) and the storyline is interesting to say the least! A martial artist competes to perform five trials. None before have ever succeeded, but he who does shall confront the 'Keeper of the Book.' Here, the plot thickens. There is another great expert who has been disqualified from entering because of what's considered to be his wrong attitude. He doesn't give up easily, however, and despite the many attempts made to dissuade him from continuing, still the lone challenger battles on. Though careful to remain in the background, the unofficial challenger (the hero) finds himself being constantly distracted from his course by a man who, although blind, is still an expert in the martial arts! Funnily enough, though, our hero always finds himself in the right place at the right time. The action really hots up when the official challenger fails at the first hurdle and dies. Our hero, now on his own, has some strange opponents. One has the power to take away his rhythm, another is a woman who abuses him. The final clash is against death."

Bruce Lee went overboard with the essence of the storyline. It fulfilled his wildest dreams and imaginations and there is no doubt at all that, had he lived, by hook or by crook, the film would have been made. The discerning reader will easily be able to make out the analogy between the plot and life itself. Our hero is, in fact, battling himself! The official challenger of course represents the thinking of orthodox people, the wayward hero, the perfect characterisation of all that Bruce held dear.

Had the Little Dragon survived his brush with eternity, there is every chance that *The Silent Flute* would have ranked alongside *Game of Death* as one of the 20th Century's finest screen masterpieces. In charge of the screenplay was Stirling Silliphant, an old buddy of Bruce's and one of the few Hollywood names to have really understood and got into the Little Dragon's super-world of Kung Fu. Bruce said in June 1970, "I first wrote the idea down in Hong Kong, but I feel with the help of Stirling and Jim (Coburn), we can have a final draft of the script completed very soon. The final will be a combination of our three personalities. The main idea is to show the various styles of the martial arts authentically."

But the project somehow stalled. Some say that an element of disagreement on the final draft of the screenplay sprung up between Bruce and Jim, although it's hard to find actual proof of this. Something caused the wheels to grind to a halt and there they have remained for over seven years.

The idea crossed somebody's mind that David Carradine could somehow take over where the Master left off and though many Little Dragon fans are doubtful over the wisdom of this unexpected move, it's arguable that surely its better the film is attempted than just left sitting on the shelf.

Carradine is certain *The Silent Flute* will now be going ahead and he's equally convinced that he will be playing the lead role. The choice, though maybe upsetting to some Bruce Lee fans, could be a good one. David's strong acting background early on and his more recent screen successes such as *Cannonball*, *Death Race 2000* and *Bound for Glory*, all pay tribute to his masterly acting abilities. Another name earmarked for a leading role in *The*

Silent Flute is Jeff Cooper, the South African martial arts specialist.

In the original concept of the film, Bruce was to take on the role of all the opposing forces and Coburn was to handle the part of the martial artist. It looks right now as if Carradine sees himself taking on the forces role with possibly Jeff Cooper taking over Coburn's part. The links are there as Jeff has long been a close friend of screenplay writer, Stirling Silliphant. Both James Coburn and Stirling still own some of the action so their agreement to David's plan is naturally paramount. Carradine however sees no problem.

Where the ex-star of TV's *Kung Fu* does see a degree of difficulty is in convincing Silliphant that the whole thing is still worth doing and in the way Carradine has it in mind. Stirling's standing and reputation in the film business is such that he no way has to get involved in something he's not a hundred per cent behind. No doubt his memories of the Master and his own pride would both tend to make him want to produce a masterpiece, or nothing at all. Carradine naturally sees it in the same way and in fact he remarked at a recent interview, "That's why I'm trying to convince (Stirling) now that he should have a hand in it. I think he would be invaluable." Still, many fans are worried that David Carradine lacks the depth of interest to put the whole thing over in anything like the way the Little Dragon would have done. To Bruce, it was to represent his first major step away from

the Mandarin film world of all-out action - violence for the sake of violence. The Kung Fu was to carry a strong spiritual meaning and the film as a whole had to be acceptable on a truly international level. Carradine obviously feels part of this when he says, "It's bringing a message to bear instead of just portraying fight scenes and bad acting."

The real answer of course is that the proof of the pudding is in the eating. Carradine without doubt has a certain reverence for the memory of Bruce Lee. At times he says he feels almost seized by the spirit of the late Master. Let's hope in a way that he is, for any amount of inspiration will be needed to produce the kind of result the Little Dragon had in mind. It has to be admitted, too, that David did squarely face the critisism of *Kung Fu* and do something about it. The early episodes contained just basic forms of Judo. Later on, however, under the technical direction of new man, Kam Yuen (who replaced David Chow) things improved considerably.

So inspired, in fact, was David Carradine with the abilities of Kam, even after the TV series was completed, he continued to study under the masterly influence of his new teacher. For a while he regularly attended classes at Kam's school in Torrance, California, then later, Kam Yuen returned the compliment by visiting David, often four or five times a week. We've yet to see the fruits of their labours. With luck, we will be confronted with a new Carradine, one who will be able to fight his own fights and without having to employ camera tricks to make it look effective.

A well produced *Silent Flute* would work wonders for the popularity of David Carradine, but if he misses, it's unlikely that Bruce Lee fans will ever give him a second chance!

THE BRUCE LEE SECRET SOCIETY

Hello again, Pam here with all the latest news and views from members of the Bruce Lee Society.

First off, how about the newly cut version of *Fist of Fury* that's doing the rounds with *Amsterdam Kill*? Don't ask me how or why, but there's a lot more been left in this time around -particularly in the famed graveyard scene. It's all there, including the gruesome part where Bruce is chewing what looks to me suspiciously like roasted dog! Let's hope this less cut version is an omen for the future. Perhaps one day we'll actually be able to see the alley fight in *Way of the Dragon*; you never know. Perhaps, too, *Game of Death* may escape the itchy fingers of the scissor-happy censors.

For those of you who've only joined recently, I'd like to tell you about our area lists. What I've done is to separate members off into various areas of the country. Each area then has all the members in it printed up onto one sheet and everybody involved receives a copy. I reckon it's a great way of putting members in touch with one another. But, there may of course be some who don't wish to be included and I need to know who. This only applies to members whose membership number is over 2,000. Earlier people have already been checked.

Finally, how about those *KFM* binders we've got for you? Society members will have their usual mail order discount. If you're not yet a member of the world's greatest Bruce

Lee Society, then NOW'S THE TIME TO JOIN! The cost is still only £3.25 and in return, there are news sheets, stickers, a membership card, photos, a badge and lots, lots more. Just drop me a line at the Bruce Lee Society, 14 Rathbone Place, London W1P 1DE... and welcome to the club! **Pam Hadden**

NOTICE

Would readers please remember that, at present, *KFM* is not running a Swop Shop. That particular service is run by the Bruce Lee Society for members only. That means, if you've got something to buy, sell or swap, then join the club!

Over the years, many readers have complained that they have difficulty sometimes in obtaining current copies of *KFM*. There are two ways around the problem. One is to take out a subscription at £4.50 for 12 issues. The other is this: If you'd like to supply your friends and make a little money for your trouble, we will supply the magazine at the following prices: 10 copies at 28p each, 25 copies at 26p each and 50 copies (maximum) at 24p each. The cost includes all handling charges. We must emphasise that this service is intended only for areas where *KFM* is difficult to locate. Also, cash must accompany all orders and no returns please! Send orders to *KFM* Bulk Buy Offer, 14 Rathbone Place, London W1P 1DE.

KICKBACK: THE LETTERS

Hi... Jenny Lee back with you again, with some great news. The editor tells me that starting next issue, we'll be running a brand new double feature on the many Bruce Lee albums that have been released, past and present. We'll be giving as much sleeve detail as possible, plus if we can, an idea of where to look for copies of your own. In some cases, the LP's are what are known as 'bootlegs' - that is, they have been illegally produced. We will obviously not be able to tell you where to find these. It's a marvellous idea and what I'd like is for readers who have something we don't mention to send in details. That way we'll be able to present a really comprehensive list. Stand by for part one next month. Now, it's letters time!

PAY WEEKLY MARTIAL ARTS SHOPS?

Dear Jenny,
Could you please tell me if there are any martial arts mail order companies in this country that will accept weekly or monthly instalments on books and equipment? I think it is a good idea as I am sure many other people would agree. It's hard on the pocket to pay out a lot of money in one go.
Mr K. Bennett, Blackpool, Lancs

Dear Mr. Bennett,
I think the idea is an excellent one! I know it's done in many other fields, but I must confess I haven't heard of a martial arts company making use of it. Some of the equipment is of course very expensive and I sympathise completely with those who can't really afford to hand over all the money at once. So come on all you mail order people, how about it!

BRUCE LEE IN PARIS

Dear Jenny,
Until quite recently, some of my friends just could not and would not believe that there are so many Bruce Lee fans the world over. Then we went on a visit to Paris with the school and *The Way of the Dragon* was playing at two different cinemas with huge crowds waiting to get in. It was fantastic! This converted my friends into avid Bruce fans, just going to show that the King's following is not declining (especially with *KFM* rolling out the brilliant posters). By the way, are there any Bruce Lee transfers left?
Steven Richardson, Seghill, Northumberland

Dear Steven,
Marvellous to hear that Bruce Lee is still packing 'em in in Paris. And don't forget that they are lucky enough to be able to see much less censored versions! And you can bet your life that the Little Dragon still has huge pulling power over here too, so your friends are in good company. For those transfers, try Cimac in Birmingham.

DISGRACEFUL BBC

Dear Jenny,
As every Bruce Lee fan knows, trying to obtain his cinema posters from the National Screen Service is like trying to get gold from Fort Knox! Then why is it that they gave at least two to BBC TV and let them disgrace the name of Bruce Lee, by showing the actual cinema poster on the series *The Goodies*, only with their version of what they thought it should have been called, smeared over the face of the Master. Examples are:- *The Big Pud* (*The Big Boss*) and *Enter With Drag On* (*Enter the Dragon*). I just don't think it was right of them to do this. They could easily have thought up original titles for the series, without making Bruce Lee look like an idiot. Lastly, as regards to your more serious features in *KFM*, I have to agree they really are great to read! Keep churning them out!
Mike Devereux, Orford, Cheshire

Dear Mike,
Thanks for sending in another really interesting letter. Actually, I missed that particular Goodies *episode*, but I can imagine how upset you felt! To a true collector, it must have been agony to see the casual way in which the posters were being used - or should I say, abused. But then, something inside me feels that nobody should be above having the odd bit of mickey taken out of them. How does everybody else feel?

SET OF BACK ISSUES FOR SALE

Dear Jenny,
After reading some of your letters, it seems to me that there is a shortage of back issues of *KFM*. Therefore I'm offering a complete set of the back issues, from issue one to twenty-four. I'm asking £10.00 for the whole set.
David Bersantie, Winsford, Cheshire

Dear David
Thanks for your offer but I've got to say, that we here at KFM, aren't too happy having hundreds of people sending you £10 in the hope of being first.

CENSORSHIP

Dear Jenny,
I am writing to you about an advert in a newspaper asking the public to give their views on censorship. I willingly wrote and I received a reply saying they had read it and thanking me. Nothing dramatic, but a start at least!
Cavan Smyth, Accrington, Lancs

Dear Cavan,
As you probably know, this very point was raised in our last issue. I'm delighted to know the ball has started rolling and for those of you who might have missed it last month, here again is the address: Jon Davey, Committee on Obscenity and Film Censorship, Dept 17, Home Office, Queen Anne's Gate, London SW1H 9AT. If enough people write, you never know, we might get a less-censored *Game of Death* as a result!

QUICKIES CORNER

David Evans, Sidcup, Kent - Marvellous to hear that colour/sound trailers are available for *The Big Boss* and *Enter the Dragon* from Thunderbird via a Blackpool firm. I agree they should be on sale above the counter.
Mr Pugh, Mile End, London - Thanks for the clipping regarding the punch-up that occurred during the *Game of Death* filming. I'm trying to find out more.
S. Green, Wrexham, Clwyd - Sorry to hear that you had trouble with Lai Choy as well - He'll be getting a strong letter from me shortly.
William Longson, Blackpool, Lancs - You're correct - *Game of Death* should be out very soon and *Fist of Fury* is going around with *Amsterdam Kill*.
James Williamson, Kilmarnock, Ayshire, Scotland - Is looking for pen pals from just about anywhere.
David Green, Bournemouth, Dorset - Yup, *KFM* No.19 still available from the mail order department.
Brian Matthews, South Shields - A Yip Man feature would be a great idea!

Unfortunately, stills from Bruce's early films seem almost non-existent.
Martin Clarke, Coventry - Thanks for your huge letter - Some of the ideas are fabulous.
Colin Jones, Rhyl, Clwyd - I love your poem - I'm only sorry it's too long to print.
Mark Ward, Wigan, Lancs - Sorry you don't dig Bruce - I guess you cant win 'em all.
William Brindle, Liverpool - Wants to know of a Kendo club in his area.

THE KUNG-FU MONTHLY ARCHIVE SERIES

At Last The KFM BACK ISSUES BINDER

For years you've been asking for it... now here it is!

Keep your invaluable collection of KFM back numbers in PERFECT condition by using the OFFICIAL KFM BINDER.

In the years ahead, a set of Kung-Fu Monthly Magazines will be worth a great deal... the more so if presented in this superb new Official Binder. Embossed with the words 'Kung-Fu Monthly... The World's Finest Martial Arts Magazine', this smart, black binder will make a beautiful addition to your bookcase.

Be proud of your collection of KFM Magazines!

Send immediately a £2.75 cheque or postal order (made out to Kung-Fu Monthly, please) to:
KFM Binder Offer
14 Rathbone Place
London W1P 1DE

Special Society Member's Price... only £2.50
(Please allow at least 4 weeks for delivery)

For a short time only, each binder bought will contain a free copy of KFM No. 5 and No. 6!!

THE POSTER MAGAZINES - VOLUME TWO

EDITORIAL

Hi there Kung Fu fans. Welcome to a very special edition of *Kung-Fu Monthly*. It's not often we can boast of having two star features in one issue, but if ever a *KFM* was a double 'A' sider, this has to be it.

To begin with, a million thanks to our associate researcher, Eddy Pumer, for all the many weeks of work he put into compiling this issue's opener, The Recordings of Bruce Lee. The wealth of material that the Little Dragon has left us is breathtaking in its enormity. Now, here at last, we offer over this issue and the next, a comprehensive breakdown of what is, or at least has been, available. In general we're sticking to the records and tapes side of things but with brief mention of 8mm film copies. Eddy dissects each disc and tape into a track by track discussion, starting with the still reasonably available four feature film soundtracks and ending, hopefully, with some real rarities.

And following on this month, we've pulled out of the bag another of our great interview scoops! There weren't many of his pupils that Bruce considered worthy to carry forward the banner of Jeet Kune Do. As most readers know, he was careful in the extreme that his 'style without style' would not join the turgid ranks of most of the other secret arts. It's therefore with great pleasure that we present the words, thoughts and feelings of one of the few. Bruce trusted his integrity and confidence - so shall we.

Finally, you'll find when you read the Society page that Pam's really been keeping her ear to the ground and there's a whole bunch of new facts on *Game of Death* so don't miss it! With you again next month...

Felix Yen

Felix Yen
Editor-in-Chief

RARE RECORDINGS OF BRUCE LEE – PART I

No one doubts the importance of Bruce Lee's film soundtracks. As a way of recalling the epic moments in the Master's films, they are perhaps second only to a copy of the film itself. And as most collectors know, available recordings are by no means restricted to simply the backing soundtrack to each of his films. There are, for instance, many other versions of the theme tunes and if you're lucky, you may even find sound recordings of some of his television appearances. And therein lies a problem for some are what are known as 'bootlegs.'

Mention the word bootleg and one tends to think more of pop stars - The Beatles, The Rolling Stones, Elton John, etc. They are recordings that have been issued containing songs or Interviews that the artist or his recording company has not given permission to be released. They are therefore illegal.

Well, you may ask, what has all this to do with Bruce Lee? The answer is that, to the best of our knowledge, the Little Dragon is the only film star to have about a dozen albums, and several singles as well, unofficially released in the UK alone. And over the rest of the world, there are probably dozens more (in Japan, in particular).

It is, of course, quite possible, too, to bootleg 8mm film and though usually poor in quality, they're worth every penny to the collector. This becomes especially so when normally censored material is included. A prime example here has to be the 8mm version of *The Way of the Dragon* that contains the rarely seen double nunchaku sequence. Some of the works we will be discussing in this feature will be genuine releases, some will be unofficial. All, however, tend to be difficult to get hold of.

A very rare, and much sought after bootleg release is an episode from the American TV *Green Hornet* series. The quality is apparently excellent and it comes complete with soundtrack. Such luxuries have a high price. You may also find 8mm copies of Little Dragon film trailers. Though much cheaper, don't forget you'll only have two or three minutes of material in comparison with many of the others which may last upwards of thirty minutes.

Cassettes of interviews are fairly easy to find. They're fascinating and great to have, but take care. Most, if not all, you're quite likely to have read elsewhere, for instance in *KFM*. Don't, therefore, expect to stumble upon something unique. And a word of warning - there are also some very poor quality soundtrack cassettes of Bruce's films in circulation that really aren't worth having at all. They've probably been recorded direct onto a hidden cassette from inside a cinema!

The main reason for the poor quality of bootlegs is that, more often than not, they're copies of copies of copies - a situation that grows more irritating to the listener on every playback. Therefore, the recordings which we will be concentrating on will be those of good quality - good for the simple reason that they have been printed from a master tape. Many we believe to be legal anyway as they have been issued by a reputable company in Japan called Toho Records. They may well have secured rights from Golden Harvest to sell the recordings.

The four main albums available for *The Big Boss*, *Fist of Fury*, *The Way of the Dragon* and *Enter the Dragon* are pretty well known. One point worth remembering though, it that Japan really went to town on *Enter the Dragon* and produced a double LP. It's a fantastic version and we'll be looking at it in more detail later on.

First though, some information on albums that are best regarded as off-shoots from the four main films. Coming on the TAM label (that's Toho Records), there's *World of Bruce Lee Part One* (LP) YX6096, *World of Bruce Lee Part Two* (LP) YX6096, *Bruce Lee* (LP) YX7010, *The Way of the Dragon* (song - single) YT1065, *The Way of the Dragon* (tight sequence - single) YT1067, *The Big Boss* (opening to film - single) YT1054, *Fist of Fury* (song - single) YT1060, *Fist of Fury* No. 2 (contents uncertain - single) YT1061,

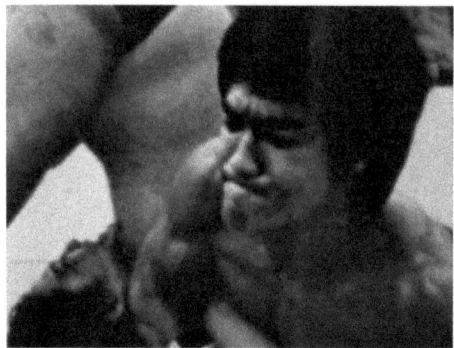

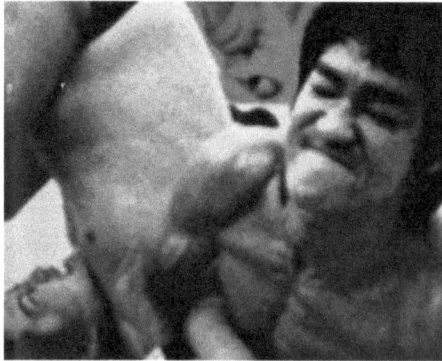

Theme from *The Green Hornet* (single) YT1073 (which also contains battle cries of Bruce that've possibly never been heard before), *Bruce Lee Forever* (EP) YT6001, *Fist of Fury* (EP) YT6002 and *The Way of the Dragon* (EP) YT6O03. Time now to deal in more detail with the four main albums. First up, *The Big Boss* - available mono or stereo with a running time 40 minutes - YX8017 (Toyo Records). While watching Bruce's first major film, you may have noticed a distinct lack of war cries. Naturally, the album reflects this and in some ways, this makes it the least interesting of the four soundtrack albums. It's hard to say exactly why the cries were excluded. It could have been that director, Lo Wei, and producer, Raymond Chow, decided to rely completely on the visual effect of the Little Dragon. Perhaps they failed to consider the impact the Master's cries were to have in his action sequences - after all, their only other screen contact with Bruce had been through *The Green Hornet* series and there was little in that to guide them! Also not included on this album is the first fight scene where Bruce's cousin gets into a scrap with some local thugs.

Side one, track one is entitled, 'Opening' and that's exactly what it is. If you remember the title sequence in *The Big Boss*, then you'll recall this music running along behind it. Track two, 'The Killing Fight,' is where Bruce Lee's two cousins go in search of two (murdered) brothers. The cousins end up at the Big Boss's mansion and soon they're slaughtered too.

Track three is called 'Search' and it relates to the part of the film where Bruce heads off to look for the missing relations. Track four is 'Fists of Justice' and it's also the main theme. Here, the local thugs from the beginning of the film gather forces to seek revenge on the Little Dragon's cousin for beating them up earlier.

They arrive at the ice factory and start a fight. Although Bruce has sworn not to get involved in violence again, he loses his temper when one of the gang takes a pendant his mother gave him. That's the signal for the battle proper to begin! Though there may be a shortage of war cries, there's plenty of moans, groans, thumps and bumps. Finally, at the end of it all, the theme tune starts again to end the track.

Track five is entitled 'Love Theme' and here Chow Mein is grieving over her missing brothers and relatives and Bruce comforts her. Side two opens on track one the 'The Banquet'. Impressed by the Little Dragon's fighting ability, the factory manager decides to make Bruce foreman. He's invited to a banquet for which the manager has hired girls, food and booze. The Little Dragon has a few drinks too many and his manager tries to persuade him to give up the search for his friends. Drunk he may be, but Bruce doesn't take the bait so the Big Boss sends over the heavy mob!

Track two, and here Bruce searches the ice factory only to find his friends - murdered, and hidden away in the ice. The Big Boss' son arrives, in time to inform Bruce that he's heading for the freezer himself! In the ensuing fight there are some interesting sound effects, including one of a saw cutting through the head of one of the gang. In track three, the Little Dragon plans his revenge. His reasons are new multiplied for, on arriving home, he stumbles over the bodies of many of his friends and relatives.

The album concludes with track four, 'The Life or Death Struggles/To be a Man.' At last, Bruce exacts his revenge by, first of all over-powering the guards, and that the Big Boss himself, in a truly epic struggle. Then, surprise - film-wise, that's all there is. However, on the album, there follows the song. To Be a Man - written by Joseph Koo, Wang Fu Ling and James Wong. It's sung by Mike Remedios.

And there we pull down the curtain for this month. Coming up soon, you'll find yet more track by track breakdowns of Bruce's films - in particular, of course, the fabulous and rather rare Japanese double version of *Enter the Dragon*. It stands to reason too, that sometime very soon, we'll also be hearing in recorded form, the soundtrack to *Game of Death*. Just how that's going to sound, KFM (at the time of writing) doesn't as yet know. One thing, however, we can be sure of - it's bound to be worth waiting for!

THE KFM INTERVIEW: ROY HOLLINGSWORTH

It's common knowledge that only a few fighters ever received Bruce Lee's seal of approval to go teaching his martial methods. Taky Kimura and Danny Inosanto are both well known now to readers of *Kung-Fu Monthly* and both have done much to honour and respect the name of the Little Dragon. Their hard and dedicated work has gone well recorded. This interview itself is something of a rare scoop. It was recorded for a British radio station some years ago - and hasn't been heard of or seen in print since. *KFM* introduces martial artist, and friend of the Master, Roy Hollingsworth.

KFM: Am I right in saying that you actually did train with Bruce Lee?

Roy Hollingsworth: Yes, for quite a number of years. I started about the end of '59, beginning of '60.

KFM: Was that when Bruce was starting to become popular?

Roy Hollingsworth: No, not really, this was very early on in his career. He was working in Seattle and was running a little school at the time. He'd taken on a few students - one of the first, was of course, Taky Kimura. I came about a year after Taky and Bruce was working then, with about 15 or 20 people. He was not long over from Hong Kong and virtually unknown at that time. Bruce revolutionised Kung Fu, especially in the United States. Right now I'm running the Bruce Lee School of Kung Fu, along with Taky.

KFM: Do you have many people coming to the school? (Editor: Remember, this relates to some three years ago.)

Roy Hollingsworth: Right now, we have a compliment of about 60. It's private and we don't charge any tuition whatsoever. It's actually a private club - there's no outside advertising.

KFM: Why don't you charge?

Roy Hollingsworth: Let me recap a little. At the beginning, even in the early days when Bruce first opened the school well, if anyone was charging forty dollars a month for lessons, then we'd be charging twenty. We were more interested in the purity of the art than in commercialising it. Bruce was a purist; he was not for the money end as he was an artist. When he died, Taky and I sat down and we talked it over. We decided to close the school down as it was in Chinatown in Seattle and move it to a different location. We decided to pick a nucleus of 50 people for pupils and we wouldn't charge a nickel.

KFM: Roy, how would you define the difference between Karate and Kung Fu?

Roy Hollingsworth: Well, there's lots of forms of both and in lots of cases you look at Karate and you look at Kung Fu and you're almost looking at the same thing. We're dealing now with individual schools of thought. Our school of thought is a lot different, our technique is a lot different. We use Wing Chun to start everybody off, which is basically the system Bruce learnt in Hong Kong, then we slowly put that into Jeet Kune Do. Altogether with the Wing Chun, it takes 4 or 5 years. The difference is a visual thing - it's hard to explain - you can't put it into words. You'll find lots of Karate and Kung Fu have the same end products just about, but Bruce's particular system is vastly different and it's Jeet Kune Do.

KFM: Would you agree that Karate is usually aggressive, whereas Kung Fu can be aggressive or soft?

Roy Hollingsworth: Yes, there's the soft and the hard form. There's many schools that have a balance of both. Then there's the hard school that's strictly force and the soft school, like Tai Chi.

KFM: Isn't Tai Chi more of an exercise?

Roy Hollingsworth: Yes, but within Tai Chi, is your system.

KFM: Where does Jeet Kune Do come in here?

Roy Hollingsworth: What Bruce was trying to do was get away from the old hardcore line of everything having to be done by numbers. What he was trying to do was get you to swim in the shallow end first, and then slowly push you into the deep end. He was trying to get away from the old code of fighting, the old code of martial arts. He wanted you to release yourself and learn to flow with your opponent. Bruce never believed too much in Kata. Don't establish yourself as a pattern fighter - learn to flow at the time with the motion.

KFM: When did Bruce open his schools?

Roy Hollingsworth: The first was in a university district of Seattle, and the one in Chinatown, in 1962, I think it was.

KFM: Roy, tell us how you think Bruce died.

Roy Hollingsworth: It's been a very controversial subject. There's been lots said and written and I would say 99 per cent of it is untrue. Exactly what did happen was this. Bruce died by taking a pill for a headache. In this pill was a drug that he was allergic to. His brain swelled up to three or four times its normal size and that was the end of him. It's as simple as that. Lots of people are allergic to this drug. If an ordinary guy had taken it, you'd have said, "Well, he's allergic to this drug and he's dead," and that would have been the end of it. But Bruce was a superstar, so he had to die a super death. It sells newspapers, magazines and that's the story.

KFM: Don't you think Bruce ended up being commercialised?

Roy Hollingsworth: To Bruce, it was a means to an end. What you see on movies wasn't Bruce Lee. In the dojo, he was an entirely different man. But he wanted to pursue the art the way he could do it effectively and that was being a movie star. It saved him a lot of time to practice his art. If he'd had a 9 to 5 job like any other guy, he'd never have made it. He'd have never made what he wanted to make out of himself.

KFM: Why did Bruce use the yin yang symbol?

Roy Hollingsworth: At the time we had the school in Chinatown, we didn't have a system. Well, some students were coming to us and saying, So and so's taking Karate and he's got a brown belt or a purple belt" or what have you, so we decided to start this yin yang symbol. It started off you had a yin yang all white, the second stage was green and white, and third stage was purple and white. There were a few others as well, but we did away with that a long time ago. It was just a thing the guys wanted as it gave them something to shoot for.

KFM: How did the grading work?

Roy Hollingsworth: It took about 4 to 6 months to get the first, all white, grade. From then on it was purely achievement.

KFM: Why didn't Bruce like classical styles?

Roy Hollingsworth: His idea was, there's no preconceived move that can possible work if the other man is thinking another way. You have a set move in your mind which is strictly classical and if the guy comes in at another angle, you're a dead man.

And there we have to leave this remarkable interview for this issue. It is remarkable in the fact that it should have lain dormant for all these years and remarkable too to the refreshingly honest answers supplied by Roy Hollingsworth. It's not often that we get word on the Master from such a close source and therefore it's useful to pick our way carefully through what he has to say.

His comment that 99 per cent of what has been written on Bruce was certainly, allowing for a little exaggeration, pretty much true at the time. A glance through many of the publications of two and three years ago reveals many a horrendous blunder. Readers have only to recall our recent double feature on misleading press information to appreciate that.

Roy's insinuation that the fables and fiction surrounding Bruce's death were largely made up by 'get-rich-quick' cash-in artists, backs up what *KFM* has said many times in the past. And it's interesting, too, to see how Roy Hollingsworth relates Bruce's outward commercial life to the Little Dragon's intentions of inward perfection. Perhaps a compromise in the truest sense!

Another point worth mentioning is the revelation of the origins of the famous yin yang sign so far as Bruce's school was concerned. By the looks of it, the Master himself nearly slipped into the trap of offering belts, grades and badges. That he later retraced these steps, is now martial arts history.

Soon, *Kung-Fu Monthly* will be picking up the threads again on this sensational interview. The second half will certainly be worth waiting for! Roy talks about how and why Bruce included many of the stunts in his films, plus his fight for realism. He discusses why many people still try to allow themselves to believe that the Master is alive and also what can be done to fight against future exploitation of the Little Dragon's star-studded career.

There's interesting news, too, about Bruce's attitude towards girls learning the arts and naturally he discusses as well, the great Jeet Kune Do rip-off. Finally, Roy Hollingsworth will be offering his own personal view on Bruce - as friend and as a teacher. Few people are as qualified as Roy to pass such opinions and we value his words on Bruce Lee, the Master.

THE BRUCE LEE SECRET SOCIETY

Hi, Pam here again, as the great *Game of Death* release date draws ever-nearer, this month I'm writing an extra-special Society column, devoted almost entirely to the sensational upcoming film.

It isn't all good news, I'm afraid. The first rumour I've heard is that many of the press release photos might be 'faked'. In fact, it's even been suggested that some have been taken from *Enter the Dragon*, with the faces of the new stars inserted by photo-trickery. I sincerely hope this isn't the case. To start with, I can see no reason why it should be necessary.

By the way, it'll be interesting to keep an eye on the amount *Game of Death* takes at the box office and to see how it compares eventually with *Enter the Dragon* and *Way of the Dragon*. The last time I saw any figures, *Way of the Dragon* had taken $27,000,000 and *Enter the Dragon* $25,000,000.

Back to *Game of Death* and it's time now for some hard facts! Apparently, the plot now concerns the rise of a young Kung Fu star called Billy Lo. Because of his rocket-like rise to fame (presumably mirroring Bruce's own phenomenal success), Billy is approached by a crime syndicate who specialise in making fortunes out of actors and sportsmen. The syndicate chief wants to sign up Billy and his girlfriend, otherwise they say they'll wreck his career. The name of the evil boss is Dr. Land and the character is played by Dean Jagger. Other stars appearing are Gig Young, Colleen Camp, Hugh O'Brien and, yes you've guessed it, Bob Wall (you can't keep him away!). Also involved in the plot, we're promised, are a regiment of motorbiking soldiers. According to our *KFM* Editor, there is every chance that well be running a special *'Game of Death* is here' *KFM*, devoted entirely to the new film. With any luck at all, that might even be the next issue!

Talking of features in the pipe-line; another goodie to look forward to is a possible interview with Norman Borine, who is the man in America running the unique Bruce Lee 'museum'. That'll certainly be worth waiting for.

A word now about Society members whose annual subscription is up for renewal (check on your membership card if you're not certain when the date actually is). It really does help us this end if you can get your renewals in as early as possible.

And that's about it for this issue. Next month the Society report will be back to normal, so I'll see you all then - PAM

Over the years, many readers have complained that they have difficulty sometimes in obtaining current copies of *KFM*. There are two ways around the problem. One is to take out a subscription at £4.50 for 12 issues. The other is this: If you'd like to supply your friends and make a little money for your trouble, we will supply the magazine at the following prices: 10 copies at 28p each, 25 copies at 26p each and 50 copies (maximum) at 24p each. The cost includes all handling charges. We must emphasise that this service is intended only for areas where *KFM* is difficult to locate. Also, cash must accompany all orders and no returns please! Send orders to *KFM* Bulk Buy Offer, 14 Rathbone Place, London W1P 1DE.

KICKBACK: THE LETTERS

And a big hello from me, Jenny, to yet another great set of letters from you the *KFM* readers! Once more, the whole question of Bruce's death is raised and I'll leave it to you, the fans, to decide on the evidence. So far as I'm concerned, the Master did die in exactly the way *KFM* has always said. I really believe that to feel otherwise is only wishful thinking. I'd say that Roy Hollingsworth has it right in this month's number two feature when he says 'Bruce Lee was a superstar so he had to have a super death.' We are convinced that the source of all these rumours was simply third-rate tricksters, trying to 'get rich quick.' I only hope one day I'm proved wrong. Some of the letters in this issue were in fact very long ones. Obviously, to fit them inside the magazine they have to be cut down - but I'm always sorry to have to do it. Please remember that when you're writing to me, the rule is always, the shorter the better. And now, over to you the readers...

BIRMINGHAM KUNG FU SHOW

Dear Jenny,
Replying to a letter from Raymond Wong which stated that, at the Birmingham Kung Fu film show, everyone who didn't get in was given their money back. But I know of at least two people who have not been refunded. They are John Sunderland and Frank McDonell. At the restaurant where we bought the tickets, John's name and address was taken - presumably for the records. So maybe Mr Wong can check and verify this. Unfortunately, both my fiends threw away their tickets in disgust after the night of the show. Were they better organised, we would like to attend more of these film shows.
Damian Sullivan, Birmingham

Dear Damian,
Thank you for letting me know the situation your end. So far yours has been the only complaint I've received regarding that particular performance, so it's likely that there has in fact been a slip-up in the refunding. If Mr Wong would like to get in touch again, I will gladly pass along the addresses of the people concerned.

CENSORSHIP

Dear Jenny,
I really do believe it's time we all got together and sorted out the censors. I recently saw *Fist of Fury* again and I was angry to see it got no mention in the publicity at all and was playing second to another piece of worthless junk. That was bad enough, but when the movie was just finishing, just as Bruce was leaving the house for the final dramatic scene, it ended, right there! Naturally, everyone screamed the house down, but to no avail. I spoke to the manager and he said it was the way it arrived.
Elvis Whetton, Streatham, London

Dear Elvis,
Believe me, I can understand just how angry you feel - it's the nearest thing I've heard to daylight robbery! To be strictly fair, though, you can't actually blame it on the censors. I'm quite certain they'd never made a decision like that. No, what's happened is simply that at one of its previous performances, somebody has obviously just snipped off the end of the reel and probably stuck it in their pocket! It's outrageous and I hope the cinema manager in question raised the matter in no uncertain terms with the people distributing the film.

KAREEM ABDUL-JABBAR

Dear Jenny,
Reading my month's copy of KFM No.36, in the article 'Adapt or Be Destroyed,' you say that the basketball giant, Kareem Abdul-Jabbar (formally Lew Alcindor) stands 7' 4" and is therefore nearly a foot taller than the Little Dragon. I have always considered Bruce to be 5'7" tall. Surely it should have read that Kareem was nearly 2' taller?
Steven Milsom, Beeston, Notts

Dear Steven,
Oops but would you believe, until you wrote in, we still hadn't spotted that awful error. Isn't it amazing what sometimes you just don't notice! I hardly need say that, of course, you're absolutely right. Kareem was indeed almost 2' taller than Bruce - all but 3".

BRUCE WOULD BE PROUD

Dear Jenny,
I am writing to tell you a little of my extensive gratitude for publishing such a fine quality magazine/poster. In fact, if the Master was able to see your valuable work, I'm sure he would be proud. To finish this letter, I would just like to say that I hope you will continue your work in keeping alive the name of the Master. Your loyal son and Master's disciple.
Mr Philip Ferris, Helston. Cornwall

Dear Philip,
Your words would I think echo the feelings of everybody here in the KFM office thank you for your letter!

IS BRUCE LEE REALLY DEAD?

Dear Jenny,
I wouldn't like to say whether or not Bruce is dead, but I read in a Kung Fu magazine that the Little Dragon was working undercover for an American narcotics bureau. In *Bruce Lee King of Kung Fu*, there is a picture on page seven which features his coffin. My sister pointed out to me that, on the right hand side of the crowd are two well known faces. Some people would that it's just a coincidence and that it isn't Bruce and Nora Miao, but if you look on pages 80 and 75 and compare them with page 77 - well, see what you think!
K.L. Wai Ling, Wheatley, S. Yorks

Dear Mr Ling,
You certainly seem to have been pulling out the stops on the research work! To start with, though, I should point out that the narcotics business was simply a story dreampt up by Max Caulfield in his book, Bruce Lee Lives, *and if you read the first few pages carefully, you'll see he admits it is only a story. So far as the picture comparison goes, I know what I think, so what about some of you readers giving me your opinions?*

QUICKIES CORNER

Rick Edwards, Coventry, West Mids - The animated Bruce Cartoon has been on the stocks for a year or two - more news when we get it. Suspect Clouse may be updating *The Man and the Legend.*

Philip Dee, Skipton, N. Yorks - I'm going to suggest reprinting the first few issues of *KFM* altogether as a sort of 'Best of *KFM*.'

Richard Lockwood, Cosham, Hants - Hope you do well in your project but, sorry, our pictures are part of a valuable collection and they have to stay in our offices.

No Name, Ipswich, Suffolk - Thanks for the *Game of Death* clip from *NME*.

Kasra Saghafi, N. Saltanatabad, Iran - Afraid the Kick and Dragon posters ran out long ago.

Steve (Bruce Lee Society No. 1439) - Thanks for the Christmas card.

Tony Walak, Mansfield, Notts - Sorry, far too many questions for the space I've got available! Most of the answers you'll find in either *KFM* or Bruce Lee King of King-Fu.

Andrew Walker, Middlesborough, Cleveland - Send 50p for *KFM* No.31.

David Vandyka, Hove, E.Sussex - To decide what's right for you, try as many styles as possible. Other people's opinions count little in the long run.

S.C.Murphy, Basildon, Essex - For a full list of Bruce's films, try and find a copy of a book by Verina Glassner.

O.Lonergan, Co.Durham - I'd say lots of today's Kung Fu champions were inspired by the genius of Bruce.

R. Chandarana, H.Hempstead, Herts - Glad you liked the Roots of Jeet Kune Do piece.

Colin Carruthers, Carterton - You'll have to advertise for *KFM* No. 1-3.

B.Lau, Ipswich, Suffolk - Bruce's *Tao of Jeet Kune Do* is available from Cimac Ltd, 606 Stratford Road, Sparkhill, Birmingham.

Colm Quinn, Limerick, Eire - Thanks for the *Game of Death* clip.

J.Stockford, Bristol - Thanks for the great sketches - they've joined our wall display!

Peter Thomas (Bruce Lee Society No. 1763), Northolt, Middlesex - Has lots of Bruce Lee magazines for sale.

THE POSTER MAGAZINES - VOLUME TWO

39

1978

EDITORIAL

Without a shadow of doubt, the name of the Master, Bruce Lee, continues to be spread far and wide. The interest shown by his public in the books, magazines and photos grows apace, especially with the coming of *Game of Death*. The legend blossoms as the Little Dragon lives on!

We've been inundated with letters on the subject of our main feature last issue which was that of Bruce's brush with the recording world. At last, over the next few months, *KFM* readers will be able to get to grips with the disc and tapes situation with our track by track analysis of what's available. Last issue we dealt with *The Big Boss* and this time, we move on to *Fist of Fury*. There's plenty of other goodies also in the pipeline, including some rare and expensive releases. This is information you won't find elsewhere, a *KFM* scoop investigation.

Number one feature this time around is a work entitled, *The Power of Bruce Lee*. Did he really win all his fights? What special skills did he have tucked up the sleeves of his voluminous garb? This month we piece together the full story of a man obsessed with success. And win he usually did, for few were able to match him in any department, be it cunning, skill, adaptation, or strength of purpose. The power behind Jeet Kune Do is the power that lay behind Bruce Lee.

Finally, stand by next issue for yet another great *KFM* competition. It's been a while since we had one so this time, it has to be something extra special - tune in then.

Felix Yen

Felix Yen
Editor-in-Chief

THE BRUCE LEE RECORDINGS

Welcome once again to the recording world of Bruce Lee. Last month we gave you a brief introduction to the intriguing memoria he left us - the sort of material that has been made available, though, sadly, much of it is no more. Last issue it was the turn of *The Big Boss* This time, to begin with, we turn our attentions towards *Fist of Fury*. Once again, the recordings hold some surprises. However, perhaps the most important change from *The Big Boss* LP is that, at last, somebody realised the importance of Bruce's war cries. They're here in full, swooping splendour - a tribute to the man who revolutionised Kung Fu and a joy to all those of us who honour his name.

Fist of Fury
LP No. YX7001 (TAM Label)
Running Time 45' 33" / Stereo.
Music by Joseph Koo, Ku Chia and James Wong. Sung by Mike Remedios.

Side One

Track one contains the main theme to the film. It sets the mood of the LP in the same way it sets the mood of the film. Suddenly, leaping out of the record grooves comes a fabulous roaring war cry from Bruce, followed by the deadly swishing of nunchakus (in super stereo). A great taster for all the dynamite action that's to follow.

The featured *Fist of Fury* song is next in line, spitting out some powerful lyrics and ending in a long, high-pitched war cry from Bruce. In fact this, and many other of the Little Dragon's screams that appear on the LP, didn't in fact occur in the film itself!

Track two is entitled 'The Death of Teacher' and naturally it concerns the burial of the Master. Bruce can hardly believe the passing away was due to natural causes and he delivers the line; "He was well, there was nothing wrong. How can a healthy man die?"

'We Are Not Sick Men' is the legend for the third track. It's the classic scene where

Bruce returns the 'Sick Men of Asia' plaque to Mr Woo of the Hongkou school and challenges them to prove it. One by one, he knocks them cold, until finally, the only man left standing is the school number two. He soon goes the way of the others! The excitement and energy the Little Dragon creates on this soundtrack is little short of remarkable. Without any visual aid, suddenly the listener is back there in the movie house - fantastic!

'I Shall Be Waiting Here' is track five and it's the well known love/parting scene where Bruce and his girlfriend discuss their future plans. The episode is strange in some ways for the relationship is never allowed to blossom. The title is also rather confusing for not once does either of them say "I shall be waiting here."

Track six is very powerful indeed. The Little Dragon stumbles upon two men who obviously have something to do with his teacher's killing. Bruce's anger comes bursting through the grooves of the record as he repeatedly demands to know why the deed was done.

Side Two

Bruce meets his girlfriend again in 'I Love You As Much As I Always Did.' In the course of their talking, he realises the interpreter, Mr Woo, has something to do with his teacher's death. Strangely, the scene where Bruce disguises himself as a rickshaw boy and finally confronts Mr Woo and kills him is not featured on this soundtrack.

Track two is where the fancy stuff begins. Bruce decides to take on the entire Japanese school single handedly. From all the sides, he is attacked - dull blows, hard cracks, smashes and bangs - he crushes somebody's head. The students lie dead around him. The Master's assistant appears and tries using a sword. Deadly swishing indicates the danger the Little Dragon has found himself in. Finally, Bruce kicks the sword into the air for it to plunge into his opponent's back.

The track breaks into a percussive background where he takes on the Russian Agent. There is tremendous poetry in their captivating battle as Bruce almost laughs his war cries. The blows come quicker and quicker, louder and louder, pounding, pounding, pounding until the Agent sinks to his knees. Bruce chops to his neck and the Russian is dead.

Only the Master of the school remains. The Little Dragon treads carefully back into the room. Unbeknown to him, the Master is waiting behind the door with a samurai sword poised over his head. The air whistles as the instrument of death misses Bruce by a fraction. A pole proves useless for defence so he grabs his nunchakus.

The Master lashes with his sword, the nunchakus retaliate - the crunch of metal and chain. The cudgels swirl faster and faster until finally, the sword is sent reeling from his opponent.

Now it's hand to hand. Deep, penetrating punches are thrown, loud and heavy, faster than can be counted. Bruce is the more accurate and he kicks the Master through the glass wall onto the lawn - the Master is slain. The Little Dragon has gained his revenge.

Track three is the finale and again, something strange is afoot. As everybody knows, in the film, Bruce returns to his school and gives himself up to the police, only on condition that his school is left alone. Finally, of course, he then makes his historic last charge and mid-air leap. For some reason, this is left out on the record.

To end the album, we return to the main theme from the first track. A fitting tribute

to what really is an incredible LP. At times, the listener must really feel the stylus is about to jump off the record. Were there to be no film - just the recording - it would stand in its own right as a masterpiece.

Time now to move on to Bruce's third great adventure...

The Way of the Dragon
LP No. YX7011 (TAM Label)
Running Time 36' / Stereo.
Music by Joseph Koo and James Wong. Sung by Mike Remedios.

What marks the difference between the cries on this album those of *Fist of Fury* is the variation in sounds that Bruce achieves. Obviously the success of *Fist of Fury* was due to

the fact that, not only was the action amazing, but so too was the soundtrack.

The Little Dragon must have realised what a difference it made in comparison to *The Big Boss*. So when his time came to direct a film (and write the screenplay), it's hardly surprising that he went to town on the war cries. And don't let it ever be thought that they were included just for the sake of it. Each and every sound uttered by Bruce, you could guarantee would be tailor-made to suit its particular situation to perfection.

On side one, track one, the music is just as you heard it in the film. The melody is easy to remember too, and that's always an asset to any movie. Track two is entitled 'The Dragon Arrives in Rome.' Landing at the airport, Bruce is met by a young lady who explains to him, the by-now-famous storyline, of the thugs threatening the restaurant. The Little Dragon promises his help.

'The Dragon's Way of Fighting' is track three and right away there's something interesting. Much of the film's first fight scene was cut in Britain but on the album it's all there. The sound of his double nunchakus spinning through the air accompanied by his screeching and whooping, the crunches as they crack into the skulls of the thugs are almost frightening. Bruce becomes an overnight hero and, for the fans, gives one of his best every displays of Chinese boxing.

Track four is simply called, 'Sharp Shooting' and it's here that the Little Dragon narrowly misses death from a gunman's bullet.

Track five is the album's title song and again, there's fabulous war cries and nunchaku sound effects to go with it.

And that's where we stop for this month. Next time, we'll continue *The Way of the Dragon* album and then move over to check the *Enter the Dragon*. After that, it'll be time for some of the rarer stuff and you'd better believe there's one or two real surprises in the pipeline.

And not only that, we'll also be letting you know just where to start looking for material you may not yet have even heard of! It's taken *KFM* many weeks of patient research to build up this dossier of Little Dragon recordings and we aim to make sure that you, the readers, can use the results. Back with you again next month for part three.

THE PUNCHING POWER OF BRUCE LEE!

It's a natural combination of three powers that goes to make up the super-power that was Bruce Lee. They are the physical, the psychological and spiritual powers - and all human beings possess them, although in differing degrees. It was the high degree to which the Little Dragon developed these God-given abilities that made him into the greatest martial artist the world had ever known.

You will probably have noticed that Bruce's physique, in comparison with a normal bodybuilder's physique, was totally different. There were no grotesque, bulging muscles on the Little Dragon. His body was streamlined and built for speed and endurance. It was a lethal weapon. And though many a weight lifter may be in actuality stronger than Bruce, put the two together in a ring and there would have been no doubt at all on the result. In many ways, it's rather like comparing a bull with a tiger. The bull has a great deal more strength but the tiger has the speed and agility to strike first.

So how did Bruce manage to develop his body to such a high degree without it becoming bulky? The answer lies deeply embedded in his unique training programme. Probably dynamic tension affected the issue more than anything else and the Little Dragon would spend many minutes of his day pitting the strength of his muscles against immovable objects.

For example, stand next to a wall with either your right or your left side facing it. Now, keeping your arm straight and pointing down, push the wall with the back of your hand, and keep pushing hard until your hand gets tired. For most people this will take a minute or two. When you stop your arm feels as though it wants to 'float' up into the air. The short exercise will have not only strengthened your arm a little, it'll also feel lighter.

Imagine doing the same throughout your body. Bruce did, and that's probably why he always appeared so light on his feet. Try and see how long you're able to keep pressing - Bruce was able to keep going for up to an hour!

Before the Master began any arduous training routine, first of all, he'd practice a warming up stage. Although he always trained hard, he also trained wisely. Well, he knew of the great damage to be done by doing too much, too quickly.

He'd start with simple exercises such as knee bends, cat stretches, toe touching, jogging on the spot and so on. Finally, when his circulation and body temperature were ready for it, he'd move to the tougher areas of his training programme.

Interestingly, he used very little in the way of external apparatus - at least in comparison to many other martial artists. He'd often rely on pitting the strength of his body against himself. For example, he'd put his hands together and push one against the other with all his might. This not only builds arms and shoulders, but also back and stomach muscles because of the great tension created.

And Bruce's neck was a pillar of strength in itself. It's obvious from looking at his photos that the thickness of his neck nearly equalled that of his head.

Suggested exercises to achieve this go as follows: rotate the head slowly in first a clockwise, then anti-clockwise motion to help get the blood circulating better.

Next, place your hands either side of your head and try pushing your head first one way and then the other. All the time, try to resist the action with your neck muscles. Following this, place your hands at the back of your head and try to push your head forward. Again, resist the action with your neck muscles. Finally, place your hands on your forehead and reverse the procedure. Building up these muscles takes time - don't expect to see startling results the following day!

One of Bruce's favourite pieces of simple apparatus was an iron bar attached by a piece of chain to the floor. He'd take the bar in both hands and pull. He did also use

weights at times, though not to the extent that weightlifters do.

Press-ups are a very popular way of building up arm and shoulder muscles but, predictably, Bruce didn't Just stay there. He'd tone up his wrists and hands by placing just his fingers on the floor - rather than the whole palm. Everyone knows by now of his one-fingered press-ups - a tribute to the strength he had in his upper limbs.

The Little Dragon did in fact use weights to develop his back muscles but after having once slipped a disc, they were used more and more sparingly. He discovered the back builds up quickly when using the following simple exercise, using a three foot plank of wood. Place one hand at either end of the plank and lift it to around six inches above the head. Now squeeze the wood as though playing a concertina, keeping up the pressure until tiredness sets in. Do the same thing behind your back.

Another exercise developed by the Little Dragon is to lay on a low table or wooden bed and, grabbing the two posts behind, lifting the entire body from the shoulder blades. This develops back, arm and stomach muscles.

Bruce was especially concerned as to the development of his stomach muscles. Much of the power and strength for both kicks and punches stemmed from this region and he built up these muscles to such an extent that they stood out. This is very rare, and usually one can only count six muscles in the abdomen area, but with Bruce you could count eight.

To help build up his mid-section, he'd get someone to drop a medicine ball on to his stomach repeatedly. Sparring also helped to a degree. Another favourite was sit-ups with a barbell on his neck. He'd often do a hundred straight forward sit-ups and then add the barbell!

Other stomach exercises he used were waist twisting, leg-ups, Bullworker stomach exercises, stretching back and forward, kicking each leg in turn into the air, and lying on the floor, keeping both legs about six inches off the ground for minutes at a time.

It's rumoured that Bruce once received an injury to his spine from a fight he had with a Japanese. The doctors, so the story goes, told him not to do any training for some time but the Little Dragon ignored them and carried on with his abdominal training. It's thought this training may have caused his early death, remember though, this is just a rumour.

The power in the Little Dragon's legs was just amazing. He could kick a 200 pound man across a room, kick a 400 pound punch bag so hard the chain snapped and kick so fast you almost felt the blow before you saw the kick coming!

To build up this power, Bruce did a lot of jogging. He covered miles a day starting slowly at first, then sprinting, slowly again and so on. He'd often follow that by riding his exercise bicycle at 40mph for up to an hour. On top of all this, the Little Dragon also quite frequently used a trampoline, doing mid-air splits and so on. Rope skipping kept him light on his feet and, he felt, taught him good breath control.

Skipping also greatly increased the strength of Bruce's ankles. Just how strong they became was clearly demonstrated in *Enter the Dragon*. In the scene where he is working out in his room, Oharra enters and the Little Dragon faces him, balancing perfectly on one leg.

It goes without saying that Bruce's training routine went far beyond just these few examples. His list of stretching, breathing and dynamic tension exercises was enormous. He tuned every fibre of his body into such a fine instrument of strength, energy, control, discipline and beauty, power could only have been the natural result.

Next issue we carry the investigation one step further. The psychological side of The Little Dragon was just as important as the physical. Well he understood the uselessness of having a superb body without knowing how to use it properly. And then we have to consider his spiritual powers. The whole of Bruce's art was based around the human spirit; the compulsion, the driving force to those years of success. Bruce summed up his feelings on this when he said, "Jeet Kune Do, ultimately, is not a matter of pretty technique but of highly developed personal spirituality and physique."

THE BRUCE LEE SECRET SOCIETY

Hello again, everyone. This month, I've left it to Jenny to spread the good news about *Game of Death*. Don't forget to read her full update on the storyline. So far as the Society is concerned, the New Year has really blasted off successfully, Though it's pretty hard work for me, the area lists look like they're doing their job and putting members in touch with one another but let me know if you're having any difficulties.

Interesting news from Alex Buttigieng (2199). He says he's heard a rumour that Madame Tussauds in London are having a wax model of Bruce made to put on display. It sounds fantastic and I'm checking it out.

Hot news from Jeff Millington (1127). He tells me that Regent Films, PO Box 54, Blackpool FY1 1SP, have just got in a new trailer of *The Big Boss*. It's in Super 8mm, runs to about 100' and it's in colour with sound. The price is £8.50 plus 25p p&p. Apparently it features Bruce's opening flying kick.

Derek Hamer (1944) has made his own Bruce Lee crosswords and puzzles book. He's really done it beautifully, with proper pages, pictures and so on. In fact, it's so nice, I'm thinking of trying to reproduce it for cost price only sale to all club members. More on that in the next News Sheet.

Meanwhile though, how about all of you working out your own puzzles or competitions. Try and make them something out of the ordinary if you can. The winning ones I'll give a prize to and probably also feature in one of the News Sheets to come.

Finally, let me remind you that subscriptions DO need to be renewed sometime! Check yours to see if the time is near. The price of joining OR renewing is still only £3.25 which just can't be bad. Don't forget, the address to write to is: The Bruce Lee Society, 14 Rathbone Place, London W1.

Would readers please remember that, at present, *KFM* is not running a Swop Shop. That particular service is run by the Bruce Lee Society for members only. That means, if you've got something to buy, sell or swap, then join the club!

Over the years, many readers have complained that they have difficulty sometimes in obtaining current copies of *KFM*. There are two ways around the problem. One is to take out a subscription at £4.50 for 12 issues. The other is this: If you'd like to supply your friends and make a little money for your trouble, we will supply the magazine at the following prices: 10 copies at 28p each, 25 copies at 26p each and 50 copies (maximum) at 24p each. The cost includes all handling charges. We must emphasise that this service is intended only for areas where *KFM* is difficult to locate. Also, cash must accompany all orders and no returns please! Send orders to *KFM* Bulk Buy Offer, 14 Rathbone Place, London W1P 1DE.

KICKBACK: THE LETTERS

Hi, it's Jenny here, and to keep the ball rolling, here's the latest information I have on *Game of Death*. The rewritten plot runs as follows: Fast rising Kung Fu star, Billy Lo (Bruce Lee) and his singer girlfriend, Ann Morris (Colleen Camp) are being threatened by a syndicate headed by Dr. Land (Dean Jagger). Despite harassment by Land's motorbike army, Bruce decides to fight back. Land strikes - during filming, his hit man, Stick (Mel Novak) swaps live ammunition for blanks and Billy is seriously wounded. He feigns death and when recovered, sets off in pursuit of the evil doctor. A mortally wounded Stick tells him where to find Land. Here's the original pagoda scenes. Billy blasts his way through the famous floors and finally confronts Land on the roof. The evil is destroyed! This new storyline sounds great and I can't wait for the April premiere.

POSTER REQUESTS

Dear Jenny,
I would like to say you have a great magazine. But I have one complaint. Could you please print other posters and pictures of Bruce such as from *Fist of Fury* where he is in the garden doing the flowing hand movements. And how about Bruce doing his thumbs up sign in *Enter the Dragon*? Seeing his rippling muscles - wow!
Pam Hornsby, Welling, Kent

Hi Pam,
Yes, I know what you mean about those muscles but the trouble is, we can only print what we can get. You must remember that the pictures we print come usually from the stills taken by a photographer on the set. If he didn't happen to have his camera, snapping at the right moment, the result is no picture.

DAN INOSANTO BOOK

Dear Jenny,
I'd just like to recommend to all Bruce Lee fans the book, *Jeet Kune Do: The Art and Philosophy* by Dan Inosanto. It's excellent. It's packed with photos of Bruce, his training equipment and his style. It puts forward not only the art of Jeet Kune Do, but the way it works in everyday situations. There are numerous unseen photos and lots of facts about Bruce. The book is for the fan and the martial artist.
Dan Muka-Bazi, Bradwell, Norfolk

Dear Dan,
Very many thanks for writing in and reminding us about this book. In fact, it is very well known to Society members as it was in the book mail order list for a while. So far as I know, it's still available in Kung Fu book shops and though expensive, probably well worth the money. Also, of couse, don't forget our superb contribution to that particular slice of history, The Secret Art of Bruce Lee.

BRUCE AND MUSICAL INSTRUMENTS?

Dear Jenny,
You asked if anyone had seen Bruce on TV. Well, about a year and a half ago, the show The Musical Time Machine was on TV. They were playing Kung Fu Fighting by Carl Douglas, and suddenly, to my surprise, I was watching Bruce fighting in The Big Boss. It's the only time I have ever seen the Little Dragon in action as I'm only 14. Now I can't wait to see them all. One last thing - did Bruce play any musical instruments?
Noel McHugh (Society No. 1489), Dungannon, Co. Tyrone

Dear Noel,
Well now, that's one appearance by the Master I hadn't heard about until now! It must have been a real shock to suddenly be confronted by Bruce when least expecting it. Who knows, maybe soon we'll be able to see all his films right through on TV. Regarding your question about musical instruments, the only thing I can find any confirmation of is that he handled a percussion track in The Way of the Dragon. Whether he did anything like that at all regularly, I doubt it.

POCKET BOOK IDEA

Dear Jenny,
Thanks for a great magazine! I'm writing in to suggest an idea that I have. It's for a Bruce Lee book with a difference. It would be pocket size (say, 3-4" by 2-3"). Then all Bruce Lee fans would be able to carry it with them all the time. In any moment of boredom, you could read about or even look at pictures of the Little Dragon - and brighten up the moment! As to contents, well, an introduction with a run down on Bruce's life story, the main contents dealing with Bruce's philosophy and his art of Jeet Kune Do. Also a run down on his films, TV appearances and so on.
Paul Wade, Boulevard, Humberside

Dear Paul,
Now that's what I call a good idea. I can see it all now - streets full of people all clutching their copy of The Thoughts of Master Bruce. But seriously, the more I think on it, the better the idea gets. Perhaps when we do our Best of Kung-Fu Monthly, we could present it in that style.

RESPONSE FROM RAYMOND CHOW

Dear Jenny,
Many thanks for putting my letter in *KFM* No.32. I promised there that I'd let you know of any reply I got from Raymond Chow concerning *Game of Death*. Well, here's my Christmas present to all *KFM* readers (as indeed it was my Christmas present from Raymond Chow). *Game of Death* is due to be released here in April and not December as originally scheduled. Finally, Golden Harvest sent along a previously unpublished photo of Bruce so would you like it for your next issue?
Dave Langley, Runcorn, Cheshire

Dear Dave,
Great to hear that you've received the fabulous news too and that premiere day is almost on us. My underground news service tells me that it has, in fact, already had a trial showing somewhere out East and it went down a storm. Finally, yes, please send along the photo as it might be one we haven't had.

QUICKIES CORNER

David Cormack, Edinburgh, Scotland - For more information on obtaining the 8mm films of Bruce Lee, contact Regent Films, 2 Palladium Buildings, Waterloo Road, Blackpool, Lancs. They seem to have a pretty fair selection.

Richard Lockwood, Portsmouth, Hants - You don't have to remind me just how blatant these Bruce Lee rip-off films are. Thank heavens the real thing is out soon.

Marlon Whetton, Streatham, London - Yes, there were cuts in most of the fight scenes you mentioned. Don't always assume though that what you see in a still photo is always actually in the film. It often isn't.

Mike Devereux, Warrington, Cheshire - Thanks for the news of the new Japanese double album *Enter the Dragon*. Actually, my spies tell me it's now available over here. More details soon.

Atul Sahai, Bihar, India - Glad to hear the magazine's getting out your way.

Michael Kellard, Ipswich, Suffolk - Yes, issues No. 27, 28, 30 and 31 are still available from our mail order department. Sorry, we have no recording available of the Bruce Lee Last Interview.

Hugh McGowan, Immingham, South Humberside - Writes to say he's got issues No. 1-5 on sale. He's looking for offers.

Ian Martin, West Croydon, Surrey - Writes in to say that he is looking for *KFM* No. 1, 2 and 3.

Ian Beaton, Barry, Glam - Thanks for letting me know that Little Dragon films still bring in capacity crowds in cinemas in this country. I must say whenever I try and catch one of the Master's films, I always end up wishing I'd got there a little while earlier!

THE POSTER MAGAZINES - VOLUME TWO

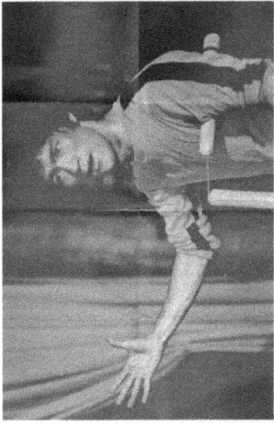

1978

EDITORIAL

Hi there Kung Fu fans. Welcome to an historic edition of *Kung-Fu Monthly*! And as usual we've two fabulous features for you to sink your teeth into - both stacked solid with Bruce Lee fact and discussion.

And not only that, there's another of our famous competitions. Pam from the Bruce Lee Society has very helpfully agreed to set the questions and arrange the judging. She gets plenty of practice from her quarterly News Sheet competitions so you can bet it's going to be good.

Feature one and it's time for the biggie! Sorry, we've postponed the Rare Recordings Part Three to bring you sizzling news of the Little Dragon's final film. At last, a stack of super-hot information has come our way on just how the film's been completed. And there's plenty of quotes too from director, Robert Clouse, and all the up-to-date news on the story behind the making of *Game of Death*. This has really got to be a fantastic scoop.

The premiere is approaching!

The support feature this month details the mind-blowing brain power of the Little Dragon. His legendary control over his emotions and the crystal clear way he handled his thoughts and ideas are already well documented. How he achieved these remarkable powers and how he linked them to the potential of his magnificent physique is described here in Part Two of *The Power of Bruce Lee*.

Finally for this month, at press time, we can't get any news of the exact date when *Game of Death* is to be premiered! EMI assure us that prints of the film are on the way and that a full publicity campaign will be mounted shortly. Probably May is now more likely than April.

Felix Yen

Felix Yen
Editor-in-Chief

GAME OF DEATH REVISED

First it's been on - then it's been off - then it's been on again! The story of *Game of Death* has been one wrought with ups and downs. Why was the film left on the shelf for so long after Bruce's death, and why has the plot been changed so drastically from the one originally envisaged by the Little Dragon? The answers to all these questions are now becoming a little clearer, thanks to a scene-setting press handout we recently managed to obtain from Hong Kong. So far as *KFM* knows, much of the information we print here has never been seen before in this country. At last, we're getting the truth behind the making of Bruce's last and most eagerly awaited film. Read on and discover the fascinating story behind the production. At last, it's *Game of Death*.

Where better to start than, for all of our readers who are eager for detailed information, with the cast list? Here it is:

Billy Lo is Bruce Lee, Jim Marshall is Gig Young, Doctor Land is Dean Jagger, Steiner is Hugh O'Brien, Ann Morris is Colleen Camp, Carl Miller is Robert Wall, Stick is Mel Novak, John is Kareem Abdul-Jabber, Pasqual is Danny Inosanto, Lo Chen is Hung Kim Po, Henry Lo is Roy Chaio, David is Tony Leung, the Surgeon is Jim James, the Doctor is Russell Cawthorne, Goldteeth No. 1 is David Hu, Goldteeth No. 2 is Peter Gee, the Boat Captain is Don Barry, the Record Producer is Jess Hardie, Steiner's Driver is Lee Hau Lung, Doctor Land's Macau Driver is Albert, the Sanatorium Doctor is Roz Hudson, Director is Eddie Lye, Assistant Director is Peter Nelson, the Referee is Stephen Nicholson.

Main credits for the other side of the camera run as follows:

Producer - Raymond Chow, Associate Producer - Andre Morgan, Director - Robert Clouse, Music is by John Barry, Special Effects by 'Far East Effects,' Motorcycle Stunts by 'Stunts Unlimited, Inc.'

The plot of the film was covered in the last *KFM*, but for the sake of completeness, here, briefly, it is again.

THE POSTER MAGAZINES - VOLUME TWO

Bruce plays a fast rising Kung Fu star named Billy Lo. Unfortunately for him, his career comes to the attention of arch criminal, Doctor Land. Land specialises in exploiting artistic and sporting talent. Billy is undecided whether or not to fall in with the evil Doctor's plans and he fears for the safety of his girlfriend, Ann.

He makes up his mind to fight back but Land strikes first by having his hit man, Stick, shoot Billy in the film studio. Billy uses this opportunity to feign death and when recovered, he goes off to combat the evil gang.

He gets to Macau and promptly kills a Karate fighter called Miller in a rigged bout. However, his way to Land is blocked by Steiner, one of the Doctor's henchmen. Land decides to finish Billy, and to do this, he captures Ann. Billy, although realising full well that it's a trap, goes to rescue her from an old warehouse.

Having just got inside, Land's army of motorbike riders come crashing into the building. Billy routs them all - including Stick, who just before dying, tells him where the boss is. Naturally, Billy sets off to put an end to the whole business, and that he does, with the

Doctor eventually falling from a roof.

The story behind the making of the film is a long and interesting one. There's little doubt that more and more information will appear as the months roll by. The first obvious point to make is that the plot as it finishes up, bears little resemblance to Bruce's original vision.

The reason for this looks to be more than somewhat to do with the amount of time the production's been sitting on the shelf. The long years since the Little Dragon's death have given other film companies the opportunity to piece together their own rip-off versions. It's therefore understandable that Raymond Chow decided to come up with a new plot.

Judging by the colourful story line, the final, revised version has more in common with *Enter the Dragon* than with *The Big Boss*, *Fist of Fury* or *The Way of the Dragon*. This may, perhaps disappoint some fans who were looking forward to the more Orientally-aimed original version. But that said, the important thing is that it's nearly ready to be shown and at last, those famous fighting scenes are to get a public airing!

It seems a long time since the early days after Bruce's death. Many fans at the time believed that his apparent demise was simply a publicity stunt to advertise his film. Despite the prophecy in the title, sadly time has proved this not to be so. The Little Dragon did, however, leave behind enough material for the film to be completed.

The going has not been easy for Chow and Clouse. The new script has had to be tailored to fit the original fight scenes and other actors have been brought in to fill the gaps. The production to date has cost, according to Chow, around US$3 million and, judging by the press information handout, a good deal of hard work has gone into the final product.

During filming in Hong Kong and in Macau, props reached mammoth proportions. A stadium that seated over 3,000 people was knocked up in only eleven days which was something of a record. We're also told that a seventy-foot wall was built to take the weight of a battery of heavy neon signs, in just a week. It's also claimed that more extras were used in making *Game of Death* than for any other Hong Kong movie.

Of interest to the technical, is the news that the special effects team (Far East Effects) had to make up 3,000 square feet of special 'safety' glass.

It's pretty clear from the new story line that hairy motorbike riding sequences are a strong feature of the film. It's *KFM*'s guess that the idea of using the bikes came along as a way of overcoming the Bruce Lee 'double' difficulties. Pictures have been seen - although not in this country yet - of a rider taking off the Master. He's dressed in the famous yellow *Game of Death* one piece suit and, wait for it, the actor is wearing one of those helmets that covers the head entirely and features a 'shaded' visor!

In the warehouse scene in the film, the Stunts Unlimited team display their skills by crashing in through the side of the building and just about managing not to damage anything, or anyone. In fact, the only mishap seems to have been a skid caused by a patch of oil.

Much of the final filming was carried out at night - often from around six in the evening to six in the morning. And such is Clouse's admiration for the man who's film he took over, he repeated shot after shot until he got it just how he wanted it. He remarked, "Bruce Lee was a perfectionist. He couldn't stand anything that didn't come up to the high standards he set himself. I wanted to make sure that *Game of Death* would be a fitting memorial to him."

Certainly Clouse knew well the way the Little Dragon's mind worked. After all, they were together on the filming of *Enter the Dragon*. And It's hardly surprising that most if not all of the other actors and film, crew felt, like Clouse, that *Game of Death* deserved nothing short of perfection. Remember, others on set included Dan Inosanto, Taky Kimura and Bob Wall.

The shooting of the final footage was not without its difficulties. The special effects people had problems trying to create heavy rain for one scene - because Hong Kong is rationed at the moment to only six hours of water a day. And to add insult to injury, nature was promising to show how it should really be done with threatened typhoons.

But finish it they did, with great cooperation from the local electricity company and Cathay Pacific Airlines who flew over much needed props from Bahrain at high speed. Clouse also has much to thank the Macau Tourist Association for their assistance during the week's location shooting on the Portuguese Island.

Bruce once said, "It doesn't matter how big or small a man appears to be. He is nothing without his integrity and ultimately a man is what he does, not what he says." *Game of Death* was designed to be an extension of just this philosophy and only time will tell whether the original intention comes through unscathed. Robert Clouse has certainly tried to recreate the atmosphere by his insistence on shooting in the East, rather than in the States. He says, "You couldn't recreate that Oriental atmosphere of Hong Kong on a Hollywood stage for a million bucks."

The final verdict lies with all of us. Would Bruce have liked it, or would he have disowned it? Not long from now well have the answers.

THE SPIRIT WITHIN

Last issue we looked into the Little Dragon's physical power, his training programme, his exercises and so on. Much of the apparatus he used was home made and ingenious and, judging by the letters we've had back from readers, the details we gave have been much appreciated. This month, however, we turn the coin over to look at the other side of Bruce's power - the enormous spiritual force that he so painstakingly developed. A powerful muscle needs to be under the tightest of control, and a superbly toned body needs only the clearest of directive influence. We investigate Bruce Lee's mental training programme to find the clues he has left us.

The psychological side of the Little Dragon was, to him just as important as any of his physical abilities. There was no point, he felt, in developing a marvellous physique only to have a brain that could not adequately control it. Indeed, Bruce once remarked that if emotional control hasn't been carefully studied, the result will frequently be failure in combat.

No matter what skill a fighter may possess, a 'tight' brain will not link properly to a 'loose' body. Outside distractions may well interfere with abilities. Bruce felt strongly that, without mental training, one's mind, courage and confidence, attitude, awareness and conquest over fear was wholly at stake.

In fact, the key word here is 'fear.' And not only does this mean fear of one's opponent; it also means fear of oneself. In a moment's hesitation, all may so easily be lost.

Sparring is an excellent way of training the mind. For the best results, opponents should be changed as often as possible so that moves won't become familiar or predictable. In many ways, that is the trouble with having just one 'style.' Without ever having even met a single style fighter a good opponent will already have a reasonably clear idea of what to expect.

Many fighters believe that, after a long time, they develop the ability to foresee an attack coming before it has even started. And more than that, it's possible to develop a technique where, by use of certain facial or body movements, an opponent can be lead into making the action you want him to make! The development of this kind of acute mental ability borders closely on the realms of Extra Sensory Perception (E.S.P.)

Such was Bruce's mental control, he was able to convince his, at times, tired body that it wasn't in fact needing rest at all! With this frame of mind successfully adopted, a fighter can keep going far longer than he would under normal conditions.

To gain full control over one's mind is to stay calm in the most tense and difficult conditions - and not to let emotions control the train of thinking. Such control will save valuable resources of energy.

One of the first mental conditions to overcome is that of worry, depression and nervousness. That state of mind wastes fantastic quotas of energy and can also be very damaging physically.

"Without control of the mind," says Bruce, "there is always the danger that a move will be made with the first thing that comes into your head. Thus, if that move comes from an uncontrolled mind, it ends up as an uncontrolled move - thus leaving you wide open." Remember though, that control of the mind doesn't mean a person should never lose their temper or cry, or laugh. The important thing is to be able to control that emotion should the need arise. It's common knowledge that Bruce had a short temper and a hilarious

sense of humour. Most of the time, he allowed these emotions their complete freedom.

The intake of alcohol presents the mind with a false picture of its immediate situation. Bruce recognised this and never drank.

Naturally, this whole discussion is very closely tied to the development of Jeet Kune Do. By studying all styles, not only was he able to extend the range of his knowledge and technique to almost infinite horizons; he also kept his mind fighting fit by constantly feeding it new situations. Putting it in a nutshell, he said, "Any technique, however worthy and desirable, becomes a disease when the mind is obsessed with it."

And just as the Little Dragon did not confine himself to one style of fighting, nor did he confine himself to just one line of thinking. Here are some interesting and relevant quotations that Bruce made at times during his life:

"The mind is originally without activity, the way is always without thought."

"Concentration is the narrowing of the mind."

"Conserve your energy - but attack decisively, confidently and with a single mind."

"To be of no mind means to assume the everyday mind."

"The mind must be wide open to function freely in thought. A limited mind cannot think properly."

"A concentrated mind is not an attentive mind. A mind not in a state of awareness cannot concentrate. Awareness is never exclusive, it includes everything."

Bruce has said that the 'body feel' is a harmonious interplay of body and spirit - and both are in separable. He was well aware that, without spirit, his immaculate physique could never have reached the perfection it did. In fact, the whole of his art was based around the spirit.

Somebody who loves, say, football will put their whole spirit into the game. The skateboarder, for instance, will never have that same feeling when playing football. Bruce once summed up his philosophy by saying that, "Ultimately, Jeet Kune Do is not a matter of petty technique but a highly developed personal spirituality and physique." Stressing the point even further, he then went on to explain that his hands, arms, feet and legs were tools - and these tools, he felt, stood as symbols of the invisible spirit.

Getting those tools into fine shape is a process in which the spirit plays a big part Bruce built his body with spirit, and he trained hard with spirit. "Training", he said, "deals not with an object, but with human spirit and human emotions." But yet, the very strength of one person's spirit can break another's. It's also true to say that that very breaking lends a feeling of great power to the victor.

The Little Dragon obviously had the experience of breaking a man - not only physically, but spiritually. He once wisely remarked that, "Our sense of power is more vivid when we break a man's spirit then when we win his heart. You can win a man's heart one day and lose it the next. But when we break a proud spirit, we achieve something that is final, absolute." The mark of any good athlete or sportsman is his ability to make it look easy. The master of his art looks comfortable, confident and fully at ease. And he is the master, for he is controlling his emotions and saving his energies. Even in defeat, he accepts the situation with composure and good grace, knowing full well that his time may come another day. There is no disgrace in being beaten. The spirit provides the will for action, the mind transmits this well to the muscles of the body which in turn perform what they are being asked. Naturally, all this takes place in just a split second - far too short a time for any constructive thought. Actions have to be instinctive and correct. The only way to achieve this happy state is with full control over the mind. Without it, the desired chain of split second events is broken. The human spirit can create and it can also destroy. It is the centre point of everything and no one ever explained this better than Bruce when he said, "The spirit is no doubt the controlling agent of our existence."

THE BRUCE LEE SECRET SOCIETY

Hi, I am here with some really hot Society news!

When member Arthur Stone (1150) told me some time ago that he wanted to produce a movie on kung fu, I knew he was going to be in for a tough time, especially as he wanted to rope in plenty of Society members. As I couldn't offer much in the way of organisational assistance, I instead placed an advert for the idea into a past News Sheet. Well, I'm pleased to say the response has been very good.

Arthur and Glynn Barker (1567) are going to produce the first member's movie, to be entitled, *The Travellers*. It's going to be made in July this year and, naturally, it will be honouring our great Master, Bruce Lee. The film will be made on location in the Lake District and basically, the plot follows the direction in which Bruce was travelling. In fact, the plot is to be a logical extension of his film career. It's set in China in the last century. A group of martial artists called 'The Travellers' help a village defend itself from a group of bandits in the mountains. Tao, a young villager, falls in love with the chief bandit's daughter and when her life is threatened, he reluctantly betrays his people. When he in return is betrayed, he goes on the rampage, eventually meeting the chief in a fight to the death. In so doing, he restores honour to his family name.

We're hoping that maybe we can make the film available to Society Members and *KFM* readers at a later date (probably around Christmas). But now is your big chance to appear in "The Travellers." We need extras to appear as travellers or bandits. Martial arts expertise is not necessary, but helpful. If you're interested, please write to Glynn Barker in Sheffield. Also, please don't forget to enclose a stamped and addressed envelope.

Finally, all the main parts are cast with the exception of a 'leading lady' - who must be Oriental. Any interested ladies out there, please write direct to Arthur Stone at Stapenhill.

Wow, doesn't it sound great? See you next month with lots more news - **Pam**

Over the years, many readers have complained that they have difficulty sometimes in obtaining current copies of *KFM*. There are two ways around the problem. One is to take out a subscription at £4.50 for 12 issues. The other is this: If you'd like to supply your friends and make a little money for your trouble, we will supply the magazine at the following prices: 10 copies at 28p each, 25 copies at 26p each and 50 copies (maximum) at 24p each. The cost includes all handling charges. We must emphasise that this service is intended only for areas where *KFM* is difficult to locate. Also, cash must accompany all orders and no returns please! Send orders to *KFM* Bulk Buy Offer, 14 Rathbone Place, London W1P 1DE.

KICKBACK: THE LETTERS

Hello, it's Jenny here with another bundle of reader's letters. Actually, it's been a while since I thanked all of you for so marvellously keeping the Little Dragon ball rolling. Honestly, nothing gives me so much pleasure as ploughing through your thoughts and opinions each month. And not only that, you've no idea just how useful the letters are in keeping the magazine informed on the current state of Bruce Lee affairs. The controversy raging right now regarding the Bruce and Linda lookalikes in our *Book of Kung Fu* is a case in point. I'm happy to say however, that this particular problem seems to have been straightened out or has it? Read on!

DAVID CHIANG

Dear Jenny,
I enclose an article on David Chiang from an Ulster newspaper. It contains part of an interview where David discusses his film career and fighting abilities. He boasts about being able to kill a man and then openly lies about Bruce. With this kind of attitude, surely he can never replace Bruce as the King of Kung Fu?
Hugh Craig, Ballymena, Northern Ireland

Hi Hugh,
Thanks for the cutting. I notice at one point that David says, "Most of all, I would like to make a really good film so that everyone would know that I'm not just a stuntman. Not even Bruce Lee succeeded in doing that." What a nerve! I find it hard to believe that the quotation it correct and in many ways, I hope it isn't!

EXCHANGE AND MART SCAM?

Dear Jenny,
Please could you help me? I am a serious martial artist and train very hard. I sent off a letter in answer to an advertisement that appeared in the *Exchange & Mart*. It said Bruce Lee tapes for sale so I sent for information. What I got back included an offer for a cassette recorder and an application form for horse race betting. Do you think the whole thing is a con?
Mr G. Hill, Warrington, Cheshire

Dear Mr Hill,
It's really hard to say until you've actually got the goods advertised in your hands. I must say I find it hard to imagine a genuine source of Bruce Lee information getting involved in horse race betting but I suppose you never know. The important thing to remember is that, if you do order something and it either doesn't turn up or it's no good and you can't get a refund - always get back to the magazine or paper that carried the advert. These days it's them who have to make sure the customer is happy.

CENSORSHIP

Dear Jenny,
A bit of bad news for all fans. I've received a letter from the British Board of Censors saying that the nunchaku scenes in Bruce Lee movies would be censored even more. This has unfortunately proved true, because when I went to see *Fist of Fury* three weeks ago, the nunchaku scenes were less than before.
G. H. Singh, Linthorpe, Cleveland

Dear Mr. Singh,
Thanks for the information. I wonder whether what you heard was just one man's opinion or whether it was an official view. The fact that Fist of Fury *was more chopped than usual may be more due to breakage - or perhaps even theft - than anything else. I know for a fact that the most recent prints of the film are far less chopped than the originals. I guess it's a matter of luck which one you come across.*

PICTURE COMPARISONS

Dear Jenny,
By now you've probably had hundreds of correct opinions about the picture comparisons of Bruce in issue No.38. I'd like to say that if maybe Mr Ling had bought a copy of *The Book of Kung Fu*, he would find our friend on page 55 sitting in mourning at Bruce's funeral. I'd take a wild guess and say he is one of Bruce's brothers. Even so, I cannot say I blame Mr Ling's sister's findings - there is a most remarkable likeness between the two.
David Ashby, Bury St. Edmunds, Suffolk

Dear David,
Thanks for sending along your interpretation of this strange old business, here's a couple of other people's thoughts on the matter.

Dear Jenny,
I think I've solved the mystery that Mr Ling wrote about in issue No.38. If he looks at page 55 of *The Book of Kung Fu*, he will see the two people he mentions are members of Bruce's family. The photo does not identify individuals but I think the man with the glasses is Wu Ngan (Bruce's long time friend) and the girl is Bruce's sister, Phoebe.
Carl Jones, St. Helens, Merseyside

Dear Carl,
That's an interesting theory but to check, I'll have to go find some other pictures of the two from that period.

Dear Jenny,
I've looked at the photo and I'm astonished how much this man looks like Bruce. I have always believed Bruce to be alive, I will always see him as being alive. Unfortunately, this is not a picture of Bruce. Standing in the picture is not the Little Dragon, but an actual member of his family. Looking on page 55 of *Super Kung Fu*, you'll note that the same person is sitting with Linda. The girl in the picture is the one he thought was Nora Miao.
Glynn Barker, Greenhill, Sheffield

Dear Glynn,
Judging by the weight of evidence from all the letters I've had in, it seems pretty conclusive that the man in the photo isn't the Little Dragon. But, that said, there still seems a great deal of confusion at to who he actually is. Wu Ngan looks like favourite at present but does anybody else have different

QUICKIES CORNER

Trevor Beaumont, Gainsborough. Lincs - I'm afraid Bruce's nunchakus shown in No.21 are unobtainable. I'm sure they were specially made him.

Valda Johnson, Hemel Hempstead, London - I'm not quite sure why you didn't find that shop advertised in the last News Sheet - I've passed the letter on to Pam. Don't forget you can buy past issues of the magazine from our mail order department.

G. Jenkinson, Rotherham, S. Yorks - Thanks for the big poster side ideas - We may take you up on it.

Stephen Daly, East Dulwich, London - Anabolic steroids have been put forward as part the reason for Bruce's death but it's not conclusive.

C. Joelson, Kirkby, Liverpool - Info on the 8mm films is in No.39.

Mr K. Close, Gosport, Hants - Bruce is buried at Seattle despite rumours to the contrary, recently. Suggest for more info you contact Pam at the Society. Also, so far as I know, there is no US fan club nearby.

Ameen Malik, Bedford - All the mail order items you mention are now finished - Bruce's *Tao of Jeet Kune Do* can quite easily be bought from Cimac in Birmingham. Sorry, Treasure Kit 2 not ready yet but hang on!

Owen Lonergan, Esh Winning, Co. Durham - the *Game of Death* suit idea was dropped as we simply couldn't find one of good enough quality.

John Paul Evans, Cardiff, S. Glam - So far as *KFM* is concerned, there is no new King of Kung Fu. There's no Wang Yu fan club so far as I know.

Mr S. Sharma, Canning Town, London - Sorry to say the Angela Mao picture wasn't ours to keep - So far as I can discover, it was borrowed from Cathay Films of Soho Square.

David Telford, Silloth, Cumbria - I'd suggest a book on weight training to answer your query. It's pretty complicated.

EDITORIAL

    Hi there Kung Fu fans. The big moment has finally arrived! Just a week ago, before putting pen to paper for this landmark issue, I caught a special showing of *Game of Death*! What I saw was the raw print with the opening sound had yet to be put on and it was completely uncut.

    I'm not going to jump into a description of the legendary viewing right here as that's been reserved for our main feature inside. But, what I do have to make is this very important statement.

    I've heard on good authority that the censors are indeed intending to remove the famed nunchaku sequence between Bruce and Danny Inosanto. At the time of writing this, an appeal has been lodged and I've yet to hear the final answer. The reaction in Hong Kong to the news has been swift. According to word I've received, Raymond Chow is now threatening to withdraw the film completely, should the censors refuse to back down. This would be a fantastic tragedy.

Kung-Fu Monthly is going to do all in its power to prevent such a happening. Assuming the worst, I suggest that every single *KFM* reader write direct to the British Board of Film Censors immediately saying, "Regarding the film *Game of Death*, I demand that the last remaining footage of Bruce Lee be left intact so that his fans throughout the country may be able to witness in full his unique skills." Add some words of your own to describe your personal feelings on the damage they are doing. The address to write is: 3 Soho Square, London W.1.

As a second line of attack, Pam is organising a petition which she, herself, will be presenting to the Film Censors. More details on that inside. Finally, may I say that I hope all this proves to be unnecessary but sadly, I fear the worst.

Felix Yen

Felix Yen
Editor-in-Chief

THEY CHALLENGED THE MASTER

The history of Bruce Lee's challenges goes back a long way - back in fact, to those well-remembered days in Hong Kong when, as a street fighter he was just beginning to hone a rough edge onto the skills that were ultimately to earn him a fortune. Let's not delude ourselves - in those days, Bruce was just as likely to lose a fight as win. He had little idea then of the theories of Jeet Kune Do. His brief was simply to survive - in the best way possible. In those days, challenges came thick and fast and egos needed to be satisfied. It wasn't until later on that prospective opponents realised the risks they were running when signing-up for a contest with the King of Kung Fu!

The early Little Dragon was weedy, thin and sickly. He had few friends and he was frequently picked on by other local kids. Try as he may, he rarely won fights and at the end of a battle, he was left lying in the gutter, dirty and bloody.

His father, Li Hoi-Chuen, was well aware of the problem and suggested he look to the martial arts as a way out of it. Together they practiced the basic tenets of Kung Fu and gradually Bruce found his health improving and his mental outlook, far more optimistic.

The young Little Dragon became positively obsessive. In an interview he later gave to a Chinese paper he said, "I was a troublemaker - aggressive and bad tempered. Whenever I met anyone that I didn't like, I would keep saying to myself, I'll challenge him, I'll challenge him."

This rather childish attitude was to stay with Bruce, more or less up until the time he went to study philosophy at Washington University. Only there did he begin to realise that one doesn't necessarily need to fight in order to win an argument or disagreement.

A case in point was a row he had with a pupil from one of the local schools. Though only thirteen years old at the time, he challenged the far older boy to a fight. A crowd of Bruce's friends gathered around and the Little Dragon began instinctively to move in strange patterns - never repeating, always changing. His opponent tried to run away but was pushed back to the battle by Bruce's friends.

The young dragon lashed out a punch but so preoccupied was he, he allowed himself to go off-balance. The boy pushed in desperation, Bruce fell over and his opponent pummelled him to defeat. Not only did the young Master lose the fight, he also lost many of his friends.

A while later on, Bruce met up with an old acquaintance and together they began discussing the martial arts - Wing Chun in particular. They fought each other to try to prove whether the style was weak and the bout was a draw. Even so, Bruce decided to accept his friend's invitation to go along and meet his teacher, a man called Yip Man.

When they arrived, there was a kind of free-sparring contest going on, the teacher versus the students. Right away, the Little Dragon observed they weren't doing very well and, rather brashly, he stepped up to Yip Man and said so.

"You can do better?" asked Yip Man, "Okay, attack me." "No, I'm ready, you attack me," replied Bruce. But before the young Dragon had got his words out, Yip Man had struck. Bruce was totally stunned. Yip Man lashed out again, this time drawing blood from the Dragon's face. The teacher struck again and Bruce fell to the ground.

Again he callenged the teacher and again and again he was hopelessly beaten. Despite, or maybe because of the thrashing, it became obvious that Yip Man had plenty to teach him. The confrontation came as a godsend. Even before he'd gone, Bruce had been well

ISSUE BONANZA! NEW 'DOUBLE' BACK

IT'S BEEN A LONG TIME SINCE BONANZA'S 6 & 7, BUT WE'RE MAKING UP FOR IT IN STYLE!

The new GIANT Back Issue Bonanza consists of:

KFM 33: Spiritual Wisdom issue
KFM 34: Golden Harvest Interview scoop!
KFM 35: Secret Art Checkout

KFM 36: Famous 'Adapt or be Destroyed' theory
KFM 37: Silent Flute revival details
KFM 38: First time in print: The Roy Hollingsworth Interview

KFM 39: Rare Recordings Checkout... part 1
KFM 40: 'The Spirit is Strong' – Bruce's ultimate battle!

Update your KFM collection with these eight incredible issues FOR ONLY £1.50!!

Rush your cheque/postal order (made out to KFM, please) to: Giant Back Issue Bonanza:
Kung-Fu Monthly
14 Rathbone Place
London W1P 1DE
Club members price... £1.20 ONLY
(Please allow at least 4 weeks for delivery)

aware that, without his gang behind him to back him up, he was nothing. This couldn't go on any longer - he had to be his own man. He studied Wing Chun hard, under the venerable direction of the old Yip Man.

Gradually, with the acquisition of new and improved fighting skills, Bruce's outlook on life began to change. He studied diligently and the story is well known of how he tricked his fellow students into going home when he wanted the individual attention of his teacher. Yip Man, however, was no fool. He had a good idea what was going on, but then again, he recognised the great talents of his cunning young pupil.

One day, an ideal opportunity turned up for Bruce to test his newly developed skills. A gang leader challenged him to a fight to the death, to take place atop a nearby tall building.

For the first time ever, the young Dragon foreswore the use of additional weapons. Never again would he find it necessary to make use of his fountain pen dagger. His skills and his senses were all he needed.

It was a testing moment for Bruce. The fight began and they circled each other slowly, neither wanting to make the first move. Other members of the gang looked on, ready to give assistance should it be needed. The leader produced a dagger and started making dangerous thrusting motions.

Bruce prepared himself for a counter-attack. He produced a lightning kick that literally booted the knife from the leader's hand. It curved away uselessly into the night air. So amazed was the leader, he allowed the young Dragon time to strike again. A powerful jab to the shoulder and a kick to the knee and Bruce's opponent was down.

The rest of the gang, stunned, looked on in disbelief. Their reaction turned to horror as their leader was dragged to the edge of the roof. Bruce turned around, gave one of his cheery smiles, and slung the injured thug over his shoulder and carried him to hospital. The doctors confirmed a dislocated shoulder and a fractured knee cap.

This none-too-pleasant fracas did, however, gain Bruce a great deal of respect from the various local heavies. They decided to keep their distance.

Not long after this famous roof-top battle, Bruce left Hong Kong for the United States, to pursue the study of philosophy at Washington University. At lunch times or in free periods, he would spar with other students and, naturally, it was only a matter of time before he received a serious challenge. Word had got round that the young Chinese student was good and one opponent in particular wanted to see how good. In many ways it was a tortuous meeting for Bruce - the opposition happened to be the best in town at western-style boxing and carried a punch like a sledge hammer.

Once again, the Little Dragon rather forgot himself and became cocky. He began making flowery moves to try and confuse his opponent. They weren't good enough! Bruce caught a smack on the jaw that sent him reeling back onto the grass. He returned for more, but all the time, the straightforward boxing style kept Bruce at bay.

The Little Dragon was very angry - not so much against his foe, as against himself. Thus began his great search for information. He bought hundreds of books on every conceivable type of fighting technique. He realised his knowledge of the martial arts had to be comprehensive and for hours he even studied films of such legendary boxers as Joe Lewis and Muhammad Ali.

His studying became almost an obsession - even while eating or while attending lessons, he'd be working hard at his fighting arts. The harder and harder he trained, the more determined he became that never again would he be defeated.

With the opening of his school, word soon spread about his reputation. Challenges from other schools came thick and fast. During one of Bruce's demonstrations, a Japanese Karate black belt started goading him. Bruce tried to quieten things down by explaining that he wasn't trying to downgrade Karate, or any other style, he was simply trying to make clear his own methods.

"You know nothing," persisted the Japanese who then told everyone not to listen to a word Bruce was saying. The Little Dragon had no alternative but to accept the challenge. They moved to a handball court and agreed certain ground rules - no poking in the eyes and no kicking in the groin.

The Japanese opened the fight with a scream and a powerful kick that Bruce avoided with no trouble at all. Before the intruder had fully reached the floor, he found himself being punched from one side of the court to the other. The blood-soaked Japanese had been defeated in exactly eleven seconds!

Word quickly spread, and instead of dissuading opposition, still the challenges came thick and fast. One such famous incident was the Wong Jack Man episode. "Let's spar first," he suggested to Bruce. "You challenged me, so I make the rules," countered the Little Dragon. "No warm-ups and no holds barred." Within minutes of the bout commencing, a group of Wong Jack Man's students were trying to break it up - to stop their man being beaten to pulp. Bruce's immediate reaction, however, was one of depression. So far as he was concerned, the fight should have lasted seconds, not minutes. That meant more training, more studying.

Before long, the film world was beckoning and Bruce returned to Hong Kong to inaugurate the final historic phase of his career. He headed for Thailand for some location shooting and there was pestered by a Thai boxing champion for a fight. Finally, the Little Dragon just had to accept. They both agreed to a number of rules and, because of these restrictions, Bruce knew the battle would last rather longer than usual.

The Thai had an amazingly powerful kick and one blow would send even the Little Dragon flying. Honours were more or less equal until Bruce caught his opponent in the chest with a strong kick. The Thai got mad and came at the Master with combinations of kicks and punches that they'd agreed would not be included. Still Bruce refused to break the rules.

Another powerful kick from the Little Dragon and the Thai went madder still, poking at Bruce's eyes and kicking to the groin. Nothing, however, could persuade the Little Dragon to sink to the same level. He simply continued to deal out legitimate kicks and punches to the head and chest. The Thai champ lost balance and Bruce delivered the last powerful kick - the champ fought no more.

The film set was the home of many of the later challenges that Bruce received. Once, on the *Enter the Dragon* set, he was talking to John Saxon about various styles of boxing when one of the extras came up and said, "I reckon you only act out your fighting. You're not for real."

The Little Dragon totally ignored him, but still the loud-mouth continued to bait him. Bruce decided the only way he'd be able to continue his talk with John Saxon was to accept the challenge. "Okay, whenever you're ready," threatened the actor. Bruce's fist blurred into the jaw of the extra and knocked him out cold. While others around applauded and laughed, the Little Dragon resumed his discussion!

Naturally, Bruce was confronted on many, many occasions - far too many times to mention here. Hopefully soon, we'll be able to recount some more of the challenges faced by Bruce Lee. Some he lost, most he won, but all were significant to the man known as the Little Dragon.

GAME OF DEATH REVIEWED

The time, 11.30am; the place, a viewing theatre at the EMI building in London's Golden Square. Leaning back in my seat, it's hard to believe that now, right now, I'm about to witness an event that's been talked about, even dreamed about, by all Little Dragon fans over the last three or four years. Thoughts flash through my mind - has the script rewrite been a success, indeed was it really necessary, even bearing in mind that the plot had been ripped off by competitors? Also, how much of the final footage was actually to be included - had Chow used it all, or was he saving some of it for a rainy day? And, of course, there was the question uppermost in my mind, how well has the double worked - how successfully has Robert Clouse pulled together the two halves of the film - the old and the new? I was about to find out!

The opening title sequence lashes out and we're away. It's a good starter, comprising partly of flashback stills from Bruce's other films. They dart around the screen like angry wasps. The primary visual aid is the Norris confrontation at the Rome Colosseum and we see a great deal of it. It did cross my mind to wonder why this should have been used so extensively, considering so much original *Game of Death* material was reputedly available. The answer gradually became clear.

Chow and director, Robert Clouse, have tried to be very clever with the storyline, but, in my judgement, posterity might well condemn them for being too clever by half. The action opens with us dropping in on Billy Lo (at times played by Bruce Lee) as he completes another scene for his new Kung Fu film. Any resemblance between this film and *Fist of Fury* is wholly intentional - in fact, it grows all the time!

The drift is obvious right from the start - Chow would have us, at least half believe that what we are watching is a flashback on the life of the real Bruce Lee. It's mostly the double at work, however, and although there is certainly some physical resemblance to the Master, the Kung Fu - though quite good is way below the class of Bruce. It's a pity too, that our double's answer to the Little Dragon's war cries sounds more like the rantings of an angry cat!

To help get us over these problems, there are frequent cutaways to shots of Bruce from his earlier Golden Harvest, films. It works rather well most of the time. The snippets are aptly chosen and really don't look too much out of place. However, another ploy used just on one occasion only - and I could hardly believe my eyes - was a shot of somebody in a chair wearing a sort of Bruce Lee mask!! I sincerely hope this doesn't end up in the final print.

It's worth my pointing out here that I'll not, in this feature, be giving you a blow by blow commentary on the entire film as that could well spoil your later viewing of it. What I will do is pick out particular areas of importance.

You may, by now, be wondering exactly who this mysterious double is. Well, the astounding news is that you're going to have to keep on wondering. Raymond Chow has decided to keep the actor's name strictly anonymous, even to the point where he hardly admits to his existence! It really is extraordinary. Some of us who caught the historic first showing were putting money on our old friend, Bruce Li, but I'm not so sure. One thing that is certain, however, is the double's non-too-inspiring voice - especially when compared to the rich tones of Bruce Lee.

Meanwhile, back inside the film, I'm going to discuss another area of the plot which is bound to stir up a maximum amount of controversy. Billy Lo, as you may recall from last issue's synopsis, is shot and badly wounded by 'Stick' the hit man, just as he is filming the final scene in his new film. Well, hold on to your seats as that final scene just happens to be an actual re-run of the last scene in *Fist of Fury*. Bruce proper flies though the air with that famous leap before we cut to the double lying badly wounded on his landing mat.

And if you're starting, like we did, to wonder just where fact starts and fiction ends, hold on to your hats for this one. Billy decides to throw Dr. Land and Stick off the trail by feigning death. To make this ruse all the more effective, a real street funeral is arranged and wait for it, because you're not going to believe it - they've used actual footage taken at Bruce's funeral, complete with shots of him in his casket!

I've got to admit the inclusion was effective, although there were mutterings of bad taste from some of those sitting around me. At least now we know why *The Man and the Legend* was pulled back to Hong Kong sometime ago as it looks like many of the funeral sequences were taken directly from it.

Apart from the fact that I found it disquieting to see the confusing mix of fact with fiction, somehow I couldn't help feeling that fuel was being deliberately added to the highly unlikely theory that the Master is still alive and that his death was just a hoax. Such ideas have only really been put around by those wishing to cash in on an apparent sensation. Of course, the most popular theory of all was that it wasn't Bruce in that casket - just a good dummy - and Chow has exploited this fable, lock, stock and barrel. And by making the storyline in many ways a parody of the life of the Little Dragon, I can't help feeling that more damage will be done.

It's not until quite late on in the film - where Billy Lo is about to confront the not-very-evil-looking Dr Land that the thunder starts to roll. It'll surprise no one when I tell you that Land's residense is, of course, the original *Game of Death* pagoda - at least from the inside. Suddenly I became aware of the sheer inadequacy of our hard working double. One moment he's running up the stairs and the next, we cut to Bruce. The effect is electric! The film, at a rather late stage, immediately bursts into full dramatic life. The truth is driven home. Bruce's films without the presence of Bruce Lee would be very ordinary indeed. The appearance of the Master gave me a feeling of flood gates being opened.

He battles Danny Inosanto in that incredible nunchaku sequence and, yes, it really is totally amazing. Why anyone should want to chop out what must be the finest, ever recorded nunchaku battle is absolutely beyond me. It seems the censors' theory is that kids will go out and make their own weapons - and possibly injure somebody. Could someone please tell me why then, we're allowed to see stabbings on screen? A kid doesn't even have to go and make a knife as every kitchen must have dozens of them! Back to the real *Game of Death*, however, and after dispatching Danny, Bruce bounds upstairs for a bizarre but riveting confrontation with sky-scraper-high, Kareem Abdul-Jabbar. Kareem is the last line of defence, so the door is now wide open for Bruce (or at least his double) to polish off the boss. At this point, some of you may be wondering why I missed out the fight scenes on all the other floors. I'll tell you why. They aren't there! It's rather obvious that Chow has indeed decided to hold back much of the prized footage so that he can keep the ball rolling with one and maybe two follow-ups. In fact, rumour has already reached me that the working title for the next film is *Bruce Lee's Last Game*.

Has it been a good idea to water down the precious remaining footage in this way? Of course, the real Little Dragon fans are bound to go and see anything that contains scenes of Bruce fighting. But, even so, there's going to be a good deal of fidgeting in cinemas around the country as the faithful await the appearance of the Master.

Obviously I've been checking the film very much from the point of a true Bruce Lee fan. What, you may well ask, is in it for the general cinema-going public? Well, leaving aside the politics, you're left with a Bond-style, martial-action thriller. I don't have to tell the true fans to go see it, but anyone hankering for an occasionally electrifying evening's entertainment would be well advised to catch a showing of *Game of Death*. The excitement's worth waiting for, and if the *KFM* petition works as I hope, the finale's a double-must.

THE BRUCE LEE SECRET SOCIETY

Hi everyone. This month's Society page is going to be a bit different this month!

By now, you'll all have heard the awful news of what the Censors are thinking of doing. I'm sure you'll all agree with me that it's an absolute disgrace. To remove THE major fight scene from *Game of Death* makes me feel like going around to their offices and chaining myself to the railings in protest!

Something has GOT to be done, AND FAST. You've already been asked to write direct to the film Censors to register your total disapproval with what they're very likely going to do. Now what I want is for YOU to help me organise the quickest petition ever in the history of Great Britain. We got around 5,000 signatures together for Raymond Chow some while ago and I'd say we ought to be able to double that.

As you'll have already read, Raymond Chow is thinking of withdrawing the film completely, rather than see the best of the action sliced up. The only way to stop this is to act fast!

Write the following onto a plain sheet of paper and try and get as many people as possible to sign their approval:

"I/we are shocked and astounded to hear of the British Board of Film Censor's decision to remove from *Game of Death*, the principal nunchaku battle scene. Bruce Lee was, and remains for many people, the greatest Kung Fu artist the world has ever seen. It is outrageous that the last remaining footage containing his unique skills should be treated in such a barbarous fashion."

When you have got as many signatures as possible post them off to: *Game of Death* Censors Petition, Kung-Fu Monthly, 14 Rathbone Place, London W1P 1DE.

Remember there is always a chance they will reverse their decision, but if, by the time this petition is collected, they haven't, I personally will deliver the signatures to their offices. No doubt many of the staff here at *KFM* will want to join me.

Lastly, may I apologise for the slightly late News Sheet last time; it was entirely due to overwork! A timely reminder to anyone reading this who isn't a member of the Bruce Lee Society; JOIN UP NOW. There's no other club like it in the world and for all the good things you get - a badge, stickers, membership card, photos, regular News Sheets It's got to be amazing value at only £3.25 a year. Contact me, Pam Hadden at The Bruce Lee Society, 14 Rathbone Place, London, W1P 1DE.

KICKBACK: THE LETTERS

Hello, Jenny here, and welcome to this very special edition of *Kung-Fu Monthly*! It hardly needs me to say that there's an awful lot happening at the moment but please don't forget to support Pam's petition for *Game of Death* as I reckon it could be one of the most important things we've ever asked you to do. More good news this month, for the first time for ages, there's a new Bruce Lee single out - and it's a real cracker! Not only has it got a fantastic disco beat, there's also Bruce Lee screaming his way through both sides (he actually says a couple of lines too!) It's great to hear a disc tribute to Bruce that totally matches him in style and action so let's try and make it a top 20 hit. The title, by the way, is *Dragon Power* and it'll be out on the Satril label on June 9th. Time now to move on to the letters!

LONGTREET SHOWN ON TV

Dear Jenny,
I'd just like to get some facts right about Bruce Lee on TV. In *KFM* No.39, Noel McHugh said that Bruce appeared in *The Musical Time Machine* in a scene from *The Big Boss*. May I correct him by saying that the scene in question was in fact the fight between Bruce and the Russian in *Fist of Fury*. Also, the TV station round my way (STV) have shown one of the *Longstreet* episodes where Bruce got the star billing. It was called *The Way of the Intercepting Fist*. Not only that, around two years ago they showed *Marlowe* where Bruce had the role of a Chinese heavy. So you see, if discerning fans keep their eyes open, they may be able to see more of the Master than they thought.
Colin Wilkinson, Falkirk, Stirling

Dear Colin,
Pardon me while I emigrate across the border! It looks to me like Scottish TV have a far more refreshing attitude than many other stations I could mention. Keep me informed on any future developments, Colin.

EXCHANGE AND MART RIP-OFF

Dear Jenny,
I would like to tell you about something that happened to me about two weeks ago. In the paper, the *Exchange & Mart*, someone was advertising a Bruce Lee tape saying it contained discussions on Bruce Lee films. I sent off for it and, 2 weeks later, I received an ordinary C60 cassette wrapped in newspaper. When I started to play it, I felt sick. There was an ordinary kid talking on it and I could hardly understand anything he was saying. He couldn't even pronounce JKD or Wing Chun and only one side of the tape was used. The ad is still in the paper, so watch out all you Bruce Lee fans. The tape cost £7.50 and I'm not exaggerating when I say it's not worth 50p.
Roy Stannard, Clapham, London

Dear Roy,
Another sad tale indeed. Apart from warning everybody else about this, I suggest that you take issue with the publishers of *Exchange & Mart*. They are responsible for the advertising the paper carries and I'm sure they'd be interested to hear what you have to say. You could also, of course, get on to the consumer protection people.

WAY OF THE DRAGON IMPORT

Dear Jenny,
In your Rare Recordings article in *KFM* No.38, you give brief mention of a *The Way of the Dragon* import from Hong Kong. Well, I also have a copy of that print and although the quality is only fair, the scenes are fantastic. It shows Bruce using the double nunchakus which has to be seen to be believed. I also have a copy of *The Big Boss* cinema trailer which lasts for five minutes. Both the print and the sound quality are fantastic.
Ian Hamilton, Sunderland, Tyne & Wear

Dear Ian,
Thanks to you, and everybody else who wrote in, congratulating us on our Rare Recordings features. It seems we've really hit a warm spot here and, though we're not going to be running it in every issue, from time to time we're going to be adding to it - particularly as more readers send in information.

GAME OF DEATH

Dear Jenny,
I have a point to make about *Game of Death* that concerns not just you there at *KFM*, but the whole Kung Fu world. I have reviewed the rewritten script you mentioned and the outcome seems to me rather anti-climatic, possibly even disappointing. The film will obviously be seen by those of us who have long-awaited the Dragon's return like the coming of Christ - almost. But the latest script doesn't look too promising. Unlike the emotional power of *Fist of Fury*, in *Game of Death*, using a stand-in could shatter Bruce's power. I'm looking forward to its release, but nobody should go expecting to see the Master's greatest work. It may just be another typical Hong Kong film.
Elvis Whetton, Streatham, London

Dear Elvis,
Point taken, Elvis, and I think there's many of us here who feel the same way. In fact, from talking to our Editor (who has of course, already seen it), the message seems to be very much to check out the amazing Little Dragon action, but, sadly, don't go expecting to see a great film.

MEMORY OF BRUCE LEE

Dear Jenny,
I went to a fair in Mansfield and on one of the stalls I came across a record called In *Memory of Bruce Lee*, by John and Rosalind. I wondered if you had heard it.
Michael Daft, Mansfield, Notts

Dear Michael,
Yes, I have heard it before. It came out pretty quickly after the death of Bruce and though it didn't make the charts, as a tribute, I thought it rather touching. And talking of singles, don't forget the one I mentioned earlier - I reckon it's a must.

REGENT FILMS

Dear Jenny,

Thank you for advertising Regent Films, I bought *The Way of the Dragon* for £32.50 and it was more than I dared hope for. It includes most of the nunchaku sequence! You don't see much of Bruce spinning them, but it does show him wipe out each of the thugs, bar one. Also, I don't know whether you know it, but some of the Colosseum fight was cut. Bruce really pounds Chuck's face with several whooshing blows that sends Chuck's head lashing from side to side. In my film, Chuck also tries to copy Bruce's dancing style and gets a punch in the mouth.

Alan Anson, Preston, Lancs.

Dear Alan,

Glad to hear that the film was well worth getting. Often it's not until you come across something like this that you realise just what has been removed from feature films.

QUICKIES CORNER

Kevin Foster, Chopwell, Tyne & Wear - Sorry, *Bruce Lee King of Kung Fu* was only available as soft back in UK.

Miss G. Kalst, Southall, Middlesex - Hope to be able to help with records soon - For the *Tao of Jeet Kune Do*, try Cimac Ltd, 606 Stratford Road, Sparkhill, Birmingham.

Zandra Simpson, Blackpool, Lancs - Only two books on Shaolin that I know of and both from the above address.

Terry Antoine, Walworth, London - Quality *Game of Death* suits never made it over here but dark blue imitations are on sale in some Kung Fu shops.

John Hill, Croxteth, Liverpool - I agree. A Bruce calendar would look great. Can't promise, though.

David Telford, Silloth, Cumbria - Bruce Lee's *Tao of Jeet Kune Do* is the only fairly comprehensive book available.

Allan Davis, Palmerston North, New Zealand - I agree, kicking posters are the finest - A pity there aren't more around.

T. Trent, Poole, Dorset - The records we mentioned are available - Try through a major distributor. Many back numbers are available - Contact our mail order dept.

W. O'Connell, Cheltenham - Bruce Lee Lives has been out of print for a while your best bet would be second hand shops.

A.Sykes, Bramcote, Warks - Bruce didn't so much change his name - His parents did it for him.

Hazell Johnson, Brixton, London - It must have been marvellous meeting Mr & Mrs Run Run Shaw - You should have sent them along to us for an interview!

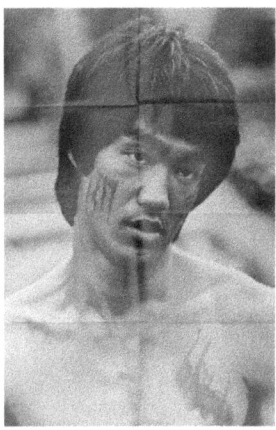

42

1978

EDITORIAL

Hi there Kung Fu fans. By the time you're reading this, the *Game of Death* film will have hit the UK cinema screens! I'm looking forward to hearing your views on it. One slice of information by the way, is rumour has it that the double was in fact played by the martial artist who won Linda Lee's audition to play the part of Bruce in her film. I'm still trying to get confirmation on that one. Whoever else it was, it seems the odds are now stacked against it being Bruce Li.

Now that many of you have seen *Game of Death*, I'm sure the talking point in your letters will be the dreadful hacking out of the Dan Inosanto fight - an insult to a superb fighter. Feature One this issue is an attempt to redeem that terrible loss. *KFM* researcher, Eddy Pumer, managed to view the uncensored print not just once, but several times and right here, he gives us a blow by blow commentary of the Inosanto action. I'm not pretending it's going to take the place of the original. On the other hand, it definitely places a good second!

Next up this month, it's time to hit the Bruce Lee LP trail again. The last two episodes sure stirred up some interest, judging by all the mail I saw on the subject. This time, we polish off *The Way of the Dragon*, then check the famous Japanese double album on *Enter the Dragon*. There's plenty more to come from this direction - you wouldn't believe the number of Lee albums that are, or at least have been, on release.

Lastly this month, have you written to the film censors yet? The address was in the last issue and have you sent us your petition for final delivery by hand, to the censor's office? I'm relying on your help to see that justice is done - I know I count on every single reader!

Felix Yen
Editor-in-Chief

BRUCE LEE VERSUS DANNY INOSANTO

Game of Death's anonymous Bruce Lee double turns in some fairly stunning fight sequences (though fans will be quick to notice the speeding-up in some places). Not surprisingly, many of these are based on fight routines featured in earlier Little Dragon films. When, however, the Master enters the set, all stand-ins are forgotten. It goes without saying that the Inosanto and Jabbar confrontations are classics - all the more disgusting therefore that half the martial feast has been sliced away to protect us, the paying customers! *KFM*'s views on this particular example of mutilation are well known - the direction and presentation of the Inosanto clash are indescribable, pure Bruce Lee. Well, not quite indescribable! Eddy Pumer has taken up the censor's challenge and, gleaned from several viewings of the forbidden footage, he offers here a detailed appreciation of the battle of the giants. We haven't tried anything like this before but we feel on this occasion, the experiment is well justified. *KFM* presents its own, uncensored report on the finest nunchaku dual ever recorded of film - Danny Inosanto versus Bruce Lee.

It's pretty well known that Bruce and Danny were the 'guvnors' of the twin cudgels. Inosanto was in fact the original teacher to the Little Dragon of this particular weapon. He, however, would be the first to admit that it was Bruce who carried furthest the exploration of the nunchaku's possibilities.

We join *Game of Death* close to the spot where the censors make their first, deadly incision. Bruce is walking up some stairs in what was the pagoda, but is now a restaurant. He's dressed in the famous and familiar yellow and black-striped one-piece tracksuit and wearing a pair of similarly styled sneakers.

On the side of the staircase hangs a thin blue stick and bag containing a pair of nunchakus. Bruce carefully slides the stick through the string of the bag and climbs the stairs. He's carrying the bag in the way Dick Whittington did in the well known picture.

Danny Inosanto sits waiting for the Master on a sort of throne affair. He's wearing a

kind of Samurai outfit and a red headband. Dan sees Bruce approaching and coolly picks up the two red sticks that lie on the table beside him. The excitement raises as he taps out a strange rhythm on the floor as Bruce does likewise.

Suddenly, Inosanto attacks to Bruce's face. The Master retaliates by lashing out at his opponent and jutting his forehead. Compounding his advantage, the Little Dragon strikes again this time sending one of the red sticks clattering harmlessly away. Bruce seizes it and does a peculiar backward hop. He raises it to his shoulder... they now have just one stick each. The Master smiles at his foe almost benignly as Danny tries another attack. He can't get near him!

Dan tosses aside his remaining stick and produces from behind his back, a pair of red nunchakus. Bruce removes from his bag his own set - yellow with a black stripe. The two of them swirl the cudgels around in menacing fashion. An interesting point here is the fact that Danny displays a quite different style to Bruce which is surprising when you consider that one taught the other. The Little Dragon's movements are very reminiscent of some of the *Enter the Dragon* sequences.

The confrontation is now starting to catch alight. Inosanto is already beginning to perspire. Both men charge, wood sliding by bone with only fractions of an inch to spare. Dan's roar (genuine) is rather more convincing than that dubbed on for Bruce. Nevertheless, the Master's insane fighting skills help overcome this distraction.

For just a second or two, the action halts. Inosanto is panting a little, while Bruce nonchalantly licks the tip on one of the cudgels. There are almost sexual overtones to the poignancy of the moment.

In a flash, the Master attacks again, cracking into the forehead of his gasping opponent. A smile of almost sadistic pleasure appears on Bruce's face as he surveys the x-shaped wound on Dan's head.

Inosanto twirls the nunchakus around himself, slowly at first, then gradually speeding up to a white hot pace. Bruce does likewise. To see these two craftsmen at work, exquisitely handling these beautiful weapons is pure joy to behold.

The nunchakus slice through the air faster and faster until, suddenly, they both chop! Yet again, a deathly hush descends. The Master this time begins the slow build up but while he does so, Inosanto strikes, catching him on the cheekbone and causing it to swell badly. Bruce retaliates but misses and pensively, he fingers his injured cheek.

Dan makes the fatal conclusion that he's getting the better ot the battle. He talks for the first time, "How do you like tha...?" Bruce lashes out in mid-sentence and smacks a stick down on to Dan's nose. The sweat is now starting to pour off the disillusioned Inosanto.

The Little Dragon stares his opponent in the eyes. Suddenly, it's obvious the clash has to be a fight to the death with no submissions, no pleadings and no feelings. There's no time either to consider the state of their respective injuries. Inosanto is now breathing so heavily, he's almost foaming at the mouth.

Bruce accelerates his sticks again and brutally lunges out catching Dan on the right wrist The Master's smile broadens! Inosanto swirls the sticks yet again and rouses his tired body for another attack. The Master switches both clubs to his left hand, leaving Dan to believe that he is about to be attacked with the two sticks at the same time. The Little Dragon outwits him with a sensational, lightning-fast kick that sends his opponent flying backwards onto the floor.

Dan recovers and once more both sets of nunchakus hit the air. Bruce jerks back as Danny aims for his head and hammers home another strike. Inosanto hurtles forwards, his sticks spinning like propellers in front of him as the Master retaliates. It's near impossible to see the deadly weapons, so fast do they move. All that can be heard is the occasional crack as sticks collide. And so impeccably do both fighters control their nunchakus, the

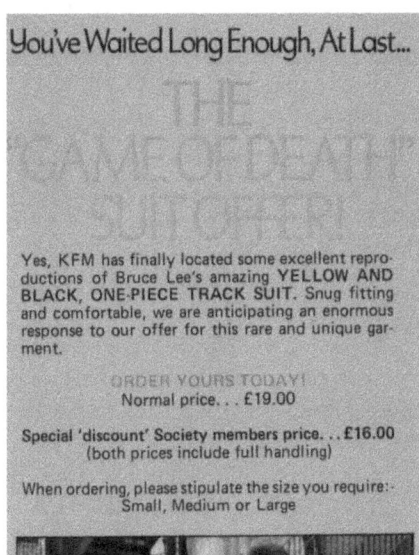

You've Waited Long Enough, At Last...

THE "GAME OF DEATH" SUIT OFFER

Yes, KFM has finally located some excellent reproductions of Bruce Lee's amazing **YELLOW AND BLACK, ONE-PIECE TRACK SUIT**. Snug fitting and comfortable, we are anticipating an enormous response to our offer for this rare and unique garment.

ORDER YOURS TODAY!
Normal price... £19.00

Special 'discount' Society members price... £16.00
(both prices include full handling)

When ordering, please stipulate the size you require:-
Small, Medium or Large

Rush your P.O./Cheque (made out to KFM) to:-
KFM Suit Offer
14 Rathbone Place
London W1P 1DE
(Please allow at least 4 weeks for delivery).

battle starts to resemble a sword-fight. Each strike is calculated to perfection, the wooden blades magically interweaving as they hurtle through the air.

The fury becomes intense as the Little Dragon gets slowly driven back, only to occasionally push forward with deadly lashes. All of a sudden, Bruce diverts Dan's attention by radically changing his weapon's direction of flow. Seizing the precious moment, the Master delivers four incredible, swirling kicks to his opponent's head. Danny reels back and crashes to the floor as a near broken man. Not wanting to waste time or to prolong the battle unnecessarily Bruce musters his final, deadly attack. As Inosanto staggers to his feet, the Master takes both clubs in the left hand and smashes at Dan's hands, held in the on-guard position.

Throwing the doomed man off balance, the Little Dragon strikes at the nerve cluster beneath Dan's armpit, cracks his knee into the stomach and finally wraps his nunchakus around Inosanto's neck. A sharp tug, a snapping sound like the biting of a crisp apple and Dan falls to the floor for the last time.

Bruce honours his fine opponent by letting his nunchakus fall onto the lifeless body and then continues on upstairs.

The making of this amazing sequence must have been a bit like playing with death itself. One misplaced move, one under-rehearsed attack and a serious if not fatal accident would certainly have been the result.

Bruce knew there was only one man in the world he could trust for such a demanding role - Danny Inosanto. There was simply no one else around who could read his actions so finely or who could react so sensitively to his immaculate timing.

It's pretty well a foregone conclusion that, had the Master lived, Dan Inosanto would have figured a good deal in his films of the future. In order to achieve such a stunning degree of realism, Bruce had to pick the people capable of responding instantly and accurately to the situations he presented to them.

KFM salutes Bruce Lee for his pure genius in capturing on film surely the world's finest-ever cinema martial battle. Pity that the British censors were not victims themselves in the first scene!

THE ENTER THE DRAGON RECORDINGS

Part two of our 'Bruce Lee's Recordings' sequence appeared in *KFM* 39. It carried us through the Tam label version of *Fist of Fury* and part way into Tam's *The Way of the Dragon*. Now it's time to polish off the *Way of the Dragon* album before diving into the Warner Brother's release of *Enter the Dragon*. Why Warners should only release this double album in Japan is a real mystery. The sales potential for it worldwide must be enormous. What in particular makes this LP really rare is that there were only a limited number of pressings ever made. It contains the entire *Enter the Dragon* film, unlike the single albums which feature only highlights.

Before attacking *Enter the Dragon*, however, it's time to check through side two of *The Way of the Dragon*.

Track one is entitled 'The Big Guy' and it's the scene in the film where Bruce does away with another would-be assassin. The background music is interesting. It's instrumental and doesn't appear in the film at all. Presumably it was specially written for the album.

Next track is 'The Threat.' This covers the splendid scene where the Master walks into a confrontation with the gang. They are trying to get the girl to sign over the restaurant to them. Bruce immediately recognises the danger and as quick as a flash, he pulls some darts from his pocket and sends them flying around the room. Several of the thugs are maimed. He threatens the Boss to lay off, or else!

'The Trap' follows. This is where the action rally catches fire. The Boss sends in three top name fighters to do away with Bruce. The first is a Korean, who only lasts a few seconds. Then the Karate Man (Bob Wall) tries his hand. Wall aims some kicks and the Little Dragon retaliates with sharp punches to the face. Bruce closes in with punches and kicks and Wall sinks to the floor. He staggers to his feet, but a kick to the solar plexis finally settles him.

Bruce sees the Boss' assistant running away into the Colosseum and follows him into a trap! He finds himself face to face with the USA Karate champion, Chuck Norris.

Track four is, not surprisingly, entitled 'The Big Fight at the Colosseum.' Bruce and Chuck get ready, their bones cracking as they go through their warm-up routines. The Little Dragon attacks with steady punching while the Karate man wades in with fierce blows. For a moment Bruce is in trouble and he has to rethink his approach. He screams and leaps forward to land heavy punches and kicks.

Chuck trails back with his back to the wall - a sitting target for Bruce's fists. Suddenly the Little Dragon snaps Chuck's knee, then follows up by dislocating one of the Karate man's arms. It's nearly over, but still Chuck won't submit. As he lunges forward with his remaining good arm, Bruce twists his head and breaks the neckbone - all is ended!

Track five is a sort of finale. It features a repeat of the title song plus a quiet, instrumental passage in the middle.

Perhaps the most memorable aspect of this album is the great variety of Bruce's war cries. They truly are amazing. Also, of course, it features the famed double nunchaku sequence.

Time now to move along to make a start on the four great sides that made up Warner Brother's double album, *Enter the Dragon*. The record number is P5526-7W, it's in stereo and the total running time is 97 minutes, 27 seconds. Music is by Lalo Schrifren and the production for the film was by Fred Weintraub and Paul Heller, in association with Raymond Chow. Director was Robert Clouse.

The album was released in 1975 in Japan and it comes complete with a free poster and libretto containing the entire script of *Enter the Dragon* - not a word has been left out! The level of quality is superb and on the copy we reviewed, there was minimum surface noise.

SIDE ONE

The signs are it's a warm summer's day. Track one kicks off with leaves rustling and birds chirping. Bruce is holding a practice fight - it's just friendly combat. Track two, and Mr Braithwaite approaches and explains about Han's tournament. Bruce isn't too impressed and carries on sparring with a small boy. Seeing the Little Dragon in action convinces Braithwaite that Bruce is his man. Track one is entitled 'The Exhibition,' track two, 'Invitation to the Tournament.'

On to the third track, '*Enter the Dragon* Theme.' This is the same musical theme heard on the single LP release. The mix, however, seems different plus you hear the sound of the plane coming into land.

'Island of no Guns' is Track Four and it's the scene where Braithwaite is showing Bruce a film of Han's island. He mentions details of the guards and he tells the Little Dragon he wants him to bust apart Han's drugs racket. The reason Bruce is selected is that no guns are allowed on the island. Finally, he's given a picture of Mae Ling, a friendly contact who's already there.

Track five, 'Sister's Death/Respects to Sister and Mother,' and here one of the Master's relatives tells of Han's tournament of three years ago. A flashback reveals how Bruce's sister was attacked by one of Han's bodyguards and, when cornered in a shed, she committed suicide. Obviously Bruce now has to avenge the death and he asks forgiveness for what he's about to do!

'Roper and Williams' is the title of the next track. Roper is having problems on a golf course regarding some money he owes. Although he dispatches the heavies, he realises his luck must run out sometime and enlists for the island trip. Williams becomes the other partner. We see him slicing up a few cops when they start hassling him. The time has come for him to make a move, too.

SIDE TWO

Track one, there's betting going on aboard the Junk. Two stick insects fight - Roper loses out to Bruce. 'Fighting without fighting.' Another martial artist, Parsons, makes a bully of himself on the boat over to the island. He asks Bruce what his style is."Fighting without fighting," replies the Master! The Little Dragon then tricks Parsons to get in the lifeboat and removes the nuisance by casting him adrift - though still on tow. The sound effects are incredible - you can hear every sound of the sea, the creaking of the junk, footsteps, laughter, just about everything.

Track three - 'Han's Island/ The Banquet/Mae Ling.' The boat lands and Roper takes a liking to Han's right-hand lady, Tania. They climb the steps up to the massive castle - men can be heard training. That evening at a banquet, Han bids everyone a warm welcome. Then he throws an apple into the air and one of his girls spears it with a dart. He repeats the trick, then the third time, the dart is thrown by Mae Ling. Bruce catches the apple and pulls out the dart. He realises it was thrown by Mae. That night they get together and she tells Bruce of some of the mysterious things that have been happening there.

Track four - 'Oharra/Tournament.' Bruce is exercising in his room when Han enters and tells him to attend the morning ritual outside. The Little Dragon continues his exercising.

The tournament begins and Williams loses no time in despatching his opponent. Roper goes next and fakes losing for a while so as to improve his betting odds. Then he really lets fly a knee to the groin and a punch to the jaw and it's all over. The crowd applaud wildly and Roper has made money from the bets Williams placed!

And there we have to leave our review for this month. Remember there's another two sides yet to the fabulous Warner album, so plenty of action to come.

And please don't send in hundreds of letters asking where this album can be bought but I'm afraid the answer to that question may be a bit tricky. Anything that can be discovered on that score, we'll pass on. Back with you all again, next month, for the final instalment.

THE BRUCE LEE SOCIETY

Hi, Pam here again, with another instalment of news for all you Society members.

First off, of course, I have to thank you for putting together the already enormous petition response. I'm going to hold off delivering it up until the last possible second, in order to make the impact as big as possible.

Once we've cleared this particular demand. I'll give a bit of time for everybody to get their breath back, and then maybe have a go at getting *Longstreet* and *Green Hornet* on the TV, with another petition! I know its hard work, but I hope you agree with me that it's got to be worth it. Television companies tend to be quite influenced by such things - particularly as in this case, we've got the *Game of Death* event to offer as proof of Bruce's continued fame.

Patricia Davies (1834) has written in asking if I know of any shop in South East London that deals in Bruce items and/or sells Chinese clothes. Okay, can any of you London members help? For the life of me I can't think of anywhere, but I'm sure there must be something, somewhere.

Reminder time, anyone wanting to find details of any British martial arts schools, the people to contact are: The Martial Arts Commission, 4 Deptford Bridge, London SF8 (Tel. 01-691 3433). They'll be able to put you in touch with registered, reliable clubs.

Hot news, member Mr. T Symons (2243) tells me that a Hong Kong magazine gives the names Chen Yao Po and Kim Tai Chung as TWO of the apparently many stand-ins used for Bruce in *Game of Death*. As you know, no names appear in the credits at all as the stand-ins say they don't want to be identified, though more likely, Raymond Chow doesn't want them to be identified.

For my full 'biased/unbiased' comments on *Game of Death*, check out the next News Sheet. I'm going to try to be fair, but factual. No punches are going to be pulled! I've seen the film twice now and believe me, there's plenty to talk about.

And that's about it for this month. Don't forget to enter our great new *Dragon Power* competition, and don't forget either, we've finally located some good *Game of Death* yellow suits and they're on offer to Society members at very reduced prices.

KICKBACK: THE LETTERS

Well, I don't know what you think, but I reckon our uncensored coverage of the chopped-out Inosanto fight is one of the best features ever to appear in *KFM*. I agree that nothing can totally take the place of the real thing but for my money, this comes pretty close. Changing the subject - it looks like I'm going to have to eat my words on the subject of Bruce's sweat glands removal. It seems at last as though there's something like positive evidence to support the theory. Finally I want to thank everybody for petition replies that have already started pouring into the office. Don't relax a moment - remember, the bigger the pile, the more effect we're likely to have! Now, it's letters time...

BRUCE ON TV

Dear Jenny,
While I appreciate the fans desire to see as much as possible of Bruce (myself included) do you not think that it would entirely destroy the mystique and atmosphere of Bruce's films to have them shown on television? After all, when you go to see him at a cinema it seems special, but people watching telly films rarely give their whole concentration and attention to it. The films shown are those, generally, that have outlived their circuit appeal. And can you really imagine Bruce possibly being interrupted by adverts for washing powder, tinned soups etc?! I believe he is better left on the cinema circuits.
Kathryn Wray, Codnor, Derbyshire

Hello Kathryn,
I must say I can but agree with you so far as the standard of viewing is concerned. Unfortunately, that's got to be balanced with the fact that many of his fans are legally, simply not able to see his films in cinemas. They really do deserve a chance to see the Master in action!

MEMORIAL FLOWERS

Dear Jenny,
In my letter to you which was published in *KFM* No.32, I said that anyone wishing to send money for flowers to be laid on Bruce's resting place should forward their monies to 'The Capitol Hill Florist Co.' My correspondant in Seattle, Taky Kimura, tells me that place has now closed down. The new address for sending flowers is: The Flower Shoppe, 1304 Stewart Street, Seattle, Washington, USA. Changing subject, to put the record straight, Bruce did have the sweat glands removed from under his armpits. I have this in writing from a member of the Lee family. Also, Bruce's old home in Cumberland Road is now a motel called 'Kam Wah Garden.'
Dave Langley, Runcorn, Cheshire

Dear Dave,
Many thanks again for writing - it sure is good to get these hot snippets of news direct from the States.

KFM - VALUE AND QUALITY

Dear Jenny,
Would you believe it? I paid £1.10 in a shop for a *Game of Death* poster of the Master, then, on buying the greatest magazine tribute there is to the Little Dragon, *KFM* No.40, what did I find but not only the usual amazing articles and features but a larger and much better poster from *Game of Death* on the reverse! All this for 35p! Guess which magazine is now ordered regularly? Two copies a month for me!
Susan Buchanan, Walton, Liverpool

Dear Susan,
I must say I admire your good taste! And if you think that issue was good, just take a close look at this one - nobody can say we don't try hard.

SWEAT GLANDS

Dear Jenny,
I, just like a lot of people, have had sweat glands removed from under the armpits. Otherwise it can be quite uncomfortable in competitions for Karate. What they do is push a hot pin through the sweat gland and burn it out. Finally, would you please give my Karate club a mention? It's the Fenham School of Karate, Morley Hill Church Hall. Telephone: Newcastle upon Tyne 886296.
Tony Pinkerton, Newcastle upon Tyne

Hi Tony,
Thanks to both yourself and Dave Langley for straightening me out on the sweat glands thing. The actual operation sounds horrible - I don't think I'll bother! I hope the club moves from strength to strength.

BRANDON LEE INTERVIEW?

Dear Jenny,
Thanks for a great magazine! I am writing in to ask if you have any plans for interviewing Brandon Lee. He's around 12 years old and I am sure many readers would like to hear his attitude to Kung Fu and his father. Keep on printing *Kung-Fu Monthly* - don't stop!
Farikh Mirza, High Wycombe, Bucks

Dear Farikh,
Now that does sound a good idea. We do have some contacts in the States so maybe such an interview could be arranged. I'm certain it would be tremendously popular!

FREE *KFM*S!

Dear Jenny,
I have in my possession four *Kung-Fu Monthly*s and one Bruce Lee poster, all of which I would like to give away to any reader of *KFM*. They are issues 4, 21, 22 and 26. Postage and packing will be free of charge but please write your address clearly.
Sandra Chalkin, Tonbridge Wells, Kent

Dear Sandra,
That's a very generous action for you to take. I suggest you pick the lucky person on a first-out-of-the-bag basis. How about some other readers offering one or two things for nothing? I think it's a lovely idea.

QUICKIES CORNER

A. Young, Cubbington, Warwickshire - I hope you don't have appendix trouble! It sounds about time you did join the Society - tut, tut indeed! Also, I agree, Cimac in Birmingham does seem a very good shop for books, magazines and equipment.
Owen Lonergan, Esh Winning, Co. Durham - Funnily enough, there is a cartoon of Bruce Lee on the way. As soon as I know more, I'll mention it in *KFM*.
Gary Ogden, Coton Fields, Staffs - Actually, the suit you mentioned is the one we weren't too happy with - It's not even black like the real *Game of Death* suit. Fortunately, all is saved, see the adverts this issue! Also, as with most Hong Kong films, *Game of Death* is dubbed. You're going to have to start searching to find a copy of *KFM* No. 1 as we ran out ages ago.
Richard Lockwood, Cosham, Hants - Interesting point - Has *Enter the Dragon* been paired with Death Race 2000 so as to cash in on the death angle?
Barry Munns, Batley, W. Yorks - I haven't heard much on Jim Kelly lately - Any readers have news of him?
Gerrard McNamara, Hammersmith, London - Sorry we have to reckon readers prefer to see repeats rather than nothing at all. Obviously though, we're still looking for fresh material.
Gerrard Heagney, Limerick, Eire - I'm biased, but I still think the best info book is our *Bruce Lee King of Kung Fu* - Check our mail order department.
D. Anthony, St. Giles, Lincoln - Suggest you take a foreign subscription for Canada - Again, check our mail order department for details.
Gordon Stephen, St. Mary's, Dundee - Details on where to buy records hopefully coming soon.
Mark Forsyth, Edinburgh, Scotland - The different names given to Bruce's films around the world are just too complicated to go into here. We'll go into it soon. Readers, Mark is looking for a male/female pen pal, 15-17 years old. Another pen pal, Allan Birrell, Carlisle, Cumbria - Likes hobbies, pop music, bird-watching, motorbike racing.

THE KUNG-FU MONTHLY ARCHIVE SERIES

KFM BACK ISSUES BINDER

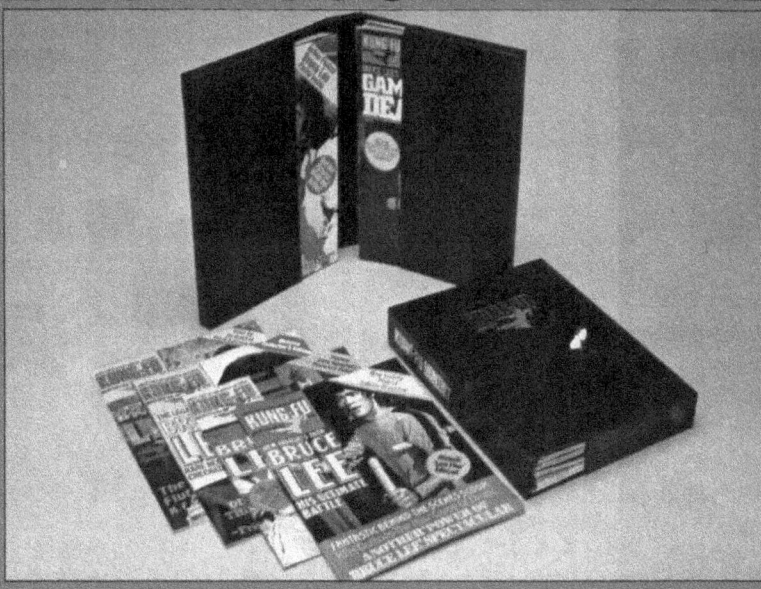

The Official Kung-Fu Monthly Back Issues Binder is already selling a storm! At last dedicated readers are able to keep their rare KFM copies in ABSOLUTELY PERFECT CONDITION.

This smart black binder is silver-embossed with the world famous Kung-Fu Monthly Emblem and makes a superb addition to anyone's bookcase.

STAY AHEAD!! If you haven't ordered yours yet (or maybe the first is getting a little full!) send immediately, a £2.75 cheque/postal order to:
KFM Binder Offer
14 Rathbone Place
London W1P 1DE

Special Society Member's Price... only £2.50
(Please allow at least 4 weeks for delivery)

SUBSCRIBE TO THE WORLD'S LEADING MARTIAL ARTS MAGAZINE

SUBSCRIBE TO KFM

It's the only way that you can be absolutely certain of keeping your collection of KFM bang up to date!

For just £4.50, you will receive the next 12 fantastic issues of the world's greatest martial arts magazine — dedicated to the memory of the incomparable Bruce Lee.

As a special service to our readers, KFM is actually making a substantial loss on the postage, packing and handling, all of which is included in the price.

Rush your cheque/postal order (payable to Kung-Fu Monthly) to:
KFM Subscriptions
14 Rathbone Place
London W1P 1DE

Please print your name and address clearly!

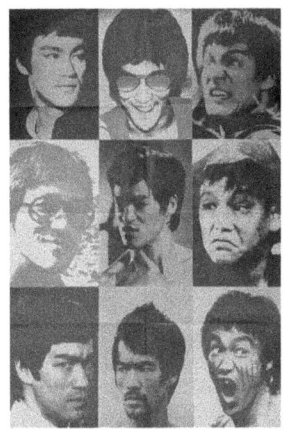

EDITORIAL

Hi there Kung Fu fans. Time to slip into gear for another unique edition of the world's finest martial arts magazine, dedicated, of course, to the memory of the Master, Bruce Lee. And this month, our main feature is really quite a surprise, for our researchers have dug deep into the pile of available literature, reports and interviews to produce the first-ever feature on Little Dragon's sparkling sense of humour.

Everyone knows that, apart from his supreme physical skill Bruce had a tremendous talent for making people laugh. His films alone tell the story - who can forget the overdose of soup incident at the opening of *The Way of the Dragon*! And then again, his wit eased him through many tricky situations. When fighting, opponents would often seem near mesmerised by his apparently light-hearted approach. They were making a deadly miscalculation.

Second up this month, we carry one step further our now legendary browse through

Bruce's recordings. This time we polish off that famous Japanese double album of *Enter the Dragon* - and what an album it is too! The quality is nothing short of superb and, content-wise, every shred of the film is there, and more. It seems, by the way, that at last, we may have some word on where to buy at least some of these great LP's. Society President, Pam Hadden, has been looking into the problem and she'll be reporting her findings in *KFM* Society news slots and club News Sheets.

And that looks to be about it for this month. Stand by - Hopefully, next issue for an amazing *Green Hornet* special. Back with you all again then.

Felix Yen

Felix Yen
Editor-in-Chief

THE WIT OF BRUCE LEE

A sense of humour came as naturally to Bruce Lee as came his desire to be the greatest martial artist of the 20th Century. From time to time during our many features on the Master, we've stumbled over some prominent examples of his great gift. In his films, for instance, he quickly realised that fighting alone - however great, was just not enough - he injected drama plus a degree of fun. But as we shall see later on, the fun-factor was in no way a contrived addition. Stories abound of his light hearted approach to life in general and there's no doubt at all that this characteristic was highly instrumental in helping shape the pattern of his cinema career. Come with us now as we probe the revealing world of Bruce Lee the joker!

It's pretty common knowledge that the Little Dragon's greatest influence - acting-wise - came from his father, Lee Hoi Chuen. His stunning performances with the Cantonese Opera Company were generally packed with high emotional content and his successes were never greater than when he was performing comedy. Whether he passed on these skills to his son by word of mouth and example or whether Bruce inherited them via the hereditary influence is hard to say. Certainly the Little Dragon bore all the signs of being a totally natural humorist.

Even at the tender age of just one month, Bruce's father made-up his son to look like a clown, with thick mascara over his eyebrows and white powder on his face. And later in life, his jokiness was to be, at times, a positive life-saver. Once, whilst being chased by a gang of thugs through the back-streets of Hong Kong, he managed to get a little way ahead - and then pulled off a neat little stunt. He leapt onto a nearby roof, stripped down to his underpants and sat meditating in the cross-legged position. When the heavies arrived, he screwed up his face and squinted to such a degree that they failed to recognise him. When asked if he'd seen anybody come by in the last few minutes he nodded, and pointed in another direction. They disappeared in hot pursuit!

During his schooldays, the Little Dragon frequently found himself in trouble with au-

thority for playing mischievous pranks. One of his favourite tricks with the girls was to give them invitation cards - not to come to his party, but to join him for the night! Though the joke was harmless enough, there were probably a few around who'd have liked to have taken him up on it; even at that early age, his good looks were coupled with great personality and charm.

In fact, Bruce developed a great liking for near-the-knuckle jokes and once started, his gag-sessions were hard to stop. James Coburn, who at one point was a frequent partner in the clowning around, remembers that a lot of the jokes were plain corny. "It wasn't so much the tag line, as they way he told them. It was funnier watching his expressions."

Chuck Norris has good reason to recall the Little Dragon's wicked sense of the ridiculous. One day, Chuck was visiting and Bruce took him into his garage where he kept a wooden dummy - especially for kicking practice. "Bruce asked me to have a go at kicking the dummy. I didn't want to because my trousers were too tight, and I was scared they might split. But he kept urging me on." Obviously Bruce got insistent and Chuck began to feel that, if he didn't do it, the Little Dragon might start thinking him incapable of performing the kick.

Chuck struck out at the dummy - accompanied by a very loud rip and Bruce immediately creased up with laughter. And to make it worse, almost at that moment, Linda appeared in the garage. Poor Chuck got so embarrassed he had to cover himself with his hands. Bruce, meanwhile, was nearly falling over in hysterics.

On the same subject, one day while of the set of *The Big Boss*, the Little Dragon was talking to support actress, Nora Miao. In a serious voice he asked her, "What do Kung Fu fighters have more than anyone else?" Nora, and one or two other people around, decided that it was obviously an important question, so they thought long and hard. Eventually, they gave up and asked him what it was. He replied, "More torn trousers," and promptly produced a pair with an enormous gaping rip in them. It was a good joke, and everyone laughed.

Bruce frequently carried his innate sense of humour into the film studios. One of the best remembered scenes has to be in *The Way of the Dragon* where a customer visits the toilet, only to discover the Little Dragon standing on the seat. His knees are bent and he's poised over the basin ready to take his trousers down! Though the impact of the joke was a little lost in the West, for Eastern audiences, it was hilarious. Well they could appreciate the difficulties encountered by a Chinese man bought up with very different toilet facilities to those normally used in our part of the world.

Again, in *The Big Boss*, he put in a truly memorable performance as a drunk while at the party thrown by the factory foreman. And in *Fist of Fury*, who could ever forget Bruce's Japanese telephone engineer disguise? Once more, many western audiences may have missed the absurdity of a Chinese actor disguising himself as a Japanese. Out East, it had them rolling in the aisles. Coming up to date, there are several numerous moments in *Game of Death*. Last issue, you'll recall our description of the Lee/Inosanto encounter. At one point, the irrepressible Little Dragon starts a sort of skipping dance around the bemused Inosanto - another delicious moment. In fact, while on the *Game of Death* set, Bruce had everybody laughing at his antics with a large 35mm camera. At one point, he was pretending to shoot the scene vertically. Maybe if it catches on, cinemas will have to start shifting their screens up to the ceiling!

Another of Bruce's more wicked pastimes was to sing, especially when there were plenty of people around. It was wicked because he had an awful singing voice, but he took great delight in seeing the pain registered on the faces of all near by him. Funnily, he really enjoyed listening to himself sing and at times was genuinely enthusiastic about it. However, he was always quick to admit his shortcomings. He once cracked the joke that, "I tell people I have a rich voice because it's well off!"

The Little Dragon often used his sense of humour to positive effect. At times, filming work inevitably gets a little tense, and Bruce was well aware of the damage such an atmosphere has on the finished product. To lighten things, he'd often start singing - badly - and cracking dirty jokes. Even the prudest of people found it hard keeping a straight face.

A man by the name of Tseng Knoming remembers the time he worked with the Little Dragon on the set of *The Way of the Dragon*. They were part way through filming an important nunchaku sequence and Bruce detected that the atmosphere had suddenly got very down. There was no way he could hit the peak form he needed while those around him were feeling low - something had to be done.

He hurried over to some musicians in the corner of the studio and urged them into playing a cha cha. Now the Little Dragon, as most will recall, was a past champion at this particular dance, and seizing an imaginary partner, he zoomed off around the studio! The atmosphere bucked up a little, but as far as Bruce was concerned, still not far enough.

He continued his one man, impromptu show by relaxing all his muscles and pushing out his stomach until it looked for all the world like a pot belly. "Bruce Lee before he takes Vitajoy," he shouted out. Then he tensed hard until his body resembled steel, "Bruce Lee after he has taken Vitajoy." He then wandered around the studio asking staff to feel his muscles. The place began to rock with laughter - even Bruce couldn't stop himself joining in!

Eating out frequently gave the Little Dragon the opportunity to turn on hilarity. One day, he accidentally knocked out one of his contact lenses. The other people at the table were worried he might flare up at this embarrassing incident. The Master, however, saw the funny side of it and, quickly, he donned a pair of heavy, shell-rimmed glasses. At once he seemed transformed into the famed Japanese telephone engineer disguise - the table rocked with the joke.

Bruce had the great ability to crack jokes even in the most upsetting situations. Once, while filming in Bangkok, he wrote to Linda complaining that he couldn't find any meat to eat, that he had trouble with his back and that he'd badly cut his hand. He signed off, "The cockroaches are a constant threat - the lizards I can ignore."

Finally, everyone has one endearing passion, and Bruce's was shredded wheat! Early one morning, Linda was awoken by a nudge from Bruce - he was looking rather concerned. She thought for a minute he might be ill or something, but no, he'd decided that at 2am, he needed a bowl of breakfast cereal! Whether he in fact got it or not goes unrecorded.

The Little Dragon was a joker all through his life, constantly entertaining people and always the life and soul of wherever he happened to be. His day was dedicated to his work, but no work can be complete without a moment or two's play. As always, Bruce was the master of the humorous interlude.

ENTER THE DRAGON
ALBUM REVIEW – PART TWO

Of all Bruce's cinema LP's, the Warner Brothers double album release of *Enter the Dragon* has to be one of the most astounding. Quality and content-wise, it stands alone as one of the finest monuments ever made to the supreme skill of Bruce Lee. Last month, we took you through the first two sides of this Japanese import, up to the point where Han's famous tournament begins. Williams has passed the first round with flying colours and Roper, too, after some feigned difficulty, polishes off his man with a sledgehammer punch to the jaw. Meanwhile, Bruce is still trying to discover exactly what secrets the island holds. We join him on side three, track one as he makes his first move.

Titled 'The Human Fly,' we hear Bruce investigating a ventilator shaft. He opens it and steps down the tunnel. Within seconds, a strange sight greets his eyes - he's looking at some kind of underground factory. Suddenly, two men are coming towards him - he climbs back out before being detected. As he makes his way back to his room, Williams, who's out for some air, spots him climbing the steep hill. "A human fly," he says to himself.

Track two - 'Oharra's Death.' Next day at the tournament, Han lets it be known that someone was seen wandering around outside the previous night. He makes it clear that such mistakes will not go unpunished. Bolo then comes on and has a field day. He utterly destroys three guards. Once the bodies have been cleared away, Bruce is called to face his first confrontation. His opponent turns out to be Oharra, the thug responsible for his sister's death. Oharra tries to impress him with a little impromptu wooden plank smashing. Bruce calmly makes the comment that, "Boards don't hit back."

Bolo gives the start signal and you can hear the crunching of gravel as the two fighters take their stances. The air is very still. The Little Dragon opens his account with a strong punch to Oharra's face. He follows it with another and his opponent sinks to one knee. Bruce's third punch fells his man who, instead of returning to a proper stance, grabs Bruce's leg and yanks at it. This foul move gets rewarded with a kick to the face - performed in mid-backwards somersault!

Han is annoyed at Oharra's poor sportsmanship, but all is settled as Bruce kicks his enraged opponent in the chest, killing him with the single blow. Oharra has not managed a single attack. Says Han, "Oharra's treachery has disgraced us."

Track three - 'Williams versus Han.' Williams is summoned to Han's study where he is accused of being the man out strolling around the previous night. Williams tells Han he wants to leave the island - a fight starts and the guards crash through the door. One by one, they get beaten and Han himself has to re-enter the battle. Williams throws a punch which is parried by Han's claw. The resulting agony provides just the distraction the evil boss needs. Williams is punched through a glass wall into an opium den. Unconscious, he is beaten to death with the iron hand.

Track four - 'Han and Roper.' Han tries to persuade Roper to join the organisation. He shows him a frightening collection of weapons, some cages containing locked up prisoners and, finally, the dead figure of Williams hanging by a rope above a pool of acid. The rope is severed and the lifeless form disappears beneath the hissing liquid. Roper is horrified.

Side four, track one - 'Nunchaku/Braithwaite.' Later that day, Bruce returns back down the air ventilator. Just as he is about to climb in, a snake threatens him. The Little Dragon grabs the reptile and places it inside a rope bag.

Arriving at the opium factory, he makes his way to the radio room. Cunningly, he tosses the snake inside and just waits! A chair flies through the window, rapidly followed by two men running for their lives. As Bruce taps out a message for Braithwaite, an alarm sounds. As quickly as possible, he finishes sending the message and leaves the room, knocking out a guard on the way.

The Little Dragon hides as other guards rush by looking for him. A man spots him and pounces - only to be dispatched with a sharp chop and a punch. Two others rush in. The background music provides the perfect match to the slow-motion action - eerie and powerful. In just one movement, the two are felled.

Suddenly, he's grabbed by the arm from behind. Bruce turns and twists the new assailant's arm while at the same time, tugging his hair. It's agony! Yet again, two more guards appear and Bruce is forced to remove them from the action with kicks to the body and face. He then dispels any lingering hope the third guard had of staying alive by tugging so hard at the man's hair, his neck snaps.

As the Little Dragon finds his way over to the cells where the prisoners are kept, the only sound heard is that of the generators humming. Without warning, ten more guards come charging at him, one armed with a long pole. Bruce ducks beneath the deadly swipe, jabs the man viciously in the back, and grabs the pole. Immediately, he mows down three of the guards, then, as a fourth rushes in, he snaps the pole in two to provide himself with a pair of fighting sticks.

The Little Dragon screams and lashes out at a new opponent with the speed of machine gun fire. He captures a pair of nunchakus and dazzles the attackers with a superb display of power and control. Faster than the eye can follow, Bruce pulled them around his body, under his arm, around his waist, across his back and around his neck.

Seeing his chance, with the man confused, Bruce smashes out at his opponent's head. The sound of wood on bone is horrifying. Still more guards rush up, and still tile Master deals with them. Realising that he's in fact hopelessly outnumbered, Bruce heads for what he thinks is an exit but unfortunately, it's a trap! Solid steel walls crash down and from above, he hears Han speak. "The battle with the guards was magnificent, your skill is extraordinary." The Little Dragon stares towards from where the voice is coming - with loathing.

Track two - 'The Big Battle.' Han summons Bruce and Roper into the arena and demands they fight each other to the death. The dual is refused, so Roper is instead matched against Bolo.

The contest is close - one, Bolo has the brawn, the other, Roper, has the brains. Several attacks are mounted but little tells until Bolo fells his man with a series of hard punches.

A punishing arm lock follows and the only way Roper can retaliate is by biting Bolo's leg! With an agonising roar, the big fighter lets go the arm and hops off on one leg. Seizing his chance, Roper kicks Bolo in the groin and then delivers a massive blow to the jaw. Roper takes his advantage well and snaps the neck of his now defeated opponent.

None of this goes along with Han's plans at all. Angrily, he shouts for the guards to take on both Bruce and Roper. Their efforts are in vain. Han screams for replacements, ordering them to kill those who question his power.

What Han doesn't know, however, is that Mae Ling has released all the prisoners. Just as Bruce and Roper are starting to be overpowered by sheer weight of numbers, the freed men arrive to do bloody battle with the guards. The Little Dragon hacks his way towards Han. As he approaches, the evil boss of the island unhooks his artificial hand and connects up a claw. They meet, and Han lashes out with the deadly, pointed steel. The Master retaliates by burying the iron claw in a wooden table. Han disconnects the arm and runs off - Bruce follows. They reach the museum and Han smashes a glass case and removes the exhibit - another iron hand, this time containing four, razor sharp blades. Bruce delivers the

immortal line, "You have offended my family and you have offended the Shaolin temple."

All around the museum, in and out of the glass cases, the great dual rages - at one point, the deadly claw rips the Master's shirt and chest, causing the famous claw marks. Bruce gets madder still and Han grabs a spear to defend himself. He hurls it at the Little Dragon, but misses as it buries itself in the wall. Han falls through a section of revolving wall into a mirrored room - Bruce follows. Tip-toeing round the room, he becomes more worried by his own reflections than by Han. He smashes as many of the panes as possible to minimise the multiple reflection problem.

The fight hots up and as Han lashes out with the claw, the Little Dragon turns on a barrage of kicks and punches. A final kick from the Master sends his opponent flying back onto the protruding spear and the evil has been overcome! Han's body continues to revolve like a stuck pig as Bruce strides past to see the battle has been won.

It's hard to lavish too much praise on this album. Nothing is left to the imagination and the quality, as has been said before, is near-perfection. Somehow, it almost seems as though the Master is there in the room with you!

THE BRUCE LEE SOCIETY

Hi everyone, welcome back to the Bruce Lee Society News column.

First off, good news that not only is *KFM* giving away the 25 copies of *Dragon Power* by the JKD Band (last issue's competition), it looks like there'll be some more twelve inchers available for the September News Sheet. Buy the way, I'm looking forward to hearing from you on your views of the record as I like it tremendously. It's quite cheered me up during the *Game of Death* problems!

As I recently reported, the Society film is now well on the way to being completed. About the time you read this, I'll be travelling up-country to meet the cast and film crew and, hopefully, to take some photographs. Providing they turn out okay, you'll be seeing the best of them in the next News Sheet. It's really exciting that Britain's first real Kung Fu movie should be the brainchild of members of the Society.

I'm just getting overwhelmed with letters from members asking for details on where to buy copies of the various Bruce Lee albums that *KFM* has lately been reviewing. Please remember that in some cases, the LP's are quite rare so don't necessarily expect to be able to 'pop down the road' to your local shop and buy them.

Three addresses which I included in the last News Sheet are worth repeating here: Soundtrack & General, 406 Brockley Road, London SE4; HMV, 363 Oxford Street, London W1R 2BJ; Magpie Records, Hopmarket Yard, Worcester WR1 1UR. All these are certainly worth trying, but don't expect miracles as in many cases, they will only be able to order.

The petition response is looking very good. By the time you've read this I'll have delivered the results to the Censor's office. I have to admit that I'm none too optimistic that they'll shift their ground, but you never know. At least they'll maybe just start to understand the upset, disappointment and wrath their action has incurred.

Something which I'd like to see happening soon is regional members organising local

Bruce Lee events. I haven't finalised plans as yet, but the sort of things that come to mind are the hiring of films, collection displays, talks, and so on. There must be lots of other things you could do as well so how about writing in and giving me some ideas? **Pam**

'78 COMPETITION RESULTS

The correct answers to the ten questions that appeared in *KFM* 40 were as follows:
1. Linda Emery 2. Guns 3. Tania 4. Maria Yi 5. Lo Wei 6. Billy Lo 7. 1964 8. A Rolls Royce 9. A Kitten (or Cat) 10. *The Big Boss*

First ten correct postcards out of the sack were sent in by:-
Frank Salmon, Gravesend, Kent / Michael Durrent, Manadon, Devon / Jasdip Singh, Rainham, Essex / P McGranaghan, Belfast, N. Ireland / Miss Lorraine Smith, Mickley, Derbyshire / Neil Devine, South Shields, Tyne & Wear / Gary Nash, Wallasey, Merseyside / Malcolm Cain, Newcastle Upon Tyne / Melanie Ogden, Coton Fields, Staffs / Miss Molly Cullen, Pengam, Gwent.

Congratulations to all of you for winning three free years membership to the Bruce Lee Society and thanks to EVERYONE for taking part.

THE WIT OF BRUCE LEE

This month's kickback is tinged a little with sadness. Following our recent review of *Game of Death*, the mail box has been virtually buzzing with interest. Most of the comments have been angry - many readers are simply despairing at what Raymond Chow has decided to do. I believe it's important that as many of these letters get an airing as possible. It hardly needs me to tell you how I feel at this moment. Perhaps the only cheery news on the horizon right now is the happy fact that *The Silent Flute* is getting good reviews so I'll pass on a release date, when I can. Stand by next issue for a unique scoop on David Carradine's tribute to the Master.

GAME OF DEATH REVIEW

Dear Jenny,
I have just finished reading Felix Yen's review of *Game of Death* and I feel cheated, disgusted, but most of all angry. To have waited four years for footage of Bruce is bad enough but Chow has no right to hold back any of it. That film of Bruce is *Game of Death*, not any double or gang of men on motorbikes. To be quite frank, I'm not even remotely interested in the rest of it. Chow is doing just what all the other magazines and films have done, which is cashing in on Bruce Lee. I feel like I've been smacked in the teeth - like I'm being used.
Alan Anson, Ribbleton, Lancs

Dear Jenny,
I've just read the sad news about *Game of Death* and it's without doubt, the worst thing that ever happened to Bruce. I couldn't even begin to describe how I feel and I'm sure this tragic news has hit me harder than anyone. If only Bruce were alive today, I doubt very much if they would try it. But he's dead, his last film only twenty-eight minutes completed and they're going to deprive us of it. They just can't help themselves, can they? It looks as though we, the fans, are going to have to think of what Bruce would have thought, and take it from there. A star sinks in the sea of his art.
A Bruce Lee Follower

GAME OF DEATH STORY IDEA

Dear Jenny,
The screen shows a back alley in Hong Kong. An old man sits telling a story to a group of excited children. The man is a greatly aged Bruce Lee (no double problems). He is relating his past adventures, the flashbacks of Bruce Lee films could easily be used. Then the old man begins: "And that was nothing to what happened to me in the pagoda." It's quite simple but in many people's minds, the simplest things are the best. If *Game of Death* was finished like this, there would be no double problems, and no need to link up the existing pieces of film - in between, you could cut back to the old man talking. I think this would have been a much better way of completing the film.
John Thomas, Bridgend, Mid Glamorgan

GAME OF DEATH DISAPPOINTMENT

Dear Jenny,
I was saddened to read how *Game of Death* has turned out. What a downfall from the film we all expected. How could Raymond Chow do this? Why leave out most of the Master's great fight scenes? Why chop up what Bruce left to make two average films, instead of putting it all into one classic? Such a film would have stood as a monument to the world's greatest martial arts exponent. I cannot see Raymond Chow's way of thinking. Maybe he thinks that by bringing out a second film later on, he's keeping Bruce Lee fans happy. Surely they would be far happier to see one complete film?
David Moore, Wakefield, W. Yorks

These are just four of the huge pile of similar letters I've had in on the subject of Game of Death. *In particular, I liked the ideas of John Thomas on how he would have completed the film. I know, some time ago, we ran a competition on the subject. Well, tell me how you feel, but I reckon this simple little ruse ranks as one of the best ever. If KFM readers can come up with these splendid ideas, probably without ever having stepped foot inside a film studio, how come Golden Harvest have botched it? I believe their pursuit of extra earnings on the footage Bruce left has actually led them away from a goldmine. A final, genuine tribute to the Little Dragon would have stood for countless years as a cinema masterpiece. It's the mistake of a lifetime.*

ENTER THE DRAGON QUESTION

Dear Jenny,
I have just read *KFM* No.41 and I think it's the best yet! Can you tell me: 1. Why was the Bruce vs Bolo fight censored and 2. How was the Bruce vs Han mirrored-room fight scene shot, without the camera and crew being filmed? I buy three issues of *KFM* every month. One I stick on the wall, one I cut pictures out of for my collection and the other I keep for my collection.
Farikh Mirza, High Wycombe, Bucks

Dear Farikh,
Answering your two questions: 1. If I could understand how the minds of censors worked, I might be able to tell you. Apparently they believed the violence to be unsuitable for our viewing. 2. The technique simply involves careful positioning of the crew and equipment - and, of course, the mirrors.

PENTHOUSE MAGAZINE ARTICLE

Dear Jenny,
On June 9th, the BBC screened a programme for teachers about the martial arts. It contained a fantastic clip of the Lee/Norris fight and an interview with Rhona McVay. Another interesting thing is that recently I saw a six page article on Bruce in *Penthouse* magazine. Also, I've just been able to obtain the hardback annual for *The Green Hornet*. Any fans who would like more details on these items, please write to me, enclosing a stamped and addressed envelope.
Gary Nash, Wallasey, Merseyside

Dear Gary,
There's certainly been a lot happening for you - Bruce Lee wise - in the last few weeks. It just goes to prove that the name of the Master is not, and will not be forgotten. Thanks, too, for your offer to the other fans - maybe this is something more readers would like to copy?

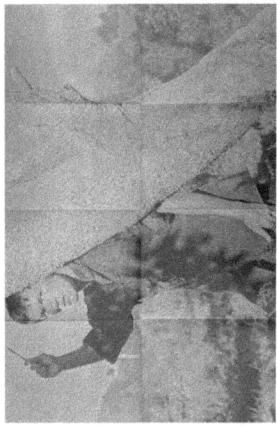

EDITORIAL

    Hi there Kung Fu fans. Just once in a while *KFM* comes up with a major Double-A edition special. Then again, we also manage to occasionally pull in amazing scoops that leave our opposition magazines floundering in the backwaters like dead ducks! This month we've managed to accomplish both in one issue! You may have thought, after the build-up and premiere of *Game of Death* - what next? I'll tell you what's next, firstly there's another of *KFM*'s blow-by-blow accounts, on a very rare animal. Secondly, there's the UK's number one close-up look at Carradine's version of *The Silent Flute*. Taking *Flute* first, regular readers will recall that some issues back we took an early glance at what was happening with Bruce's pet project. No, we're able to pull out all the stops! The full storyline, behind the scenes glimpses, biographies of the stars, production details - for the first time ever, read about it right here in *KFM*.
    And how about the second half of our double-A issue? One glance at the front cover

should have given the clue - the staff of your favourite Kung Fu magazine are proud to bring you a scene by scene account of an episode of the famed TV series, *The Green Hornet*. The show in question was entitled *The Silent Gun* and the action, as you will see, was pretty dramatic. This is the only time, to my knowledge, that a *The Green Hornet* episode has come under such close scrutiny so let's savour the moment.

In case you hadn't heard about it, *Game of Death* is out and doing the rounds! Although, at the time of writing, confirmation has yet to come in, it seems the hacked out nunchaku battle may have been replaced by another of the fights filmed by Bruce. This could have something to do with Raymond Chow's declaration that, he would withdraw the production if the Inosanto clash were censored out. More word on this as I we get it.

Felix Yen
Editor-in-Chief

THE SILENT FLUTE: CARRADINE COMPLETES THE LEGEND!

Not long ago, *KFM* brought you news of the latest developments surrounding Bruce's pet project, *The Silent Flute*. We outlined how David Carradine had interpreted the Little Dragon's famous legacy and how he felt, in some way, that the spirit of Bruce was helping him in his quest. We gave a brief outline of the story and a run through of some of the other actors present - like the South African fighting star, Jeff Cooper. Now, as opening day draws nearer (as usual, no date is fixed at time of writing), the world's greatest martial arts magazine is able to offer the full story - dedicated, as is the film - to the memory of the Master. We make no promises, but maybe it'll go just a little way towards making up for the *Game of Death* disappointment. Let's hope so!

THE SILENT FLUTE CAST LIST

David Carradine ... The Blind Man/The Monkey Man/The Rhythm Man/Death. Jeff Cooper ... Cord. Roddy McDowell ... White Robe. Eli Wallach ... Man in Oil. Erica Creer ... Tara. Christopher Lee ... Zetan. Anthony de Longis ... Morthond. Earl Maynard ... Black Giant. Heinz Bernard ... Ferryman. Ziporra Peled ... Ferryman's Wife. Jeremy Kaplan ... Monkey Boy. Kam Yuen ... Red Band. Elizabeth Motzkin ... Japanese Woman. Bobby Newman ... Thug Leader. Roy Friedman ... Young Monk. Ronen Nabah ... Beautiful Boy. Michal Nedivi ... Boy's Mother. Nissim Zohar ... Boy's Father.

The Executive Producer is Richard St. Johns. The Producers are Sandy Howard and Paul Maslansky. The Director is Richard Moore. The Writers are Stirling Silliphant and Stanley Mann.

The film opens to an ageless ritual. In the presence of a blind flute player (Carradine), a string of 'empty hand' martial arts opponents do battle, one after the other, with Morthond the Dancer. Each time, Morthond is the victor, and each time the judge, White Robe, places a coloured stone in a dish. Chanting accompanies the rite.

But there is a young hothead called Cord (Jeff Cooper) who can contain himself within the rules no longer. As his time arrives, he disgraces himself by attacking with two closed-fist Kung Fu punches. Morthond collapses but is immediately awarded the Medallion of Victory. "I won," complains Cord. "Morthond is a dancer - I am a fighter." White Robe, however, will take none of Cord's arrogance. He directs that Morthond will be the one to seek out the invincible Zetan, defeat him, and thus gain the Book of Enlightenment. Cord is furious and storms away from the Amphitheatre. He decides that it will be he who conquers Zetan - not the fallen Morthond.

Later, as Cord rests by the roadside, he is disturbed in some odd way by the blind flute player who strolls by. Morthond appears, before he sets off to seek enlightenment and Cord follows. Some way along the road, the blind man passes them, looking far too self-assured in his step. They see him enter a castle and immediately there are sounds of battle. Cord rushes in to see the sight-less stranger dispatching eight muscle-bound thugs - his staff cuts the air like a sword and Cord's amazement is heightened when he realises that the blind man somehow always seems to be facing his opponents. And so caught up is he in this famous victory, he fails to notice the stranger's sudden disappearance.

Cord wanders off in aimless fashion, only to hear once again the lilting of the blind man's flute. The air is filled with unanswered questions. The flautist ignores the pleadings of his new disciple and continues on his way as Cord stays with him.

Suddenly, uproar, as they pass some shrieking Monkey Men, Morthond staggers out from the bushes - near dead, and ashamed at failing, his First Trial. Cord takes the Medallion, then puts Morthond out of his misery. He goes to investigate the Monkey Men in their cave dwellings and is confronted by the leader, Jungar. Recalling the blind man's earlier tactics against the thugs, Cord overcomes his initial fear to win the battle. With his dying breath, Jungar directs him towards his next trial in the search for Zetan.

Cord crosses a desert and passes a man who is dissolving himself in oil - to banish lewd thoughts, he declines an offer to join him! Over fertile land, then into another desert and Cord meets with the Rhythm Man - a Turk named Changsha. Our searcher asks many questions, but all he is offered in return is the lovely Tara. Though aware that she may be his Second Trial, he succumbs to her charms. His weakness is rewarded in a terrifying manner. Come the morning, the entire camp is gone - with the exception of the crucified Tara!

Cord's grief is mollified only by the appearance of the blind man, who offers nourishment and wise words. He agrees to Cord staying with him only if he asks no questions. The young searcher agrees. It's a promise he finds hard to keep. Time and time again, the Blind Man does the most peculiar things and each time Cord has to ask why. The final encounter

to stir him comes when the Blind Man deliberately disfigures a beautiful child. Cord can contain himself no longer - how could anyone do such a thing? Carradine explains that it is he, Cord, who is blind! Because of his beauty, the boy was already a tyrant. The parents were now free of this burden. Cord is deeply humbled and he realises there is even more than he thought to the blind old Sage.

Inside a ruined fortress our searcher meets his next Trial. His opponent is non-human, maybe Death itself, and is called Panther Man. Cord summons up his recently acquired wisdom to defeat the apparition (played by Carradine). His wisdom and strength are starting to look impressive.

Changsha again crosses his path, and once more Cord is tempted with worldly goods. This time, however, he refuses, saying he seeks only Zetan. Their confrontation takes place the following morning and though at times, Cord finds it hard to understand the reality of what's going on, his powers, both mental and physical, see him through.

The Trials now over, he is told that the way is across the water. Cord crosses and meets with Zetan - a strangely gentle looking figure who lives in a beautiful monastery. "When do we fight," asks Cord. Zetan, however, insists that he simply practice the procedure whereby he becomes Keeper of the Book. Confused, and despite being warned that opening the book would prove more alarming than anything that's been before, he turns over the pages and each is a mirror!

Cord realises that the truth lies in himself! Zetan offers the alternative of him either staying at the monastery or returning again to the normal world. Realising that the Blind Man himself faced a similar choice some time ago, Cord makes the same decision - and flees the monastry. High in the mountains, he once more crosses the path of the Blind Man, playing a flute that's silent to all but Cord. The Sage asks the young man what he found. "Everything," replies Cord.

Taking hold of the flute, Cord himself begins to play - hesitantly at first, but improving with every note. The two of them dance in Celebration.

And thus was told a tale that owed much to folklore and legend, and even more to Bruce Lee. The Master had devised it as a way of blending the best of Eastern mysticism with the finest of exhibitions of the martial arts. Philosophy, wit and bravery were all combined in the film that was to prove to the world that not only was the Little Dragon the ultimate fighting machine - he was also a considerable actor. Sadly, that ambition was never to come alive.

It was left to Carradine and a talented team of film makers to complete the vision. Stirling Silliphant and Stanley Mann worked to transform the Lee/James Coburn story into a credible film script. Kam Yuen, the Hong Kong born and American raised martial artist worked with Carradine on the fighting scenes. The combination was well proven - they had already done good things with the later episodes of TV's *Kung Fu*. Other martial artists brought in included Tom Ascencio, Wilber Chang, Mike Vendrell, Leo Whang, Rob Gardner, Donnie Williams and Janet Watson.

There's plenty more we could say about the film - but that's better kept in cold store until after it's been seen. Suffice to emphasise that it's obviously got to be at least worth a look and if it's as good as it sounds on paper, it could be a sensation. Whichever way it works out, it's good to see that the talent of Bruce Lee is still making itself felt, all these years after his tragic death.

THE GREEN HORNET
THE SILENT GUN – PART ONE

Time first for a resume of *The Green Hornet* plot. The scene opens with a rainbow ray of *The Green Hornet*, silhouetted in the right hand corner of the picture. Stills flash onto the screen in quick succession as the announcer repeats the time-honoured words, "The Green Hornet - a sought after criminal, but protector of the lives of decent citizens - with his aid, Kato. His true identity is known only to his secretary and the District Attorney." The Hornet is of course otherwise known as Britt Read and his daytime occupation is as the owner of the newspaper, The Daily Sentinal. Bruce plays his butler/manservant, Kato, and he shares Britt's secret hideout. When duty calls, the Little Dragon transforms into a masked chauffeur - not an ordinary one, mind you, but a driver with a deadly art at his fingertips.

The entrance into the Hornet stronghold is via a huge poster for Candy Mints, and through several holes in the wall. The image of the pair, unlike *Batman* which comes from the same stable, is fairly modest. Whereas for the Dynamic Duo, the scene is set around

the corny dialogue, Bruce and Van Williams (Britt Reid) intend the lines to be taken seriously. And when, at times, the script falls a little short of its intentions, the two heroes more than compensate with fine performances.

The episode here is titled *The Silent Gun* and Richard Bluel is the Producer, William Dozier the Executive Producer, Leslie Martinson, the Director and Ken Pettus, the Writer. It's a Twentieth Century Fox production.

The scene opens in typically dramatic fashion. A funeral is in progress and a police car pulls up with the D.A. and a detective in the back. They're after a man called Bannister and, sure enough, he's there in the crowd. The trouble is, they're a shade too late!

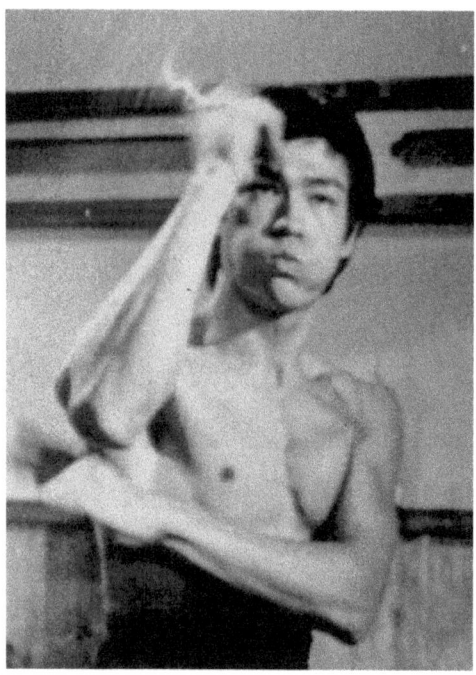

To the horror of the other mourners, another man pulls a gun and fires off a shot. Bannister falls dead into the grave of his father, though strangely, no one had heard a shot. The bullet had been fired from, yes - you've guessed it, a silent gun!

The D.A. gets on the trail and he contacts Britt with details of the post mortem. The amazing news is that the bullet was fired from a 17 calibre gun - a totally unheard of device. The dead man's girlfriend contacts Britt with a surprising deal. Thinking she might be next for the chop, she offers to tell all she knows in return for $2,000 - enough for her to leave town. Britt agrees.

Later, back at the hideout, he meets up with Kato. Bruce is wearing a white jacket and black trousers (a little too short for him), plus a white shirt and black bow tie. The reserved dress belies the ferocious personality hiding underneath. The D.A. arrives and as he comes through the wall, an alarm sounds in Britt's living room. The Hornet shifts a couple of books on a shelf, which turn out to be leavers, and the D.A. comes down in a lift, while the fireplace rises up. Pure corn maybe it is, but the visuals are most impressive.

The D.A. has a hot lead - Bannister's father was a retired gunsmith who had recently been working on some new kind of silencer. The phone rings and brings even more disturbing news. A man in a lift has just been shot and robbed of $5,000 in negotiable bonds but no one heard the gun being fired. "We better destroy this gun fast," mutters the D.A. "Let's hope there's no more than one gun," replies Britt. The D.A. leaves the way he came - Britt returns the leavers, then asks Kato to get the Black Beauty ready.

What, you may wonder, is the Black Beauty? Over to Britt's garage for the James Bond-type answer! To all intents and purposes, there's just an everyday car parked there. Bruce switches the positions of a couple of spanners and a panel on the wall lights up. He pushes a button and four clamps rise from the floor to grip the car. He pushes some more, and the entire floor swings over and upside down to reveal Kato and the Hornet's strange looking roadster, the Black Beauty. The Candy Mints poster open up and off they roar. The critical may notice that when the D.A. was there, it was broad daylight, yet minutes later they leave in the dead of night!

A switch of scene now to Britt's office at *The Daily Sentinel* where his assistant is meeting Bannister's girlfriend. Just as she's about to spill the beans, our two heroes burst in. The Hornet fires a burst of green gas into the assistant's face while Kato grabs the girl.

At this point, the viewer could be forgiven for feeling slightly confused. However, Britt checks the man is asleep, then offers the money for the girl's information. No one could accuse the show of being short on cliches. When asked by her how he knows so much, the Hornet replies, "I know about a lot of things!"

The story comes out that, in a craps game, Bannister had blown $2,000 of the money they'd put aside for a wedding. When he tried to get it back, he just got worse in debt. Someone called Al Trumm had put one of his thugs onto Bannister who, realising he couldn't meet the money he owed, instead stole his father's secret weapon - the silent gun - as alternative repayment.

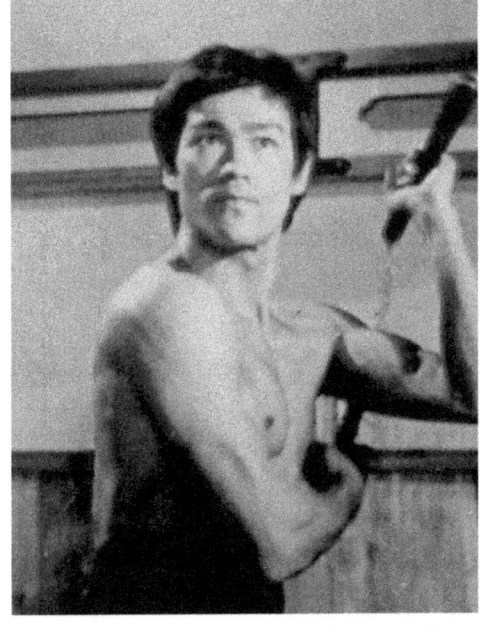

Bannister's father found out and was about to tell the police when he was run over by a car - driven by Trumm. It was made to look like an accident, but Bannister knew better. He decided to tell the police himself, and that, rather neatly, brings us round to the opening scene where the law arrives just too late to save him.

The first real fight sequence is fast approaching. Kato and the Hornet drive over to the thug's flat and leg up onto the balcony. Through the window they can see two guys - one of whom is identified as Big Dan Carley. Big Dan and the other man both leave and Britt and Kato climb into the room. The place has been ransacked and the thug, who's called Renner, is dead.

Suddenly, Trumm enters the room, flanked by two henchmen. Seeing the possibilities of the situation, he announces, "It's the Green Hornet and he's just killed Renner." He covers them with a gun and tells one of the bodyguards to call the cops.

At last it's time for a glimpse of the Master at work, be it short and sweet! Bruce kicks a box from the floor into the face of Trumm, giving Britt time to jump in and grab the villain's gun-hand. The Little Dragon continues the action by slugging one of the thugs on the jaw. Then in a moment of pure magic, he leaps through the air to deliver an elbow jab to the back of the other thug's neck, followed by a powerful blow to the stomach. Both bodyguards are out for the count and Trumm is now covered by the Hornet.

The burning question is, of course, where is the 'silent gun' - and Britt asks it. Trumm just laughs at him, until Bruce throws a straight fingers jab that snaps to a stop just milli-

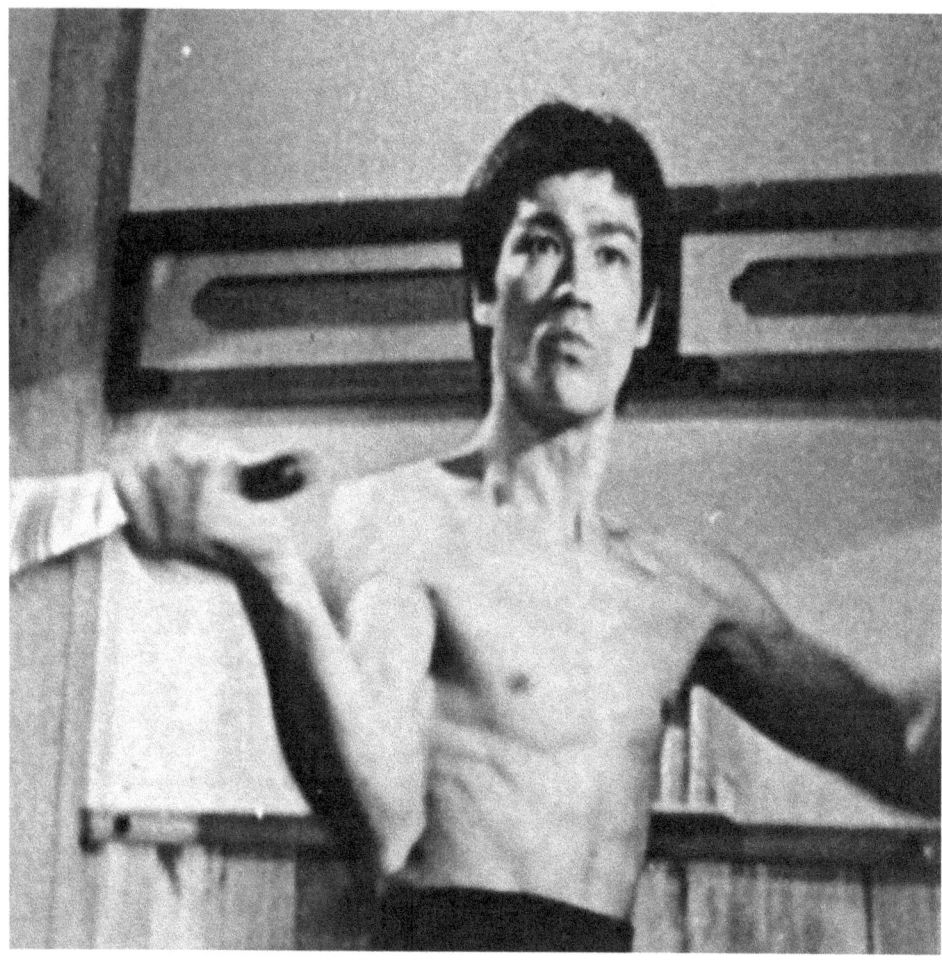

metres from Trumm's throat. "Okay, okay I've got it stashed." "I want it," says Britt. "So do a lot of people," sniggers Trumm.

The Green Hornet spends a while convincing the villain that they aren't the only people interested in the weapon. Trumm makes out he's not scared of anyone, but eventually, he agrees to a deal where they work together with Big Dan Carley over possession of the gun.

It's obvious here that the Hornet has something up his sleeve - another plan has been hatched.

And that's where we'll leave the plot for this month. Next issue, in Part Two, you'll find that Bruce loses no time in warming to some more action - this time with the aid of some very similar darts to those he was later to use in *The Way of the Dragon*.

It's easy to see, watching this episode, why Bruce soon found himself taking over most of the limelight. Van Williams, as Britt, did a very competent job, but somehow he could never match the charismatic, star quality of Bruce. Maybe in a roundabout way, this was why the show never really took off in the way everyone had hoped. But for the true Little

Dragon fan, it has to be a real treat. Not only do we view a magnificent, though perhaps none too sizeable, dose of Bruce in action - we also catch a slickly produced and fun slice of entertainment.

It's not often that one gets to see the Master outside of the influence of the somewhat shambolic Mandarin film industry - such moments are to be savoured. Hopefully soon, we'll be seeing some of these golden episodes on British TV screens. Meanwhile, hang on won't you, for next month's second instalment of Bruce Lee as Kato in The Silent Gun.

THE BRUCE LEE SOCIETY

Hi everyone, Pam here again with, this month, a report on the delivery of the *Game of Death* censorship petition.

On Thursday, July 13th, myself and photographer Rick Kemp, turned up on the doorstep of the British Board of Film Censors, armed with over three and a half thousand signatures. The bundle, plus several hundred words I'd written myself, were accepted most graciously by Mr Ferman, Secretary of the Board.

We got to discussing the nunchaku battle in *Way of the Dragon* and Mr Ferman made the point that, originally, the scene was included for general release. Apparently it was only after many complaints from the public, the police and local authorities, that the section was chopped out. It seems there were a number of instances of kids badly injuring themselves and those around them, with homemade varieties. I asked him why, therefore, the scene was now back in position. Mr Ferman was surprised to hear the news! He said it must have been done without his knowledge and that any public showing of the reinstated battle was illegal!!! However, that said, Mr Ferman admitted to being quite a fan of Bruce Lee and said he hated cutting anything out of the films.

I made the point that, if kids were mimicking Bruce in action by making and using nunchakus, surely that meant the 'X' Certificate system wasn't working? Why penalise serious fans of the Master because of a badly administered law? Furthermore, most of the public reaction took place some years ago, when Bruce had just died and the craze was still raging. Now, with a much more mature following, I can't see the same problem existing.

We also argued over where exactly the line should be drawn between violence that is acceptable and violence that is not. My feelings are very strong. How on earth can some of the more recent gory and bloody hackings, maimings and butcherings that all too frequently nauseate me when I go to the cinema, be acceptable? Yet a super-skilled display by the world's leading practitioner of an ancient weapon be unacceptable? I think he agreed that the whole business was very unfair indeed!

Mr Ferman is putting the letter I gave him to the Board and the answer I receive will obviously be passed on as quickly as possible to you, the fans.

In the next News Sheet, I'll include a much fuller account on the whole affair but let's just hope that, by then, the future for skilled, cinema martial action will be a good deal brighter!

Lastly, just take a look at the adverts page this month. The offer open for new members to the Society is absolutely stupendous! By the way, don't feel at all left out all you present members as there's something similar lined up for you in the next News Sheet!
Pam

KICKBACK: THE LETTERS

And right away, it's a big hello from me, Jenny, to another edition of Kickback. First off, and late extra news, not only is *KFM* offering a close-up look at David Carradine's *Silent Flute* but hopefully next month, we'll also be able to tell you just how good the film actually is. That's right, our Editor will be reporting on a sneak preview to the first ever showing in Britain - another *Kung-Fu Monthly* first! It's hardly surprising that our letters this issue still tend to reflect reader's views on *Game of Death* - after all, it is the number one talking point of the moment. But, how about this month's Society membership offer? Where some more magic copies of *KFM Scrapbook* came from, heaven only knows, but come they have. If you have been thinking about joining up, then there'll never be a better time than the present. Get those applications off to Pam by return, I'd say. Now, it's letters time!

DRAGON POWER ERROR

Dear Jenny,
Having read through the *Dragon Power* competition in *KFM* No.42, it seems to me there's been a gross error made somewhere. According to the newsflash from Satril Records, the disc was released on June 16th and only 5,000 copies of the 12" version were released. Elsewhere, however, you say that the record was released on June 19th and that 15,000 copies were released. Who was right?
Ian Grant, North Shields, Tyne & Wear

Dear Ian,
Thanks for pointing out what looks on the face of it to be somewhat conflicting information. Funnily enough, in some ways, both were right! Originally (when the newsflash was put out), the date of issue and the quantity were correct. Then, problems with pressing and enormous pre-release demand caused the changes.

CENSORSHIP FAILURE

Dear Jenny,
It seems to me that the British Board of Film Censors is concerned about the effect on youngsters who may be over-awed and mislead into believing that they can use the nunchaku as well as Bruce. If this is so, the system of issuing X certificates is not working and the Board would be better occupied in attempting to correct their system, rather than in depriving cinemagoers of some of the best action ever filmed.
A.D.P., Eccles, Lancs.

Dear A.D.P.,
Bravo! I honestly couldn't have put it better myself. And in fact, that's also a point Pam Hadden made to the Secretary of the Board when she handed over the petition. Perhaps rather than keep leaning on the B.B.F.C. (who, to an extent at least, seem to be on our side), we should try directing our efforts towards cinema legislation that isn't working.

GAME OF DEATH DISGUST

Dear Jenny,
Firstly, congratulations on producing such a fine magazine. Secondly, I must express my anger at the way *Game of Death* is being treated. To save half of the footage for a follow-up makes me wonder whether they really are interested in the Little Dragon's farewell - or simply keen to make more money. Here is my own tribute to Bruce:
Bend with the wind, I remember it well his outlook on life, and yet he fell but remember this fact now he's laid to rest that those who leave early are often the best, of him this fact could truly be spoken he left much more than one heart broken he was smiled upon, then left, but why? Loved by so many, too good to die. But none of us grieved when he went away for he went to the right place, on the right day such a man is always respected and such a short life should be expected. For as I have said, the good will die young but out of his body another has sprung And when I think, we must all pay a fee why must we pay with the likes of Bruce Lee?
Phil Boardman, Manchester, Lancs

Dear Phil,
Regular readers will know that poems only occasionally find their way into KFM *Kickback* .but this has got to be the exception. I think it's superb! I especially like the first verse. Congratulations, Phil, on writing lines that sent shivers up my back. Okay, everybody, there's a challenge for you - mail in some more works like this and I'll print the best of them.

BRUCE LEE'S NUNCHAKU SKILLS

Dear Jenny,
I have a Chinese friend in Hong Kong who says it only took Bruce one year to learn his nunchakus. I, however, have read that it took him ten. Who is right? By the way, I'm giving away three full colour, giant posters to the first person who can tell me what Bruce had on order shortly before his death.
Brian Jenkin, Redruth, Cornwall

Dear Brian,
It's really a question that's a bit hard to answer. I'm pretty sure that he'd acquired tremendous mastery over the weapon within the space of twelve months. But then again, I'm sure he'd have been the first to admit that, over the years, time honed an even finer edge on his abilities. Thanks, by the way, for picking up on the idea and making your kind offer. If enough free offers come in - given away on a first come, first serve basis - then maybe I'll start another small column.

QUICKIES CORNER

Gary Daniels, Hayes, Middx - Try writing to Nora c/o Golden Harvest Ent., 8 Hammer Hill Road, Kowloon, Hong Kong. No pilgrimages planned right now - the cost is just too enormous.

Marlon Whetton, Streatham, London - If Pam says that *Enter the Dragon* somersault was done by a double, then I'm sure it was.

Paul Nayman, Linthorpe, Cleveland - Glad you liked *Dragon Power* so much - it looks like *Top of the Pops* haven't noticed it yet, try writing and demanding.

Michael Cooney, Holborn, London - I agree, the double's war cries were an embarrassment.

John Hill, Croxteth, Liverpool - I'm not surprised to hear that *Game of Death* was pulling capacity crowds to your local cinema in London's West End as it was the top film for some weeks back.

Gary Stubbs, Witherwack, Tyne & Wear - Sorry, *Exit the Dragon, Enter the Tiger* stars the notorious Bruce Li.

Patrick Phillips, West Kirby, Merseyside - Apologies for not answering your long letter more fully. No way do we intentionally try to make out that Karate is inferior to Kung Fu. Bruce's films were full of obvious fantasy - it should do no harm to echo those sentiments.

COMPETITION RESULTS

Time now for the news you've all been been waiting for - the *Dragon Power* Competition results! Receiving a free signed 12" copy of the record will be: Miss Cynthia Nazareth of Ashford in Kent, Michael Metcalfe of Radcliffe in Lancs, George Fitzgerald of Battersea in London, Paul Short of Foxhill in South Yorkshire, Ahmad Latif from London, R. Rolph of Barking in Essex, Mr K.L. Gill of Burnley in Lancs, Miss Clare Humphreys of Warrington in Cheshire, Gary Harness from Nottingham, Mr S. Ward of Slough in Berks, Mike Devereux of Orford in Cheshire, Derek O'Toole of Basingstoke in Hants, R.S. Richardson of Stockport in Cheshire, Mr K. Pryor of Kingsley in Northampton, Miss Ann Leyland of Pemberton in Lancs, Ann Perren of Milton in Hants, Mr Lee Baker of Oadby in Leics, Bruce Hussain of Fenton in Staffs, Roger Bayntun of Walton-on-Thames in Surrey, Martin Lea of Acocks Green in Warks, Premdas Napar of Southall in Middx, Miss Kerry Beaumont of Wigan in Lancs, John Donaldson of Edinburgh in Scotland, Miss H. Midgley of Barnsley in South Yorks and Richard Milney of Barry in Glam.

Congratulations to the winners and thanks to the thousands of you who took part.

THE POSTER MAGAZINES - VOLUME TWO

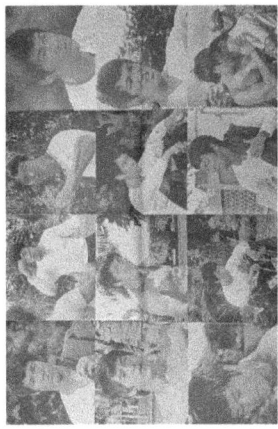

1978

EDITORIAL

    Hi there *KFM* fans. If someone asked me to sum up the flavour of this issue in just one word, then the one springing most readily to mind would be 'Celebration.' 1978 hasn't been without its disappointments - *Game of Death*, both in what the makers did with Bruce's legacy and in terms of the scenes the censors decided to mutilate, has given us little cause for joy. So why, you may ask, should this be a celebration issue?

    The answer, I'm delighted to say, lies in David Carradine's interpretation of the Master's *The Silent Flute*. Maybe we don't actually see a single frame of the Little Dragon in action but what we do get is his great influence and his undoubted message - spiritually he is with us. And David Carradine seems to have thrown himself into Bruce's pet project almost as though his life depended on it. Just how well he's done you can judge for yourselves by reading my review. Last month we told you what the script was calling for. Now, right here, you can read Carradine's Catalogue of success.

The Silent Flute review is a long one, but there's still room for Part Two of our check out of *The Silent Gun*. Bruce Lee as Kato in the *Green Hornet* proved to be an inspired piece of casting, to the degree eventually where he actually ended up overtaking Van Williams in the popularity stakes. There may not be quite the dynamite martial action we came to expect later from the Master, but as a starter to his Western World show business career it was more than enough.

Finally this month, may I offer my congratulations to Pam Hadden as she heads off into year three of the Bruce Lee Society. While the club has gone from strength to strength, one thing that hasn't changed is Pam's tireless work in keeping the BLS right up on its toes as the world's number one appreciation society. I wish her many more years of success.

Felix Yen
Editor-in-Chief

THE SILENT FLUTE: THEN AND NOW

Last month we brought you another exclusive first with a run down on Carradine's version of Bruce's legendary and intended epic, *The Silent Flute*. We gave a full check out of the stars and a line by line appreciation of the plot as it now stands, we also expressed the hope that our Editor would be able to sneak a preview in time for a write-up, this issue - and he has! But there's more - not only will you find here his impressions of how Carradine and the crew have interpreted the great legacy, we also bring you a detailed report on how Bruce himself conceived the idea - why, after so nearly starting the project, was he finally forced to abandon it? Read on for some surprising answers.

Probably by now, quite a few of you have already seen *The Silent Flute*, but let me say immediately that, to the best of my belief, David Carradine has done it. Though at times the Master is painfully missed, the spirit of his intentions live on! If ever the fans needed something to lift them out of the disappointments they found in *Game of Death*, then this is it. It's a beautiful production to be missed by no one.

But we move ahead too far so let's return first to the days when the Little Dragon was first planning to create a definitive film on the martial arts. The idea for such a film had been on his mind for quite a while. Now Dame Fortune had struck - at last he was in a position to carry out his desire - to film the ultimate display of his art and genius. The initial move was to consult James Coburn and scriptwriter, Stirling Silliphant. He showed them his roughed-out ideas and immediately they were hooked! It's not surprising they took to it so quickly. Both had known Bruce for gome time and both knew the passion that burned within him. They decided that being too close to the source of inspiration might possibly bring them to produce a script that was overloaded with self-indulgence. They had to remember that, ultimately, the movie needed to show commercial success.

A couple of things were tried. First of all, they hired a writer, who's work proved such a disaster, he was fired again almost immediately! Stirling then tried handing the project over to his nephew/ Silliphant and Coburn were starting to realise that they had already stepped back far enough from the script to see it in its true light - and at once, ideas started to flow. They were sound, positive ideas that not only remained true to Bruce's original concept but were also commercially viable. Their labour of love looked like it was certain to flower into a truly magnificent motion picture.

All three of them turned aside other work they bought to see *The Silent Flute* finished. Each Monday, Wednesday and Friday, they would meet up, having pledged with each other that nothing would interfere with the project until the day of completion. Little did Stirling know, the day he took the finished work along to Warner Brothers, the blind alley into which he was heading. Yes, they loved it but unfortunately, they then decided the production would have to be shot in India, where they just happened to have some 'blocked rupees.' In other words, they had money there which they couldn't take out of the country. Bruce's project seemed the ideal way to use it.

It was a sad blow for Bruce because it was going to be more than tough trying to shoot a Chinese film on location in India! Many would have given up then and there but the Little Dragon, being an eternal optimist, decided to set out and see what the country had to offer. Alas, the trip proved fruitless, and so disillusioned did all three become, they simply ended up squabbling amongst themselves. The project got shelved indefinitely.

Later it came to light that, many of the themes within *The Silent Flute*, borrowed heavily from Bruce's own attitude to life; his spiritual, mental and physical outlook. The story traces the path taken by a young martial arts students and sees the problems confronting him when faced with an out-of-control ego. Gradually he is able to take charge and with the courage he finds, he defeats the finality of death to discover his spiritual rebirth. There's one line which stands out as a sure example of the Little Dragon's battle with the contradictions of life, "I'm not even sure what trials I passed through or how I came to be here. I still have doubts, many doubts, like how, without more struggle, can I resolve them?"

Now, in a preview theatre, it was time to view the finished work and to see the discarded reins that David Carradine had so aptly gathered to him. Sitting in the small movie house waiting for *The Silent Flute* to begin, I suddenly became aware of that feeling of anxiety I have always experienced before seeing one of Bruce's films. What was going to happen to the Master's concept? Would they distort it? Would they abuse it? Would they commercialise it beyond all recognition?

Forty or so lucky members of the film business took their places and the murmuring died away, the lights dimmed and the curtains parted to reveal a pitch black screen. Slowly we became aware of one of the most beautiful sunrises ever to have been photographed. On screen top right appeared the philosophical note: "Although two birds tied together have four wings, they cannot fly." It blueprints the theme for the rest of the film. There's nothing to be gained in simply reiterating the plot, as recounted last issue. Rather, from here on in, I shall be pointing out the things that, for one reason or another, have stuck in my mind.

The Blind Man (David Carradine) sits playing a long flute and, visually, the setting is superb. Unfortunately, the flute we see and the sound we hear coming from it don't fit together! The instrument we see looks something near a bass flute, the notes we hear

come from an alto. Most, however, will not worry about such trifles.

Watching the fights progress in the amphitheatre below there's a warm feeling that, although Bruce's genius for choreography is surely missed, still the result is no disgrace - in fact it's good in comparison to most other martial arts films. The final battle between Cord and Morthond will remind many of *Enter the Dragon*'s opening sequence. The circling and the smile playing upon Morthond's lips are direct pinches from Bruce's psychological approach to combat.

Later, while Morthond and Cord are walking along the road, bickering with each other (strange that two such mighty warriors should descend to such a mundane level) the Blind Man passes by. Attached to his toe is a bell. Though not explained, the reason for this is presumably that it offers a simple form of radar. Throughout the film, the Blind Man walks and fights without hesitation as obstacles in his path prove no problem at all.

Carradine's fight scene in the castle with the eight thugs is excellent. Though his actions are much slower than those Bruce would surely have achieved, his handling of the staff is really effective - casual and sure. In fact it's fair to say that, since his *Kung Fu* series on TV, Carradine has raised his fighting abilities by a very high degree; he's far more fluent and positive. Bruce explained to a young student in *Enter the Dragon*, "Never take your eyes off your opponent, even when you bow." Though blind, Carradine manages to face all his opponents in combat.

Later, after the fall of Morthond, Cord comes once again upon the Blind Man. Here Carradine is sat in a quite remarkable set. Surrounded only by rocks, the air is filled with flying doves. Cord has a hundred questions to ask and this is where many of Bruce's philosophies appear in the script. Obviously, much of the scene was written by the Little Dragon. Every question put by Cord is answered by the Blind Man who puts Cord into the position of asking the questions of himself. It's a memorable scene and pure Bruce Lee.

It's a superb moment when Cord meets the first time with Changsha the Rhythm Man (also Carradine). A black giant (Earl Maynard) has very professional battle with Changsha. The giant's huge fists plough into Carradine - who easily avoids them. He takes a leaf from Bruce's fight against Bob Wall in *Enter the Dragon*, adding a sort of dancing shuffle. In fact, as the battle continues, Carradine's style becomes more and more like the Master's. Maybe the statement he made after seeing *Enter the Dragon* is true - that he feels the spirit of Bruce Lee within him.

Dodging the giant man's kicks and thrusts, Carradine lands a crippling punch to the solar plexis - and it's all over.

Further along the film footage we come upon some astounding camera techniques. Cord stumbles into an old fortress and immediately everything turns bluey-green. Carradine as The Panther Man becomes the centre of many shimmering, sharp-angled shots and the general feeling of evil is the best I've witnessed since seeing The Exorcist.

Eventually Cord arrives back at Changsha's camp and so begins the most stunning scene in the entire film. The battle between the two is heralded by a roll on the drums and immediately Carradine smiles the Lee smile of total self-confidence and begins circling his prey. The choreography is masterly - time and again they meet each other with inter-twining punches and kicks. They look an absolutely equal match. It has to be said that David Carradine has finally got it dead right. Imitating he may be, but every little movement and every gesture of his hands and that smile, its pure Bruce Lee. The drums beat faster and louder, the battle grows ever more furious. Beautiful camera cutting between Changsha and the other characters that Carradine plays lift the tension to a fantastic peak.

Finally, Cord rises to the occasion and he strikes the winning blows, the apparitions fade and the seeker after the Book has won. The film totally captures the atmosphere of victory and gives me a feeling only ever previously experienced when watching the Master's own epic confrontations.

What follows is a masterly change of mood. The camera pans across glistening water to a serene shot of the island where Zetan holds the Book and suddenly the atmosphere reeks of mysticism. Cord makes the short journey and arrives in a paradise land where stands the ancient monastery. One can almost catch the wafting scent of the beautiful flowers which surround it - everything is at total and absolute peace.

Zetan himself appears - a role that's perfectly carried out by former arch villain, Christopher Lee. On this occasion, however, somehow he seems to epitomise wisdom and contentment all rolled into one. A poignant moment is when Cord strikes an aggressive stance - and Zetan hands him a rose. Cord refuses the gesture. It's interesting to recall that Bruce was putting the basics of *The Silent* Flute on to paper during the flower-power era and it may well be that Zetan's action resulted from his experience of those times.

Cord, having taken over the position of Keeper, our hero returns for his final, joyous meeting with the Blind Man. The final shots are breathtaking. As the two dance and make music in celebration, the camera slowly pulls back until all that can be seen are two minute figures in the far distance surrounded by mountains and canyons.

I'm sure most of the fans will agree that Carradine's *The Silent Flute* comes as near to Bruce's wishes as anything could, without the Master actually being there. There's one small mystery that has yet to be solved. Bruce intended in his original version to play five parts but Carradine, however, only takes on four.

What happened for that matter? What is the elusive fifth role?

Having read this report, I'm sure most of you will understand the very high esteem in which I hold this amazing production. In just about every aspect, it shines out as a compelling example of just what is possible when the genius of Bruce Lee meets the talent of top class actors and Kung Fu artists under conditions of sheer professionalism. Not wishing to rub salt into the wound but *The Silent Flute* is simply everything that *Game of Death* isn't.

Will Raymond Chow now learn a few lessons and at least make passably good use of the remaining Bruce Lee footage? I recommend he go see *The Silent Flute* and maybe then he'll be able to work out for himself just what caused the *Game of Death* disaster.

As for David Carradine, well there could have been no better way for him to have cleared many people's lingering doubts. The man is good and he seems sincere about what he's doing and, what's more, his martial arts ability has increased by a million miles since the *Kung Fu* series on TV.

Let's hope for a worldwide box office smash. If David Carradine really is possessed of the spirit of the Master, then there's no better way for him to show it than by turning out more productions along these same fine lines. The sentiments, the philosophy, the fighting, the camera skills - it's all there. Only Bruce is missing and somehow, one distinctly gets the feeling that he isn't really that far away!

THE GREEN HORNET AND KATO
THE SILENT GUN – PART TWO

Last month we took you part way through *The Green Hornet* episode, The Silent Gun. To recap the story so far, A man by the name of Bannister owes hoodlum, Al Trumm more money then he can lay his hands on. He decides to offer instead a gadget that his father has recently perfected, a silent gun. Bannister's father finds out about the deal but, on the way to tell the police, he gets bumped off by Trumm. While attending his father's burial, Bannister himself makes up his mind to tell all. It's too late, Trumm has him silenced too. In the meantime though, Bannister's girlfriend spills the beans to our indominatable heroes, Kato (Bruce Lee) and The Green Hornet (Van Williams). The two break into Trumm's flat, which gives us the first chance of seeing Bruce flex his martial muscles. Finally a deal of some sort seems to be in the offing between the Hornet and Trumm, although it's obvious the duo have something up their sleeves. We rejoin the story.

Just prior to the confrontation in Trumm's flat, Kato and the Hornet had seen someone else checking out the hoodlum's hideout - a thug by the name of Big Dan Carley. Wasting no time, the two pay him a surprise visit. As usual they slip in through a window (does no one lock their windows these days?) and immediately we catch some hot action from the Little Dragon. A henchman is obliterated by two sharp blows to the head. Another goes for his gun only to find himself stuck through the arm with darts (very similar to the ones later used in way). Carley tries to pull his shooting piece from a drawer and Bruce

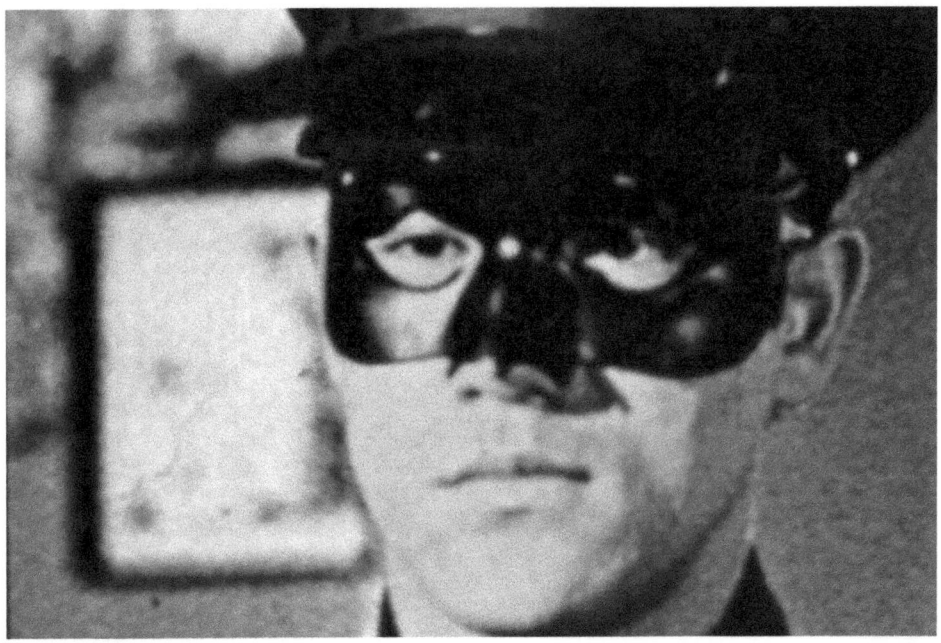

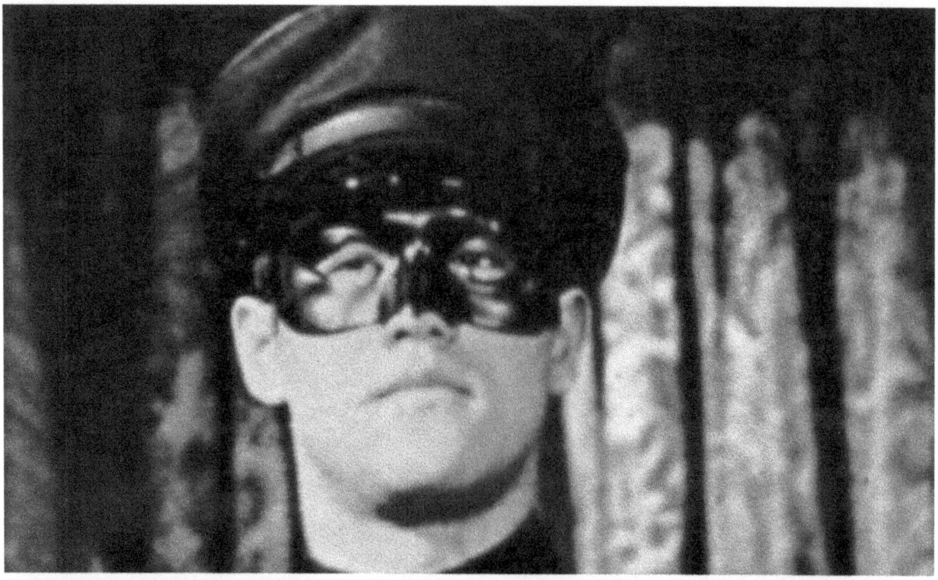

issues a deadly warning in the shape of another dart that buries itself in the wood, just inches from the searching fingers. Relative calm descends and the Hornet offers the silent gun to Carley. At first the thug plays ignorant, then he agrees to a meeting sometime soon.

As Carley casually lights up a cigar, Bruce sticks a microphone under his table. Kato and the Hornet leave via the window and as they head off down the road, they switch on a receiver and tape recorder. Carley is on the phone to Trumm.

Between them they decide that The Green Hornet will be bumped off at the meeting.

Later, after playing the tape to the District Attorney, the duo decide they have to go through with the meeting.

The scene switches to Trumm's car. He and Big Dan are in the front and the Hornet is sitting behind. There are problems - Bruce is parked in an alley listening for a signal from the Hornet that Trumm's car is passing. He hears it and starts to follow, but almost immediately, the police recognise the famous Black Beauty and they start chasing Bruce. Trumm, Carley and the Hornet arrive at the hoodlum's office - the silent gun is produced - and right away Carley traigs it on the Hornet. Our hero is not surprised. He slams a cupboard door on Carley's hand and makes a break for it. During the chase, the Hornet manages to temporarily blind Trumm by squirting him in the eyes with oil from a can. Carley, however, creeps up behind and begins the usual 'I've got you at last' routine.

Bruce arrives outside the garage where the Hornet seems about to breathe his last. A press of a button and several rows of what look like shotgun barrels beneath headlights of the Black Beauty. However, flaming rockets appear, which successfully shatter the garage door (in very spectac-

ular fashion) and Kato drives in through the debris. The Hornet dodges out the way and Carley shoots blindly. Unfortunately for him, the bullet slices through a nearby hot water pipe and a jet of steam burns into the thug's face. Bruce leaps from the car but no more help is needed. Instead, the Little Dragon grins from ear to ear in his immaculate, boyish manner and remarks, "One greased and one hard boiled!" A beautiful finale. And that's all there is to know about The Silent Gun. Perhaps it's not the most original of film scripts and for sure, the fans could do with a far heavier dose of the famed Bruce Lee action. But all that said, as such rarities as these find their way onto 8mm film, so the horizons broaden for the true Little Dragon collector. Where The Silent Gun leads, more will follow.

THE BRUCE LEE SOCIETY

Hello, Pam here again with this month's news and views on the world famous Bruce Lee Society!

To begin with, apologies all round to Third Year Members for the lateness in arrival of their new kit. I've tried to be ambitious and, unfortunately, we're paying the penalty in the amount of time it's taking. Hang on in is what I say! Actually there's a good deal of re-working going on to make the various kits more standardised, and here's more or less what I'll be doing. The basis of it all will be special 'Year Stickers' - which will follow the yin/yang design of the Second Year brooches. Everyone, new Members and old, will be receiving an updated version of the scroll, which will remain current all the time they're Members of the Society, taking the place of any others they may have had. After each twelve-month period of membership, I'll be sending you the next Year Sticker to affix to the scroll in the area shown. Easy, isn't it! And what's more, the new membership card you get sent on renewal each year will also carry the appropriate Year Sticker.

One particular aspect of the three-monthly News Sheet that's growing in popularity is the "Member's Picture" section. Each issue now carries quite a few snap-shots, and it's great to see. Now, therefore, it would be a good moment to say a word or two about the sort of picture that will print the best. It needs to be clear and in focus and preferably with a fairly uncluttered background, such as a wall or the sky. Finally, and just as important, our design artist tells me that he definitely prefers to use black and white rather than colour. It's going to end up black and white eventually, so I suppose that makes sense!

After all the bad news, it's been refreshing to hear some good for a change. I'm talking about David Carradine's *Silent Flute* and, I've got to admit it, there was a time when David was my pet hate! Now I'm happy to say all is forgiven and in fact, he's really helped salvage the year of the *Game of Death* tragedy. After you've seen *The Silent Flute*, write and tell me if you feel the same way. How about sending in some local review? I've seen some good ones already.

That's about all I've time for this month. Remember, if you still haven't managed to find time to join our Bruce Lee Society, it's never too late. The subscription is still just £3.25 a year and the person to write to is me, Pam Hadden, at *KFM*, 14 Rathbone Place, London W1P 1DE. See you next month!

KICKBACK: THE LETTERS

Hi, Jenny here with yet another monster sack of reader's mail! And when I say sack, I mean sack! Really, since the start of the *Game of Death* controversy, the number of letters we've been getting in has risen to epic proportions. Most, I'm sorry to say, register various shades of disappointment with Raymond Chow's efforts, ranging from the upset to the plain outraged! I think now it would be timely for me to make the comment that, okay, it's been done and most of us have hardly had a good word to say. But the world has got to keep moving and there are other battles to win. The dead hand of censorship continues to gnaw away at the Master's genius and still British TV refuses to commit itself to showings of *Longstreet*, *The Green Hornet*, and so on. The Death battle is over - others are only just beginning! And now, the letters...

AUSSIE CORRECTIONS

Dear Jenny,
You may not know me, but I've been a member of the BLS for nearly two years now, and a close friend and pen pal of Pam Hadden, the President. While looking through my collection of *KFM*, I came across a letter in *KFM* No.21 from a fellow Aussie in N.S.W. In his letter he said his relatives sent the magazine over to him each month, and I must say I found your reply highly amusing. However, you made a mistake, it's 'ya' and not 'ye.' To avoid any further error in true blue, fair dinkum (Ha Ha) Aussie replies, I've taken the liberty of drawing up a mini dictionary of Aussie slang! G'day - good day; cobber or mate - friend; bonza - good; ripper - fantastic; true blue - real; fair dinkum - true, no lie; micky - fun or sport.
Wesley Fleming, Daw Park, Adelaide, S. Australia

Hi Wesley,
It's great to be talking to one of Bruce's Australian fans! How about writing back and letting us know the scene your end? For instance, do you have the same censorship problems we have in Britain? Finally, if I have any more problems with Aussie slang, I'll know where to go for help!

BRUCE LEE RECORD SUPPLIER

Dear Jenny,
I thought I'd send in the name and address of where to get Bruce Lee records. The best place I've found is Flyover Records, 15 Queen Carolyn Street, Hammersmith Broadway, London W.6. The phone number is 748 1595 and the man to speak to is Lou Raynor. If you write for information, remember to enclose a SAE.
Eddy Pumer, Capital Radio, London NW1

Editor's Note: *There was no response to Eddy Pumer's letter.*

MORE GAME OF DEATH FOOTAGE?

Dear Jenny,
I see Raymond Chow has held back footage from *Game of Death* to make follow-up(s). What is he doing? There are strong visual images in Bruce's last-ever fight sequences which cannot be carried over into another film. For example, the yellow and black colour theme of the nunchakus and suit is mirrored, to an extent, in the interior of the pagoda (yellow curtains, etc.) It's my guess that all this originates from the yin/yang symbol. It's a strong image, far stronger than the mirror sequence in *Enter the Dragon*. Let's face it, Chow's action is ludicrous and hypocritical, particularly in respect of his comment in *Photoplay*. I quote, "*Game of Death* is our tribute to a friend who became a legend." He should have added, "And if I can stretch it into another film, I might make more money." Finally, Jenny, can you tell me where I might get a copy of *Dragon Power*?
Graham P. Williams, Mayhill, W. Glamorgan

Dear Graham,
Some pretty constructive criticism there and I must say I agree with every word of it. For Dragon Power, write to Satril Records, 444 Finchley Road, London NW2 2HY.

GAME OF DEATH - A POSITIVE TAKE

Dear Jenny,
I would like to take this opportunity of thanking *KFM* and its many readers for at last getting *Game of Death* tuned out, for I'm sure that without all the pleadings and petitions, the film would still be collecting dust on the shelves of Golden Harvest. Even though it is disgusting that the best fight sequences were cut, I still think we should chalk it up as one to us all.
Dave Ashby, Bury St. Edmunds, Suffolk.

Dear Dave,
Without actually talking to Raymond Chow himself, it's hard to say exactly how much effect we had with our hard work. The one point that keeps crossing my mind is, if he did take a little interest in what we were asking, what a pity he didn't take more notice of the, 'How to finish off Game of Death*' competition results that I mailed to Golden Harvest some time ago. So far as I'm concerned, ALL the winners gave better storylines than the one he eventually used.*

SPOOKY GOINGS-ON?

Dear Jenny,
We recently heard a strange story concerning Bruce. One day he rebuked a photographer for using a flashlamp - he found it 'glared' on his contact lenses. Just a few weeks later, he died and one of the people who came along to see the fans paying their last respects was this same photographer. He leaned over to take his shots, but each time he tried, the flash attachment refused to work. In desperation, he turned and tried a shot of the crowd - the camera worked perfectly!
Michael McDonnell & Norman Kavanagh, Kilmarnock, Scotland

Dear Norman and Michael,
These kind of stories make my flesh creep! I must say I'd like to hear it verified from the lips of the photographer himself.

QUICKIES CORNER

Russell Clayton - *Dragon Power* actually made the top of several disco charts - unfortunately the good old Beeb failed to pick up on it, so that was that.
David Telford, Silloth, Cumbria - *Tiswas* sounds quite a together programme - Perhaps they'll be showing more on Bruce soon.
Dave Evans, Sidcup, Kent - Thanks for the long letter - I guess we all feel a bit cheated.
Jean McMillan, Royston Hill, Glasgow - The poem is lovely - You may have been brought up on Fred Astaire, but I'm glad you've made the conversion!
Paul Wade, Boulevard, Hull - Come on readers, you tell me! What is the book that Bruce is reading in the Kickback page picture in *KFM* No.37?
Dave Stuart, Bidston, Merseyside - Believe it or not, yes the scene was actually taken at Bruce's funeral .
Elvis Whetton, Streatham, London - I'm glad somebody liked *Game of Death*! The battle cries sounding like a drowning rat is the best description I've heard yet.
Mike, Birkenhead, Merseyside - A Raymond Chow interview would be revealing - We'll work on the idea.
Peter Thomas, Northolt, Middlesex - He's got Bruce Lee magazines and books for sale at low prices.
M. Campion, Audley, Stoke-on-Trent - Sorry, I reckon the 'Would Ali have beaten Bruce?' discussion to be very tiring! I don't think so, but who can prove it?
Robert Firkin, Halesowen - Glad the magazine has got you started in learning the martial arts.
Stephen Sinclair, Rutherglen, Glasgow - *KFM* No. 2, 4, 10? Try our Collector Packs mail order advert.
Martin Connor, Airdrie, Lanarks - Actually, we're still toying with a 'Best of' idea. Do join the club, Pam will be happy to welcome you in.
Paul Sheerin, Sandyhills, Glasgow - Send your photo request to: Warner Brothers Ltd, 135 Wardour Street, London W1 - Good luck with the book
John Gallagher, Rochsoles, Strathclyde - I'm as sorry as you are that the Water Margin series has finished - It will indeed soon be time to start pushing for *Longstreet* and *Marlowe*.

THE KUNG-FU MONTHLY ARCHIVE SERIES

NEW KFM COLLECTORS PACKS!
Your last chance to obtain many rare back issues including Issue 1

Recently we have reorganised our warehouse and discovered a few hundred or so copies of very rare back issues of KFM. These are certainly the last remaining copies which still exist other than those already in the hands of collectors. We are therefore dividing all back issues into 'Collectors Packs'. Orders will be serviced strictly on a first come, first served basis. Refunds will be made when stocks are exhausted.

Many of you will already know that copies of early issues often pass hands privately for very high prices and we regularly receive offers from collectors around the world of up to £10 or more for individual copies. To give everyone a fair chance, we have always declined such offers and this policy will continue. We have little doubt though, that this really is your final opportunity to acquire back issues of many early editions.

To order, follow the instructions carefully and please note the following points:

- All orders can only be serviced on a first come first served basis.
- Prices include all postage, packing and handling charges.
- On certain early editions, the condition of the copies may not be 'mint' although we will not be despatching any seriously damaged copies.
- All orders are subject to availability.

- A FREE KFM binder will be sent to anyone ordering 5 packs or more.
- Orders can only be accepted for whole packs, with the exception of the first pack which contains KFM Nos. 1, 2 and 3. These first three issues are available individually while stocks last.
- All packs contain five issues as indicated, except for Collectors Pack No 1 which contains these issues.
- All previous back issue offers, including 'Back Issue Bonanzas' are now closed.

COLLECTORS PACK No. 1
Contains Nos. 1, 2 & 3
£5.00 per pack
Individual issues £2.50 each

COLLECTORS PACK No. 2
Contains Nos. 4, 5, 6 7 & 8
£4.00 per pack

COLLECTORS PACK No. 3
Contains Nos. 9, 10, 11 12 & 13
£4.00 per pack

COLLECTORS PACK No. 4
Contains Nos. 14, 15, 16 17 & 18
£2.50 per pack

COLLECTORS PACK No. 5
Contains Nos. 19, 20, 21 22 & 23
£2.50 per pack

COLLECTORS PACK No. 6
Contains Nos. 24, 25, 26 27 & 28
£2.50 per pack

COLLECTORS PACK No. 7
Contains Nos. 29, 30, 31 32 & 33
£2.50 per pack

COLLECTORS PACK No. 8
Contains Nos. 34, 35, 36 37 & 38
£1.75 per pack

COLLECTORS PACK No. 9
Contains Nos. 39, 40, 41 42 & 43
£1.75 per pack

Write your order carefully indicating which pack(s) you require. Enclose your name and address with your order, clearly written in capitals. State how much money you have enclosed. Please do not send cash. Make your cheque or postal order payable to Kung-Fu Monthly. Send your orders to: KFM Collectors Packs Offer, 14 Rathbone Place, London W1P 1DE.
KFM Bruce Lee Society members may deduct 10% from the listed price. However, you must write your Society number after your name when ordering.

THE POSTER MAGAZINES · VOLUME TWO

EDITORIAL

Welcome, everybody, to a smash edition of *Kung-Fu Monthly*. And when I say smash, I mean smash! To begin with, you've probably already noticed the great new photos. It must be obvious to everyone that locating unseen pictures of the Master gets to be progressively more difficult all the time. However, I'm delighted to say our researchers have turned up trumps yet again. Believe me, over this and the upcoming issues, there's going to be quite a few surprises in store!

And talking about surprises, how about feature one this month? If there's one area that's been in need of a tidy-up for a while now, it's the power-packed story of just how Bruce acted, and reacted, behind the scenes while he was shooting all those legendary movies. It's common knowledge that he was the nearest thing to a human dynamo the Mandarin film industry had ever seen. What's less known is the sheer scope of his involvement - script writer, fight choreographer, star actor, ideas-man and even occasional cameraman! The Little Dragon let no detail slip by in his quest to produce only the best; hairstyle, scenery, sound effects - all were important and all demanded his attention.

This month, in part one, we reveal much of the behind-the-scenes activity that surrounded the making of *The Big Boss* and, in addition, Chuck Norris gives some personal comments on what it was like working with the King of Kung Fu. There's word too on Bruce's technique for achieving total visual impact with the fight scenes. The Master never aimed to miss - he knew the camera wouldn't lie.

Second-up this issue is a track by track breakdown of the new *Game of Death* album. After the disappointment surrounding the film, perhaps it's partly to be expected that the LP suffers a similar fate.

Felix Yen

Felix Yen
Editor-in-Chief

BEHIND THE SCENES WITH BRUCE LEE – PART ONE

Dotted around the world are a few lucky people - lucky because he had the honour of watching Bruce Lee, the Master, at work on a film. If you asked them to give just one word that summed up what they saw, that word would be Charisma. A gift maybe it was, but the Little Dragon certainly made it work hard for him. It's easy to forget that the final product you see rebounding off the screen represents in fact hour upon hour of preparation, concentration and rehearsal. Whether it was a fight sequence or a talk scene, still Bruce would settle for nothing less than perfection. This month, *KFM* turns the key to this previously unlocked door to reveal an astounding world of total cinema dedication.

Right from the word go, one important facet of the Little Dragon's mental make-up was to stand him in good stead - his film and theatre experience, he learnt, and learnt well. Even at the tender age of just six years, he absorbed the wisdom of professionals while making an early film. And naturally, this wealth of experience was to pay off in many ways. Later on, superstars like Steve McQueen, James Garner and James Coburn were to seek his advice. On one occasion, his close friend, Unicorn Chan, asked if he'd handle the choreography of *The Unicorn Palm* - a film in which he was starring. Bruce of course obliged, but not only did he spend precious time devising and perfecting fight routines, he also studied other aspects of the movie as well.

For instance, on this particular occasion, it's recorded that he supervised some of the scenery and even made sure that Unicorn's hairstyle was right for the part. Well, he knew that starring roles require the maximum of visual impact. It was in fact, on the insistence of Unicorn that Bruce later received a photo and name credit on the posters - the Little Dragon took it as a great compliment.

Bruce used the occasion of his first starring role in a feature film with relish. *The Big Boss* was to be a testing ground and right from the start he worked hard to produce a totally different approach towards the making of the tight sequences - compared to those that were still being churned out in the traditional Kung Fu movie manner.

It's hard to believe now, seeing the movie, the tensions that existed within the studio. His fellow actors frowned upon the then-strange and unorthodox approach and hardly a day would pass without arguments. Offset, he eventually changed most of the script - in fact, he later commented, "You wouldn't believe all the stuff I rewrote." The temperature on set was too hot, there was a lack of fresh food and, the last straw, he seriously cut a finger.

The first major blow-up occurred with Director, Lo Wei. It was really just an accumulation of all the problems and Bruce was growing steadily more and more disheartened. When, finally, the production was complete, there were, without doubt one or two people around who'd have been delighted to see this cocky upstart fall flat on his face.

They were out of luck. At a film premiere in October 1971, the audience went wild - stamping, clapping and cheering, although the Little Dragon was mobbed outside the cinema and acclaimed the new Hong Kong superstar, little did they realise he was destined to become a world famous screen figure. Offers came pouring in for the diminutive Chinese sensation, but he rejected them all as he had his heart set following up with a new movie to be entitled, *Fist of Fury*.

If *The Big Boss* had called for several weeks' preparation, then *Fist of Fury* demanded months! Yet still he was receiving little in the way of help from some of the cast members and, to make matters worse, his feuding with Lo Wei was becoming intolerable.

Fist of Fury was also the first of the Master's films to incorporate a nunchaku battle and some of his fellow actors thought it crazy to be swinging sticks around in a film studio. But Bruce persisted and day after day he trained, cajoled and urged his opponents to gain the necessary degree of precision. It must have been a bit like making a Kung Fu film and running a martial arts school at the same time!

And everything that the Little Dragon arranged for *Fist of Fury* had to be just that much better than that which he had put into *The Big Boss*, kicks had to be higher, punches faster and the general effect, even more sensational. The more perceptive will notice that he also began at this point to take more notice of his acting and he started developing his sense of humour.

Bruce once remarked, "The simplest things are always the most effective." A classic example to illustrate this train of thought lies in the character he dreamed up for the role of the telephone man. No mounds of make-up for him - he just donned a pair of glasses (that he owned already) and turned on a permanent grin.

But don't go away thinking that ideas like this were two-a-penny. Often, even the easiest of ideas take ages to think up. Every night, he would pore over the script for the following day, trying in every way he could to improve it to hone it into shape.

The soundtrack was another problem. As most readers will probably by now know, Chinese films are nearly always shot wild - that is, the sound is added on later in a dubbing studio. Bruce realised that here lay another area that required his urgent attention as many a Mandarin film would turn out a farce after careless work in the audio suite. He spent days adding on all the effects such as the swirl of the nunchaku and the thump of each punch. Not only did they have to sound correct, they had to be added at exactly the right time and the most curdling war cries had to be carefully placed to achieve maximum impact.

It was felt by some people that the strenuous yelling might well have been at least partly responsible for his later blacking out. But even that apart, he worked away in the dubbing suite, often until he was nearly ready to drop. It's hardly surprising that the gruelling work was soon to take its toll. Such was Bruce's unbarring sense of perfection, not a single frame was allowed to be shown until he'd worked upon it. That work could take days, if not weeks. The fruits can be seen in any frame of any Little Dragon film you care to mention. Each is a work of art.

As Bruce's involvement behind the scenes grew more and more demanding, it became obvious that he'd have to formalise the situation, he did this by founding his own film company, Concord. *The Way of the Dragon* and *Game of Death* (in its original form) were projects that came directly from the Master's hand. In fact, he actually wrote, produced and directed *The Way of the Dragon* - the film was entirely his idea. It was typical of Bruce

that, before he'd even begun thinking about using precious film footage, he'd spend great deal of time working out essential detail and making important decisions.

Chuck Norris spent quite a while with the film and at times he had the privilege of working closely alongside the Master. He comments, "Bruce was a genius at creating new ideas. This is what amazed me about him - his inventions - the new things he would create and develop." It's hard to think of a greater compliment from a fellow artist.

The Little Dragon was never one to look for the easy way out. For him, true realism equalled hard and sometimes dangerous work. The double nunchaku sequence in *The Way of the Dragon* was one of the hairiest choreography scenes ever filmed. Challenging the sticks were quite a variety of deadly weapons and, without meticulous rehearsal, accidents would almost certainly have occurred.

Even with the best laid plans thing is going to go wrong elsewhere and during the shooting of *The Way of the Dragon*, tempers frequently frayed as a result of minor, though often painful injuries. Bruce's technique was amazing. He knew, to achieve total visual credibility, he had to do more than just aim blows that stopped short of actual contact. Such an attack could never really look right. He insisted that a slight touch had to be made. When rehearsing for a particular scene, he'd carefully explain to everyone what was going to happen. Then he'd do it in slow motion - perhaps twirling a pole slowly around to end up gently tapping his opponent's cheek. Gradually he'd speed up the move until it took place at normal rate. Bruce Lee was a master at this for two reasons - not only was he skilled enough to be able to just touch his man, although to all intents and purposes, it looked like a savage beating was taking place, he was so good at it that the actor at the other end of the pole actually believed he was going to survive! And that's as much as we've got time for this month. Next issue, we'll wrap up the feature with part two, and there'll be quotes from Bob Wall outlining just what sort of preparation went into their epic battle, details of some of the things that went wrong both behind and in front of the camera and, finally, an indication of the pressure under which Bruce constantly found himself working. Did he simply take on too much by trying to do the work of four or five people? Check out next issue!

GAME OF DEATH ALBUM REVEALED

Most readers should be more than familiar with *KFM*'s regular review of Bruce Lee albums. In fact, one that must be mentioned straight away is a new 'single LP' version of the famed *Enter the Dragon* Warner Brothers (Japanese) double album set. Numbered P-10016 W, it contains most of the speech from the film and is also worth buying for the photo booklet inside. But on to the other feature this month and it's one that, like it or loathe it, we simply couldn't miss out. Stand by for a review of the recently released *Game of Death* album.

The most impressive thing about the whole LP is the cover! The front contains a picture of Bruce, taken from the waist-up in his now legendary tracksuit. A trendsetter if ever there was one, it shows well in a negative black and white kind, of impression. Bruce's face conveys a truly sinister expression. The positioning of his fingers and thumbs are exaggerated and the words Bruce Lee's *Game of Death* run one after the other into a coffin; they're coloured blood red. The reverse cover shows a similar shot, though this time he's holding some nunchakus.

Over part of the image lie the words, 'Bruce is Back' and within this great lettering, are some amazing shots from the film. A further bonus with the album is the accompanying libretto and poster from the film (in fact it's the same picture as appeared on our *Game of Death* Special). The entire sleeve and extras are very well designed in every way, but, sadly, what lies within is little short of disappointing.

The actual quality of the recording is hard to criticise as it's as near as I've heard to being faultless. The trouble is, nearly all the tracks are simply variations, or worse, repetitions of the main theme. Only one track stands out as being unique. But, that said, if the cover doesn't make you want to buy the LP, then this track should! Let's start, however, from the beginning.

John Barry is possibly one of the greatest film composers of our time - he has, for example, a string of successful James Bond themes to his credit. His composing style is truly distinctive. Unfortunately, he seems to have tried the same formula here, but the Bond-style of music just sounds horribly dated against the film. The worst part is around the end sequence where Bruce and Abdul Kareem Jabbar are engaged in deadly combat - the air is thick with fury but what do you hear? Creeping into the background come lush

string and brass orchestrations that lend as much impact to the bloody proceedings as a wet rag. Compare the overall result with, for instance, Lalo Schifrin's score for *Enter the Dragon*. While Lalo's music wrenches every last drop of drama and emotion from the action-packed battles, Barry's sounds like it was composed to accompany a Sunday afternoon tea party.

SIDE ONE

Main Title - 'Bruce Lee Theme' (2'43")
It's this theme that's scattered throughout the rest of the album in varying degrees. One person who listened to it felt the melody would be more suited to a biblical epic than a martial arts film.

Track Two - 'Will This Be The Song I'll Be Singing Tomorrow?' (2'36")
This is a lush string arrangement with the usual attractive John Barry melody line. To be honest, it's the sort of thing you more normally hear whilst finding your seat in the cinema. The best thing I can think of to say is that it's probably good to drink nightcaps by!

Track Three - 'Gathering Speed' (5'46")
The main title theme starts up (again!), followed by some long sustained notes from the string section with a scattering of percussion. A rhythm finally picks up as the main theme returns, this time with Bond-style bellowing horns. The drum arrangement gets rather weird - it sounds like something out of a seedy jazz dub.

Track Four - 'A Matter of Survival' (3'58")
Yes, right again, another variation of the main theme - this time slowed down a little. The tedium is relieved by some good atmosphere percussion that comes creeping in towards the end. More like that would certainly have improved things. Finally on this track, it had to happen, there's a trumpet playing Goldfinger.

Track Five - 'Will This Be The Song I'll be Singing Tomorrow?' (2'21")
Shades of Track Two - it's the same thing again but this time with vocals added. However, the lyrics themselves are really quite well done (though as far as I can see, they're not credited). The singing is competently handled by Colleen Camp.

SIDE TWO

Main Title - 'Bruce Lee Theme' (2'43")
It's the same theme again as you heard on Track One on the first side. The only difference here is that, at the end, someone attempts to imitate some Bruce Lee war cries.

Track Two - 'Everything at Hand' (2'47")
We're treated here to a moody string introduction which sounds to my ears something along the lines of Swan Lake. So what do you think follows it? One guess is all that's needed - it's that main theme again!

Track Three - *'Game of Death'* (2'53")
This piece went in the film with the section they showed of the real Bruce Lee funeral. In a sick sort of way it's used quite effectively.

Track Four - 'Will This Be The Song I'll Be Singing Tomorrow?' (2'21")
If you think this is a misprint, well you're wrong! Outrageous as it is, the song appears here for the third time.

Track Five - 'Face of with Hakim' (3'30")
Sorry, we haven't a clue what the title means either but apart from that, this last track has to be by far the most exciting on the whole album. In the film it, covers the (missing in the UK) Inosanto nunchaku sequence. Despite the fact that it features someone else trying to imitate Bruce's frightening screams, it does give the listener a pretty good idea of

just how furious the scene turned out to be. Right at the end, you can hear the infamous snapping of Inosanto's neck and even on record it sounds hair-raising. Check back to the issue where we reviewed the battle, then play the track - it's quite a stunning experience.

After Bruce has dealt with Dan Inosanto, he tackles Jabber. Unfortunately the record fades out into oblivion.

You can probably judge by what I've said so far that the album, at least in my book, comes a poor bottom of the class when compared to other LP's available from the Bruce Lee classics. I really got the impression that the music was written for nothing in particular originally and it just happened to get slotted into *Game of Death*. There are many moments in the film when, for my money, the orchestration in no way enhances the action that's going on around it.

We've been told time and time again, by Raymond Chow and by Robert Clouse, that

Game of Death was to be their ultimate tribute to their old friend and nothing was to be spared in making the film an epic to end all epics. That the film itself failed by a million miles to measure up to these pious words has been mentioned a number of times over the last few issues. The more cynical among us might say it's only right that the LP finds a similar level.

The album is available on the TAM label, YX7037 and you'll be able to buy it from either Flyover Records or HMV Oxford Street.

Surprising as it may sound, to date there's been no less than thirteen albums released in the name of Bruce Lee - and we're told that several more and definitely on this way. Add to that over a dozen singles and EP's and you'll begin to appreciate the astounding news that the Little Dragon has had more records out than many of today's rock superstars!

This month in our Discography Part One, we're revealing a complete checklist of Bruce Lee's albums. All of the records, depending on availability, can be bought from either HMV Records in Oxford Street, London W1 or Flyover Records, 15 Queen Carolyn Street, Hammersmith Broadway, London W6. Costs are around £8.50 for single LPs and £15.50 for doubles. Although several of the compilation albums are duplicated, it's well worth having them for the pictures alone.

The World of Bruce Lee (Double) TAM label Record No. YX6095/96. This contains a compilation of *The Big Boss*, *Fist of Fury* and *Enter the Dragon*.

The Bruce Lee Big Special (Double) TAM label Record No. YX6097/98. This contains a compilation of *Big Boss*, *Fist of Fury*, *The Way of the Dragon* and *Enter the Dragon*. There's also some great pictures.

Fist of Fury (the original soundtrack) TAM label Record No. YX7001. The record contains some of Bruce's best war cries.

Enter the Dragon (with highlights from *The Big Boss* and *The Way of the Dragon*) TAM label Record No. YX7005. This is the Chinese version.

The Way of Life (mostly *The Way of the Dragon* but with several instrumental tracks) TAM label Record No. YX7010. The record contains the famous double nunchaku sequence.

NOW FOR THE FIRST TIME IN THE U.K.!
TWO SUPERB NEW BRUCE LEE BOOKS BY THE EDITORS OF KUNG-FU MONTHLY

The world's greatest martial arts magazine is proud to announce 2 sensational new additions to the Bruce Lee library: with BRUCE LEE IN ACTION we turn the emphasis on the supreme fighting talents of the worlds greatest martial artist. With WHO KILLED BRUCE LEE? we shed some light on the clouded circumstances surrounding the Master's mysterious death. You simply cannot afford to miss either of these lavishly illustrated volumes.

10% discount to all Society members.

Priced £1.75 each or £3.00 for both.
Rush your P.O./Cheque (made out to KFM) to:-
Bruce Lee Books Offer
14 Rathbone Place
London W1P 1DE
(Please allow at least 4 weeks for delivery).

Limited Stocks Order Now

JOIN THE BRUCE LEE SOCIETY
And stand to win a "chance-in-a-lifetime" prize!

The Way of the Dragon TAM label Record No. YX7011. This has the original soundtrack.

Bruce Lee Dragon Sounds Special TAM label Record No. YX7025. It includes the theme from The Green Hornet.

Game of Death TAM label Record No. YX7037. It's the original music soundtrack.

The Big Boss TAM label Record No. YX8017. Here's the original soundtrack.

Enter the Dragon (Double) Warner Brothers label Record No. P5526-7W. Japanese release, it contains the entire film soundtrack with all dialogue.

Enter the Dragon Warner Brothers label Record No. P10016W. A single album with highlights from the double version. Again, Japanese.

Enter the Dragon Warner Brothers label Record No. K46275. This has the music only.

The Ballad of Bruce Lee (by his brother, Robert Lee) Sunrise Records label Record No. LP-R905. It includes songs about Bruce.

All in all, the list represents a superb collection dedication to the Master, Bruce Lee.

THE BRUCE LEE SOCIETY

Hi everyone, Pam here with more word of the Bruce Lee Society.

The first thing I've got to mention is Carradine's *Silent Flute*. As many of you may know, it ran its premiere at London's Columbia cinema in Shaftesbury Avenue for three weeks, up to around mid-October before it promptly disappeared! At the time of writing this, the distributors are being very and it's proving impossible to get word on dates for national release. I've no idea what might be holding things back but as soon as there's any news, I'll be sure to let you know.

Next I have to drag out an old chestnut that hasn't been mentioned for a while. Yes, it's SAE time again! Gradually more and more letters are starting to arrive without stamped and addressed envelopes. Please remember, if there's no SAE, you're not likely to get any reply.

There's been quite a bit of talk lately about the possibilities of arranging some sort of Bruce Lee convention. As Jenny mentions in Kickback, probably the best way to organise it would be through the club. However, before going to an awful lot of trouble, I'd like to be sure that the interest is really there. Therefore, I'd like anyone interested to write in with their ideas such as where it should be held, whether it should be restricted to Society members only, and so on. Possibly a good date to hold it would be around four month's time to celebrate *KFM* 50!

Talking of meetings, as you'll probably recall, the area lists I worked out were specifically designed to enable members to meet each other and I even hoped that local enthusiasts might hold meetings together. So far I've not heard a peep that this is happening, so to help things on their way, anyone who would like to see this kind of thing happen, but who so far has been unable to make suitable arrangements, please write in telling me what the problems are and I'll help however I can.

Finally, some bits and pieces; If anyone knows of a shop in Derbyshire where members can buy Bruce Lee books and magazines, could they please write in and give me the address. Arthur Stone is still busy editing the Society film and if the convention idea comes off, let's hope it'll be ready for then. Lastly, I've still had no reply to my letter to the Censorship Board. It looks like it's time for me to send a reminder!

KICKBACK: THE LETTERS

Hi, it's letters time come round again! Something I've just got to mention - it seems there's been another of those 'Bruce is still alive' rumours sweeping the country! The gist of it all is that Bruce has been seen in Red China by a traveller who was passing by. Presumably the idea is, that when things got a bit too hot between the Little Dragon and one of the Secret Societies, he decided to fake his own death and funeral, and then hop over the border. Rumour also has it that a film is on the way to confirm the story. Let me say that I don't think we're ever going to see the film because I simply don't think it's true! I've said it before and I'll say it again - of course nothing could be greater than Bruce still being with us. But facts are facts and it's going to take some pretty strong evidence for me to believe anything other than what I know. Now, the letters!

JEET KUNE DO MAGAZINE

Dear Jenny,
A short time ago I bought a magazine published in Hong Kong that was called *Bruce Lee and Jeet Kune Do*. It was all about the filming of *Game of Death* and it names Bruce Lee's doubles. Firstly, the man to act in the silent scenes - like walking or standing - is Chen Yao-po. His eyes and face look like those of the Master. Secondly, the man doing the fight scenes is Kim Tai-chung. He's from Korea and is an expert in Taekwondo. Apparently, he later changed his name to Tang Lung. By the way, in the fight between Bruce and Jabbar, the giant basketball player is wearing a blue jacket. In almost every single one of the stills from the film he's wearing just shorts. Why is this?
Paul Marston, Plymouth, Devon

Dear Paul,
Thank you for a most informative letter as it really does help when readers take the trouble to write in and let us know things they've seen or heard about. Regarding the Jabbar puzzle, he did shoot some more footage for the revised version so possibly the person in charge of continuity made a silly mistake.

FAN MEETING

Dear Jenny,
I am interested in the possibility of arranging meetings of Bruce Lee fans - like those that have occurred for Elvis and Marc Bolan. It's a great idea and should have been thought of long ago. You could have Kung Fu demonstrations as well as films of Bruce.
Bruce, South Shields, Tyne & Wear

Dear Bruce,
Funnily enough, Pam Hadden from the Society and I were discussing this very idea not a week ago. My feelings were that this was something the Society could best arrange. Pam agrees it would be great to do, but she feels a little caution is needed before jumping in the deep end. Check the Society page for more details.

GAME OF DEATH FIGHTS

Dear Jenny,
I have it on fairly good authority that the three fights used in *Game of Death* (Hapkido, Nunchaku and Jabbar) were the only ones filmed by Bruce and that there is, unfortunately, no more in the pipeline. I don't know why everyone seems to think Bruce canned more. Overall, I was surprised at the film's direction and quality - both were very good. Also I thought Bruce's absence was very deftly handled by Mr Clouse.
David Leeming, Bamford, Gtr. Manchester

Dear David,
To take your first point, I have it from an ex-staff member of Cathay Films U.K. that there is more film in stock. In fact, I hear from a source we have in Hong Kong that the follow-up film is already being planned. Secondly, like it or loathe it, so far, I've received over five hundred letters about *Game of Death*. To the best of my knowledge only three of these registered any sort of approval!

BRUCE VS KAREEM ON WORLD OF SPORT

Dear Jenny,
Some Saturdays ago, I was bored watching television when suddenly, on World of Sport, up came the famous Lee/Jabbar clash from *Game of Death*. My brother and I looked at each other in amazement. How I wish I'd had a video recorder handy. P.S. *KFM* is No.1.
Paul Colgan, Rathfern, N. Ireland

Dear Paul,
Yes, I was watching then as well. Doesn't it seem strange that they show a clip from something most of us could go out now and see, yet we still can't get a showing of, say, The Green Hornet.

MORE BRUCE ON THE BOX

Dear Jenny,
The last letter I wrote was to tell you about Bruce on TV and you published it in *KFM* No.41. Since then, I've written to Scottish TV asking for more Bruce Lee on the box. The reply I received was nice, but very, very disappointing.
Colin Williamson, Hallglen, Falkirk

Dear Colin,
Well done on keeping up the pressure. If others try too, they're just going to have to change their tune.

GAME OF DEATH COLLECTOR'S SPECIAL

Dear Jenny,
The *KFM* Special Collector's Edition of *Game of Death* is absolutely fantastic. Why not do a special collector's edition on all Bruce's films?
A. Liddell, Billingham, Cleveland

Dear Mr Liddell,
Now that's an idea! I'm putting it straight to the KFM Editor.

ENTER THE DRAGON BOTTLE SCENE

Dear Jenny,
I've just seen *Enter the Dragon* again and I'm pleased to say that the bottles' scene has been restored to the Lee/O'Harra fight. It's all great stuff but, having seen it, I honestly can't understand why it was removed in the first place. I've seen other films containing scenes I consider far more violent and they remain uncut. Let's face it, our wonderful (?) Censorship Board are biased against martial arts films.
John Lees, Moodiesburn, Glasgow.

Dear John,
Couldn't agree more. By the way, keep quiet about the re-insertion of the 'bottles' sequence, I suspect the Board don't know about it right now!

QUICKIES CORNER

Chris Smith, Hattersley, Cheshire - Thanks for reminding us that there's lots of stuff available from the Kung Fu Supplies Company, 199 Johnson Road, Flat 7C, Wanchai, Hong Kong.
Keith Yates, Cannock, Staffs - Yes, suits are still available.
Paul Taylor, Westgate, Lancs - *The Green Hornet* & *Longstreet* not scheduled for TV right now - Write to your local station. *KFM* No.12? Check with our mail order department.
Stephen Fletcher, Belfast, Northern Ireland - Regret time doesn't allow me to answer all letters. Information on where to buy records appears regularly both here and in Society News Sheets.
Chris Elson, Walsall, Staffs - *KFM* No. 31 & 32 available from our back issues department.
Stephen Hill, Birkenhead, Merseyside - The miniature coffin carrying the 'In memory of a once fluid man...' quote dates back to Bruce's LA teaching days.
Stephen Syndercombe, London - Thanks for the 8mm info - We're checking.
Alison French, Watford, Herts - A Really lovely poem, though a bit long to print this time. I'll keep it by in case I can arrange a book of reader's poems.

David Jones, Heath, S. Wales - Lots of new pictures at last. We're investigating the Elvis angle.

Mike Devereux, Orford, Cheshire - re *Game of Death* - Maybe the doubles weren't too bad - but I'm sorry, I can't rate the script, production or acting of the imported stars.

Carl Northern, Newfoundpool, Leics - Sorry to sound a cynic but Carradine's 'Bruce's spirit is inside me' stuff just sounds like good promo.

Paul Hnatuszka, Leek, Staffs - Glad the Lee/Inosanto fight report made good reading.

Mohammed Afzal, Ashington, Northumberland - I agree, Jabbar's blue top must have come from a later filming. But was it a shirt or a jacket?

Tahir Abdullah, London - There's no re-release dates set for *The Big Boss*, *Fist of Fury* or *The Way of the Dragon* right now.

David Vandyke, Hove, Sussex - I'm sure Chow's decision to hold back material was made for business reasons - didn't do much for the film, though!

Ansar Mahmood, Aylesbury, Bucks is 21 years old, he's got lots of hobbies including sports and languages and of course, Bruce Lee. He wants a Danish pen pal to help his studies on the language.

STOP PRESS!

A few pieces of last minute news! Firstly, we hear from Cimac Martial Arts in Birmingham that arrangements are in hand to bring over Dan Inosanto for some tuition in Jeet Kune Do. The trip is tentatively pencilled in for next summer and the cost of an intensive week's course will probably come out at around £100 all in.

Second item is, further to Pam's comments, plans are very much in hand for a Bruce Lee Convention to be held in the spring of '79! The celebration will be timed to coincide with the 50th edition of *Kung-Fu Monthly*. Much more on that soon.

What a marvellous occasion! To celebrate the upcoming fiftieth edition of *Kung-Fu Monthly*, the Bruce Lee Society is going ahead with organising Britain's first Bruce Lee Convention. I shan't go into too much detail here so check the Society page for more on that. Suffice to say that, if ever the knockers needed proof of the still-growing fame of the Master, this is going to be it! Not wanting to bite off more than she can chew, Pam Hadden will be restricting the number of people coining to 400. it sounds a lot, but I've got a hunch that tickets will be selling fast so book now to avoid disappointment!

This month's issue hits the start button with part one of a really superb new feature. With the help of ace *KFM* researcher, Eddy Pumer, we unreel some of the forbidden footage that the censors have decided is unsuitable for us to see. Bruce's own views on censorship are discussed first - then it's time for us to dive into a selection of the more famous omissions. As with the Lee/Inosanto clash that was so disgracefully chopped from *Game of Death*, where appropriate, we take time to describe the blow by blow action. Check out the genius that's been denied us.

Secondly there's part two of our 'Behind the Scenes' investigation. What was it really like to work alongside the human dynamo by the name of Bruce Lee? Bob Wall talks some more, as does editor, Kurt Hirshler. There's more word too on his dubbing room blackout and a look at a very exciting new 8mm film. Its great reading!

And that's about it for this month. Back on the Convention again, keep an eye on the upcoming *KFM* issues - there's bound to be lots happening. If the ideas keep flowing the way they are now, we'll be in for a great day.

Felix Yen

Felix Yen
Editor-in-Chief

Acceptance, denial and conviction prevent understanding. Let your mind move together with another's in understanding and sensitivity. Then there is a possibility of real communication. To understand one another, there must be a state of choiceless awareness, where there is no sense of comparison or condemnation, no waiting for a further development in order to agree or disagree. Above all, don't start from a conclusion." - Bruce Lee.

If the Little Dragon were with us today, what would his opinion be of the way censors butcher his films? A studied look at the above quotation gives us some strong clues. It is Bruce Lee speaking and it's pretty clear from what he's saying that he wouldn't have thought too much of a man who - put in the position of defending 'good taste' didn't fight to remove much of the out-of-date and hypocritical overtones of censorship. Today's 'scissormen' accept the basic traditions of the job as gospel, thus the new films of today suffer from the denials and convictions of many years previous. Such blindness prevents strict comprehension of the content of a film. The secret lies in understanding with sensitivity. If only the board of film censors were to invite a cross-section of the public to preview a film in a form of a jury then they'd surely end up with a far better idea of what to leave in and what to take out.

Then, to reiterate the words of Bruce Lee, "There is a possibility of real communication. To understand one another, there must be a state of choiceless awareness where there is the sense of comparison or condemnation."

KFM recommends that the old method of censorship be done away with and a new one adopted, one based on direct contact with the public. The censor himself would be able to base his judgments on the reactions of those around him - no more would he have to exercise judgements purely on the grounds of tradition, comparison and, of course, his own in-built prejudices. Working in today's confined methods of censorship encourages the 'waiting for a further development in order to agree or disagree' type of attitude.

The censoring of the entire nunchaku sequence in *Game of Death* makes a good case in point. Pre-judgement had obviously already been made, that, should there by a nunchaku sequence in the new Lee film, out it would automatically go. Such consideration and sensitivity! "Above all, don't start from a conclusion." Read right through Bruce's words again and you'll see that he's even asking you not to take the quote, itself as a final opinion. "Let your mind move together with others." If you agree or disagree with what he said, or, come to that, would like to add to it, let's be hearing from you.

In most countries around the world, each of Bruce Lee's films has, one way or another, been subject to censorship. Over this and an issue ahead, we're going to be running through as many of the cuts as we can, outlining the damaging effect they've had on the whole.

It's generally accepted that *The Big Boss* suffered the worst hacking - possibly because it was the first film of its kind to be given a full-scale release in the western world. Take the scene where Lee's cousins refuse payment to keep their mouths shut about the heroin being smuggled out in ice blocks. Around the west, their subsequent stabbing to death was deemed quite acceptable, yet in many countries, their later chopping-up was sliced out of the film. Often, all one is allowed to watch is the saw starting up and the bodies being pushed towards it. Only in Hong Kong itself, so far as we know, has the entire scene been left in for public viewing. There, the fans could witness the cutting-up and the remains being pushed into the ice-making machine."

Bruce starts to search for his cousins, and his boss, sensing problems, invites him to dinner. This scene also tends to be omitted, or at least badly slashed, for the girl who accompanies him at the meal, a bottle of brandy later, invites him back to her place for a good time. Despite the 'X' rating of the film, many a censor decided the glimpses of bare flesh to be too much for the public to take and promptly removed them (including a full frontal of Bruce, with a chair covering the necessaries!) So Bruce continues the search for his family, eventually discovering the chopped-up bodies in the ice blocks - alongside the clear, but suddenly, in come the henchmen carrying knives. Though most of the fight survives the censor's onslaught, many countries removed the sequence where Bruce embeds a saw into a man's head and scythes through the neck of another.

The fight continues outside and the Little Dragon polishes off all but the son of the boss. However, as they face each other, one of the fallen thugs regains consciousness and creeps up behind Bruce. What many of the fans still haven't seen is the Little Dragon grabbing the man's crotch (without even needing to look behind him) and pulling the attacker forward. The thug passes out cold (not surprisingly).

The final sequence, where Bruce battles with the boss himself, usually starts with him

running down the street holding a bag of prawn crackers. For some reason, in many versions of the film, we don't see him actually buying them. And quite a few cuts often get made in the fight itself. This is pure sacrilege to the real fans, though to be fair, you wouldn't know the parts were missing if you hadn't seen them in the first place.

Fist of Fury is usually the film that ends up with the least cuts. It's also the first time on the big screen that we see Bruce using nunchakus, and in most cases, the censors let it through. The question springs to mind, why on earth was the Inosanto/Lee confrontation in *Game of Death* so rudely rejected? Two scenes have frequently been omitted from *Fist of Fury*. First, right at the beginning where Lee's girlfriend talks to him in his den, asking him why he continues to be so depressed over his teacher's death. The second scene shows Bruce roasting a dog over a fire, before finally, he takes a huge bite out of it. Both these scenes, long missing in UK

Fist of Fury prints, have recently been reinstated. Strangely, the censors seem to have no knowledge of the reinsertion so better catch the frames quickly, in case they're removed again! But all these savage cuts pale into near insignificance when compared to the butchery of the often-removed, double-nunchaku scene from *The Way of the Dragon*. The original is a gem of artistry! First, Bruce produces one pair of sticks as the heavies arm themselves with long poles then he produces another set. Both he twirls casually around before tucking them under his arms.

Two thugs rush forward and a quick swing of both sets of cudgels sends them staggering back in either direction.

Another man comes up on Bruce from behind and he promptly receives a reverse twirl to the skull from the Little Dragon's left-hand set. Another, approaching from the right receives similar punishment from the other set. The Master hasn't yet looked at either of them! Somehow his uncanny senses have registered their presence and judged the distances.

Taking three paces back, he rotates the nunchakus in his left hand, strikes another man down who comes too close, then proceeds to perform aerobatics with them swirling each set of nunchakus in complimentary sequences. First clockwise, then anti-clockwise. Flying round like two giant catherine wheels, finally they're restored to their original, under-arm position. It's hardly surprising that the rest of the gang look on in stupefied amazement. They decide to charge Little Dragon - always a perilous decision! The sticks fly in all directions - a giant of a man crashes into a stack of boxes, another flies back and a third nearly makes it to Bruce before being dispatched by a nunchuku to the stomach. The carnage is complete - to left and right, thugs lie at Bruce's feet. He twirls the sticks and collects them once again under his arms. Slowly, most of the gang recover from the onslaught, and Bruce, throwing one set aside, continues to wind the other about his body, finally coming to a halt in the now-familiar 'left-hand spread, out in front' stance. The gang gathers for a second, extremely foolish attack. One is immediately brought down with a direct hit as another is surprised by a Lee back-kick which hurls him into oblivion. Bruce resumes his original position as of the larger thugs approaches with a vicious-looking iron bar. It's no problem as the Master wraps his nunchakus round the bar and rips it from the villain's grasp. He follows up with a blow directly to the centre of the head. The others look more than shaken as the giant slumps to the ground.

But it's not over yet. The gang still have a few more cards in the pack and the odds are still heavily out of Bruce's favour. Tune in again soon for the continuing blow-by-blow run through of the famous *The Way of the Dragon* double-nunchaku sequence. And we'll also be sorting through *Enter the Dragon* and *Game of Death* to check out the sections the censors didn't want some of us to see. Stand-by for part two.

It's time once again to take you behind the scenes with Bruce Lee. Last month, we showed just some of the intense activity he turned on while filming his epics and in this issue, we carry the story one stage further. It's easy to view the Master in full, dynamic action and murmur words like 'brilliant,' 'amazing' and 'fantastic.' Certainly all three adjectives would quite adequately describe his genius. Yet Bruce's fire burned brighter!' Many a Hollywood star is said to have turned in an inspirational performance. Few, however, could claim to have so real creative influence so far and so wide. Bruce didn't just star in a film - he was the film. In a Lee movie, just about every frame that flickers the screen, in some way or other, bears his stamp. In the words of his supporting actors, "His work-load was phenomenal." The story continues...

It's well known that Bruce went to tremendous lengths during rehearsals to get everything right. No one sat around while the little dragon was perfecting another scene. Yet, come the actual filming, not even did he manage to give even more, he expected all the other actors to do likewise. And he was well qualified to take an interest in what went on around him. Bob Wall related once during filming, "He's not only a great a martial artist, he's also a good actor, as well as a good technician. He believes in spontaneity. After instructing us in what to do in the fight scenes, we shot them over and over until he felt it looked exciting. Wall went on to say that, before filming, Bruce taught him how to take punches and kicks without getting hurt while still not making the action look contrived. Bob Wall also told of how well Bruce controlled his kicks and punches. In fact, such was the Master's obvious expertise, after the first qualm of two, most of his screen opponents soon became quite reassured as to their eventual fate!

Enter the Dragon was the most eventful of all the Little Dragon's major feature films and there were many 'behind the scenes' incidents. The often-censored bottle clash between Wall and Lee took hours of preparation. Clearly the dangerous action had to be timed, literally to a fraction of a second and although all had gone safely during the run-throughs, tragedy struck on the first take. As always, Bruce was trying to improve on perfection and with the camera rolling, he struck out at Wall with such speed, his dazed opponent had no time to drop the jagged bottle. The resulting impact gave the scene rather more realism than anyone had expected.

More problems occurred, such as one with the cobra in the underground control room. Bruce was running through putting the snake into the sack and the cameraman were finalising shooting angles when suddenly, the cobra struck and the Little Dragon paid the price for a moment's distraction.

Luckily for all concerned, the snake had been largely de-venomised and the wound was not too serious. Anyway, he insisted on carrying on with the shooting until the scene had been canned to the Master's usual high level of satisfaction.

Often Bruce practiced scenes completely alone which was a marvellous way for him to dream up new ideas. That's why he was always able to arrive each day at the film studios with fresh moves in mind. Kurt Hirshler, the man who edited *Enter the Dragon*, once said of him, "I got a genuine education working with footage of Bruce Lee. He's so lightning fast

and yet everything is perfect. There aren't even any signals he gives - not a hint that he's going to throw a punch." It's no fluke that the first work on the lips of anyone who sees him in action is 'perfection.' A great deal of off-set rehearsal went on in the Little Dragon's personal time, long after everyone else had forgotten about work for the day. It wasn't just by chance that he'd appear each morning with bundles of bright ideas!

One of Bruce's greatest difficulties was in teaching the Chinese actors what was required of them. Many had no experience whatsoever in either fighting of filming and so far as the Little Dragon was concerned, that was simply not good enough. Not only did they have to learn the basics, they had to learn them thoroughly. Most martial arts films are notable for the appalling level of acting and fighting from the support cast. Not so Bruce Lee's films - no way was the Master going to 'spoil the ship for a hapeth of tar.'

Probably the most tragic incident of all, and one that's already been well related in these pages, came when Bruce was dubbing the sound onto *Enter the Dragon*. Suddenly, one day while he was slicing-in his war cries, his body gave way. It was a hot afternoon and the air inside the tiny Hong Kong dubbing suite was, to say the least, oppressive. The Little Dragon had other things on his mind than just *Enter the Dragon*. As one film was finishing, so a multitude of other projects were getting under way and adding to the pressure.

He had decided to take a break in the rest room where the air was cooler but no sooner had he got inside that he collapsed. Semi-conscious and on hands and knees, when somebody approached, instead of asking for help, he pretended to be searching for his

NOW FOR THE FIRST TIME IN THE U.K.!
TWO SUPERB NEW BRUCE LEE BOOKS BY THE EDITORS OF KUNG-FU MONTHLY

STOP PRESS
Bruce Lee in Action has completely sold out!

The world's greatest martial arts magazine is proud to announce two sensational new additions to the Bruce Lee library: with THE UNBEATABLE BRUCE LEE we uncover a veritable treasure chest of previously unknown facts and figures on the world's foremost martial artist. With WHO KILLED BRUCE LEE? we shed some light on the clouded circumstances surrounding the Master's mysterious death. You simply cannot afford to miss either of these lavishly illustrated volumes.

Priced £1.75 each or £3.00 for both.
Rush your P.O./Cheque (made out to KFM) to:-
Bruce Lee Books Offer
14 Rathbone Place
London W1P 1DE
(Please allow at least 4 weeks for delivery).

Limited Stocks Order Now

glasses. Pride became his downfall.

Somewhat recovered, he returned to the dubbing theatre to continue work. There, he collapsed completely and lost consciousness - the state was accompanied by acute vomiting and convulsions. Little did anyone around at the time realise, the incident was soon to be repeated; only this time, it was to take his life.

To see Bruce's films, it's hard to comprehend the effort and striving that went into their making. And it was all done for you and me - the fans - who were the ones who really mattered. He was a man who found perfection, then tried to reach beyond it.

There a 'behind the scenes' film now available. Shot on Super 8 and entitled *Enter the Dragon: On Location*, it shows the Little Dragon in his characteristic organising role. You see him discussing *Enter the Dragon* with Fred Weintraub and then rehearsing the fight sequence with Bob Wall.

Another tit-bit is where Bruce works out with extras, pointing to camera angles and so on, and you can also catch Roper being thrown by one of Han's daughters into the lap of another. Time and again, the Little Dragon runs through the action, seeking a near-impossible degree of perfection.

Possibly the most exciting segment of the telling and spectacular film is where Bruce lines up the scene in the underground factory where he battles opponents with a long pole. Surrounded by the film crew, we see him practicing the routine with the help of an extra.

The six foot pole whirls everywhere and on one run-through, we actually see a young boy being struck lightly several times on the side of the face. He is being shown just how hard a blow the weapon will land once the cameras are turning. Sure enough, the cameras roll and Bruce, after beating off several attacking extras, gets finally to the young boy. The pole comes whistling through the air and, to all intents and purposes, it really does look as though it strikes the actor a savage blow on the head. Scene over, the extra gets up and Bruce gives him one of his famous broad grins.

His uncanny knack of effecting true martial realism while at the same time not seriously damaging the rest of the cast was some sort of chance gift. Hours of work with a video recorder had taught him the art of faking battles to a high degree of realism. With the right camera angles, it became difficult for even an expert to detect whether blows were genuine or acted.

But the Little Dragon was never one to keep things to himself (it will be well remembered that many of the enemies he had in LA were after his throat for blowing the secrets of the East). Time and time again, he'd spend precious hours showing an unenlightened newcomer the ropes of Kung Fu fighting - the lessons had to be good as mistakes could be fatal!

That Bruce's tireless patience was to reap astounding reward is now a matter of proven fact. The back-breaking work load he set himself was eventually to rub off on many a Mandarin martial arts film. Behind the scenes, the Little Dragon, at times, resembled a human tornado. He geed-up studio technicians and actors alike when problems were weighing heavy. He taught just about everybody in sight the rudiments of cinema fighting. He wrote, produced, directed, checked costume and make-up, and even at times, took over the cameras.

Anyone else would probably have found himself in hot water. After all, nobody likes being told what's what by someone who's employed to do a totally different job. But with Bruce, the problem rarely arose behind the scenes, as in front of the scenes, his personal magnetism saw him through.

Hi. I'm here again with some stupendous word on the event everyone's been talking about; the coming Bruce Lee Society Convention. Actually you'll see most of the information is in the big advertisement elsewhere this issue. What I want to say is just this. If all goes to plan, May 19th 1979 should turn out to be a momentous date for the UK fans of Bruce Lee. It's something I've often thought about doing but somehow it's taken a long time for me to actually pluck up the courage to make a start!

Okay, maybe it does sound a bit corny, but I say it again, the success of the Convention will depend, not just on me or on you, but on everyone. All of us this end will do everything we can to make sure things run smoothly and all we can do now is await your interest and enthusiasm. Right now, I don't know whether there's going to be two or twenty thousand people wanting to come; the only thing I will say, is that, if you want to be sure of getting in, BOOK EARLY! There's no way at all that we'll be able to exceed the top figure of 400 people. Quite a few of the things we're not sure of, have obviously not appeared in the advertisement. One of the most exciting, and remember, this is NOT yet confirmed, is that we may be getting a copy of a film that's never (to my knowledge anyway) been seen in this country. It's a compilation of many of Bruce's childhood films and rare is not the word!

All of you will by now have received the December 1978 News Sheet and I hope you find it a good read! Remember, the special member's Christmas card that went out with it is also available as a mail order item. They cost £1.00 for a bundle of ten (including envelopes) and should make pretty handy, all-purpose greeting cards for all Society members.

That's it for me this month; stand by for much more follow-up news on the Convention! **Pam**

Isn't it wonderful news about the Convention? I'm sure I echo everyone's thoughts when I wish Pam the very best of luck in organising it. Indeed, long may the Bruce Lee Society continue to expand and prosper! This month it's been especially hard picking out the letters to print. Often some of the most exciting letters I get are the longest and of course those are the ones I haven't room to include, except maybe in part. So if you see one of your letters here and only a quarter of it's been used, I hope you're not going to be too upset! Remember, wherever possible, keep things short and sweet.

THE GREEN HORNET

Dear Jenny,
Following on your *The Green Hornet* feature in *KFM* No. 44 and 45, I thought you might like to know a few other points of interest. To start with, the mask they used wasn't the original choice of design. The first was an exact replica of the one worn by the old radio Green Hornet and it fitted over the nose and mouth instead of the eyes. William Dozier, the producer, dropped that because it would muffle the lines. The second was similar to the final one chosen, except the eye slits, sloped upwards and were more pointed on the cheek. On the Hornet's mask there was no Hornet sign. The third of course, we all know. In the Preying Mantis episode, co-starring was Mako, the great Japanese fighter, who played the evil leader of the Tong. Bruce, as Kato, wants revenge on the Tong because they smashed up his girlfriend's restaurant (sounds familiar), ambushed Kato and dumped him in a trash can! The final battle takes place in a Buddhist Temple where Kato confronts the entire Tong. First, he uses his darts as in *The Way of the Dragon*, but Mako deflects them with a metal hand fan. Bruce wipes out three of the attackers by using their own three-section staff. He performs a similar trick on another man, using a Bo, which resembles a walking stick.
Finally, Kato faces Mako and after a series of deadly punches, kicks and blocks, he disposes of the last of the evil.
Paul Marston, Mutley, Devon

Dear Paul.
I just had to print that one almost in its entirety - thanks, it's great stuff!

US MARTIAL ARTISTS

Dear Jenny,
I read *The Silent Flute* article in *KFM* and eagerly await its arrival here in Runcorn. You may not know it but there are a couple of named martial artists with bit parts in it. One is USA heavyweight champion, Everett Eddy, there's the man with the flying feet, Eric Lee and finally, the greatest Karate star the USA has ever had, ex-world heavyweight champion, Joe Lewis. By the way, in reply to David Carradine's newspaper spot the other week, Bruce Lee's spirit entered our hearts and soul in 1973/74 - not 1978.
Dave Langley, Runcorn, Cheshire

Dear Dave,
Thanks for the information and by the time you've read this, according to the distributors, you should have caught The Silent Flute. Thanks too for the other letter you sent in. For the benefit of all the readers, Dave is in fairly regular touch with Taky Kimura. Well, over the phone the other day, Taky asked Dave to pass on to all KFM readers his best wishes for a Happy Christmas and New Year. Dave, on our behalf, returned the compliments.

FIST OF RIP-OFF!

Dear Jenny,
What a rip-off! Recently I went along to see a film called *Fist*, starring Chen Lee. The advert for the film showed Bruce Lee's famous leap from the end of *Fist of Fury* so I arrived thinking that was what I was going to see. Instead it was some creep called Chen Lee doing his best to imitate Bruce.
J. Roe, Blackpool, Cork, Ireland

Dear J. Roe
How many more of these rip-offs are we going to get? I suppose the only real satisfaction to be gained from the whole sorry business is that it proves that Bruce's name and image are still magic ingredients when it comes to attracting good box-office figures.

LOTS OF QUESTIONS

Dear Jenny,
I thought you might be interested in some of the facts I've researched on Bruce Lee. Did you know that apart from having one leg longer than the other, one foot had no real heel - it was just 'fat.' Another physical disability was that he had only one testicle. Changing the subject though - Twenty doubles were used in the making of *Game of Death* and the money spent by Chow came to HK $4.5million. Before Bruce died, some of the world's most famous stars and athletes were invited to appear in *Game of Death* including Ali, Pele (who actually met with Chow), James Coburn and Steve McQueen. Also, did you know that, after completing *The Big Boss*, Bruce was attacked on a plane by a gang of Japanese people? Soon after, he made the first suitable anti-Japanese film he could, and that was *Fist of Fury*. Lastly, it's said that Bruce was planning to smuggle a one million dollar sword into Hong Kong via the post. His death, however, intervened.
Agi Georgiou, London

Dear Agi,
Sorry it's taken six tries for you to get a letter into KFM but your patience has won through. A couple of the things you've mentioned I've heard before, but, as you say elsewhere in your letter, much of this comes from Chinese magazines. Without dismissing any of it out of hand, I must say I'm a little dubious. There's no doubt that some of the information coming from that quarter is made up. Sensations equals sales! Confirmation from reliable quarters will be welcomed.

ENTER THE DRAGON DOUBLE ALBUM

Dear Jenny,
I can give the good news that the *Enter the Dragon* double album (reviewed *KFM* No.43) is available from Flyover Records in London, a company who deals mainly with Japanese imports. There's also a single I know of called *Forever Bruce Lee* that's sung in Japanese. The B-side is *The Way of the Dragon*.
KFM Reader, Cleveland

Dear Anonymous Reader,
Thanks for sending in word on Flyover - they really do seem to be the major source of Bruce Lee recordings in this country and they're also very friendly people to deal with.

Toby Boulesteix, Yelverton, Devon - Congratulations on getting *KFM* No. 1-43. A book for each of his films is something we've been considering for a while - Pictures are the problem.
Neil Haggar, Eastbourne, Sussex - I afraid you're right - Bruce Li is just cashing in on Bruce Lee. Some say, however, that his fighting is improving.
John Simpson, Greenhills, Glasgow - Thanks for the most amazing letter I've ever had! It must have taken ages.
Noel Hyland, Dublin, Eire - I haven't heard that Chow's following *Game of Death* with *Towers of Death* - I shouldn't be at all surprised.
Paul Ruderham, Cheetham Hill, Salford 8 - Correct, you'll only hear Bruce's voice in *Enter the Dragon*. By the way, readers, Paul's offering two giant Lee posters, plus a complete *Enter the Dragon* soundtrack to the first reader to correctly identify Bruce's first martial arts instructor. Write to him direct.
Miss Lorraine Lee Mellor, Sheffield - Sorry, I'm no relation of Bruce. If you want to contact Bruce Li in Hong Kong, I suggest you approach the Run Run Shaw Film Company.
Susan Reibanks, Skipton, N. Yorks - Another lovely poem filed for the future.
Dave Ashby, Bury St. Edmunds, Suffolk - *Game of Death* soundtrack is available - Glad *KFM*'s worth the wait.
Michael McDowell, Kilmarnock, Scotland - Your friend's drawing flatters me!
Tony Cole, Middlesborough, Cleveland - Great to hear that the newly re-released *Fist of Fury* is drawing fantastic crowds. As you say, the King lives.
Charldene Li-Hua, Heme Hill, London - Another lovely letter! Yes, isn't it fabulous to see all the reinstated scenes.
Mr M Gibbard, Mucclecote, Glos - *Wisdom of Bruce Lee* and *Bruce Lee in Action* have so far only been published in America. We're still hoping for better things over here.

Welcome, everyone, to yet another scoop. Really, they seem to come so thick and fast these days, it's getting unusual not to be featuring a first of some sort or other. In fact, it's such a biggie that we've put aside the second half of last month's major feature, which should now appear next issue; So, what is it, you're all asking? Well, we all know that Bruce had to undergo a fairly rigorous screen test for his part in *The Green Hornet*. Having now seen a copy of the film of that test, I can reveal that it's absolutely sensational! That means (for the first time ever, so far as I recall) *KFM* just has to turn over the whole of the issue to a report on this rare and amazing clip.

And it certainly is compulsive viewing. Having seen it once, it's one of those things you've gotta keep seeing over and over again. Once, twice, three times just isn't enough! *KFM* super-sleuth, Eddy Pumer has already spent days studying it more or less, frame by frame. There's no way he intends to miss a thing in this month's vital report. The sight of a slightly under-confident (though still ultra-skilful and charismatic) Little Dragon going through the martial motions for a top American TV mogul is one I'd never forget. And don't you forget, we expect to be screening it at the Convention!

Lastly, Jenny's been showing me all the mail we've had in recently and congratulating us on the great new pictures that have been featured over the last few issues. Well we know of the fans' lust for fresh Bruce Lee material. It gets tough, but don't worry - as long as you keep crying out for new pictures, we'll keep on unearthing them!

Felix Yen

Felix Yen
Editor-in-Chief

BRUCE LEE'S GREEN HORNET SCREEN TEST – PART ONE

In March of 1966, Bruce and Linda Lee returned to Los Angeles with high hopes of the Master taking star billing on a new TV series entitled *Number One Son* but it never happened. For film director William Dozier however, there were other ships in the sea. At the time he was just getting ready to go into production with a re-run of the old, 1930's radio spoof, *The Green Hornet* and, would you believe, all that remained for him to locate was a good looking Chinese actor with a sound command of the English language! One of the major reasons for Bruce clinching the role was the way he conducted himself during an amazing screentest and fortunately for all of us, posterity has been kind. A filmed copy of the great moment recently found its way to us via a backstreet shop in New York. Ace *KFM* sleuth, Eddy Pumer, was assigned the job of reviewing this sensational scoop.

"The only reason I got the job was because I was the only Chinaman in all California who could pronounce Britt Reid," so joked the Little Dragon to news men after being told the part was his. Although the joke is a well-repeated and often heard remark, considering the supreme quality of the action he had offered in his screentest, such modesty was truly unbecoming.

I first caught this remarkable strip of film, courtesy of a well known TV studio that will remain nameless for reasons of confidentiality. For me, it's always a strange and exciting moment when I manage to catch up on fresh material of the Master - though he's been gone so long, still there's always something new around the next corner.

Lights dimmed and we were ready for action. While still in darkness, a voice suddenly blurted out. "Production 263 - 05 - 224 - 10 Text X 1." Presumably they shoot so many screentests, each has to be prefaced with a code for easy recognition. I think to myself, "I bet they don't get too many like this one, though!"

Faders up and all of a sudden, we see a very nervous looking Bruce Lee. He's 24 years old, clean shaven and wearing the older-style short hair. His suit is dark and very loose cut and his shirt, dazzling white. Around his neck is a tie that's tightly wound into the smallest of knots.

He's sat on a chair with his legs crossed and his hands held together. The studio set looks suspiciously like an ordinary office or living room. There's a sofa, mantelpiece and so on, and Bruce is looking somewhat to his left, presumably towards the Director.

A voice commands instructions, "Now Bruce, look into the camera lens and tell us your name, age and where you were born." The Little Dragon obeys, and goes on to explain that

he left Hong Kong in 1959 and that he's been acting in movies since he was six years old. "Now look over at me as we talk. I understand you've just had a baby boy." Bruce chuckles, "Yeah, he's kept me up for three nights." The director asks him how movies are made in Hong Kong, and Bruce replies that, because of the heat and noise of the day, most of the shooting goes on during the hours of twelve midnight to five in the morning.

"You told me earlier today that Karate and Jujitsu are not the most powerful forms of oriental fighting. Which are the best?" asks the Director.

Bruce clears his throat nervously and noisily, puts on a brave smile and responds, "Well, it's bad to say the best, but in my opinion, I think Kung Fu is pretty good."

The Director asks him to explain further. "Kung Fu originated in China and is the ancestor of Karate and Jujitsu. It's more of a complete system and it's more fluid. By that, I mean, it's more flowing. There's a continuity of movement, instead of one movement, two movements and then stop."

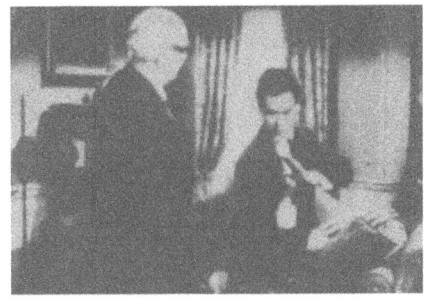

The Director continues by asking Bruce to look into the camera, while at the same time explaining how Kung Fu may be compared to a glass of water (obviously the point had already been raised in some previous conversation). As Bruce starts to reply, he speaks as much with his facial expressions as he does with his voice - slight smiles, nods to one side, a squinting of the eyes and over-pronounced shaping of the mouth. He goes on, "Well Kung Fu... the best example would be a glass of water.

That's because, err, water is the softest substance in the world, yet it can penetrate the hardest rock, or anything... granite, you name it."

Bruce squints his eyes a little, frowns and shifts his head from side to side. "Err, water is also insubstantial. By that, I mean you cannot punch it and hurt it, you cannot grasp hold of it. Every Kung Fu man is trying to do that, to be soft like water and flexible - to adapt to the opponent."

Aware probably that he's not performing in his more usual, exuberant style (imagine yourself in that situation), he nervously looks to his left, then remembers he's been asked to look into the camera and quickly turns his head back again.

He's asked, "What's the difference between a Kung Fu punch and a Karate punch?"

"Well," replies Bruce, "a Karate punch is like an iron bar... whack! A Kung Fu punch is like an iron chain with an iron ball attached. It goes 'whang' and it hurts inside!"

And that's the end of the first, smaller part of the Master's *The Green Hornet* screentest. Next he's told to stand up and demonstrate some actual Kung Fu. Bruce looks a little apprehensively towards the Director, then nods his okay. A voice from somewhere shouts, "Cut - print it," and the screen goes blank. Even the mere anticipation of screentest fighting action is enough to set any true Little Dragon fan's pulse a'racing. The atmosphere was tense in that tiny TV studio. What we were about to see was a seldom shown, rare sequence of frames of the world's greatest martial artist, at work under extreme pressure. No one, not the Director, the assistants, the cameramen or crew had any idea of what was about to happen. In fact, it occurred to me later, that, had they known what was coming, they possibly wouldn't have risked using a member of their staff as the fall guy or the victim of Bruce's superb demonstration.

The screen fills once again Bruce is standing and being pictured from the waist up. He's asked to give a three-quarter angle to the camera, then a profile showing his right side. Then it's time for a left three-quarter and a left profile. Finally, he's requested to look directly into the camera.

The camera pans back, and the Little Dragon is asked to perform movements in the style of the classic Chinese theatre. Bruce explains before starting, that in Chinese theatre, there are several standard characters. He begins with the warrior.

A practical demonstration of bending the knee of his right leg, he raises and straightens it out in front of him; all the while, he retains perfect balance on the left leg. The movement is then repeated while balancing on the right leg.

Then, being theatre, he shows how the girls walk. Chuckling to himself he slips into the routine, walking along with shoulders raised and taking only tiny steps forward. He says, "One can tell one character from another simply from the way he walks or by his actions. It's these movements that represent the character."

Then came the moment I'd long been awaiting as Bruce is asked to do some Kung Fu. Obviously very nervous now, he explains, "It's hard to do it alone, but I'll try to do my best".

The situation is relieved a little by the Director sending out on to the set, the rather elderly victim mentioned earlier. The fun begins. Bruce, of course, is perfectly happy as to the man's welfare, but, having caught the atmosphere of slight apprehension, he giggles and remarks: "Accidents do happen!" Unlike the old man, all of us watching lick our lips in anticipation.

BRUCE LEE'S GREEN HORNET SCREEN TEST – PART TWO

Warming up to the demonstration fight, Bruce strokes his nose with his thumb - a characteristic we've got to know well through his movies. He says, "There are various kind of fights. It depends on where you hit and what weapon you will be using. To the eyes, you will use the fingers." Bruce throws a lightning, demonstration jab to illustrate his point. You barely see his arm move, and it's at this moment, that one realises the truth of what's been said about the Little Dragon's actions being slowed down in his movies. For that eye jab to really work from a cinema viewpoint, there are no two ways about it - it would have to be slowed down to gain any real appreciation. Come to that, compare speeded-up antics of all the Bruce Lee lookalikes!

But back again with the action, and the old man's starting to look even more scared. "It's okay, I won't hurt you," sooths Bruce and, still in complete control, he rapiers another vicious jab to the eyes.

"And to the face..." The Master's fist flashes through the air so fast, you can actually hear a smacking sound. Again and again, the old man comes within a millimetre of serious damage.

The Director himself comes onto the set to move the two men around for a better camera angle. The view we get is certainly an improvement. Bruce demonstrates three

enormously fast, backhand punches, explaining that a lot of the punch's power comes from the waist. Whap! Whap! Whap Each blow kisses the air against the man's jaw.

Sensing the hapless victim's air of desperation, the Director asks the Little Dragon to back off a little. The studio crew, meanwhile are now laughing at this incredible display of martial arts. The atmosphere on the screentest set is unbelievable - the old man looks terrified while Bruce, a shade embarrassed, laughs and kids with his hand to his face.

"And then of course, Kung Fu is very sneaky. The Chinese always hit very low, from the high and back to the groin." In a split second, his fist travels from jaw to groin.

However mind boggling things have been so far, it's nothing compared to what follows. They ask Bruce to repeat the routine but from the other side. He moves the man across a few feet and gets asked by him whether his amazing reactions come naturally. Before the Little Dragon can answer, the film crew start chuckling again.

All the movements are repeated, but this time in super-quick succession. The effect is just impossible to capture in print. Only with the eye can one appreciate such skill and superbly flowing motion.

To put this whole bizarre scene into perspective, it's worth reflecting that Bruce was performing his miracles under considerable duress. He needed to display his very best while wearing a most uncomfortable-looking suit (the trousers are far too short for him!). He had nerves of his own to conquer, plus an opponent who needed to be kept reasonably at ease. Even an experienced martial artist would have flinched in the face of the Master's onslaught but the old man put on a gallant display.

But there's more to come! Bruce thrusts out again with pointed fingers faster than anything he'd done so far. "There's the finger jab," affirms the Little Dragon. "The punch," Bruce's jacket flies around him with the sheer power of the movement. "The back fist and then low."

"And of course they use legs..." Although he's standing no further than a foot and a half from the old man, his right leg snakes out, first at the groin, then the head. "Straight to the groin, then come up!"

Both movements are executed in just a split second and scarcely have they been completed before Bruce continues, "Or if I back up a little bit..." thrashes out a right leg to the unfortunate man's forehead. Laughing, the Little Dragon pats him on the head and remarks, "He's kind of worried!" It's an understatement. The stooge looks rigid with fear.

But it never takes long for the thinking observer to realise the precision behind Bruce Lee's power. At the same time as the Little Dragon's frail opponent was mentally checking his last will and testament, the Director confidently predicted: "He's got nothing to worry about." From just these few minutes of unique martial artistry, he had gleaned enough to be confident that Bruce was in full control of all his actions.

The laughter dying down a little, the Director asks, "Now show us once again how a good Kung Fu man would coolly handle it and walk away." Bruce is just preparing to go into the routine when the 'pips' go. The old man, still attempting to protect his necessary parts, looks well relieved. "Cut it," says a voice from the wings.

We move now to the third scene. The effect is stunningly beautiful as Bruce outlines some of the traditional stances of two different styles. "Test two," says the voice, and we see a repeat of the previous scene, only this time, without the old man.

The Director asks the Little Dragon to demonstrate some of the differences between Jujitsu and Kung Fu.

"Well, you will often read in a magazine that if somebody grabs you, you will do this and this, and then and then and then and then. Thousands of steps before you do a single thing. And this kind of magazine would teach you how to be feared by your enemies and admired by your friends. But in Kung Fu, it always involves a very fast motion. For instance, if a guy grabs hold of your hand, it's not the idea to do so many steps." Bruce slams his foot onto the floor before continuing, "Just step on his instep and he'll let go. This is what we mean by simplicity. The same thing in striking - it has to be based on a very minimum of motion so that everything will be directly expressed. Oooh!" Bruce shouts and stamps on the floor again.

All the time he's talking, Bruce uses his hands to add expression. "Doing it gracefully;" not yelling and jumping all over the place. Byah!"

He stands straight for a moment, with his hands together. They part to nervously pat his thighs while he awaits a new instruction. He looks down and laughs politely, slightly embarrassed that he might have gone too far. He decided to speak on, "Kung Fu can be practiced alone or with a partner. Practicing along alone involves forms, imitating for instance a crane, a monkey, a praying mantis." He demonstrates the crane and stretches his arms out to either side. Interweaving, they whirl around to portray the neck, head and beak of that great bird. He turns to face the camera, arms still flowing at incredible speed. Suddenly he lashes out a punch, then a kick that almost reaches the ceiling. "Byah!" A fierce jab stabs the air. Slowing, he finishes the routine back again on the stance. Straightening up, he looks over and nearly bows towards the Director.

"Show us one more and then we're all finished," and Bruce, who is pulling at his suit to

NOW FOR THE FIRST TIME IN THE U.K.!
TWO SUPERB NEW BRUCE LEE BOOKS BY THE EDITORS OF KUNG-FU MONTHLY

The world's greatest martial arts magazine is proud to announce two sensational new additions to the Bruce Lee library: with THE UNBEATABLE BRUCE LEE, we uncover a veritable treasure chest of previously unknown facts and figures on the world's foremost martial artist. With WHO KILLED BRUCE LEE? we shed some light on the clouded circumstances surrounding the Master's mysterious death. You simply cannot afford to miss either of these lavishly illustrated volumes.

Priced £1.75 each or £3.00 for both.
Rush your P.O./Cheque (made out to KFM) to:-
Bruce Lee Books Offer
14 Rathbone Place
London W1P 1DE
(Please allow at least 4 weeks for delivery).

Limited Stocks Order Now

get it back into shape, replies, "Okay, I'm glad to hear that!" He laughs and laughs again. Then he goes on, "You have the tiger, using claws to claw the face." He takes a fencing stance, but with fingers shaped like a claw. Then, rather like the action of scooping sand out of a bucket, each hand and arm, in turn, flows outwards and upwards. In fact the movements are quite reminiscent of his actions in *The Way of the Dragon*, at the point where he's about to knock down the fat man in the back alley.

Bruce finishes and proceeds to tug at his shirt sleeves, to bring them down below the level of his jacket sleeves. "Thank you very much," says the Director. Bruce smiles and thanks him back. He got the job!

One thing that's immediately obvious from looking at this rare clip is that the Little Dragon would have been far better off ad-libbing or writing his own scripts. Indeed, one of the critics once went so far as to write, "I can tell the producers of *The Green Hornet* how to improve their show - they should let the Hornet's sidekick Kato, write his own dialogue."

Bruce himself felt that the series was too straight and that it needed a sort of James Bond element. Nevertheless, the Little Dragon toured the country to help promote *The Green Hornet*, dressed of course in the black suit, chauffeur's hat and famous mask. He loved playing the extrovert, whether at work or play!

And soon, too, he had to learn to come to terms with the adulation of the fans. With the instant TV exposure, being mobbed in streets started to become commonplace. At times, people's enthusiasm was almost irritating, and he once told *Black Belt* magazine, "It can be a terrifying experience. Once, when leaving a Karate tournament, I started to make an exit through a side door, escorted by three Karate men. I was practically mobbed outside and I had to get out through another side door." Soon, the Master was to leave *The Green Hornet* series far behind him in his battle to achieve world acclaim. And that in a way, is what makes this unique reel of film all the more valuable. For it shows us Bruce Lee as we seldom see him - off guard and, if you like, in the raw. There may have been times when he spoke better, performed more coherently and showed more confidence but it doesn't matter! For any true fan of the Master, a chance to see this film is a chance not to be missed and I didn't.

THE BRUCE LEE SOCIETY

Hi... Pam here again! For ages now I've been wanting to organise some sort of Society book list. For the fans, finding out where to get hold of particular titles is often a time-consuming business and it would obviously be a good idea to bring as many as possible under 'one umbrella'. I'll be announcing more details soon, but perhaps in the meantime, anyone interested might like to drop me a POSTCARD ONLY please, listing the sort of selection you'd like to see.

Following on a brief mention in Kickback this month, Ian McNaughton (2445) writes in to tell us more on Golden Harvest's latest kung fu signing, Jacky Chan. Apparently he has a pretty good background in traditional acting and Golden Harvest are confidently going ahead with a movie aimed at the international market, entitled *The Fearless Hyena*! It's said by a spokesman that, although he has a long way to go before challenging the Master, he has the ambition to become a world star. Unfortunately, a critic describes him thus: a squat and muscular young man with a rubbery face that's dominated by a massive nose. Anyone for Kung Fu comedy?!

Now for something I don't like hearing about. Word comes from Graham Waggett (2602) that his local ABC cinema in Derby was recently seen advertising for its 'Screen 2,' 'Bruce Lee in *Fist of Fury Part 2*". If Graham's right, then I suggest that somebody gently reminds the management that it is in fact, Bruce Li who 'stars' in the epic, before they get accused of ripping-off the fans. Come to that, I wonder what EMI might think about any such false billing!

Lastly, thanks to so many of you for responding so well to my call for word on whether you'd attend a Bruce Lee Convention. Now the day is actually drawing near, please make sure you come. For details, check the big ad that appears elsewhere in this issue.

KICKBACK: THE LETTERS

Hi everyone, and in this, the year of the Great Convention, it does my heart good to introduce another batch of super-fine letters. I've got a little story to tell you this month! One day, not long ago, I popped into a shop in London that specialises in stocking valuable items on stars - to sell to the likes of you and me. Well, I asked him who he kept most on and which were the big names. His top five best sellers are: James Dean, Elvis Presley, Marilyn Monroe, Clint Eastwood and, that's right, Bruce Lee. Apparently, in this cream of the cream company, the Little Dragon now ranks number two in the order of sales importance, with only Clint Eastwood ahead of him! And I'm told interest is still on the rise SO it seems there's every chance that Bruce will soon be hitting the top spot. I find that news incredible and further confirmation (as if we needed it!) that the Master's magic is still a giant force to be reckoned with. Phew, how about some letters!

UNDISCOVERED BRUCE LEE FILM

Dear Jenny,
I've read in a leading movie magazine that while Bruce was making *The Big Boss*, he was also working on a film entitled, *He Walks Like a Tiger*. It said that it was along the same lines as *Game of Death*, with most of the fights and acting being handled by Bruce. Apparently the film has been a very big secret and only now has it been taken off the shelf.
Wesley Fleming, Adelaide, S. Australia

Dear Wesley,
All I can say is - amazing! It's all new to me, so it sounds like time for some investigation. Watch this space!

WISDOM OF BRUCE LEE

Dear Jenny,
I am writing to ask when the book, *The Wisdom of Bruce Lee* will be available? It was advertised a long time ago in the magazine and still members of the Society are unable to obtain it.
Paul Wade, Boulevard, Hull

Dear Paul,
We've had literally hundreds of letters in regarding this book, so I've been making a few enquiries. The problem is that, originally it was written especially for an American company. It was advertised in KFM *because they promised to send over a quantity for mail order in this country. They never did! Their first-print editions sold out almost immediately and we missed out having any. Since then, there've been several attempts from this end to do something about it, all unfortunately to no avail. I'm glad to say that nowadays we seem to have overcome the problem. American publications such as* Bruce Lee in Action *have indeed been available through our mail order. We haven't given up on* The Wisdom of Bruce Lee *yet though!*

NUNCHAKU - BAD PRESS

Dear Jenny,
I enclose a news clipping from the *Lancashire Evening Post*. In essence, it reports on the arrest and subsequent fining of a Chinese teenager who, it was alleged, was about to enter into nunchaku combat in a Preston carpark and I'm really worried as to the effect the article will have on the serious nunchaku practitioner. In the evidence, he gave, Inspector Russell Gorman claimed that the weapon is capable of smashing six house bricks with one swoop. I think this is highly unlikely, if not impossible. Secondly, it says in the article that Mr. Wong (the youth arrested) recognised that the nunchaku could be used only as an offensive weapon. It's a pity they hadn't taken the time to watch the beauty of Bruce in action with the flail and realised the speed and accuracy required to master it. Surely this puts it apart from something like a bicycle chain? I'm not trying to make excuses for Mr. Wong, but I feel only one side of the picture has been painted. Its incidents like this that give the martial arts world in general and Bruce in particular a bad name.
A. l'Anson, Preston, Lancs

Dear A. I'Anson,
Point taken and all martial artists carry the responsibility of protecting the good name of their sport.

FIST OF FURY SINGLE

Dear Jenny,
You said *KFM* No.38 that you were unsure of the contents of the single *Fist of Fury* No.2. Well, the 'A' side is the *Fist of Fury* theme, but it's not Bruce Lee, it's someone trying to imitate him. The 'B' side is from a film called McQ. Also, beware of two other singles. Both are *The Way of the Dragon* and neither feature Bruce. They do, however, have Bruce on the front cover (in colour) and a black and white inside.
Graeme Warwick, Glasgow

Dear Graeme,
Thanks for sending along the info. This sort of letter really is a great help.

THE BEST EVER PUBLICATIONS

Dear Jenny,
Congratulations for keeping the standard of *KFM* as brilliant as ever. Also, I'd just like to say that *Bruce Lee in Action* and *Who Killed Bruce Lee?* are the best-ever publications concerning Bruce.
Mark Gibbard, Hucclecote, Glos

Dear Mark,
Modesty usually forbids me from printing letters like this. However, on this occasion, it looks like it sorta sneaked through.

BRUCE LEE DOUBLE BILL

Dear Jenny,
Two weeks ago, the North West had a double treat - *Enter the Dragon* and *Fist of Fury* together. At the cinema in Widnes, the two nights that I went, the place was packed. It's nice to know that the Bruce Lee fans are still great in number and even growing. Also, I would like to apologise to the Empire manager because I couldn't resist taking the poster.
A.M. Harmer, Frodsham, Cheshire

Dear A.M.,
It goes back to what I said at the start, that all the signs are that the Master is more than holding his own; he's on the way up again! Tut, tut about that poster - you could try asking! What about all the fans who came along after you and who don't get to see it?

BEST MARTIAL ARTIST NOMINEE

Dear Jenny,
I am writing to you to nominate who I think is the best martial artist, now that Bruce is dead. His name is Jason Pai Piau, and though he's not reached Bruce's standards, he outclasses any other martial artist I've seen. Do you have any information on him?
Steven Robertson, Queenslie, Glasgow

Dear Steven,
You've really got me going with this one! The name certainly rings a bell - in fact I think I've seen him in action. Anyone else help?

KICKBACK QUICKIES

Elvis Whetton, Streatham, London - I've gotta agree, UK film censors DO seem to have double standards.

John Walsh, Possilpork, Glasgow - Sounds like there's enough good material left for Chow to make a knockout film - will he do it?

W.A.Rysztogi, Walkley, Sheffield - Reading *KFM* at night makes you late for work? You better think of something else to tell the boss!

K. Stokes, Newport, Gwent - Thanks for the info that good Bruce stuff is to be had from The St. Martins House, opposite the Bull Ring centre in Birmingham.

J. S. Walker, Walsall, Staffs - You've got a lot to catch up on! Why not join the Society and get jawing to Pam?

Michelle Scully, Blackburn, Lancs - Thanks for checking out possible convention places - maybe we'll try up there next time.

David Taylor, Poplar, London - He says send 60p (cheque or postal order) plus SAE, he'll send back a copy of the 12" single *Dragon Power*.

A. Ferrin - A nice long letter - Let's keep our eyes open for Jacky Chen.

Rochelle-Huen Chang, London - Gotta agree - It was tragic the way they scissored out Dan Inosanto.

Stephen Mullings, Springwood, Yorks - Good question, what were bottles doing in the *Enter the Dragon* battle? Presumably to show Oharra's complete disregard for honour.

Mr R C Symes, Dukes Town, Gwent - If Chris Kent did the war cries in *Game of Death*, I'd rather he didn't do any more.

Adrian Mitchell, Cookstown - If you want to contact a Hong Kong studio, I suggest you write C/O Golden Harvest, Soho Square, London W1.

David Coombs, Small Heath, Birmingham - PG said that Bruce had no respect for Yip Man. I find it hard to believe.

Chris Ebon, Walsall, Staffs - He's looking for a Chinese girl pen pal. He's into Bruce and travelling.

THE POSTER MAGAZINES - VOLUME TWO

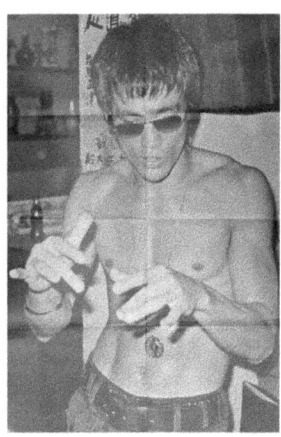

EDITORIAL

Welcome to issue 49 of *Kung-Fu Monthly*, just one before the magic 50! As you can probably guess, that's going to be something of a sensation! Apart from containing a full report on The Bruce Lee Convention, there'll be one or two surprises that you'll just have to wait to find out about. To say that reaching 50 is an amazing achievement would be the understatement of the decade.

We intend to be celebrating every way we know how.

But enough of next month and back to the present. First off, we deal with one of the most contentious talking points of the present time - the situation regarding the huge number of Bruce Lee 'rip off' films. Good or bad, most of them make their money by judicious use of lookalikes. Entirely apart from the ethics of it all, is it really fair that the public should be confused in this way and more than that, what effect is it having on Bruce Lee's own reputation? Read part one to of our startling new insight and let us know what you think!

The second feature this month is devoted to another revealing look at the forbidden footage - the scenes in Bruce's films that, for the most part, the censors would prefer us not to look at. Many times in *KFM*, we've ranted on about the absurd censorship laws in this country and indeed, it starts to look as though we may actually be winning the battle. Lately, one or two prints have been doing the rounds with a good deal more left in than previously so let's just hope it hasn't been a mistake!

Lastly, back with the Convention again - a million apologies to the hundreds of fans who applied too late to get a ticket. Obviously to start with, we had no idea just what the response would be, though 400 seemed like a pretty good guess. As it turned out, the final figure was over triple that!

Felix Yen
Editor-in-Chief

THE BRUCE LEE RIP-OFFS!

Steve McQueen, James Coburn and Danny Inosanto stand before Bruce's coffin, their heads bowed in grief; flowers are strewn across the wooden box. It's July 20th, 1973 and as the stars pay their last respects, so too are the public mourning in the streets. The death of Bruce Lee is making a profound impact upon the history of Hong Kong.

Believe it or not, this scene is for real - it's part of *Bruce Lee, the Man and the Myth*. One of the better Little Dragon films going around the international movie circuits, this one stars the well-known, Bruce Li. Though more or less a re-enactment of Bruce Lee's life (and true fans will recognise many of its inaccuracies and shortcomings) still when it comes down to brass tacks, the picture is yet another attempt to capitalise on Bruce's box office pulling-power. More on this film later!

It takes no real talent at all to look like the Little Dragon - let's call it an act of nature. But to be able to act out one of the Master's tight sequences - now that's something else! And herein lies the basis of my contention that nine out of ten of these films are not only a rip-off, they're also a downright insult to Lee the man and Lee the artist.

Imagine you have two cakes, both apparently identical. One, however, is filled with real cream, the other with some kind of confectionary substitute. Placed side by side, the onlooker might find it very difficult to tell one from the other; the colour, the shape, the smell - everything seems the same. Only by actually taking a bite will the cake enthusiast be able to make a proper judgement.

That bite is what separates Bruce Lee from all the other Kung Fu cinema artists. Another actor might look fine on screen - simply because he is imitating the Master. Nothing, however, can match the flavour of the real thing. A copy is only a copy.

"You can't fool all the people all of the time!" Over the years, we've heard at the *KFM* offices of quite a number of fans who, on seeing one of the imitations, thought in fact they were looking at the genuine Bruce Lee. But that's only because they hadn't seen a Little Dragon film before. Once the omission had been put to rights, none of them ever wanted to waste more time on lookalikes.

There are literally hundreds of these rip-offs being shown around the world (mainly in the States and Hong Kong). And of course in some ways it has to be seen as a great compliment - after all, imitation is supposed to be the sincerest form of flattery.

They tend to fit into three different categories. First off there's the borrowed format variety. One such example is a movie entitled *Bruce Lee's Secret*. The synopsis folder features a painting of Lee's face and has pictures spread around it of a lookalike (the imitator in fact bears a distinct resemblance to Bruce Li although the star of the epic is credited as Ho Tsung-tao; maybe this is Li's real name).

Well, the storyline is supposed to be about the Master during the time he was teaching Kung Fu in San Francisco. Some ruffians start bullying one of Bruce's friends (who, by the way, just happens to be a restaurant owner - shades of *The Way of the Dragon*). 'Bruce' naturally beats hell out of them they crawl off to tell their boss what happened. The boss tries again, only this time with greater numbers (sounds even more like *The Way of the Dragon*!). 'Bruce,' of course, does his number again and knocks whole crew for six and so impressed are the waiters at the rest rant, they ask him if he'll show them his style of boxing (yes, beginning to shape up nicely like a *The Way of the Dragon* rip-off). The boss tries buy off our hero to go back Hong Kong, etc but to no avail. There's only one alternative - to bring in another champion.

It's with relief that I'm able report that the alternative champion is not in fact, a Chuck Norris lookalike! (although the idea must have been tempting). The boss' saviour turns out to be a certain Chin Yung-chi and, just by way of a slight twist to the plot, he goes round and destroys Bruce's school while he is out (hey, that's not from *The Way of the Dragon*, we've suddenly switched to *Fist of Fury*!). Anyway, as you'll all be able to guess, 'Bruce' gets his revenge in the big fight - end of story.

Another in the long list of imitations that fit into this category is a Run Run Shaw production that boasts the name, Bruce Lee - Father of Jeek Kune Do - that's right, Jeek not Jeet. They've managed to cash in on the Master and his art in just one, mis-spelt title; once more, the star looks like Bruce Li.

On to the second group of rip-offs and here, only the physical side of the Master has been borrowed - the scripts are, to the most part, original.

The Magnificent is one - it's a competently made movie that features some quite excellent workout scenes. The storyline, however, gets a little confusing at times. What it does have is a new star - wait for it - Bruce Lai! Sadly, his deficiency in skill is all too apparent on screen and thus he only appears for a few minutes.

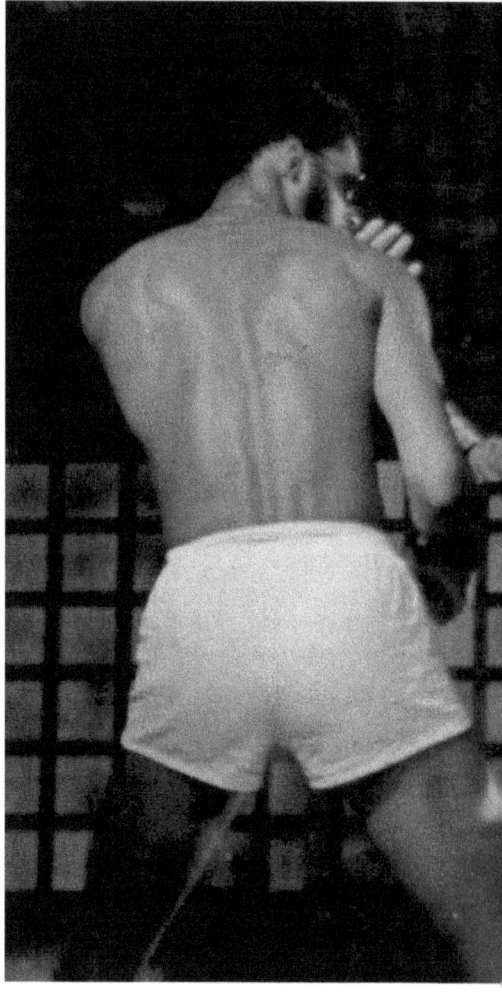

Meanwhile, an excellent martial artist by the name of Casanova steals the show (with, in part, a superb double kick). Against all that, however, is a sickening statement we came across in the film's press release - the makers claim it to be a bigger letter than Bruce Lee's films. It isn't, and anyway, what's the point in going out of one's way to try and alienate a good number of the potential audience?

The producers of this movie (Asso Asia Films) have already come out with another offering entitled *Bruce Against the Odds* and another, *The Dragon of Fire*, is in on the way. Both are said to be aimed at the Bruce market, although neither have been heard of so far around the British circuits. Dragon Lee is another of the film star lookalikes. Unfortunately for this particular gentleman, nature has endowed him with a 'bulging muscle' kind of body which bears little resemblance to the streamline physique of the Master. He stars in *Enter Three Dragons* (let's hope casual film-goers don't mistake 'three' for 'the' - the other dragons being played by Ron an Clief and the man who did such a great job in *Enter*

the Dragon, John Saxon. Clief is one of America's popular martial artists and recently he's starred in a highly movie, *The Super Weapon*.

One of the latest offerings to fit into this second category is *Dynamo*, starring Bruce Li. In it, he wears the famous yellow tracksuit with the black stripe (shades of *Game of Death*, of course) and if that doesn't grab you, how about this for a title - *Clones of Bruce Lee*! *Fist of Fury Part 2* turned out nearer to the Master and in fact we've received one or two fair reports on it. It's said that parts three, four and five are in the pipeline, though whether they star Li is not clear.

Lastly, before leaving this section, mention must be made of what, so far as we know, is the only comedy made about Bruce Lee. If the Master were alive today, there's no doubt at all that he'd belly laugh over this one. Entitled *Enter the Fat Dragon*, the hero of the piece is fat, blubbery and extremely unattractive! Further to the film's credit is the fact that the star was in fact a good friend of Bruce Lee.

Finally, we come to the third kind of film imitation and here we find that actual clips of the Master have been included within the theme. These usually claim to recount at least, part of the Little Dragon's real life.

Two very similar films are *The Real Bruce Lee* and *The Young Bruce Lee: The Little Dragon*. Both include frames from Bruce's child movies - mostly from *The Orphan*.

The Real Bruce Lee stars Bruce Lee, Bruce Li and the new so-called superstar, Dragon Lee. The poster for the film proclaims "He's back" and "We positively guarantee the real Bruce Lee." And they're right - they've incorporated some early footage taken of Bruce when he was fourteen. On the poster however, they've included pictures of him taken when he was twenty-eight; they're placed above one of Bruce Li who, with dark glasses, is looking amazingly like the Master.

At one cinema alone (The Milgram in Philadelphia) it's said to have taken $50,247 in just one week and with that sort of popularity, it should certainly be worth a look. Unfortunately, there's no news yet of a British release date.

The Young Bruce Lee: The Little Dragon stars Bruce Lee, Bruce Li and Lee Hsaio Lung and it was written and created by Dick Randell and Larry Dolchin, with Randell also producing. The early footage comes from no less than four of the Little Dragon's childhood efforts - one in fact, where he's only six years old. The roles he takes are various - a likeable little scallywag who gets into all kinds of scrapes, a carnival barker, a member of a Chinese soap opera company and (very true to his own nature) a young hoodlum going round looking for fights.

From these rare scraps of film, the plot shifts to San Francisco and eventually (with the help of the lookalikes) we see him becoming an internationally famous superstar. There're also clips from the actual funeral.

And that's all there's space for this month. Next time round, as promised, we'll be looking closer at *Man and the Myth*. In particular the spotlight will be falling on Bruce Li - just how good is he getting these days? As the world's most prolific impersonator, his is a name that just can't be ignored.

CENSORED – PART TWO!

A guy with a dagger in his hand slowly approaches Bruce. The Little Dragon jolts forward - but it's a false step, a feint. Three times he makes to move, the fourth time it's for real. The nunchaku hurtles to their target. Bruce leaps into the air and delivers the final strike on the back of the neck, using the weapon as clubs. Maybe you've seen it before or probably you haven't! We're back on the trail of more censored scenes. Right now we're standing in one of the ultimate danger zones- it's the alley fight from *The Way of the Dragon*.

Another thug charges in, but is brought to a halt with four rapid blows from the sticks, the last dumps him on the floor. Bruce is sweating hard, his face twisted in furious concentration. Gradually the odds are turning his way. There're only a few of the attackers left now.

Another man is urged forward but against this super-human lighting machine, he's powerless. Twice he's kissed by the flails, and kicks to the ankle and jaw see that he takes no further interest in the proceedings. Three to go, and a fat man with a pole demands another of his compatriots attack. Stopping three feet away from Bruce, the luckless victim-to-be threatens with a knife. It's the last thing he does as one sharp blow to the centre of the forehead settles his fate.

Just two are left now and the fat man urges the other forward. The Little Dragon decides to switch technique. Keeping hold of the nunchaku (one stick in either hand) he simply butts the guy in the gut, followed by the jaw. Not even bothering to watch the figure crumple to the floor, he switches his attention to the last in line.

And this is usually where we cut back into censored versions of the film. Those not realising the back room hacking that's been going on should be forgiven at this point for wondering how suddenly, all these bodies are lying in the alleyway. Just remember that Bruce would have been as upset with the butchering as anyone. Why nunchakus should be singled out for such barbcrous treatment remains a mystery to this day.

Of course, it has to be said that censorship of Bruce's films wasn't always the result of action from the Censorship Board, for instance, in *Enter the Dragon*, the original version didn't, as is normal these days, open with the contest. Before the duel, there should be a scene where Bruce walks through the grounds of a temple, talking to the head monk. This segment was removed in most western countries because it was felt the fighting made for more of an opening impact.

Then, later on, the love scene with Mae Lin usually gets omitted. True the frames add little to the story, but why chop those and yet leave all the others in?

The famous fight with Oharra got decidedly tampered with, to the extent that the final death blow is rarely seen in some countries. Often, the last known cut is where Bruce's kick to the chest sends his opponent reeling back into the onlookers. That has become the killer blow. What in fact happened originally was that Oharra recovered from the punch, grabbed hold of two bottles and having smashed them together to leave just the jagged necks, lunged back into the fray.

It's pretty well known now that these bottles were real, not for Bruce, the sale sugar-glass that any other actor would use (and of course he received fairly serious injuries while shooting the sequence). All this makes it even more irritating that our lords and masters have decided that we cannot see it! Oharra therefore makes his rush at the Little Dragon in a state of blind anger and Bruce uses this vulnerability to kick one bottle clean out of his hand. Another strike topples the maddened fighter.

Then follows a sequence of shere magic. Bruce jumps high in the air to land on Oharra's neck with his feet delivering the coup de gras. The action is in slow motion and once the Little Dragon has landed the deadly blow, the slow motion continues as the camera cuts to a close-up of his face. Were that final shot taken at normal speed, undoubtedly the audience would have missed the continuity of his feelings.

NOW FOR THE FIRST TIME IN THE U.K.!
TWO SUPERB NEW BRUCE LEE BOOKS BY THE EDITORS OF KUNG-FU MONTHLY

STOP PRESS
Bruce Lee in Action has completely sold out!

The world's greatest martial arts magazine is proud to announce two sensational new additions to the Bruce Lee library: with THE UNBEATABLE BRUCE LEE, we uncover a veritable treasure chest of previously unknown facts and figures on the world's foremost martial artist. With WHO KILLED BRUCE LEE? we shed some light on the clouded circumstances surrounding the Master's mysterious death. You simply cannot afford to miss either of these lavishly illustrated volumes.

Priced £1.75 each or £3.00 for both.
Rush your P.O./Cheque (made out to KFM) to:-
Bruce Lee Books Offer
14 Rathbone Place
London W1P 1DE
(Please allow at least 4 weeks for delivery).

Limited Stocks Order Now

Bruce's face turns from red anger to the registered shock of having taken a life in battle to, finally, the ecstasy of revenge now found, though tinged with sorrow. "Why?" he seems to be asking, "is all this necessary in the first place?" There's a kind of tragic stillness as he steps aside.

This wonderful scene from *Enter the Dragon* frequently gets dumped on the scrapheap. It seems it's okay for us to see breadknife stabbings in full, gory detail, and to witness bullets blowing apart skulls, yet Bruce Lee dealing with a bottle-wielding maniac is too much for us. Sometimes I wonder if censorship boards are clean off their rockers!

We'll finish off the *Enter the Dragon* censorship with something that wasn't. It really censorship at all - at least not in the normal sense of the word.

The original script had Bruce killing Han in the weapons room - up to that point, no one had come up with the idea of the mirrors. However, whilst on location, Robert Clouse (the Director) and his wife Ann happened to stroll around a boutique, the interior decor of which consisted of many thin strips of mirror. He noticed that, as she walked along, her image seemed to shatter from mirror to mirror. It gave him a marvellous idea!

Quickly the script was rewritten to take in a great new finale sequence. In fact, it was quite a blessing for Bruce who at the time was nursing a painful groin injury. Much time was spent on working out the best positioning of the mirrors, to disguise the Little Dragon's legs.

The expense of it all was enormous, in fact it was quite the most costly scene in the film. Moves were planned out and marks were made on the floor with coloured tape and numbers. Reams of notes detailed what shots were to be taken from which angles. One of the most difficult problems to solve was keeping the camera reflections out of the field of vision.

During one sequence, it turned out that Bruce would have to kick Han in the head from a distance of three inches! Unhappy about how it would turn out (not that he couldn't do it) he decided it might be better to try something else. People around the studio couldn't help but wonder whether he could do it anyway and Bruce agreed to put the move to the test. His agreement with Clouse was that, if it looked okay in the rushes, in it would go.

So, from early morning until late at night they battled on to record the entire scene and the next day when they saw the prints, they knew they had a winner. Even the three inch kick looked amazing. So what, you may wonder, has this to do with the business of scissoring? Well, just this. So wrapped up were they in getting things right (they shot variations that all in all, there must have been around an hour's worth of usable footage. What we see of it in *Enter the Dragon* lasts just ten minutes or so and that means there's perhaps over forty minutes of mirror sequence material that's never been seen by the viewing public!

Where is it now? One theory is that it sits collecting dust on a shelf somewhere in Warners, possibly never to be seen again. Wouldn't it be fantastic if that, plus other cast-offs from *Enter the Dragon*, were laced together into one long feature?

They could call it The Making of *Enter the Dragon*. As a B-feature to one of his regular movies, it would be just astounding. Already of course there's *On location with Enter the Dragon* available on Super 8mm (from Regent films) but a full length movie in its own right - what a knockout! Lastly we come to *Game of Death*. Love it, hate it or just plain put up with it, there's one thing you can't deny - the chopping out of the Bruce Lee/Danny Inosanto nunchaku clash was one of the major censorship gaffs of the year. A detailed breakdown of this missing segment has already been given in *KFM* No.42 so there's no point in going into it in detail.

Let's just realise what a scandal it was that cinema-goers were denied the thrill of seeing a world master performing his art at the very height of his genius. Someone, somewhere should be hanging his head in shame.

Eventually as time passes and some sort of sanity returns, I'm confident that the scissor-men will get to realise the enormity of what they have done in the sullied name of censorship. Then we will be able to see what Bruce wanted us it, see rather than having to make do with the decisions of a third party - one that probably doesn't know its arts from its elbow.

THE BRUCE LEE SOCIETY

Hi, Pam with you again, and one thing I'm not going to be mentioning is that Convention! I'll have lots to say in next month's 50th issue tribute.

One idea that is worth outlining, though, is this one. For years now I've had request after request for the Society to arrange regular film shows, for us to hire out cinemas for the showing of Bruce's films (preferably not censored).

And it wouldn't have to stop at that. There are many other titles going around that, for one reason or another, fans of the Master would probably enjoy seeing; names such as David Chiang, Wang Yu and maybe even Bruce Le, spring immediately to mind. Considering the interest everybody demonstrated by coming to the convention, I'd say that those film events are now a very real possibility and without a doubt, the time has now come for us to check the availability of the movies concerned.

That's where you come in. I'd really appreciate as many members as possible sending me in postcards, listing the ones they'd most like to see. Obviously we'll be looking to show all the Bruce Lee material we can, so don't bother including *The Big Boss*, *Fist of Fury*, *Way of the Dragon*, *Enter the Dragon* and *Game of Death* titles. Concentrate on lesser known material that you think is worthy of a place.

Changing the subject, I'm delighted to say that the book list I introduced in the last News Sheet is quite a success. I had a feeling that bringing rare volumes under one roof (so to speak) might be a popular idea, but results have exceeded even MY cautious optimism. Keep letting me know of any new titles you think should be included! I can't promise that I'll be able to find all of the more items of Bruce Lee literature, but I'll certainly be trying as much as I can! And that's it for this month. Take care. **Pam**

KICKBACK: THE LETTERS

Hi again, Jenny here; there's so many great letters this month, I'm leaving out the quickies to concentrate on the full length stuff but it'll be back to normal in *KFM* No.51! It's a bit hard, but we've all been sworn to say nothing about the Convention - until next month. I can see the point because, after all, where better than *KFM* No.50 to rave on about Britain's first Bruce Lee Convention. What I will say though is that letters are already beginning to pour in with messages of congratulations. There may have been the odd technical problem but I think most people found the atmosphere incredible. It may come as no surprise to everyone who came along, that Convention No.2 is already going through the planning stages.

BOOK PHOTO QUERY

Dear Jenny,
If you refer to page 2 of *Bruce Lee in Action* and the front page, plus pages 4, 25 and 26 of *Who Killed Bruce Lee*? you will notice a half inch long, crescent-shaped scar on Bruce Lee's right cheek bone. This scar is also visible in many other early photos. How did he receive it? Also, we've looked closely at many pictures of Bruce in his coffin and so far, we've yet to see the mark. Could it be due to heavy make-up or perhaps not!
Norman Kavanagh and Michael McDonnell, Kilmarnock, Scotland

Dear Norman and Michael,
Yes, I've noticed the skin blemish myself, but to be honest, I'm not certain exactly which incident was the cause of it. No doubt I shall be well and truly put in the picture over the weeks to come! So far as the coffin mystery goes, I suspect your guess is right. Heavy makeup would indeed be the likely culprit as you suggest.

MORE NUNCHAKU POSTERS

Dear Jenny,
Please could you suggest to the Editor of *KFM* that he has more posters of Bruce using the nunchakus and also wearing the gloves from *Enter the Dragon*. Another thing - would it be possible to reprint the posters only of *KFM* No. 1, 2 and 3 and also to do a Bruce Lee calendar, with pictures of Bruce for every month? Finally, may I say that it's amazing to see that *KFM* has gone on for so long and still it keeps up to a good standard. I can't wait for *KFM* No.50 to come out.
John Hill, Croxteth, Liverpool

Dear John,
Believe me, we'd love to print more nunchaku and glove pictures - the only trouble is finding them! The calendar idea is one that's come up before and it certainly bears thinking about for next Christmas. Lastly, regarding KFM No.50, I also can't wait to see it. The last I heard, they were even discussing including one of those flexi-disc records!

GAME OF DEATH SEQUEL RUMOUR

Dear Jenny,
I read in a Chinese magazine that a lot of the scenes originally filmed for *Game of Death* are now being put into a sequel that's entitled *Tower of Death*. Scenes include a fight between Chieh Yuan and Chi Hon Tsoi. Also it says there is an epic battle between Bruce and Dan Inosanto that takes place against a country background, with Dan using kali sticks and Bruce, his nunchakus. Lastly, I have just purchased the *Game of Death* soundtrack and in your review, there was a slight mistake. The track you say is called 'Face of with Hakim,' on my copy it is in fact called 'Face off with Hakim.' The meaning then becomes quite clear.
Paul Marston, Plymouth, Devon

Dear Paul,
Although we've already touched on the *Tower of Death* business in a previous issue, it's worth picking up on it again for the following reason. Word has it from a film industry source that plans may have been changed for the follow-up. I hear, that, early in May, Raymond Chow visited the States and while there, he arranged a meeting with Steve McQueen. The speculation is that Steve may become the link man to some 'Genius of Bruce Lee' type of production - adding flow to the hours of action cuttings that Golden Harvest have to choose from. Lastly, sorry about the goof regarding the 'Face off with Hakim' track - suddenly it all makes sense!

WHO'S KNOCKING BRUCE?

Dear Jenny,
I am writing in reply to Agi Georgiou's letter in *KFM* No.47. I, too, have read the magazine he quotes from (*Real Kung Fu*) and it seems to do nothing but run down Bruce Lee. It remarks for instance how Bruce failed to attend Yip Man's funeral, without making mention of the fact that be didn't even know of the death until some three days later. In fact, Bruce was very angry that no one had told him in time and he was heard to say: "You know those sons-of-bitches (referring to Yip Man's students), they live right in the city and never called me. Dammit, they carried out their jealousy too far." I, as Phil Cook pointed out in a previous letter, agree that the magazine also implies that Jeet Kune Do is just a mock-up of Wing Chun. Misguided fans might easily get the impression that Bruce was a phoney and a liar. Finally, I hope you keep up the great work of producing a brilliant magazine.
Peter Jagger, Kings Norton, Birmingham

Dear Peter,
Thanks for some wise-sounding words and hopefully, these days, most of the knocking-type magazines have gone on to pastures new.

BRUCE LEE AND PUNKS

Dear Jenny,
I'm a punk and a dedicated Bruce Lee fan. And I believe in Bruce Lee's philosophies. As far as I can tell, I am the only punk with Bruce Lee connections as anyone who claims to be a punk and who thrives on fear and violence, should be ignored. My understanding of punk is, a taste for the music, the right to say what you like, a rebellion against other styles, plus a show of individualism. I am not narrow-minded and I like lots of things other than punk. I choose to be a punk because I like it. My punk name is GOD, which as you know is an abbreviation for *Game of Death*. I chose this in respect to the Master and his worthy beliefs. I never involve myself with violence or trouble.
John Simpson (GOD), East Kilbride, Scotland

Dear John,
It's good to know you can find unity in two such different world. Actually, some would say that you're in good company.

BRUCE LEE CASSETTE

Dear Jenny,
I've just received the latest *KFM*, and what an issue!! The Bruce Lee Censored File and Behind the Scenes made fantastic reading! Regarding the picture of Bruce sitting down holding open a file, notice on the bottom left-hand corner of the desk, there is a cassette with what looks like a picture of Bruce on the cover. Any suggestions on what the title is?
Mike Devereux (1061), Orford, Cheshire

Dear Mike,
Thanks also for sending along the list of film and TV studios - addresses like that are worth having! On to the letter, the cassette is not one that I can remember seeing before so come on fans, out with those magnifying glasses for some instant detective work!

NEWS FLASH!

Since Jenny compiled this month's letters column, the great news is that, she had it right - a special flexi-disc will definitely be included with *KFM* No.50! And recent Convention-goers will need no reminding of the words recorded on it - James Coburn, paying personal tribute to Bruce Lee in a stunning and off-the-cuff speech lasting nearly five minutes, where he reveals the warmth, understanding and depth of communication that existed between them. James tells how much he now misses the inspiration - his friendship with a man who, quite literally, gave it all away. Thanks to Eddy Pumer, this unique recording becomes available to *KFM* readers on the very day that, we celebrate our 50th birthday. Though there has to be a small increase in cover price (one month only) to cover costs of manufacture, I hope you will feel as excited as I do by the result.

THE KUNG-FU MONTHLY ARCHIVE SERIES

THE BRUCE LEE SOCIETY, in association with KUNG-FU MONTHLY, is delighted to be able to announce.

BRITAIN'S FIRST BRUCE LEE CONVENTION 1979

No, we can hardly believe it either! At last, KFM, Society President – Pam Hadden – plus friends are presenting the event we've all been dreaming of all these years. Naturally there are many, many points still to be finalised, but here's what we're able to tell you right now.

1 The venue is the Acklam Hall, in London's Notting Hill Gate; the Convention will run approximately 10.30am to 5.00pm on Saturday the 19th May, 1979.

2 It looks like we'll have to set a ceiling on delegates of just 400. That means you'd better book early – in fact, to avoid disappointment, BOOK NOW!

3 By and large, entry to the hall will be by pre-paid ticket (at a cost to the general public of £3.25. . . Society members, £3.00). However, there MAY be just a few tickets on sale at the door – BUT WE CAN'T GUARANTEE IT.

And how's this for some of the attractions we hope to have lined-up for you.

● The moment everyone's been waiting for. . . come and view Way of the Dragon – FREE OF ALL EUROPEAN CENSORSHIP! That's right, it'll include the famed 'double nunchaku' sequence. What a great scoop for the Convention!

● Another fantastically rare reel of film. . . as described recently in KFM, catch a viewing of Bruce Lee as he makes his actual screen-test for the Green Hornet series!

● Collect as you enter the hall our unique Convention Kit. . . don't worry about price, it's inclusive with the ticket. Inside there'll be an info sheet on the story of KFM and the Bruce Lee Society, a rare Game of Death film brochure (courtesy of Golden Harvest), plus a commemorative Convention Scroll.

● You might like to visit our Swop-Shop Corner. That's where fans will be able to barter and bargain to their hearts content . . . if you've got anything to sell, swop or give away, BRING IT WITH YOU.

● Among all the great stalls we expect to have lined up for you, don't forget to drop by the KFM stand. There'll be rare Bruce Lee books, back issues, a one-day only chance to join the Bruce Lee Society at a specially reduced price AND special souvenir Convention T/Shirts, Drinking Mugs, Brooches (all naturally in black and yellow!).

● On top of all that, we're arranging for a top-class martial arts display, . . . food and drink will be on sale for most of the day . . . Master of Ceremonies will be our old friend (and ex-Cathay Films man), Roy Byrne. . . there'll be on-the-spot prizes, competitions and probably much more besides!

That's the kind of line-up we're mid-way through assembling! But, apart from anything else, it'll be a chance for Society members and fans to get to meet each other **for the first time ever on a national scale.**

Come along and support the Bruce Lee Convention – it's undoubtedly going to be one of the major events of 1979. Remember, it's just £3.00 for Society members, £3.25 for everyone else.

Send your cheque/postal order (made out to KFM) to:

Bruce Lee Convention
Kung-Fu Monthly
14 Rathbone Place
London W1P 1DE
(Please write your name and address clearly – IN BLOCK LETTERS)

A SPECIAL COMPETITION

We'll be making time on the day for a rather unusual competition. Anyone wanting to enter should accompany their ticket application with a statement on the subject, 'Why Bruce Lee was the greatest' – using not more than 200 words.

The best ten of these will be picked out by President of the Bruce Lee Society, Pam Hadden, and the authors will be asked on the day of the Convention to take the microphone and repeat their words to the fans present. The contender raising the biggest cheer will be adjudged the winner.

THE POSTER MAGAZINES - VOLUME TWO

EDITORIAL

    It's with great pride and a sense of enormous privilege that I hereby rip away the wrapping from this historic 50th issue of *Kung-Fu Monthly*. I hope you feel, as I do, that the Convention, plus the James Coburn message, have somehow almost magically combined to make this *KFM* edition literally second to none. By any reckoning, it has to be a mind-blower. On the front cover, you may have detected something rather unusual -a record! On it are engraved those now famous words of Mr James Coburn, paying personal tribute to 'his brother,' Bruce Lee. Capital Radio's Tony Myatt introduces. As a mark of our respect to both you the readers and to Mr Coburn, we have raised the cover price this month, sufficient only to pay for the extra costs - and not a penny more. I hope you feel the small increase (for this month only, of course) to be well worthwhile.

    Feature one in this slightly topsy-turvy edition centres naturally on the Convention. I've taken it on myself to write a detailed account that covers not only the day's events, but also the trials and tribulations that led up to it. I often get readers asking for more inside information on the workings of *KFM* - well, here's your chance to grab some unusual reading. Feature two just had to be the story of James Coburn's friendship with Bruce Lee. Eddy Pumer dissects the background, then launches into an account of his meeting with the great film actor himself. I must say it makes one of the most absorbing reads I've come across in a long time and, according to Eddy, there may yet be more info to come!

Lastly, on what usually is he Society report page, just for this month, Pam Hadden and I pay tribute on the occasion of the magazine's 50th birthday. Phew... what an issue!

Felix Yen

Felix Yen
Editor-in-Chief

BRITAIN'S FIRST BRUCE LEE CONVENTION 1979

No Convention of this kind can take place without a great deal of prior organisation and ours proved no exception. First hatched in the *KFM* offices during the autumn of 1978, right away the idea presented a whole host of problems.

"How many fans are likely to attend?" was the first question to be considered - after all, that would decide the size of the hall needed. We guessed at around 400 but as events were to prove, we got it wrong! The next question was "When?" Well, May 5th, 1979 was mooted and booked - then, horrors, we'd forgotten it was Cup Final day! The event was quickly shifted to May 12th, but two weeks later, the Cup Final was also shifted to May 12th! Finally we settled on May 19th. Would the clash have mattered anyway? It was a question we weren't prepared to try answering.

The venue itself proved only a little less mobile. With just a few weeks to go to D-Day and with Notting Hill Gate's Acklam Hall as the choice, suddenly it became clear that we needed somewhere much larger. The magic 400 figure had been blown apart within days of the first advertisement appearing in *KFM* - the hunt was on for more space.

At last (it felt like weeks, though in fact it was only days) the Gods directed us towards the London University Union building. It seemed in many ways to be an ideal choice - there were canteen facilities, a built-in 16mm movie projector, plus accommodation for over 600. We booked it! Without warning, however, the public's imagination seemed to catch hold. Nationwide did a lengthy splash (including clips from Bruce's films, an excellent display from Mr. Ooi's team and an interview with Pam Hadden), London's *Time Out* magazine gave the Convention and Bruce Lee a half-page write-up and even some of the daily papers dropped the word. Demand grew yet again!

Saturday, May 19th, was the day when, borrowing the sentiments of James Coburn, the circle was rejoined. At last, words were to be ended and promises were to be put to the test. Under the auspices of *Kung-Fu Monthly* and its famous sister society, excited fans poured into London University's soon-crowded Union building to take part in Britain's first - possible the world's first - Bruce Lee Convention. As an experiment in taking the temperature of the Little Dragon's continued popularity, it was successful beyond all our expectations as an historic event, and for many it proved to be, quite simply, an unforgettable experience.

Come the day, over 800 crammed into the Union building. I already exceeding the official maximum, we, sadly, had no option but to turn away the hundreds of fans who turned up during the day without tickets. Looking back, I confidently predict that, given even bigger premises we could eventually have attracted over 1,500 fans. What a sock in the eye for the 'Bruce Lee's popularity is in decline' brigade! Next year we'll be prepared for upwards of 1,500 fans. But enough of the preliminary - what of the Convention itself? From 7.30am, the *KFM* staff began stumbling through the back door to the hall, tired from a shortened night's sleep and wondering if it had really been such a good idea after all! As if to prove it was, an amazing sight greeted the bleary eyes. Already a queue was forming at the main entrance as eager fans, staging their hours-long vigil for entrance to Britain's first Bruce Lee Convention.

Work on the hall, plus adjoining rooms, raged on at amazing pace as posters seemed to appear virtually from nowhere. In fact, a passer-by dropping-in on this strange sight could have been forgiven for thinking that all hell had been let loose. Of course things fell behind schedule - in fact, how on earth everything got ready by 10.30am remains to this day, one of life's great mysteries!

Doors opened and in poured the fans, which I have to confess that I found it one of the most terrifying moments of the whole day! Suddenly, all these people had actually arrived and they were expecting something important and dramatic to take place. Would we satisfy them? For about the first hour, most of the fans appeared perfectly happy to explore their new surroundings, to mingle among the stills and to grab a coffee or two upstairs. The stalls in fact proved magnetic attractions throughout most of the day. Flyover Records had on sale an excellent selection of Bruce Lee albums, the North London Martial Arts Centre offered a fine range of equipment and the *KFM* stand naturally carried a tasty selection of books and magazines, plus all the specialities of the day - Convention T-Shirts, Mugs, Brooches and so on. Indeed, so popular was this particular area of the building, at times customers were standing early twelve-deep. And so keen were they to reach the piles of goodies, gradually the stalls were getting pushed back into the wall behind, with the poor people serving, jammed in between! At one point, *KFM*'s Roger Atyeo had to mount the table to appeal for order! At last, around 11.15, the action on stage was due to begin and unfortunately, that's also where all our troubles began! The production, from Capital Radio's Tony Myatt, was the first casualty. Tony got unexpectedly called away on urgent business and Roy and I had to step in. Lucky, we thought, that the remainder of the day's words were already on tape. Then came a double catastrophe. First of all, the slide projector gave up the ghost and then the sound system failed! The audience displayed quite remarkable patience as heroic attempts were made to patch things up but eventually though, it became clear that: a. the slide projector was finished for the day and b. the sounds wouldn't be back until after lunch.

To our rescue came a team of martial artists from the Tang Soo Do club, admirably stage managed by their main-man, Mr. Hock-Lye Ooi. The conditions they performed under were far from ideal - normally such a stage would have been considered far too small. Somehow they did it - a superb display of accuracy and control, carried out under very trying circumstances. There were very close shaves and at one point, a flying brick skimmed over the twin turntables of the PA system and another found its way into the face of an assisting, though inexperienced, *KFM* editor. Three stitches in the local hospital were needed to sort him out!

The display was, however, just what was needed to carry the action along to lunch, and an hour's breather for us to sort out some of the technical problems. Once the sound system was fixed, the number one priority was to get *The Way of the Dragon* ready for screening. Yes, you've guessed it, unbeknown to most of the fans, there was some nail-biting goings on there too. The film had arrived on the wrong kind of reels for the projector and only hours of laborious hand-winding by our marvellous projectionists saved the day!

Around one o'clock, the great moment began and at last, all went smoothly. There's little need for me to recount the reaction of the fans to an uncensored showing of *The Way of the Dragon* - the popping of camera bulbs and the cheers, oohs and aahs, said it all.

The essay contest was also a great success. It takes a good deal of nerve to stand on a stage in front of 800 people and to read out loud something you've written. Our competitors performed most courageously and they all fully deserved the prizes they received.

The audience, too, was with them all the way with enthusiastic cheering to lighten even the faintest of hearts. Winners (first place was a draw) were: Will Johnson from Barrow-in-Furness and someone, I'm sorry to say, who's name has been lost (could he write in please)! Both essays were extremely well thought-out and written.

Will, in fact, then agreed to join other luminaries on stage for the 'You ask us' spot and soon it became obvious that his great fund of knowledge was proving very useful in steering the team through some tricky questions.

Sharing the limelight with him were Society President Pam Hadden, Capital Radio's Eddy Pumer, *KFM*'s Bruce Sawford (following a triumphant return from the local hospital) and Roy Byrne - ex of Cathay Films. Handling the microphone was co-organiser of the event, Irene Campbell.

The Green Hornet Screen Test followed next, and again it was nail-biting time. Each attempt to start the 8 minute clip resulted in a break in the film. Only with super-precise control over the projector were we able to show this rare reel. And, boy, was it worth it! I'll admit to having already viewed it on a small TV screen/but that was nothing compared to the full 8 by 10 blow-up. The fans seemed positively spellbound as a nervous Bruce paraded his talents before an impressed producer. A second showing, this time for the camera-freaks, became very much the order of the day.

And if that weren't enough to send the hundreds away happy, still to come was our magnificent coup de gras - of course, the James Coburn tribute. There's no point in me going into the content here but suffice to say that, as a fitting end to Britain's first Bruce Lee. Convention, it's hard to imagine anything more suitable. You could've heard a pin drop as James released those honest and powerful words -it was one of those unforgettable moments.

And that was it for 1979. Next year, who knows! Already we're searching out a larger venue, and included in the list of attraction, will almost certainly be another uncensored Bruce movie, plus that Dan Inosanto/Little Dragon clash that was sliced out of *Game of Death*. But it's still early days - stay tuned to *KFM* for more details as they come available.

THE JAMES COBURN TRIBUTE

Probably the landmark of the first British Convention was that most fitting of finales, the James Coburn tribute. If ever fans needed confirmation of the esteem in which the Hollywood stars held Bruce Lee, then this must surely have been it. Of course there's a story behind the famous Coburn/Little Dragon friendship and that to start with, is what *KFM* researcher, Eddy Pumer, will be telling now. Later in this feature, he switches to the drama of the day when he actually visited the famous movie star to make the unique, May 4th 1979, recording. The importance of the interview should not be underestimated - James was one of Bruce's closest friends - perhaps even the closest. It's not often we're able to publish a new, first-hand report on the Master, so we're doubly happy that it coincides with *KFM*'s 50th issue.

It all began when Stirling Silliphant telephoned Coburn, raving about this guy called Bruce Lee. James had a great interest in the martial arts so, naturally he asked Stirling to pass the message back that he'd like him to ring some time. Bruce duly made contact and finally they got together.

Straight away, Coburn asked the young Chinese man for a demonstration and he got it! Bruce gave him a cushion to hold to his chest, then he placed a chair some feet away behind. It was the now-famed, one inch punch. Whack! Coburn went flying back into the positioned chair, and such was the force of the punch, the impact caused the seat to topple over, leaving him to roll backwards into the sofa. It was that magic moment which brought the two men together and soon they became the best of friends.

And that's friends in the truest sense, for they were openly honest with each other. Coburn could and would make comment on Bruce's acting and, in turn, Bruce gave Coburn the insight into his capabilities as a martial artist. "Bruce gave me the tools," explained James Coburn, "but it was up to oneself to develop a way of using them. Bruce didn't teach, he allowed oneself to. He would place you in circumstances where you could evolve yourself."

From that first meeting, they went on to train together for the next three to four years, working out as often as three days a week. It seems Bruce's place was favourite, because of the range of apparatus at hand. The sessions lasted about an hour at a time and Coburn relates, "Bruce would be highly charged with a force - you really felt high when you were working out with him." After, they'd relax and talk a while, with Bruce relating just about everything to the martial arts!

James Coburn was no stranger to the martial arts, and even before meeting the Little Dragon, he'd used what he already knew in the Flint films. It was enough for him to be able to remark that, "The first time I met him, I had no doubt that he was the greatest martial artist that had ever witnessed - probably the greatest of all time."

Having seen the Master in action live, Coburn insists that what you see on the screen is real - there were no tricks, no stand-ins. Of course, we all know that Bruce couldn't jump over a fourteen foot gate or twirl two 12-stone men around him or lift a man and a rickshaw into the air. James, here, is referring specifically to the fight sequences.

"He had to slow himself down sometimes, to make it look more lifelike," and Coburn also confirms that, often, the Little Dragon's scenes were shot at slightly higher than usual rate, so that when they were played back at normal speed, one could actually see what he was doing. Otherwise the action tended to look rather 'Mickey Mouse,' and sort of blurred.

Gradually they evolved ideas on the *Silent Flute*, the basic theme being that it was to be esoteric rather than physical. They were both very firm in their convictions on how it should be done, so maybe that's partly why James, although being none too impressed with Jeff Cooper, still to this day, refuses to see the final picture.

James Coburn last saw his friend three days before the tragic death. Stirling Silliphant rang James with the shattering news but, as Coburn explained later, to start with, he thought it was just one of Bruce's jokes. Several days later, however, he was facing the grim reality of the Master's funeral. He spoke the last words at the graveside:

"Farewell brother, it has been an honour to share this space in time with you. As a friend and a teacher, you have given to me, have brought my physical, spiritual and psychological selves together. Thank you. May peace with you."

And so to my meeting with the man himself.
First of all, I must personally thank Ms. Lynsey de Paul for her very great kindness and co-operation in helping me make contact with a man I've been trying to get in touch with for over three years. And of course, there has to a very special thank you to James Coburn himself for paying such a fine tribute. I know, too, that my appreciation should rightly be extended to cover every single person who attended the Convention. A brief look at all the wonderful letters this month on the Kickback page is all that's needed for Mr. Coburn to be assured of the very warm reception he received.

It was five o'clock in the evening as I stepped out into the street to hail the cab that was to take me to my long-awaited meeting. It was a glorious, sunny afternoon and warm - so warm.

But I felt even warmer inside knowing that, at last, I was to meet the man whose relationship with Bruce Lee had been as close as anyone's - perhaps closer. I gave the address to the driver of the light blue cab. "I live just round the corner from there," said the cabbie, and suddenly I just knew everything was going to go well.

I arrived outside the beautiful house at around 5.30 feeling totally calm, yet excited, in a serene kind of way. There was a light breeze, and birdsong was everywhere. A ring on the bell, and standing there, looking taller even than the door, was the man I had come to see - James Coburn. He greeted me with a welcome smile that reached almost ear to ear and showed me into a homely and comfortable-looking lounge. On the coffee table lay a flute. I asked him if he played it, and he raised it to his lips. The haunting sound immediately turned my thoughts towards *The Silent Flute* - why, oh why, had he not taken the part in the film? It was later that he informed me of the problem with Jeff Cooper.

Placing the instrument back on the table, he explained that the only reason I was sitting there that afternoon was that I'd come to talk about Bruce and not his own personal career. He said, "I'll do it for Bruce."

I showed him my own copy of *The Tao of Jeet Kune Do* and asked if he'd seen it. "I've heard about it, but I don't have a copy." It was obviously right that he should have the copy that I'd bought. Flicking through the pages, he remarked, "He wrote about four of these kinds of books when he was laid out in hospital with a bad back. A man who produces such works, when in a state of total inactivity, is a true artiste."

He thanked me for the copy and looked distantly at the picture. At times, it's hard to put one's emotions into words. They have to be felt rather than spoken. Looking at James Coburn, I knew that, though he felt so much, he could tell his experiences with Bruce, but not his emotions. He explained his feelings the first time he saw 'this little Chinese guy.' "To look at him, you wouldn't think he had so much power. He was the most perfect physical specimen I've ever seen. His skin was like velvet - you could almost see through it to

the very fibre of his muscular tissue. Every muscle was honed to perfection - not just the basic muscles, but every muscle, because each one was just as important as the other."

He went on to explain that Bruce aimed at building a streamlined physique - not like those pumping iron boys! "Bruce was the Nureyev and Nijinsky of the martial arts." I asked how Bruce accomplished such a beautiful physique and he explained that it was through the proper combination of weight training, exercises and dynamic tension.

"Bruce's back was so strong that, when he put it out, the only way of clicking it back into place was for him to use his back muscles to swivel it back round and into place again. He suffered badly with his back and was on cortisone for some time."

Altogether I was with James Coburn for about an hour and a half (although originally I'd expected it to be for just a few minutes). After ten minutes, I asked him if he'd say a few words for the convention. "What do you want me to say?" he asked.

"I want you to say what you would say if you were there in person, in front of 700 people. Reflect back on your experiences with Bruce. How would he feel if he were there himself?"

Obviously this was an almost impossible request! How can anyone put into a few minutes, that which he has experienced over a period of more than four years? He was silent for maybe 2 or 3 minutes, deep, deep in thought. I started the recorder and he spoke...

FIFTY GOLDEN ISSUES: FROM THE EDITOR

So, we've notched up 50 issues - against all the odds, we've made it!

And current figures tell me the magazine is selling more issues now than it was this time last year. The tide is on the rise.

Probably the more normal thing at this point in a 50th issue would be for me to wander thoughtfully through the years, picking out milestones and generally patting myself on the back. No, not this time! When there's a first-ever Convention to report on and an exclusive, personal tribute to Bruce, paid by a human being of the calibre of James Coburn, then I think *KFM*'s birthday should be seen in its proper context.

There is no need to look back when there is so far to look forward. A half-century is a significant moment, yes, but an end unto itself - never. No sooner are we 50, than we are 50 and a day - even as we celebrate, the stars will have moved on!

So where to for the future? What path still lies untrodden? Which tales have yet to be told? Strangely, the answers seldom come readily to mind - they seem instead to have a habit of finding their own way on to the pages of *KFM*. Come to that, was it just timely that James Coburn happened to be in the country only days before the Convention?

There are still very many people in this world some, close relations - who could reveal fascinating insights into Bruce Lee. And we have yet to finally excavate that enigmatic character. That a man could come into this world, and be able to see exactly what was needed of him - and could conquer all but one of the frailties of being a human being is reason enough for us to continue publishing *Kung-Fu Monthly*. It's hard to imagine any other person casting such a strong and watertight impression on the minds of millions literally millions - of dedicated fans and followers. That I have been given the honour of editing the only magazine that's truly dedicated to his living memory is a responsibility I can never ignore.

Bruce Lee's name has survived the rantings of ignorance, the sense-less hackings of scissor-happy heathens and the full force of the 'cash-in' industry. I have no doubt whatsoever that, after another 50 issues of *KFM*, he'll still be standing up on a hill, way ahead of us - waving and beckoning for everyone to follow.

Felix Yen

Felix Yen, *The Editor*

THE BRUCE LEE SOCIETY

It hardly needs me to say that, in terms of 50 issues of *Kung-Fu Monthly*, the Bruce Lee Society is something of a newcomer. But that said, we are about to enter our 4th year and that, I feel, is no mean feat in itself.

People ask me, "What's to be gained by joining the Society, when much of the information we're after will appear in the magazine anyway?" That's an easy one to answer! Anyone who's ever been a member of an efficiently and enthusiastically run club or society will vouch for the difference. There is a strong sense of belonging - and purpose, too and a feeling that you really do count in the things that matter. When a decision is taken or a step is made within the Society, there is every possibility that you could have been one of the voices behind it.

And not only that, in some ways, *KFM* also caters for the more casual fan and perhaps the newcomer who has yet to feel the full force and energy behind the Bruce Lee movement. Once that person experiences the need to become more actively involved, there's only one place to go looking - The Bruce Lee Society.

And there's plenty of work to get down to. High on our urgent list is to petition the TV to show the *Green Hornet* series. According to one information source, the reason we haven't yet seen it, is that it's 'too violent for kids viewing time and not adult enough for later in the evening.' That's the sort of nonsense we're out to defeat. Then of course, there's the old chestnut of the ever-elusive Bruce Lee TV documentary. Maybe now there's been a successful convention, we'll be able to convince them the error of their forgetful ways.

There're also other lands to conquer! We've certainly got quite a few members from Europe and around the world,, but nowhere near enough. I know that the Master's following is not just restricted to the British Isles - all that's missing is proper communication. It's a tough problem, but one I'll be working on.

I value the enthusiasm of every single member of the Bruce Lee Society and also the work they put into spreading the good word. There's nothing quite like fighting for something you know to be right - it's a great feeling. I hope every single fan who's a member now will still be with us when *KFM* No.100 comes along. I'll be there if you will.

Pam Hadden

Hi - it's Jenny here, with a rather special edition of Kickback. Naturally it's special - being the 50th issue is reason enough! But, apart from that (and just for this month) *KFM* joins forces with the Society on the Letters Page to bring you the fans' reaction to the Convention. Actually, I have to admit to having kept what's known as a low profile on the day itself - partly because I found the size of the crowd so staggering. The atmosphere was electric and, for me, it's something I'll remember for a very long time indeed - at least until next year's Convention, anyway! Let's see what the letters have to say about it...

CONVENTION PRAISE

Dear Pam,
I must write down my feelings about Saturday's Convention before my sides split. I'd say not one of the many fans could deny walking away from it with a lump in their throats and tears in their eyes. I know I did after hearing James Coburn's thoughts and fond memories of Bruce Lee (I wish I had the same memories). Just by listening to James talk, you could tell, like all of us, how he carries a burning admiration for the Little Dragon. In fact for me, the last 15 minutes of the Convention were like hearing, for the first time, that Bruce had died that morning - that's how much it moved me. I am still on the crest of that unbreakable wave. I have felt a power within me ever since leaving and I can't remember feeling so low and then so high, on anything in my life. Most of us arrived as strangers and left as friends - all because of two words, Bruce Lee. Well done all of you on a 100% success and I look forward to 1980's mammoth Convention. The word must be spreading like a forest fire with a hundred mile an hour wind behind.
If all the water on the Earth tipped at once, it could not douse the light burning in the middle of Bruce Lee's universe of fans.
Cary Dean, Ryde, Isle of Wight

Dear Cary,
I really hope you don't mind Pam passing your letter on to me. I'm including it because, as a summary of one person's emotions following a day at the Convention, I think it's just about unbeatable. Thanks for penning such expressive lines.

MORE CONVENTION PRAISE

Dear *KFM*,
Fantastic - First Class - it couldn't be greater. Of course, I'm talking about the Bruce Lee Convention '79. I can't wait for No.2 - it will be superb! I know there was a bit of a push and rush for the Bruce Lee gear, but what do you expect?! I felt very sorry for Felix and Co. getting frustrated behind the stalls and sweating and feeling very thirsty - and being pushed towards the windows. Lots of gratitude, too, for Pam as her work finally paid off!
M Gardner (2340), Cirencester, Glos

Dear Pam,
Firstly I'd like to say a big thank you to all who helped in making the Convention as wonderful as it was. You deserve a lot of praise for the time and effort that went into it. The uncensored *The Way of the Dragon* was amazing, the screen test was a piece of history and the James Coburn farewell speech was very touching. I'd also like to say thanks for letting me take part in the 'Why Bruce Lee was the greatest' competition.
Graeme Warwick, Glasgow, Scotland

Dear Graeme,
Again, my thanks to Pam for passing this letter along. I'm glad you had such a good day, Graeme, and congratulations to yourself and everyone else who took part in the essay contest. I was amazed at how well you all did!

CONVENTION HIGHLIGHTS

Dear Pam,
I must congratulate you on the fantastic success of the Convention - what more could a Bruce Lee fan ask for than the astounding double nunchaku sequence? What really made my day was actually holding the nunchakus that Bruce warmed up with before shooting the nunchaku scene in *Fist of Fury*.
Colin Joelson, Kirkby, Liverpool.

Dear Pam,
Just a line to say how much I enjoyed the Convention. I must say I was a bit surprised at the seating arrangement, I would have thought there would have been enough seats for everyone. Needless to say, it was worth standing for - I'd stand on my head if I had to! I thought Bruce's Green Hornet Screen Test was just fantastic and I loved the epilogue made especially for the Convention by James Coburn.
Mrs Chris Hurn, Kings Lynn, Norfolk

Dear Chris,
Once more, I hope you don't mind me borrowing your letter from Pam's file! I'm sure you'll understand the seating problems as soon as you've read this month's story behind the Convention. Hopefully, there'll be no need for you to stand on your head next year! The next two letters also come courtesy of Pam.

WAY OF THE DRAGON UNCUT

Dear Pam,
I'm writing to say how much I enjoyed the Convention. To see *The Way of the Dragon* again in its entirety was fantastic and the Screen Test was incredible. All Bruce's charisma was there and although he was obviously nervous, the arrogance that is much part of his appeal was still in evidence. I'm looking forward to next year's with great eagerness.

Dear Pam,
Thanks for a great Convention. I enjoyed every minute of it. I've never seen the famous double nunchaku scene from *The Way of the Dragon* before and I was totally amazed; so much so that I joined in on all the appreciative whistling and clapping. I think that you, Eddy Pumer and the others dealt with that annoying (whistling) microphone admirably, and I hope Bruce Sawford's head is okay - seriously! I saw your guest spot on *Nationwide* on Friday 18th and it was great to see the two Bruce clips as well. Again, thanks to you and everyone else who helped with the Convention (especially Eddy Pumer for the Screen Test and the James Coburn message) and - yes - I'll be there next year!
Andy Aylett, West Wickham, Kent.

Dear Andy,
Your letter provides a great way for me to finish off. Other name checks that have to be made are: Irene Campbell and Jane Rackham for their brilliant organising; Roy Byrne, for holding the show together so admirably; Mr. Hock-Lye Ooi for arranging such a marvellous martial arts display; and the staff of the Union building for being so friendly, helpful and patient.

SORRY YOU MISSED IT

BUT WHY NOT JOIN IN THE GREAT BRUCE LEE CONVENTION SELL-OUT?

Despite enormous demands on the day — and what a day! — all of you will be glad to hear that there still remain, small quantities of First Convention Souvenirs.
If you weren't able to make the day itself, this may be your only chance to update on things that are bound to become Collector's items in the very near future.
Remember, most of the Convention Souvenirs on sale here will NEVER be repeated as offers in this magazine!
BUT... some stocks are very low. Order now to be sure.

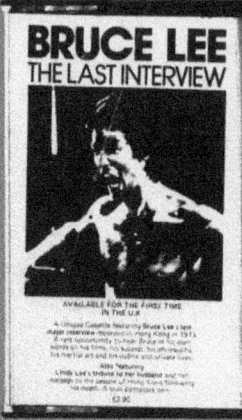

BRUCE LEE: The Last Interview

AVAILABLE FOR THE FIRST TIME IN THE UK.
A Unique Cassette featuring Bruce Lee's last major interview recorded in Hong Kong in 1973.
A rare opportunity to hear Bruce in his own words talking about his films, his philosophy, his martial art and his public and private lives.
Also featuring
Linda Lee's tribute to her husband and her message to the people of Hong Kong following his death.
A true collectors item.

Price: £4.00 (inc. p&p)

Convention T-Shirts

There are still a few medium size T-shirts available at £2.75 (inc p&p).
Sorry — small and large sizes are completely sold out!

Souvenir Brooches

Whether you were able to attend the Convention or not, you will be proud to wear this handsome enamelled brooch finished in black and silver. Price 85p (inc p&p).

If you order goods to the value of £5.00 or over, you will receive a Bruce Lee memorial scarf absolutely free of charge!
10% Discount to all Society Members.

Send your cheque/postal order (made out to KFM) to: Kung Fu Monthly, 14 Rathbone Place, London W1P 1DE. (Please write your name and address clearly — IN BLOCK LETTERS).

THE POSTER MAGAZINES - VOLUME TWO

1979

EDITORIAL

    Hi there Kung Fu fans. And how about that last issue! Maybe we couldn't get anyone to print us a double-sized edition of *KFM* (as I had been hoping) but you've got to admit that the James Coburn flexi-disc was an absolute knockout. That was our first-ever "Disc-zine" - you can be sure there'll be plenty more to follow.

    Now for some good news and bad news. It's not often that I take a swipe at anyone in this column, but I reckon the time has come for EMI! Over the last few months (in fact, ever since the Convention), we've been secretly planning a Bruce Lee Film Festival - tentatively it was pencilled-in for December 1st. Well, you'll be stunned to hear that, despite our being able to hire a really super cinema, EMI just wouldn't say yes to our having the movies. You want the good news? I suggest you take a look in Pam's Society News column!

    Feature One this month is a real monster. You may remember that we printed a Bruce Lee Astrology Chart in *The Book of Kung Fu*. Well, this month, there's a new version and believe me, revelations is not the word! What's more, next month in part two, our lady of the stars steers into hitherto unchartered waters; she tunes in to the time after Bruce's tragic death to try and discover what the future had in store for him. Maybe you don't believe in astrology, maybe you don't. Whichever way, it makes for interesting reading.

Last up is part two of our long-awaited 'Bruce Lee Rip Offs' feature (Part One, you'll remember, appeared in *KFM* No.49). As you can imagine, letters have flowed in a'plenty regarding various ploys and dirty tricks that some film companies dream up in order to boost sagging box-office sales. Unfortunately, it's pretty clear that the Little Dragon caught the sharp end of the stick, so far as this particular game is concerned. No other star has suffered quite so much in the same sort of way.

Felix Yen

Felix Yen
Editor-in-Chief

THE NEW BRUCE LEE STAR CHART

It's quite a few years now since *KFM* commissioned its first ever astrological chart of Bruce Lee. That one (see our *Book of Kung Fu*) covered the period from his birth, through to his death. Recently, however, we had the sensational Idea of asking a well-known astrologer to not only run through that period again (no two people see things in exactly the same way) but to also look ahead at the years after his death! We wanted to know, had Bruce Lee lived, just what sort of life he would have had ahead of him. Both the new appraisals are absolutely stunning. This month, in part one, we look at the re-take of his lifetime chart; next issue, incredible as it seems, we'll be checking out the future that was so cruelly denied him.

Need it be said that Bruce Lee chart shows somebody who would deviate some way from normal and accepted behaviour (The rare 'T Square' between Pluto, Venus Mars, Moon, Jupiter and Saturn confirms it). It's clear that he would ruggedly resist pigeonholing and the 'Splay shape' (the general appearance of the chart) emphasises his hatred of strict routines.

Having a number of planets in the potentially erotic sign of Scorpio, he possessed not only a great depth of sexual passion, he would also be passionately interested in any field of life-politics, work or play. In fact, according to the chart, a peculiar intensity, coupled with a sense of purpose and a determination to do nothing by halves permeated his whole personality. Indeed he had the strength to battle against any odds, such was his will to win.

He also appears to have had a hitherto unexpected quality and desire to systematically build up a career, followed by a great urge to destroy it again. But more than anything else there is magnetism, excitement and an aura of mystery (Satellitium in Scorpio) and although this'll be nothing new to his fans, it's worth mentioning that his chart simply

shouts these characteristics!

Although, career-wise, the signs don't automatically say 'Kung Fu,' it does seem as though he needed to tax his abilities to the fullest. Indeed there are indications he would have made a master criminal - perhaps through a sense of resentfulness. Also, as we all know, Bruce was not a man to make an enemy out of; it seems his sense of grudge would be long lasting. There are strong indications that he was drawn to the underworld and all forces of darkness, and Mercury in Scorpio in the 1st House shows that he thoroughly enjoyed self-discipline, and testing himself. In fact he'd have made a good soldier or sailor.

The Little Dragon could be a steadfast and dependable person (8 planets in fixed signs). He saw things clearly and realistically - possibly too much so as escapism and drugs are strongly marked (Pars Fortuna and North Node in the 12th House).

Mars in Scorpio in the 1st House suggests that he had an accident prone tendency

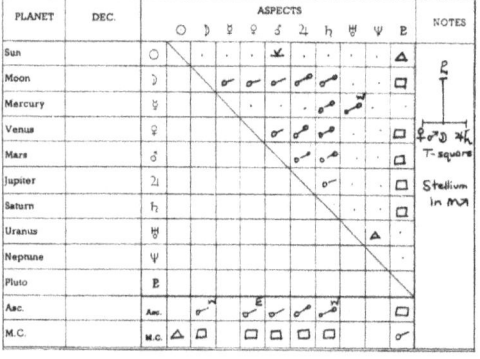

and also that he overtaxed his strength; compared to us mere mortals, however, he had a very high level of energy (Mars in opposition to Jupiter). Few will be surprised to learn that his chart shows problems with headaches. And he had an inclination to expend energy wastefully, which sometimes caused nervous tension (Mercury in opposition to Uranus).

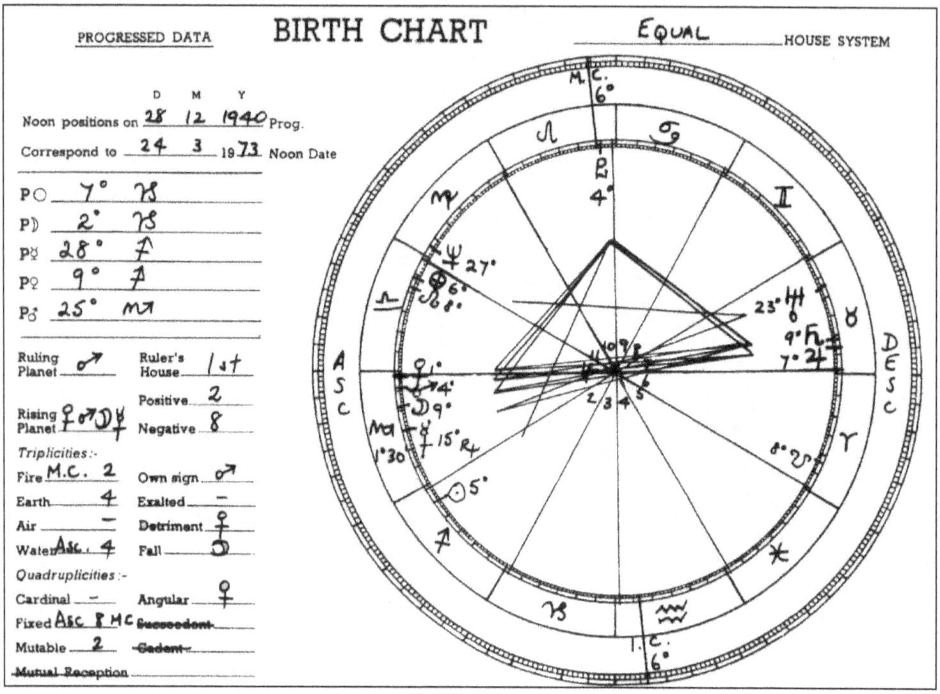

Bruce's chart shows great infectiousness, freshness and zest, but he was also hasty, impulsive and perhaps over-enthusiastic and blindly optimistic. (Ascendant in conjunction to Mars). He liked to be spoilt and indulged frequently his enjoyment of good living, food, company and in particular, the accumulation of money; in fact it's likely he might eventually have been interested in oil companies, big business and the Stock Exchange, (Venus in Scorpio in the 1st House).

He must, too, have been a possessive and jealously inclined person who enjoyed risk-taking; certainly, although courageous, he did sometimes rash into things (Moon in conjunction to Mars).

An exaggerated rebelliousness had to be channelled into positive outlets (Mars in opposition to Jupiter) and there are also signs of great inner restlessness and a lack of temperance and also an inability to maintain an even flow of energy (Mars in opposition to

Saturn).

Underneath he knew he lacked a sense of purpose and so he drastically over-compensated, becoming obsessive about his objectives, sometimes without considering the feelings of others (Mars square to Pluto). He had an enormous power complex and he was always ready to get rid of the old and bring in the new - he found it easy to dispense with people.

Peter Lee, one of his brothers, said: "Ever since he was a little boy, he always liked to be on top." In fact he had a great need for recognition and in order to sublimate this desire, when he was young, he tended to identify strongly with heroes, thereby sometimes losing his own persona. I suspect, too, that he felt a sense of mission, possibly even believing that he was in some way "chosen" (Sun trine to Pluto and Pluto in conjunction with Mid-heaven in Leo in the 10th house).

Mentally, not only was Bruce incisive, he was also thoughtless and fairly self-centred! And though shrewd, he could sometimes be sarcastic and malicious when talking (Mercury in Scorpio in the 1st House). It's also true that he could be hard and abrupt, with a tendency to plot and scheme (Mercury in opposition to Saturn).

Though, superficially, he may have had many friends, I believe only a few were what you would call close. It seems he could lose his temper over small things, perhaps even becoming coarse! He looked to have an exaggerated sense of drama-a good thing perhaps for a film star, but harder, I dare say, to live with in real life.

The Little Dragon's chart shows an enormously inflated ego and a larger-than-life approach to most things (Mid-heaven in opposition to Jupiter). His hunger for fame was real enough, but it was coupled with a degree of fanaticism and a desire to exploit people. He probably suffered from extremes of feeling that veered from love to hate, anger to pity

and happiness to misery. He'd make sacrifices if it meant furthering ambitions (Jupiter in conjunction with Saturn in the 7th house) and he had a single-mindedness and a feeling of continual discontent that, together with supreme endurance, led him to constantly seek for new horizons.

There are very strong indications that Bruce found it hard being faithful in marriage! (Jupiter in the 7th House). Indeed there seem to have been unusual conditions surrounding his relationship with Linda (Uranus in the 7th house) certainly the choice came as a surprise to the Little Dragon's friends. They were not expecting him to marry a quiet, sensible, middle American, and although Linda describes her marriage as "idyllic," Bruce's chart suggests that he may have suffered through a need for freedom of expression. Indeed, the partnership may at times have seemed dull and burdensome (Ascendant in opposition to Saturn).

In an astrological chart, the 7th house represents partnerships and marriage. Here we find the zodiacal sign Taurus, which tells of the marriage partner. This shows a reliable, solid, faithful and gentle girl - obviously Linda Lee. But the many oppositions between the first and seventh house indicate problems. His Scorpionic side, while revelling in her quieter nature, would crave and yearn for excitement with the opposite sex (Venus square to Pluto). The stars indicate a full-blooded philanderer!

And there must have been disappointments with his emotional relationships (Venue in opposition to Saturn), for although he could be jealous and possessive with loved ones, still he couldn't take those relationships at all seriously. I wonder in fact if his mother was inadvertently the cause of this attitude with Moon in opposition to Saturn, there is every chance that she adversely affected his self-confidence.

Overall, Bruce Lee's 'birth to death' chart shows tremendous dynamic energy and a great, all-encompassing love of life. But there was also a make or break side to him and obsessive attitudes ended up being coupled with sheer charisma. To be honest, with so many volcanic elements in the horoscope, death at thirty-two comes as no surprise.

Elizabeth Banks

THEY CASHED IN ON BRUCE LEE

So huge is the whole area of Bruce Lee rip-off movies, we could, if we liked, spend the rest of this feature just briefly outlining each one. However, such revelations of the vastness of the problem would do little more than confirm out worst fears so instead, *KFM* research Eddy Pumer, has decided to take an in-depth look at one in particular of these 'cash-ins' - *Bruce Lee, The Man and the Myth*. It stars, of course the greatest (or at least, the most famous) imitator of them all, Bruce Li.

If there were to be some sort of prize for the actor who'd rung-up tills most often in the Bruce Lee lookalike market, there's little doubt that Li would win it hands down. And, like him or loathe him, general consensus among fans puts him top of the overall performance list. Indeed, there are those among us who feel that he's even becoming a halfway reasonable fighter - something that wouldn't have seemed possible a few years ago.

In *Bruce Lee, The Man and the Myth*, Li portrays the Master from his college days through to his death. It's a fair attempt at realism in that many of the incidents that *KFM* included to the 'Challenges' and 'Behind the Scenes' features are meticulously recorded - for instance, his constant attempts to keep the cast in good spirits, and the challenges he was always getting from punks.

The screen opens to Bruce joking with friends outside of his university; he's keeping them amused with coin tricks (it's exact details like this that places this film a notch or two above its rivals). Immediately it's obvious thai Li has been working hard - check out the sunglasses, the walk and that inimitable smile.

The basic theme of the movie is Bruce meeting the constant challenges of punks and upstarts. An attempted robbery at a petrol station where he's working leads to the Master's famous, though brief, confrontation with a Karate champion. The opponent is left twitching on the ground.

The clock moves round to Long Beach and we're treated to some real footage of the audience. Unfortunately, it's Li we see actually performing in the arena! Of course, the upshot of that occasion was the 20th Century *Green Hornet* deal, but we see Bruce with his heart and mil on bigger and better things.

Back in Hong Kong, another slice of realism, we are confronted with Bruce's actual long-time buddy Unicorn Chan (playing himself). We glide over the Little Dragon's meeting with Raymond Chow and Lo Wei and thence into the shooting of *The Big Boss*. There's interesting stuff here for we see Bruce, just as he's preparing his fight scene with the foreman of the ice factory, being challenged by a fighter with a knowledge of Thai boxing (check *KFM* No.40 for word on the real thing).

It's a good sequence and, apparently, people who were present at the time of the actual clash were asked to give details - the realism is impressive. Later we see Bruce visiting a Thai boxing match - checking out a few points. A good thing too, for the next day the punk returns with a few friends! Set amongst ruins, this sequence is perhaps the best the movie has to offer and, for once, Li really looks as though he's going through one or two paces.

The boxers attack from all sides and one shot shows Li perform an *Enter the Drag-*

on-type, back somersault over a useful kick to somebody's teeth. All in all, his gymnastics are pretty good. After the fight, however, the head man comes over and tells Bruce that he's a great martial artist and concedes that Kung Fu is better than Thai boxing. Li's reply is badly scripted: "Don't you forget that my Kung Fu is the best," etc, etc. Maybe Bruce Lee was a bit cocky but you can bet his reply would be a bit more subtle than that!

The next scene is amazing, it shows Bruce Li sitting in a cinema acknowledging wild applause during a *The Big Boss* press showing, and for a moment, you're fooled.

The dark glasses and the broad grin are near perfect and the 'Linda' sitting beside him also passes the lookalike test.

But not everything's right. At his home, we see Bruce working out in a gym that's equipped with not only the apparatus we've come to know so well - there's also gear that I'm pretty sure he never used to have. After eating Linda's meal (proteins and vegetables), we see him returning to the gym to use some electronic gadget that's supposed to strain the muscles, it's been said that the device contributed to his headaches and eventual blackouts.

On to Rome, and the shooting of *The Way of the Dragon*. Once more, some suspicious-looking characters challenge him but this time the result is rather odd. It looks as though Li is going to produce a pair of nunchakus - then suddenly it's all over! Could be there's been some censoring, but on the other hand, maybe it's just a neat way of overcoming Li's failings in that department. Anyway, so far as I know, in real life, no such fight ever took place (readers, please correct me if I'm wrong!). Maybe the scriptwriter just ran out of ideas.

Later, while working out one evening, Bruce experiences an excruciating pain in the head. Could be the occasion was added in the film for a little extra drama. It has been reported, though, that the Master frequently suffered headaches before he finally died.

On to *Enter the Dragon* and this time, it's one of the extras who challenges Bruce. Though based on a real-life scrap, this particular episode is a gross over-elaboration. We see Li making a hot parody of the Little Dragon's fancy footwork (though the spring is not quite the same) and he throws in some impressive acrobatics for good measure. In fact, in the real version, all it took from Bruce Lee was one solid jab for the challenger to 'sleep easy' for the rest of the day.

Further into the film, we see Bruce utilising more electronic equipment and training to the point of near exhaustion. Three thick wooden boards go flying across the room as he 'one-inch' punches them - the camera work is generally very good, especially with the different facial angles.

A strange thing happens at this point in the film; though *Enter the Dragon* has been completed, we see nothing of *Game of Death*. Considering the detail afforded to the other productions, the omission is most unexpected.

We cut instead to the bedroom of a lookalike Betty Ting Pei where Bruce, complaining of another headache, get handed the fatal tablet.

From here on in, strange things happen. Betty returns to the room to find the Master in a coma. Now, what would you do if you found someone in a coma? Surely, ring for an ambulance? No, nothing that obvious for Betty; she rings Raymond Chow.

Now, surely if you were Raymond Chow and you'd just received a call to tell you that Bruce Lee was in a coma, then the first thing you'd do would be call an ambulance? Wrong again! We see Raymond burning-up precious time driving over to Betty's flat. On arrival, seeing Bruce nearly lifeless on the bed, surely then he calls the ambulance? Still wrong - he calls a doctor! Finally the doctor arrives and he rings for an ambulance. So what actually did happen on that night? If this really was the way it happened, why all the time-wasting?

Thousands and thousands of mourning people line the streets - some in controllable grief. Bruce Lee is dead and it's 'for real' time as we're treated to actual footage of the funeral. There are shots of James Coburn, Steve McQueen and Danny Inosanto, plus the Master's close family, all wearing expressions of disbelief and despair. The press photographers snapping away make it look like a fireworks night.

Again, is it right to put the fact with the fiction? Some time ago, during its review of *Game of Death*, *KFM* voiced the opinion that this sort of mixing can easily leave a nasty taste in the mouth. Balanced against that, of course, is the point that such real life footage would probably remain eternally hidden from the fans, were it not for films like *Bruce Lee The Man and the Myth*.

Be that as it may, there in a coffin at the Kowloon Funeral Parlour, lies modern history's greatest martial artist. Everyone, stars and Linda alike, pay homage among the flowers. Later, the cameras move to Lake View Cemetery, Seattle, we see fresh pictures of Bruce's grave, described in *The Life and Tragic Death of Bruce Lee* as: "A place of peace and calm where the rain lightly falls, keeping the country fresh and green." It looks over Lake Washington, a place Bruce dearly loved to visit.

The camera pans back on to the Master's gravestone and, amidst breathtaking views of the mountains, a narrator speaks the incredible words, "Bruce Lee died at the age of thirty-five." THIRTY FIVE!!! To think this is one of the better rip-offs.

Its still not quite the end, however, for we're next treated to a variety of different 'endings.' Was he attacked by a gang armed with scythes, did a wise man urge him to vanish for ten years? It's interesting that, for the latter rumour, we see Bruce leaving for Asia. Remember the story a few issues back when a traveller in Red China apparently reported

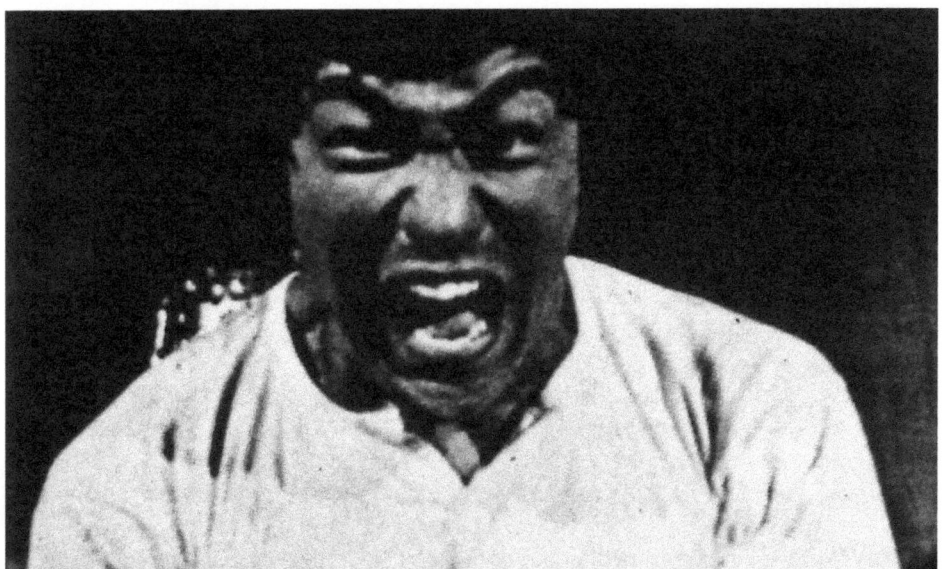

seeing the Master?

And there finishes *Bruce Lee The Man and the Myth*. As rip-offs go, it's something of an exception. Most of these productions give little or nothing to Little Dragon fans - at least here they are able to see some shots of the real Bruce Lee.

Interestingly enough, by that sort of reckoning, *Game of Death* itself might be described as a 'better' kind of rip-off. Think about it - other than the end sequence, it's no different than from any other Bruce Li movie. Maybe that's why Linda Lee kicked up such a stink about it and wanted the title changed. If only Chow had kept with Bruce's original line!

The trouble with rip-offs is that the likes of Bruce Li are still around to make them - while Bruce Lee is gone. Shallow parodies of real genius may make a certain amount of money, but no way can they ever replace the real thing. Accept them, maybe, but accept them for what they are - a deliberate attempt to cash-in on the work of a man who, quite simply, without equal; Bruce Lee - Ultimate King of Kung Fu.

THE BRUCE LEE SOCIETY

Hello, it's Pam here with another column for members of the Bruce Lee Society.

This month, there's "news" to report. For some time now, we've been planning a Bruce Lee Festival for December 1st and everyone here has been looking forward to another really great day. Rank had kindly offered us an enormous and beautiful cinema in North London and so as far as we knew, securing the films was just going to be a formality. How wrong we were!

Our first request to EMI was met with point blank refusal as EMI/Warner now control Bruce's 35mm movies in this country and our second try, to the next-to-top man, was greeted with a, "Well, probably no; we're doing something around that time ourselves so we'll let you know in two months or so." Both he and I knew that, if a cinema was to disrupt its normal schedules, arrangements needed to be made there and then, not eight weeks later.

May I, through this column, remind EMI of one or two things? Firstly, it's largely been *Kung-Fu Monthly* and the Society that have kept the Bruce Lee flag flying in this country. The fact that EMI can still fill their cinemas when showing Little Dragon films is largely down to the enthusiasm of the very people they are trying to slap in the face. Of course it isn't only *KFM* readers and Society members who pile into the theatres but we, however, are the pacemakers, the leaders of the movement.

Another thing is that EMI felt that such a showing might affect their own plans for re-releasing Bruce's films around the same time. Well, the most we could have crammed in would have been perhaps 1,500 fans; a flea-bite of a figure compared to the number EMI would attract on the national circuit. And not only that, the publicity surrounding such a great festival would almost certainly have helped BOOST box office receipts for any Lee films running at the same time; remember how the newspapers and TV took to the Convention? Looked at from any direction, their decision is mean and self-defeating.

Want to know the good news? Despite the meanies at EMI, the Festival is ON!!!!!! Some very wonderful friends have come to the rescue with the offer of, and it's hard to believe it, the ORIGINAL, UNCENSORED CHINESE versions of *The Big Boss*, *Fist of Fury* and *Way of the Dragon*! In celebration of this great victory, I hereby declare that forever more, the last week in November shall be known as BRUCE LEE WEEK. By an amazing stoke of fate, it will also of course coincide with the Master's birthday.

And how else could we have topped such a week than with the organising on the 7th day of the world's first-ever Bruce Lee Film Festival? Check elsewhere this issue for further details on what is bound to be another splendid event.

Society members, and for that matter, ALL other readers of *KFM*, BOOK TICKETS QUICKLY! I promised you a great Convention and you got it. This time I'm promising an amazing Film Festival so don't you dare miss out!

KICKBACK: THE LETTERS

Hello, Jenny Lee here again with another monster sack full of reader's letters. Straight away, however, let me say how over-the-moon I am to hear that we really are going to have a Bruce Lee Film Festival. I must say, for a while I was beginning to have my doubts, but Pam's report of the coming Bruce Lee Film Festival has just about shot me out of my seat! I'll be interested to hear what you, the readers, have to say about EMI giving us the thumbs down! And still on the brighter side, how about this month's ultra-controversial, Bruce Lee Astrology Chart? Judging by the reaction here in our offices, I have a feeling we'll be hearing quite a lot more on the subject. What's more, I've just taken a sneaky look at Part Two and all I can say is hold on to your hats next month. By the way, if you would like your own chart done by the same lady (though be warned, it's hard work and the service is not cheap), give me your enquiries and I'll make sure they get passed on.

KFM IS THE BEST!

Dear Jenny,
May I suggest you give Eddy Pumer an OBE for the work he did compiling info on *The Green Hornet* Screen-tests 1 & 2. Don't let go of him. Can you tell me why Ed Parker is depriving the world of his film of Lee at Long Beach in 1964? Is he waiting for an offer to suit him or is he just selfish. I don't understand why a person will keep something to himself that could make millions of people happy (get the violins out!) Agi Georgiou's medical report on Bruce was half right. In fact, that is why Bruce had to leave the army. Also, he said Bruce had one leg longer than the other, when in fact it was the other way round; he had one leg shorter than the other (only joking).
Andrew Horner, Frobsham, Cheshire

Dear Andrew,
What can I say? With jokes like that, you'll soon be putting Tony Blackburn out of a job! Actually, the Ed Parker business is a little bit strange. We've had feelers out for some time now to try and make contact with him. Until we do get word through, I think it's wrong for us to jump to the conclusion that he's just selfishly keeping things to himself. You never know, he might not even have the film anymore!

KFM IS THE BEST!

Dear Jenny,
Congratulations on reaching the 50th edition of *KFM*. Your superlative magazine is an excellent contribution towards keeping the memory of Bruce Lee alive. Other Kung Fu magazines fizzled out after the first few issues but *KFM* is still supplying fans with superb action posters, up-to-date news and reviews on the Master. Let's see *Kung-Fu Monthly* on the magazine counter for years to come!
Andrew Waite, Bradford, Yorks

Dear Andrew,
Thank you for such a marvellous letter of congratulations. All of us here are as pleased as anyone that we've reached the magic fifty. And while I'm on the subject, equal thanks must go to all the other fans who have written in saying the same sort of things. See you at issue 100!

GAME OF DEATH QUERY

Dear Jenny,
Please could you explain this newspaper cutting dated Friday June 8th 1979. "Colleen Camp has been offered a part in *Game of Death*." Surely she was offered the part years ago? The paper also says that Bruce dies in the film but in the picture I saw, he didn't. Is this a new *Game of Death* or don't the papers realise the film has been released?
Neil Haggar, Eastbourne, E.Sussex

Dear Neil,
Yes, I did see the cutting - in the Daily Mirror, if my memory serves me right. In fact, I rung up their newsdesk to find out what went wrong, and all I got was some lame excuse about how they'd got the story from one of the big news agencies, as though they were in no way to blame for printing such nonsense. All I can think is that the agency somehow send out information from the wrong file. it's all a bit of a giggle though!

PHOTOGRAPH RESPONSE

Dear Jenny,
I have just received *KFM* No.49 and I am replying to Mike Devereux's question about the Bruce Lee picture on the left hand corner of the desk (*KFM* No.47). My suggestion is that it is an off-set shot of *Enter the Dragon*, because in a Chinese magazine I have seen near enough the same photo. Bruce is wearing his black Mandarin suit with hands behind his back, looking on at Han's men training.
Steve Shea, West Vale, Liverpool

Dear Steve,
Mike certainly seems to have stumped the fans over that picture. In fact, yours is the only suggestion to so far have reached us. I must say I agree the clothes look decidedly 'Enter-ish' to me.

DATE CLARIFICATION

Dear Jenny,
Perhaps you could clear up for me what appears to be a mix-up of dates. In *KFM* No.48, March 1966 is said to be the date of Bruce's screen test. But, more important, it is said that Bruce's son, Brandon was born in February 1965. Therefore, should not the date in *KFM* No.48 be March 1965, instead of March 1966?
Don Quinn, Ballysimon, Ireland

Dear Don,
There's no way round that one - it seems to me you've just got to be right! It just goes to show how easy it is to take someone else's word for something, without thinking it through properly.

GAME OF DEATH ALBUM

Dear Jenny,
In issue 46 you reviewed the *Game of Death* album and said that it wasn't much good. I agree that the majority of the record is just variations of the main theme and I also agree that "Face off with Hakim" is by far the best track. To me, though, the record isn't as bad as you made it out to be. In fact, I like both the theme and the film.
Dennis Armstrong, Killingworth, Newcastle

Dear Dennis,
So far as the album goes, I'm not really sure whether we were too hard on it or not. Perhaps what it is. is that somehow, when it's for Bruce, I just always expect: the best. The music is averagely good but I was hoping it would be amazing - when it comes to the Little Dragon, nothing less should do!

KICKBACK QUICKIES

Steve Walpole, Outlane, Huddersfield - Yes, I think you're right - most of the imitators are just the same guy; he's got a lot of names though! (By the way, I thought readers might be interested in the rip-off picture caption in *KFM* No.49. The film title and starring name were those given in the original press hand out. We know it as the Legend of Bruce Lee".
W.J. Rice, Tremorfa, Cardiff - I must make it clear that we are nothing to do with this forthcoming "Bruce Lee Jamboree" (although I'll give you no guesses where they got the idea from). No so far, as I know they're not real fans.

"John", Greenhills, East Kilbride - Glad the mention was a bit of a tonic - Here's another for good luck!

P. Wigley, Swingate, Kimberely, Notts - Fans, he's after *KFM* Nos. 1, 2, 3, 7, 8, 29, 30, 31.

G. Connell, Workington, Cumbria - Glad to hear from such a "long-time" Bruce Lee fan. Thanks for a nice letter.

Tony Parker, Derby - Have you tried our mail order department for *KFM* No.9? (Thanks for the pictures, by the way).

CFN Kendrick, Barker Bks, - This gentleman is desperate for *KFM* No.2 - anyone help (£5 offered).

Ian Hamilton, Sunderland - No, the Long Beach Tournament (so far as we know) was never properly filmed.

Shaun Ullah, Great Horton, Bradford - Super-8 films from Regent films (0255 49823).

Paul Short, Foxhill, Sheffield - Thanks for the info that Jason Piau starred in: *Super Dragon*, *Stranger from Canton* and *Black Dragon Revenges the Death of Bruce Lee*.

Barry Mason, Dodworth, S. Yorks - Glad you found the *KFM* staff so helpful - we do try!

Alan Davidson, West Drayton - Yes, there've been several letters in about that *Kentucky Fried Movie* sequence - Funny or not, I agree it might have been better to have used someone with a bit more expertise than that!

WE'VE DONE IT!!!

JOIN US AT THE WORLD'S FIRST-EVER

BRUCE LEE FILM FESTIVAL

December 1st
At the Gaumont State Cinema,
Kilburn High Road, London N.W.6.

Showing will be the original, CHINESE versions [with English sub-titles] of:

BIG BOSS — COMPLETELY UNCUT!
FIST OF FURY — COMPLETELY UNCUT!
WAY OF THE DRAGON — COMPLETELY UNCUT!

See ALL of Bruce Lee's Mandarin movies — exactly as he wanted you to see them... without the usual horrific censorship.

At last, we've put together the perfect partner for the BRUCE LEE CONVENTION. YOU can attend the BRUCE LEE FILM FESTIVAL by sending a cheque or postal order [made out to KFM] for £3.00 [Society members] or £3.50 [non-Society members] to

Film Festival Tickets
Kung-Fu Monthly
14 Rathbone Place
London W1P 1DE

The extra 50p will entitle non-Society fans to become Associate members of the BLS for one year only. Their only entitlement will be the possibility of attending film shows organised through the Society.

UNIQUE OFFER

Become a full Society member AND attend the Festival for only £5.00. This remarkable offer (which saves you £1.50) must close on November 30th.

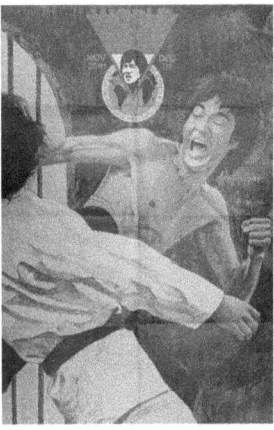

52

1980

EDITORIAL

Hi there Kung Fu fans. Welcome aboard the ship for segment 52 of the "never ending" *KFM* saga! Of course, I know everything has to end sometime, but the prophets of doom have been predicting our downfall - as sales of the magazine continue to rise - for so long now, I sometimes wonder if fate hasn't organised them just to spur us on to greater things.

And talking of prophets and fate, it's time to check out our amazing number one feature. "The Stolen Years" makes for one of the most fertile and enlightening articles that I've ever read. I have to be honest and admit that, until recently, my feelings on astrology have always bordered on the sceptical. However, the power and insight of Elizabeth Banks' words have decisively helped tip the balance.

Second-up this month is, something rather unusual from *KFM*'s ace reporter, Eddy Pumer, has done it again with a contribution that ought to be subtitled: "The influences that lead to *The Silent Flute.*" *Flute*, of course, was in many ways to represent the high point of Bruce's mystical searchings - it actually mirrored his own battles through life and it was designed to help him break away forever from Asia's then somewhat ham-fisted approach to cinema production.

Culminating Eddy's piece are some hitherto unreported words on the Master, recorded by the man who seized a major role in Carradine's version of the epic, Christopher Lee. Read on - it's good for you.

Lastly, don't forget about our plans for World Bruce Lee Week and our sensational Film Festival that goes with it (details elsewhere in this issue). Tickets are selling like mad and although the cinema is big, we've gotta draw the line somewhere!

Felix Yen

Felix Yen
Editor-in-Chief

THE STOLEN YEARS

Last month in Part One, I took you through Bruce Lee's Astrology Chart covering the period from his birth to his death. It was a saga of excitement, high potential, genius and grave misfortune. This month I shall be attempting two things - firstly to look rather more closely at the months leading up to the Master's tragic death, and secondly, to examine in close detail the way his life might have run had not fate stepped in so dramatically and finally. I believe it's the first time that this latter judgement has ever been attempted.

With Bruce Lee's progressed Ascendant in conjunction with his progressed Mars, the year of 1973 meant heightened energy, overwork and strain. The manifestations would have been a great need to rush, to drive fast and to overdo everything. Unsurprisingly it also indicates a strong tendency towards headaches - indeed problems with the head in general.

Careerwise (Progressed M.C. trine Jupiter natal), 1973 would have been Bruce Lee's year. He was approaching his full potential (Progressed Sun trine Jupiter radical) with financial and social affairs blossoming. But the coin was two-sided. The malefic (bad) aspects indicate an agony/ecstasy personality to 1973. Bruce may well have felt that the great fortune on the horizon was also a bringer of worries.

In March 1973, his personal affairs suffered: disappointments would have been likely and he may well have been hurt (Moon progressed square Venus radical). With progressed Moon also square Ascendant, domestic difficulties and a possible breakup of a relationship are clearly evident.

Transiting Saturn opposition Mercury radical would have made the Master depressed and there could have been upset due to friends or relatives. And during April, the Little Dragon would have felt a blocking of progress, frustration and a cramping of style (Moon

progressed quincunx Pluto radical). Indeed he would likely have indulged crazy risks and gone to extremes; signs are too of great strain and edginess. During this highly critical period (which, extends into May) he'd have needed total quiet and rest. It doesn't surprise me, therefore, that with the high work load he had during this time, he collapsed and went into a coma.

Not only that, during March, April and May, with transiting Neptune (the planet of escape and drugs) square radical Jupiter (which can indicate good spirits and luck), Lee might easily have been inadvertently overdosing with drugs - be they something like Dilantin prescribed by his doctor or perhaps marijuana.

And so to the fateful July - an extremely interesting section of chart for any astrologer. Progressed Moon trine M.C. would show a "coming before the public." In most cases that might mean something like a major TV appearance - for the Master, it was a public funeral. As he lay in his coffin, thousands of people, friends and fans alike, trooped past in mournful respect and awe. A final clue - progressed Moon conjunct progressed Sun indicates a great change in one's life - quite probably to do with health. This speaks for itself.

Right from the end of June and into July, progressed Neptune was conjunct radical Sun - drugs were a prominent part of his life, and indeed, his death. With transiting Saturn opposition Mercury radical there are good reasons for believing it was a nerve racking and strenuous period. Worse, during July transiting Saturn was also square Neptune radical, lending to the Little Dragon, indecisiveness, confusion and worry. This aspect particularly indicates his demise. Saturn is a dark, heavy and deathly planet; a square shows problems and Neptune, as has been mentioned, is the planet of drugs and ultimate escape - in this case, meaning death.

Another malefic aspect to Saturn comes from Jupiter (transiting Jupiter square Saturn radical) - and a sign of difficult times and, with progressed Mars trine M.C., possible accidents.

But enough of what was because it's time now to look past the fateful day of his death, to speculate what may have happened to Bruce Lee, had not fate so cruelly wrenched him from us.

In January 1974, he would likely have turned his talents to writing a film script (Pro-

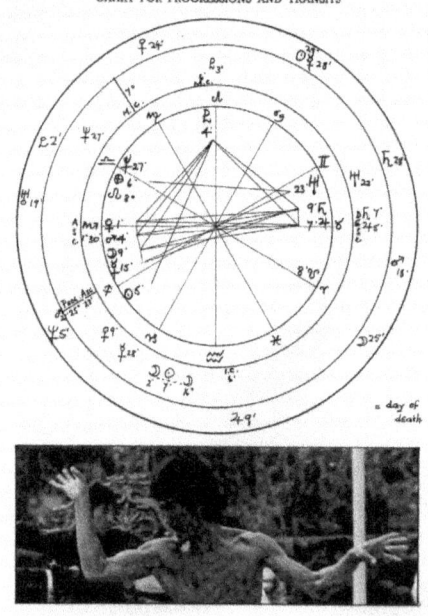

gressed Moon sextile radical Mercury). From the years 1973 to 1975 (Progressed Mars sextile progressed Neptune) business enterprises would have prospered, although during 1975, the Master might well have needed some able assistance (Mercury progressed square progressed Neptune) to cope with unusual phobias and fears, deceit and self-confusion.

Nevertheless his career would have been at its zenith and he would be looking for new projects, new avenues and new enterprises (Progressed Sun sextile radical Moon and Progressed Ascendant sextile radical Neptune).

Come 1978 he would have felt the mental strain brought on by over-activity (Progressed Mercury quincunx M.C. radical). 1979, however, would have been an interesting year (Progressed Ascendant semi-sextile radical Venus). The signs are he would have been swept off his feet by a romantic attachment and there would have been difficulties over this, possibly through his partner's indiscretion or thoughtlessness.

It looks as though 1981 was to have been THE year in Bruce Lee's life, in particular with regard to a change in direction of his career (Progressed Sun sextile radical Mercury). Interestingly the previous year (1980) shows a great period of business and literary interest (Progressed Ascendant sextile radical Moon). Putting two and two together, I think he may well have abandoned acting and gone into film directing and scriptwriting with, as usual, very good results. Signifying this completely new approach is Progressed Ascendant trine radical Pluto.

The years of 1982 and 1983 (Progressed Ascendant conjunct Sun and trine M.C.) indicate a peak year in relation to his career and public standing - more than likely through universal acclaim with the new career started in 1981. Both these years show hard work, but a proneness for accidents and Bruce, though perhaps over-anxious and impulsive, would generally have benefited.

There would have been trouble ahead in 1984 (Venus progressed opposition radical Uranus), with difficulties and breakups in domestic life.

Finally, looking a full ten years ahead to 1989, the Little Dragon might well have suffered the legacy of overwork - a nervous breakdown (Sun progressed square progressed Uranus). There are, however, indications that this may only have spurred him on to even greater things (Sun progressed square progressed Neptune).

Looked at astrologically, Bruce Lee's death was no accident. So what, you may ask, might have happened if he had been warned of what was in store - that the planets were in bad alignment and therefore he was facing a very dangerous situation? Again, astrologically, it just wasn't to be; there is no warning message shown in his planets.

And call it fate, call it karma, Bruce's chart is haunted with frightening aspects depicting drugs, frustration, accidents and death. He left this world at the very time he was destined to leave - we do not rule the stars, they rule us, and the Little Dragon (in this respect at least) was no different from any other mere mortal.

Kung-Fu Monthly would sincerely like to thank Elizabeth Banks for her magnificent, probing insights into the "star" world of Bruce Lee. For someone whose first hand knowledge at the start was simply that the Little Dragon was a world famous martial arts movie star - well I find her understanding astounding and her predictions, real food for thought.

The Editor.

BRUCE LEE AND CHRISTOPHER LEE

Once Bruce Lee had got his first taste of movie success - when still just a child - his burning ambition was to become a real film 'star.' At that time, the cinema productions in Hong Kong were very much in the style of the old Chinese theatre - a bit like *Coronation Street* goes East, and certainly inappropriate for the majority of Western audiences. From very early on, Bruce saw and understood the problems. His plan of campaign was to gradually build on his growing fund of knowledge, until such time as he was able to pull Hong Kong's cinema skills into line with the West. Still, however, he would Insist on retaining his unique Oriental heritage and, in many ways, *The Silent Flute* came to epitomise that ambition. Eddy Pumer reports...

Recently, I had the great privilege of viewing one of Bruce's early movies entitled *Thunderstorm* and surprise, surprise, the Little Dragon is now being credited as a 'Superstar.' As we all know, at the time he was nothing of the sort - the picture titles have been re-edited in order to change the billing. No doubt the film sells all the better for it!

Bruce has what are known as walk-on parts - he comes and goes throughout the movie and most of the time, his acting might best be described as highly emotional. He looks about eighteen years old, has greased back hair (which makes his ears appear to stick out) and his cheeks are decidedly chubby. Yet the facial expressions are pure Bruce Lee - the frowns, the scowls, the broad grin and the constant sharpness and sparkle in the eye.

His energy and enthusiasm for the part is positively overwhelming and he overshadows his fellow actors, even at this early stage of his career. And although the movie is by most standards, the usual Chinese theatre kind of production, even here there is something new and refreshing in the Little Dragon's approach.

The first thing that any newcomer to Bruce Lee films notices is his incredible facial expressions; and then they see too, his grace of movement and controlled exaggeration, it's all there in *Thunderstorm* and it's obvious that, even from very early on, he knew many of the answers. He learnt and he remembered.

In fact, Thunderstorm contains no fight sequences whatsoever, despite the fact that Bruce was heavily involved in the martial arts at the time of its making. But his training shows in his lightness of step - some of his movements have a near ballet-like quality.

And so the Little Dragon continued to study his way around the film world. Wisely, he left no stone unturned and he learned about direction, production, lighting, camera techniques, set design, costume design and even the work of the makeup department.

During the time he was studying at University, the idea gradually came to him - why not marry his two great loves - martial arts and the movies into one power-packed effort? Not the usual 'blood and thunder' sort of thing, more pure and realistic fighting combined with a up-to-date storyline. Little did he know, he was already stepping forward onto the path that so nearly led to *The Silent Flute*.

America really opened his eyes to what he still had to learn. Yet learn he did, and as most people now know *The Green Hornet* was soon to become his stepping stone to Stateside success. And it was a double-sided coin, for never before had the western world experienced a man like Bruce Lee - either on or off the screen! The martial arts/movie

chemistry had begun.

Of course, the Little Dragon's heart was always back in his homeland, and soon that wealth of experience travelled back with him to Hong Kong. Like a human tornado, he turned the Chinese movie industry upside down, shaking out years of cobwebs and adding whole new dimensions for the Eastern fans. After *The Big Boss*, he became a star, after *Fist of Fury*, Bruce Lee was a hero and, finally, with *Enter the Dragon*, he found himself transformed into the first Oriental superstar.

The Master's success led many a known film actor to his door including the great James Coburn. A special formula evolved between them. Coburn ribbed Lee about his acting (describing his style as 'arch!'), Bruce on the other hand retaliated by joking about James' martial arts shortcomings. This freedom of speech was to act as the final seal to their friendship.

Thoughts turned to their working together on a film script. Once a week, they'd go along to Chinatown for a meal and talk and talk and talk. Philosophy was usually a favourite for the agenda, followed by what Bruce would call the 'practicality' of self defence. Thoughts flowed and one day, to quote Mr Coburn, they came up with the idea of "Mak-

ing a movie about a man whose yoga was martial arts and his evolution into finding and coming together with his own soul—becoming complete again; which is essentially what happened to Bruce."

The result was *The Silent Flute* - at last a dream was to come true? Well, no, not quite, for troubles lay ahead and temporarily (Bruce thought) the script had to be shelved. In fact, the original manuscript and notes on the film are still held by James Coburn to this day.

It's no great secret that, although he was delighted that the film was eventually made, Coburn had his reservations. However, his doubts about the talents of Jeff Cooper were swayed a little in the knowledge that David Carradine and Christopher Lee were to star in the film.

Coburn's feelings about it all have been fairly well recorded. Recently, however, I came across a rare interview with Christopher Lee where he talks of the film's philosophical content, its spiritual meaning and its evolutionary cycle of a man who finds himself living through many trials. Taking this interview at face value, I believe that all the original ideas and emotions expressed by Bruce in the script are contained within the movie. The Master, of course, isn't in the picture but, as Christopher Lee explains, his spirit is.

"It has a strange, mystical, out of this world, no specific time quality; I think it looks stunning. The fights are excellent, the young man, Jeff Cooper, is more than adequate (you know, he's not so glamorous as Joe Davis) and David (David Carradine) is David - he does it very well. My only qualm when I did it was that the audience might be slightly disappointed, when he's building up to this great confrontation with the world's greatest martial artist and they think they are going to see the greatest martial arts fight ever staged on the screen. But of course it was absolutely right that this is the only possible ending - in that they find themselves in the mirror.

"This is the only possible ending and it is the right ending - that of course, martial arts is not just physical but spiritual. The man I play has been through all the physical aspects - the stepping stones in the Buddhist religion - and he's reached a kind of spiritual nirvana. But he's getting, I suppose you would say in a supernatural sense, rather bored with it all. Rather desperately he's saying, release me, take my place.

"I believe the film is very good, although I don't know what the audience will think. It's done tremendous business in Paris - something like $130,000 - $140,000 in the first two days."

Christopher Lee is happy that *The Silent Flute* has been faithful to Bruce's original concept. "It hasn't changed; it was always that and the man at the end, Zetan, must be the personification of everything carried to the enth degree - which means spiritual perfection. That is, as I understand, the ultimate aim of anybody connected with the martial arts - that you do become spiritually purified, through physical contact, and soon."

Over the years, I've heard many reasons for Bruce holding back on *The Silent Flute*. Disagreements over the script, inappropriate choice of location by the film company, sheer pressure of work, and so forth. That always makes me suspicious that there's something, something far bigger and much more important, that's not so far been said.

For Bruce Lee to literally build his career up the ladder of success with *The Silent Flute* as the uppermost rung, only for him to sidestep the pinnacle of his ambition, smacks strongly of mystery. *KFM* continues its investigations.

WORLD BRUCE LEE WEEK
NOV 25TH – DEC 1ST 1979

Once more the Bruce Lee Society takes a vital step forward towards ultimate, world-wide recognition of the Master.

Kung-Fu Monthly was the first magazine of its kind anywhere and it remained true to its goal and survived when every one of the others fell by the wayside.

The Bruce Lee Society, once formed, marshalled its forces and succeeded, where the rest just came and went. The Society organised the world's first Bruce Lee Convention and so well was it received, others now try to copy it in almost every detail!

It's really rather flattering. The fame and charisma of the Master was enough to spawn a bumper crop of lookalikes and rip-offs but now it seems as though The Bruce Lee Society is getting the same treatment. As I say, I'm truly flattered.

What all this adds up to is SUCCESS. At last, the Bruce Lee movement is reaping rewards and that's largely down to all the years of hard work that you and all of us here have been putting in together. That others now see an opportunity to cash-in on it is proof enough that the job has been well done.

But for the Bruce Lee Society, enough is never enough, and to celebrate the next stage of our development, I've declared World Bruce Lee Week to run November 25th to December 1st. Every year I intend *KFM* and the Society to celebrate this unique event in the Bruce Lee calendar.

Of course there have to be objectives for each of the seven days, otherwise the week would ring very hollow indeed. Therefore, following now are my suggestions for the work to be carried out-during those celebrations.

DAY 1

(Sunday 25th November) A time of relaxation and meditation on the thoughts, sayings and words of the Master. Decide how YOU will live this week in a way Bruce would have approved.

DAY 2

(Monday 26th November) Time to start work on a campaign to spread the Master's word to as many people as possible. Contact local newspapers, radio and TV stations etc, to tell them of the 7-day celebration and to ask that they report the event in some way. Talk to them about your feelings for Bruce Lee and impress on them the size of the worldwide movement and the success of the Society.

DAY 3

(Tuesday 27th November) A very important day, of course, for it is time to celebrate His birthday. Perhaps consider what Bruce might have been doing now but be happy in the legacy He left with us. Essentially, however, it's a day of fun, and in that spirit it would be appropriate to hold a party, relaxed and informal.

DAY 4

(Wednesday 28th November) Let the real work begin! From today, until the end of the week, see how many new recruits you can find for the Society. Remember though, they must be interested in the aims of the Bruce Lee movement; a passing whim is not enough. Let me know how many new members YOU find; prizes will be offered to those who introduce five or more new faces.

DAY 5

(Thursday 29th November) Thursday is petitioning day. If there is something you'd like to see shown at your local cinema or on TV, or perhaps there's a film that hasn't yet been made, but you think should be, or maybe you just wish to protest about savage and senseless censorship. Whatever it is, this is the day to take action to let those in authority or command, know your view on their actions. Of course praise too, where praise is due.

DAY 6

(Friday 30th November) A day for tidying up loose ends. Your last chance to meditate on the implications of the world's first ever Bruce Lee Week, to introduce new members to the Society and to prepare yourself for the Bruce Lee Film Festival.

DAY 7

(Saturday 1st December) At last, the great day has arrived, the true culmination of a week's work and the finest possible way to bring to a close World Bruce Lee Week. Join hands with your brothers and sisters at the first Bruce Lee Film Festival.

You'll find all the details elsewhere in this issue of *Kung-Fu Monthly*. You can't afford to miss this, the seventh day of World Bruce Lee Week; celebrate along with us on a unique occasion. We remember the legacy of the Master and once more, in the words of James Coburn, "the circle is rejoined."

KICKBACK: THE LETTERS

Hi everyone, Jenny here again with the pick of letters. Before that, though, I'd like to sneak in some news about Bruce Lee recordings. It's pretty unofficial, so let's treat it as rumour rather than cast iron fact. To start with, it seems that a re-release is in the air for the *Dragon Power* 12" single - apparently demand from the fans is so great, the company can no longer rely on existing stocks. The date may in fact coincide with our upcoming Bruce Lee Film Festival. A definite fact is that *Dragon Power* is to be featured on a new JKD Band LP, due for release at the same time. Lastly, there's every chance that the band will soon be recording a follow up single entitled Leeway. Sounds great!

WHAT A TRIBUTE!

Dear Jenny,
One Saturday afternoon in August, I had a browse in a stationery shop and picked up the *KFM* No.50 magazine. My friend, who works at the record bar, immediately played the tribute single. Sixty customers or more were completely spellbound and at the end, they gave a hearty round of applause to Coburn's speech. Surely final proof of the Little Dragon's popularity in 1979.
Paul McKenna, Pollock, Glasgow

Dear Jenny,
I would like to know whether or not the artist performing on the *KFM* No.50 record is Bruce Lee. I believe the record is a tribute to him, although it doesn't actually feature his voice.
P. Wigley, Swingate, Notts

Dear P. Wigley,
The cries you hear in the background music and the first voice you hear are those of Bruce Lee. They were reproduced with kind permission of Warner Brothers Limited and Satril Records.

WHAT'S HIS NAME?

Dear Jenny,
Could you please settle an argument me and my friend are having about Bruce Lee's son. He says that his name is Brendon, but I say it's Free (or Three). Could you please settle this once and for all.
Danny Lee, Dunstable, Beds

Dear Danny,
Sorry to say that you're both wrong! I don't know where Free came from, but anyway, his real name is Brandon, not Brendon. KFM is still making considerable efforts to try to get an interview with Brandon - after all, he's growing up now and it would be extremely interesting to find out how he compares with his father.

BIG BOSS SUPER 8 TRAILER

Dear Jenny,
Recently I bought the *The Big Boss* trailer in Super 8mm colour/sound and in it there are lots of spelling mistakes: "Inventor of Jet Kuen To" and "He is Peerless" and "Throughout Amena and Asia." I wonder, is it a misprint or has it been done deliberately? Has anyone else bought these films and noticed this?
Clive McKenzie, St Anns, Nottingham

Dear Clive,
I must say I haven't seen the reels you describe. However, it seems to me from what you say that the translations, have been done abroad - probably in the East. People over there do sometimes get themselves in a terrible tangle with the English language.

JAMES COBURN TRIBUTE RECORD

Dear Jenny,
Firstly I'd like to congratulate *KFM* on the James Coburn Tribute record - it's fantastic, especially the start. I had the whole family listening to it and I asked my mother, what does "It's like a finger pointing at the moon, don't concentrate on the finger or you will miss all that heavenly glory" mean. She said she'd have to think about it, but I can't wait that long.
Gerard Sammon Artane, Dublin, Eire

Dear Gerald,
Actually, the line tells quite an interesting bit of philosophy. To me, its saying don't concentrate too hard on the means to an end - otherwise you might end up forgetting about the real goal. If that doesn't make things any clearer, take for example, the novice martial artist. To start with, his aim is clear - to achieve total control over his physical and spiritual self. As time goes on, however (and this often happens), the student may become far more interested in his training technique, how much he can impress his friends, and so on - he has lost sight of the "moon" and is busy instead concentrating on the "finger."

Next, a letter passed on to me by Pam.

KFM SUBSCRIPTION

Dear Pam,
I'm a soldier currently serving a 16-month tour in Northern Ireland - I'm also a member of the Bruce Lee Society and a great fan of Bruce Lee. At the moment I'm having a bit of trouble getting *KFM*. As you can probably understand, I can't just walk off camp to the nearest newsagent and buy my favourite magazine, like I can in England. I was wondering if it was possible to order it straight from you at *KFM*.
Colin Quinton, BFPO807

Dear Colin,
A sad story like that neither Pam nor I could pass by. Until such time as you return to England (let us know when, won't you) your KFM *will be mailed to you direct, courtesy of* KFM.

A COUPLE OF QUESTIONS

Dear Jenny,
First may I say well done on a truly great magazine. Quite recently I had the honour and pleasure of personally meeting Mr Dan Inosanto and I took some photos of him. I will send copies to any *KFM* readers who can answer my two questions. 1. Where can I obtain a licence to purchase martial arts weapons? 2. What were Bruce's measurements- ie, chest, forearm, waist, etc.?
Ian Clark, Rotherham, S. Yorks.

Editor's Note: *Jenny didn't respond to Ian Clark's letter.*

KICKBACK QUICKIES

Paul McLoughlin, Dublin, Eire - Glad you liked reading *Who Killed Bruce Lee* - It's one of our best, I reckon.
Anthony Thorpe, Stoke Newington, London - You ask about any electronic training aids used by Bruce - Well, I seem to remember something used for muscle toning, does anyone know of any others?
James Norman, Birkenhead, Merseyside - Slicked back hair in *Fist of Fury* - You're not thinking of *The Big Boss*, are you?
Richard McColl, East Kilbride, Scotland - I agree, Bruce Lee was a Master above Masters.
George Brannon, Moodiesburn, Glasgow - Thanks for the news that USA Columbia Records are doing an album of *Game of Death* complete.
Anthony Dure, London - James DeMile was indeed an early pupil of Bruce's.

Pete Matthewman, Chesterfield, Derbys - Wants to know how Bruce developed those huge back muscles - Anyone help?

Gary Dinsdale, Norton, Cleveland - Writes to tell of the new *Bruce Lee* album (YX-7045). He reckons it's good, barring the fact that two of the tracks feature Bruce imitations.

Mark Gardner, Cheltenham, Glos - Yes it's nice to know that we got it so right that the organisers of the "other" convention felt it necessary to crib ours all down the line. Even so, I'm glad for the fans that it was successful.

Thomas Hamilton, Govan, Glasgow - *KFM* Nos. 46/47 are available from our mail order department.

Bryan Bath, Romford, Essex - Glad you liked the official Convention so much - Plans are already well ahead for next year.

Steve Ambler, Illingworth, Yorks - Good work on outlining the 8mm movies available - I'll print the list soon if I get the chance.

Paul Wade, Boulevard, Hull - Okay, I agree, any film that contains footage of Bruce has got to be valuable!

Nisar Ali, Handsworth, Birmingham - The water colour looks very good - if you can take a good quality colour slide of it, we might be able to use it in *KFM*.

EDITORIAL

Hi there Kung Fu fans. Here I am toughening up the reflexes for another punchy edition of your favourite *Kung-Fu Monthly*!

And straight away, may I thank all of you who came along to the first Bruce Lee Film Festival for giving me such a great time. I had a pretty good idea of what the crowd would be like from the convention, earlier on last year; well, I wasn't let down! The people, the excitement and the interest - everything was simply "Bruce-beautiful" on the day.

So what, you're probably wondering, are we serving up for this month? Okay, Part One and Part Two join up for - you've guessed it - a sensation! I think the word has well and truly got around that Pam Hadden of the Society recently embarked on a journey that I'm sure everyone would give their eye teeth to go on - a pilgrimage to Hong Kong. And I am delighted to hear from her that the trip was all she ever dreamed it would be - welcomed in style as the leader of the world's major Bruce Lee Movement, Pam tells me she spent ten unforgettable days, drenching herself in pure nostalgia. Read her amazing story right here in her version of "Hong Kong meets the Bruce Lee Society."

And looking ahead to *KFM* No.54 kind of ties in with this month. While she was in Hong Kong, Pam located a huge file of Bruce Lee newspaper clippings - dating right back to when the Little Dragon storm had still to brew itself into a fully fledged hurricane. Much of the detail in these lengthy reports has never before been published in the Western World. Next issue we're able to staunch that omission with the first in a series of information-packed articles, headlined "The Hong Kong Papers." Stay in touch!

Felix Yen

Felix Yen
Editor-in-Chief

THE GREAT VOYAGE OF DISCOVERY
PAM HADDEN IN HONG KONG

"On the 9th August, 1979, Pam Hadden - president of the Bruce Lee Society - set out on a trip that she had been planning to make for years; the destination was Hong Kong! What happened to her while she was there - the people she met - is detailed right here in one, sensational, double-feature report. It's a very personalised account, for the words pour direct from her own pen, and for readers who are unable to embark on that momentous journey for themselves (and let's face it, that means MOST of us!) well, I guarantee Pam's ultra-descriptive account of her pilgrimage to that holiest of lands will serve as the finest of substitutes. *KFM* brings you - literally - the journey of Pam Hadden's lifetime!

"Hong Kong!" I suppose that for any fan of the Master, next to "Bruce Lee," those are two of the most magical and inspiring words imaginable, for there lays the true roots of the legend that was the Little Dragon. For nearly six years I'd been planning the trip, so you can imagine my feelings as I climbed on board the plane at Heathrow. Not only was I very apprehensive, it was somehow as though I was walking in a dream.

If I needed reassurance that I was awake, well it wasn't long in coming as the plane got grounded at Frankfurt with engine trouble for four hours! At long last, though, we were on our way again with only stops at Bahrain, Bombay and Bangkok before final touchdown at Hong Kong.

After what seemed like an eternity, the Captain announced he'd be landing in about 10 minutes and as butterflies came and went, I glued myself to the window to await the first glimpse of the airport or harbour.

At last, the wheels touched down and even before we'd stopped rolling, I was first up and heading down the aisle for the exit. If I'd had an ejector seat, I'd have been out even sooner! Walking down the steps, I was suddenly near to tears as there was no question of it being anywhere else. Somehow I seemed to recognise the bustle, the chattering and the skyline that reminded of a miniature New York.

My "base" was the YMCA on Waterloo Road in Kowloon. I decided on that area because that was where there would be most that related to Bruce. I was close by a large main thoroughfare called Nathan Road and I spent many hours just strolling along it taking in the atmosphere. Strange fruits, exciting aromas, people carving away at skilful designs; all was perfect and intriguing, except the heat! It was during the monsoon season and most of the time, the perspiration just poured off me. It wasn't long before I learnt that it was a mistake to rush around in my usual British fashion!

But it was time to turn my attentions to my quest; the search for the memory of Bruce had begun! To start with, results were a little discouraging. Of course everyone knew the name "Bruce Lee," but apart from a poster and a book in Chinese, shops-wise there didn't seem to be a lot to add to my collection. I must admit to being disappointed but wouldn't you? At last, on Wednesday 15th August, things really got mining.

I met Mr. Robert A. Burton, Vice President of International Distribution at Golden Harvest. The company had already been informed by their London office that I was dropping by on a visit and over lunch at the Peninsular Hotel, we chatted generally about Bruce and Hong Kong. Mr. Burton is American and he's worked for Golden Harvest for 2½ years out of the 15 years that he's been out there. The meal in fact was superb, as was Mr. Burton's company. I felt at ease as soon as I met him and was eagerly looking forward to a visit to those famous studios.

We drove down Hammer Hill Road, and as we entered the gates, I started to feel again, that stirring of emotion that had affected me all the way over during the flight. I thought the buildings to be just large warehouse type wooden structures, approached by a dirt track. However, although to some extent this description is right, one thing omitted is the new and luxurious block of offices nearby.

Mr. Burton was called to the phone so he suggested I just carry on walking around taking pictures - until he was free again. The only proviso was that I didn't trip over cam-

eras or get caught up in some Kung Fu film! I'd heard that new Golden Harvest protégé, Jackie Chan (tipped to replace Bruce Lee) was filming there and I was promised a meeting with him during one of the breaks. Meanwhile, I just strolled around, thinking to myself, "I wonder if Bruce Lee stood here" or, "I wonder what buildings Bruce filmed in?"

Wandering around between scenery and buildings, I was astounded at the simplicity of it all as it seemed unbelievable that it was here that a good part of Bruce Lee's films were made! I returned to the offices and fleetingly saw Raymond Chow. He was very busy - we smiled - and he carried on upstairs. As I stood talking to Raymond's secretary, Betty Kwong, a man came in and immediately I was struck by his nice smile and lively personality. Surprise, surprise, it was Jackie Chan himself and believe you me, the "rubber-faced, flat-nosed" description is more than a little unjust. Sure he doesn't have Bruce's good looks (how many people do!) but Jackie comes over as a sort of Chinese Charles Bronson. And there's no real attempt at billing him as some sort of Bruce replacement as he's more of a comedy actor, and anyway, his style of fighting is quite different.

Later, Mr. Burton took me round to see Bruce Lee's old dressing room, but as fate would have it, the door was locked; Jackie, the present occupier, was out shooting and he had the key with him. Ah well, you can't win them all! And on our travels we came across a street scene set, specially designed for Jackie's new film and I noticed that every bit of space seemed to be used to advantage. Mr. Burton pointed out that, although the studios were not as spectacular as near rivals Shaw Brothers, Golden Harvest didn't suffer the same overheads as Shaw's as they didn't keep a regular payroll of actors, but rather they employ them as and when needed. Presumably Golden Harvest's object is quality rather than quantity.

Back in his office, Robert Burton put me right on a certain question that's been cropping up for years; the change of coffin mystery that dates back to the time Bruce's body was being flown back to Seattle from Hong Kong. Various papers at the time reported that the casket had been opened and tampered with - speculation was rife that he had been prematurely buried.

In fact, I was told the casket had been damaged in transit. Also, because of pressure changes, apparently things can happen to bodies in flight. Unfortunately, because it was necessary to change the casket for Bruce's burial in the States, all sorts of rumours started up about somebody being buried in the Master's place.

Director of International Advertising and Public Relations, Russell Cawthorne entered the conversation (by the way, a final credit to his name is that he also played the part of a doctor in *Game of Death*). I asked what had happened to Bruce's old training equipment and was told that much had been given away to the Little Dragon's old Hong Kong school (I'm waiting for a reply right now to discover whether we might be able to borrow some at a later date). Mr. Cawthorne has also promised to try and find anything else Bruce might have owned.

Both Robert Burton and Russell Cawthorne seemed impressed at the functioning of *Kung-Fu Monthly* and the Society and they expressed themselves keen to assist in any way possible. Making a good start, they sprang one little surprise; a quick phone call to the *Hong Kong Standard* and an interview was fixed up for me on the following day, with a Mr. Ken McKenzie! Generally very "wary" of such things, I went along with it and ended up pleasantly surprised. Not only was Mr. McKenzie completely "for" Bruce Lee, he also

gave us a write-up measuring 18" by 4" and he missed nothing! Not to be misquoted and not to have one's words twisted around to make the story better came almost as a shock.

But enough, for the time being of Golden Harvest; I had a mini tour to start on and also a VERY important person to meet!

It was time to begin my investigations in earnest! I'd luckily already met up with a "safe" and very charming escort at the hotel, and as he had some time to spare, he happily agreed to help me on my whistle-stop, fact-finding tour of Hong Kong. The first destination, we decided, should be Bruce's old home, so, armed with camera and car, off we set. On the way, we passed by Queen Elizabeth Hospital so we briefly stopped at the ambulance bay to see if the vehicle which took Bruce there (number A43) was anywhere around. I couldn't see it, so I made do instead with taking some pictures of the casualty door and the driveway, etc. I thought once or twice about actually going inside, but I decided that might easily annoy someone - and foul up the whole thing. For the same reason, Happy Valley Cemetery (shown in *Enter the Dragon*) was also off bounds.

One more stop on the way to Bruce's house and that was at Betty Ting Pei's apartment and the place where Bruce was taken ill. I found some discrepancy about the number, so I took pictures of three separate blocks as it's better to be safe than sorry!

Up to that time, I'd tried to put an awful thought out of my head but now I couldn't avoid it any longer. Driving towards Bruce's old house in Cumberland Road, the rumour I'd heard kept coming back to me, that the place was now being used as a "house of ill repute," somewhere for "gentlemen" to take their lady friends for an hour or two. I didn't want to believe it, but as we drew up outside, my worst fears were confirmed. It took me a minute or two to fight back the tears that I could feel welling up. How could his house be used for such a thing? Eventually I told myself, well, whatever it's being used for now, it was Bruce's home and that's all that matters.

I left the car and approached the doorman. "Was this Bruce Lee's house?" I asked him. He told me, yes, did I like him? "Like him? Oh yes I like him!" I asked if he minded me taking some pictures and he happily agreed for me to carry on. I took shots of the house, the garden, the entrance - but what I'd have given to have gone inside. My escort friend saw how upset I was and when I told him how much I would have liked to have been able to look around the place, he soon got me laughing again by saying with a big grin, "It could be arranged quite easily!" (if you get his meaning). As we drove away, I wondered to myself just what Bruce would have thought about it all.

Part two of my search was - you've guessed it - to try and track down Bruce's brother, Robert. My friend came to the rescue. He suggested I contact Hong Kong TVB and try their Public Relations Officer, Miss Betty Young. Betty agreed to contact Robert and then call me back. This she did, and the unbelievable message was that Robert would be phoning me at the hotel shortly! It just didn't seem real and I simply couldn't convince myself that he would actually call me.

Suddenly the phone rang and I fell over the furniture rushing for the telephone. Trying to sound composed I came out with a very original greeting, "Hello?" A soft, American-Chinese accent asked, "Is that Pam Hadden? This is Robert Lee." POW! ZAM! Fighting for composure, I gurgled agreement that I'd meet him in the lobby of the hotel at 7.30pm - and the call was over.

I was there by 7.10, and feeling VERY emotional. Here I was, about to meet Bruce's brother, a man who I admired as a singer in his own right. I remember thinking as I waited, about specific tracks on Robert's albums - ones that were very special to me. It helped stave off the panic!

All at once I saw a good-looking guy walk through the door wearing a smart cream suit, white shirt and cream tie - even minus the beard, I knew it was Robert. Other people in the hotel recognised him immediately but he came over to me and asked, "Pam?" We shook hands and one lovely smile later, I was instantly aware that I was in the presence of the Lee charm.

Robert put me at my ease immediately and asked about the Society. We chatted generally and I discovered that he married his wife, Sylvia, on December 18th, 1977 - in the States. She's a singer and actress who works under the name of Sum Sum. He also confirmed that his mother was living permanently in Los Angeles, with sisters Phoebe and Agnes, and that brother Peter was now Assistant Director at the Hong Kong Observatory.

The conversation changed tack and I asked about the Long Beach Tournament Film

and did he know of its whereabouts? Robert confirmed (as we'd all suspected) that the only copy was in the hands of Ed Parker and his feeling was that Ed would only let go of it if he was sure it wasn't going to be used for commercial gain. Obviously therefore, he might relent for a convention (I'm looking into this right now).

I asked Robert what sort of questions he usually gets asked. "Everything under the sun. It's surprising what they can think up!!" I agreed and gave as an example, one of the questions a fan had once asked me, "Did Bruce wear pyjamas?" Robert gave his charming smile, and in reply to that questioner, I am now able to say in all truth that yes he did!

Robert is extremely proud of his brother and it shows all the time. He told me that his mother, Grace, had now finished the book she's been writing, called *The Untold Story* and she might soon be going to countries like Japan to promote it. He confirmed, too, that Linda had not remarried and that Brandon (now 14 and very much the young gentleman) is often seen escorting his mother around. Robert also mentioned that Brandon is now quite like Bruce in looks and also that he IS continuing to study the arts under Danny Inosanto. Asked if he thought Brandon might follow in his father's footsteps, Robert is inclined to feel that there is a strong possibility.

I decided it was time to pop a controversial question: I asked him, "Robert, what did you think of *Game of Death*?" "I didn't like it" - he replied, "Except when Bruce appeared," he added, smiling. I asked whether he thought Bruce would have been disappointed had he seen it. "He would have hated it as it wasn't what he had in mind at all."

I changed the subject and asked, "Did you ever meet James Coburn?" "Yes, several times," replied Robert. "He's a nice guy. Bruce and I used to go to James' place a lot." Robert lived in the States for 10 years and spent a good deal of time with Bruce and his friends. And was James Coburn really Bruce's best friend? "Oh yes, definitely, they got on great together."

That settled, I decided to ask about one or two of the other questions that crop up regularly. I sprang a difficult one, "Was Bruce a bully when he was a boy?" Robert hesitated.

"Come on - honestly!" He smiled that charming smile: "Well - yes. Often he'd fight twice a day." I said that I presumed it was fighting that prompted him to take up the martial arts - at the age of 13. "Yes, he went to Yip Man and other instructors and picked up everything he could." I had to ask, "Did Bruce actually attend Yip Man's funeral?" Robert replied very much in the affirmative. And how about the story of the sweat gland removal - was it true? Robert laughed and replied: "No, it wasn't."

And what about his own career? Were there just the two LPs, *Ballad of Bruce Lee* and *The Boat Song*? Robert confirmed that so far that was all, adding though that a new one was on the way. I asked him about the track, "Parting," on *Ballad of Bruce Lee* - it's credited to both Robert and Bruce, so who did what? "It was a joint effort really. Bruce wrote the poem and I did the music arrangement." Another question the fans are always putting to me, and one I had to pass along - did Bruce smoke or drink? Robert replied that, generally speaking, he did neither. However, shortly before his death, when visiting him one day, Bruce asked Robert for a drink of wine. Robert was surprised; "What! You - drink wine?" It was that unusual!

Lastly I asked another of those questions that crop up time and again. "Can you say anything about the electrical equipment that Bruce is supposed to have trained with? Robert confirmed that his brother had indeed used such a piece of equipment. Apparently you are supposed to start with it tuned to No. 1 and then to progress to the maximum position - No. 8. But Bruce didn't start at the bottom: "He went straight in at No. 8 - that's how he trained."

Robert had to leave as he was due to see his wife's show that evening. I thanked him sincerely for his kindness in talking to me for so long and for answering some fairly direct questions. All I can say about the man is that he really is a devoted fan of his brother. His pride when he talks about him shows clearly through. Also, on occasions, I caught a little of Bruce in the way he smiled and looked, and he has all the openness, charm and hospitality of the Chinese people. I keep my fingers crossed that everyone will be able to see him later this year because there's just a chance that he'll be able to make it over for the next convention!

My last hours in Hong Kong brought home to me all that had happened in those few, short days. I went to the top of the Sheraton Hotel and looked across the harbour at the boats, and further away, the peak stretching up into a dark sky. Even though all dreams have to end sometime, one thing I can say; seeing Hong Kong, Golden Harvest and Bruce's home was reward enough, but meeting Robert as well made me feel as though I'd put out my hand to reach the moon, only to come back with the stars as well!"

THE BRUCE LEE SOCIETY

Thank you, thank you, thank you for coming along in such huge numbers to this country's second major Bruce Lee event of 1979; the first ever Bruce Lee Film Festival. It made a wonderful "last chapter" to my Hong Kong trip!

I think all those there will agree that this time the venue turned out to be near ideal because, size-wise, we filled Kilburn's massive State Theatre with only a few seats left to spare. That means over 1,700 fans piled in. You just don't know how relieved I am that NO ONE had to be turned away.

And I thought, too, that the projection work was excellently handled and the sound system, crystal clear. My congratulations to all the technicians concerned. Sadly, plans are afoot to convert the enormous auditorium into three screens, but if that gets delayed a while, I think we shall be looking no further for a site for the 1980 Convention.

I hope everyone enjoyed the little tit-bits that were included at late notice; first it's James Coburn, then this time it's a greetings message from Robert Lee! Bruce Lee-wise, I must say I loved that snippet from *My Son Ah Chang* (I can't wait to see it in full at the next Convention) and, of course, that very rare Golden Harvest tape that we played last of all, had to be the most fitting of finales.

Last, and definitely not least, I have to hand a warm vote of thanks to Eddy Pumer for his superb compeering work. Only he could have carried us over the one disappointment of the day; a chunk missing from *Fist of Fury*, presumably removed by a scissor-happy projectionist.

By the way, it's vital that I tell you the following disastrous news. Once the reels that we were showing wear out, and already they're looking somewhat "tired," I'm told there can NEVER be any replacements! That's not the case with the usual, English dialogue, censored version, just the uncut originals. Therefore, what we were showing is a slice of history that will quite soon disappear forever, which is a sad, indeed tragic fact. Take my advice and see them while you're still able to.

A quick change of subject. I've been thinking for a while about the possibility of having a bronze bust or statuette made of Bruce so recently I checked out some details. We can have a bust (life size) at a cost of around £200; a full-size statue (also life size) would set us back around £1,000/£1,500. So, what I want from ALL you members are suggestions on the siting of a Bruce Lee bust/statue and whether you would be willing to contribute the required amount. Please write to me via the Bruce Lee Society BUT ON A POSTCARD ONLY PLEASE.

Just time for a last minute "scoop". Most of you will know about that rarest of rare books; Bruce's own *Chinese Gung Fu*. Over the years, I've had hundreds of enquiries about it and now, exclusively for Society members, I've managed to get hold of some reprints. They're available DIRECT FROM ME so just send £4.50 inc postage (Outside Britain, add £1) to me at 14 Rathbone Place, London W1P 1DE. Please make cheques/PO's payable to Pam Hadden.

Lastly of course, a quick word on the one and only Bruce Lee Society. Our strength lies in our membership and not like most appreciation societies, a collection of half interested fans, the BLS can truly boast the most dedicated and active followers in the land. If YOU feel that YOUR enthusiasm fits the bill, then WE NEED YOU! Become a part of the great, worldwide Bruce Lee Movement. Send a cheque or postal order for £3.25 (made out to *KFM*, please) to: Bruce Lee Society Subscriptions, 14 Rathbone Place, London W1P 1DE.
Pam Hadden

KICKBACK: THE LETTERS

Hello, it's letters time again and, as usual, it's Jenny here in the "hot seat." First off some interesting news - I have it on the authority of the British distribution company, Enterprise, that both of Chuck Norris' smash sellers in the States are due for imminent release over here. Apparently they'll be kicking off around the Manchester/Liverpool area about the time you're reading this with *Force of One*, followed a short time later by *Good Guys Wear Black*. It's then planned for the two movies to spread their way around the country. By the way, one extra titbit is that it's on the cards for Chuck himself to jet over here for some special appearances but don't worry, *KFM* will be watching out for him! Now, on with the letters!

EASY FOR SOME

Dear Jenny,
First the Convention and now the Bruce Lee Film Festival - and both situated in London. Although it may be easier for you folk to organise an event somewhere nearby, would it not be fairer to stage the Festival in Scotland, or at least nearer to Scotland?
Paul Lang, Downfield, Dundee

Dear Paul
The great news is that plans are very much in hand for a "North of Britain Film Festival" (stay glued to the pages for more on that!)

BRUCE LEE VERSUS POPEYE?!

I read the rip-off article in KFM No.49 and it was said that Enter the Fat Dragon was the only comedy that had been made about Bruce. Well, I've seen another. It was called Dragon Lives Again and the film starred Bruce Leong; the storyline concerned Bruce Lee's life after his death (and if that confuses you, I'm not surprised). The movie has "Bruce" ending up in another world after he dies, and there are a group of people who want to revolt against the King. Among them are Dracula, James Bond, a Clint Eastwood type character and a blind man. This group also oppress people and the film is largely about how "Bruce" opposes them. He opens a gym and one of the people he teaches is Popeye (yes Popeye!) who is never without his pipe and who becomes stronger with every mouthful of spinach. It's a very strange film.
P. Jagger, Kings North, Birmingham

Editor's Note: *Jenny didn't answer this letter.*

LIVING A LI

I'd like to tell you that I, for one, will never see a Bruce Li picture again. Having viewed Fist of Fury Pt.2 and Exit the Dragon Enter the Tiger, how anyone can think Li even resembles Bruce Lee is beyond me. And in Fist of Fury Pt.2, in the end fight between Li and the new master of the Japanese Karate school, Li receives cuts that try to make him resemble Bruce Lee at the end of Enter the Dragon. Before going, I'd been interested to know, what Li's physique was like in comparison to Bruce's and I was disappointed. Li appeared to me to be a massive blob of bulky muscle.
Barry Munns, Staincliffe, W. Yorks

Dear Barry,
I'll say it again, what really irks me is that, here is a man who is making a lot of money out of the originator - who was a hundred times better and, because he's dead, can't fight back.

STARCHART APPLAUSE

In *KFM* No.51, you really excelled yourselves. It was full of the usual high standard of information and fine sharp pictures of the late, great Master. And this month it had something extra - I think it was the astrology rundown on Bruce, a great idea.
Mr Gilbert Ross Lochgilpead, Argyll

Dear Gilbert,
I'm very happy to know that we agree on the excellence of Elizabeth Banks' "star-charting."

KICKBACK QUICKIES

Steven Garvey, Irvine, Scotland - Thanks for your kind comments on the magazine; so far as I know, the suits are still available - check with our mail order department over price, sizes, etc.
Alan L'Anson, Preston - Would like someone who has the *Game of Death* album to record the fight scenes for him (he has a silent 8mm film). Please write direct to him.
Sondra Chen, London - Thanks for details of the very strange goings-on at your local cinema - the information has been passed direct to Golden Harvest who are investigating.
Paul Miller, Hanley, Staffs - Yes, there is a chance of the Film Festival moving north - Check out 'Easy for Some" in the letters.
Jonathan Terry (?), Wollaton, Notts - Thanks for a very nice card.
Eustace Clarke, Stoke Newington, London - Felix Yen passed on your message - We'll try and fix you up with the two issues, although I can't guarantee it will be possible.
Thanks to whoever sent along the copy of *Strike Out* - A club magazine; very professionally done if I may say so.
Gilbert Ross, Lochgilphead, Argyll - What an appalling clipping from the *Daily Express* - I've passed it along to Pam for some sort of action.
Ray Uings, Swancombe, Kent - Could you be more explicit about the sequence removed from *Enter the Dragon*?
G. Connell, Workington, Cumbria - Sorry, the mugs are long gone; suits are probably okay. Yes, Brandon is still practicing the arts.
Keith Kerr, Ryton, Tyne & Wear - Afraid we missed it this time - A calendar is definitely being planned for next year.

THE POSTER MAGAZINES - VOLUME TWO

1980

EDITORIAL

Welcome Bruce Lee fans to the 54th edition of *Kung-Fu Monthly*! The big talking point in our offices at the moment is, of course, the disgraceful re-editing of the Little Dragon's, films; the British Board of Film Censors' intention has, I believe, been to remove every single nunchaku sequence, plus other fight scenes besides. Not only is this outrageous, it also appears to go against everything their Mr Ferman recently told us. Battle has commenced - more news on the Society page!

    We all need some cheering up after that - and boy, have we done it this time. Our own, incredible Eddy Pumer walked into *KFM* the other day carrying the actual film script for Bruce Lee His Life and Legend. Ring any bells? No? Well, that was the movie that Linda was planning on making - and never did. Not only does Eddy report on this final draft, he also turns up some startling revelations in the process.

    Follow up this month is part one of the promised, "Hong Kong papers." As you'll probably know. Society President Pam Hadden recently brought back from Hong Kong, some rare newspaper clippings that span much of the time that the Little Dragon was grabbing public attention - both before and after his tragic-passing. This month I have chosen to relive the days following July 20th, 1973. How did the people react to the death of their own local superstar? Read on for some detail that may surprise you!

Lastly, apology time - two name checks that should have been given in *KFM* No.52. Thanks go to Mike Childs and Alan Jones (and special thanks, too, to *Cinema Fantastique*) for the Christopher Lee interview.

Felix Yen

Felix Yen
Editor-in-Chief

THE BRUCE LEE PAPERS – PART ONE

"Bruce Lee is dead. Hong Kong's popular hard-fisted, quick-kicking screen hero collapsed suddenly at his Kowloon Tong home last night and died shortly afterwards in hospital." Thus was the death of the Master (Inaccurately) reported by one Hong Kong newspaper in its July 21st, 1973 edition. There were other "misunderstandings" as well - who he was with at the time and why he died are just two. There's no doubt that, for reasons we can only guess at, the truth was distorted - even turned over on its head - and discrepancies between the various press articles seem quite absurd - even laughable now. *KFM* takes yon back to that fateful moment and releases the news, just as it was released to an aghast, disbelieving Hong Kong public all those yean ago.

This same account compounds its opening mistake with a quite fictitious report of the final hours, "Mr Lee, according to sources, went for a walk in his garden in the evening before he was scheduled to meet Golden Harvest Studio boss, Raymond Chow and Australian actor, George Lazenby, of James Bond fame, to discuss a new film. He retired to the house soon afterwards, complaining of not feeling well. He lay down to rest." In actual fact, as we now know, he was with Hong Kong actress, Betty Ting Pei.

The following day's edition takes the distortions even further. "According to friends of the family, Bruce collapsed while taking a stroll with his 28-year old wife, Linda, outside their luxury home." And "He was taken to Queen Elizabeth Hospital at 11.15pm by his wife and Mr Raymond Chow and a close friend. Despite efforts to revive him by a team of six doctors, Bruce died. 15 minutes later - with his Swedish-born (really?) wife giving him a last kiss on the forehead." Thus the fabrication has become even more elaborate; still no mention of Betty and what happened to the ambulance that took him to the hospital? Also, according to some reports that have come to light since, there are even doubts that Linda was in the country at the time (although I find that hard to accept). Passing on to cause of death, the July 24th edition reported doctors as pointing out that, although further examination would be necessary, preliminary checks suggested that: "death was caused by a burst blood vessel in the brain.

Meanwhile, Chow announces he will make a documentary film the moment the body is claimed from the hospital to the departure to America". He also announced a traditional Chinese funeral be held at Kowloon Funeral Parlour at 10am on the morrow.

On the same day, in another newspaper, we first come across a theory that has persisted to this day: "Rumours sweeping the Chinese community suggest bad feng caused the death last week of star Bruce Lee. Lee's sudden and untimely death last Friday in lately led to a neighbour saying that he knew something bad was in the offing because a tree in the star's home in Kowloon Tong, was struck down by Typhoon Dot".

The paper goes on to report that bad luck comes to those living in the area and, as a result of the superstition, most Chinese people shun the place for fear of bankruptcy and destruction. This of course, is why Bruce had the bad feng shui deflector erected on the roof of his Cumberland Road home. Interestingly, we get a brief technical description of the deflector. Known as a "pat kwa," it is a wooden frame (octagonal in shape with a mirror at its centre. Bruce's had disappeared during the Typhoon!

And the report cites two other reasons for bad feng shui. According to legend, Kowloon Tong (which translated means nine dragon pond) was, for several centuries, where nine dragons lived. "With the emergence of the 10th dragon in the area, Bruce Lee himself (his Chinese name meaning Little Dragon), it caused rivalry and anger among the dragons for their habitat. But since he was only a "Little Dragon," the older and more powerful dragons killed him." The final cause of the bad feng shui lay in the titling of his latest film. Named of course *Game of Death*, film director, Lo Wei, had already warned of the possible consequences of choosing such a name. Lo in fact went on to cite an event which had happened some ten years before, where a road accident killed off an actor who at the time was starring in a movie entitled *Rendezvous with Death*. July 26th, and the truth will out! A spokesman for the Fire Services Department confirms that Bruce was not taken to hospital from his Cumberland Road home - rather it was from Betty Ting Pei's flat in Beacon Hill Road. Newsmen who visited the place in search of more information were being met with the flat reply, "she's not at home." Indeed, police visited the apartment, but left once they found no suspicions of foul play. It was also becoming clear that "cause of death" was a complicated one, for the autopsy report had still to be released. Coroner, Mr C.K.E. Tung, was deliberating on whether or not to call for an inquest. And at 10am on the same day there occurred the biggest funeral in the modern history of Hong Kong.

The papers were full of it. Vivid descriptions of the hordes of fans and sightseers - all anxious to take a last look at a superman finally laid at rest and many of them broken in grief. "Reinforcements of more policemen were needed when the crowd became wild. Many people had been there since early in the morning in order to have a good position for a look at the funeral."

It was obviously not at all easy for Linda. Dressed in a traditional Chinese mourning gown she "bowed to every visitor who paid their last respects to her husband. She burst into tears many times during the whole service." With her were Brandon, Shannon and Bruce's brother Peter and his wife. We're told that among the stars and personalities who turned up were Nora Miao, Nancy Kwan, Lo Wei and George Lazenby. Betty Ting Pei was conspicuous by her absence.

Inside the $40,000 bronze casket, only Bruce's head was visible and - probably due to

the heavy autopsy examination - his face was caked with makeup. He wore his suit from *The Big Boss*.

One final and intriguing paragraph that appears near the end of this article, dated July 26: It was reported a few packets of powder were found on Bruce Lee when he was admitted to Queen Elizabeth Hospital."

And so, the newspapers of July 27 had the task of reporting Linda and the two children's quiet departure from Hong Kong's Kai Tak Airport. Also on board was the bronze casket containing the physical remains of a man whose spirit, power and ambition, though stripped of mortal form, were to live on in the minds of millions of devoted followers the world over.

This time there were no wild scenes; only fifty or so people were there to see them off and that included 20 or so reporters. The family arrived shortly after 8am with some friends and relatives and at an impromptu press conference in the nearby restaurant. Golden Harvest man, Choi Wing-cheung, read out in Mandarin, a statement handwritten by Linda. She sat close by, we're told, wearing sunglasses and an all black suit and looking "strained with grief." It read: "It is my wish that the newspapers and the people of Hong Kong will stop speculating on the circumstances surrounding my husband's death. Although we do not have the final autopsy report, I hold no suspicion on anything other than natural death. I myself do not hold any person or people responsible for his death.

"Fate has ways we cannot change. The only thing of importance is that Bruce is gone and will not return. He lives on in our memories and through his films. Please remember him for his genius, his art, and the magic he brought to every one of us. For we who knew him very well, his words and thoughts will remain with us forever and influence the rest of our lives.

"I know the people of Hong Kong loved Bruce and are proud of his achievements which have brought world attention to Hong Kong, so I appeal to all of you to please let him rest in peace and do not disturb his soul.

"These are my personal feelings and those of his close friends and I would appreciate it if you will honour and respect my wishes."

With these words, the remainder of the Lee family left Hong Kong for Seattle. And as much as the people could understand those wishes, still the mysteries remained unanswered. Why were so many lies told during the hours after his death - lies that would obviously "crack" at the slightest investigation? What, too, was Betty Ting Pei's part in it all? Since that day her career hasn't exactly blossomed - she's married and to some people, appears a near recluse. Many of Bruce's old friends believe there's a lot more that Betty could tell - facts that would shed a great deal more light on the death of the legend that was Bruce Lee.

THE FILM THAT NEVER WAS – PART ONE

The place: a film studio in Burbank, California. The people: superstar, Barbra Streisand, her partner Jon Peters, Chuck Norris and Robert Clouse - plus hundreds of young hopefuls. The occasion: an audition to find the man to play the Little Dragon in Linda's forthcoming movie, *Bruce Lee His Life and Legend*. Several years ago, *KFM* reported briefly on that very occasion, commenting that the film was to be based on her *Life and Tragic Death of Bruce Lee* (American title: *Bruce Lee - The Man Only I Knew*.) That was the last we ever heard of the project - that is, until very recently. Eddy Pumer reports...

On that fine spring day in 1975, the "hopefuls" crowded into the studio and lined up, waiting to give their own individual impersonation of the Master. The winner was announced, a 23-year old and his name, Alex Kwon (real name, Kwok Ki Chung). Proclaimed as hot favourite to replace Bruce, you may recall our feature on the man in *KFM* No.15.

For some time he worked closely with Robert Clouse, Linda Lee and Chuck Norris - in the hope of capturing not only the Little Dragon's actions, but also his spirit. But just as things were beginning to click into gear, misfortune struck. It seems (although we're not altogether certain) that the Streisand/Peters production company, Barwood, pulled out and as a result of the consequent lack of financial support, the whole project had to be abandoned. An alternative theory has been mooted that the movie was actually begun, if not completed; it's said the result turned out way below expectations.

Whatever the reason, not a lot more was heard of Alex Kwon. Clouse went off to resurrect *Game of Death* (and in the process, pickaxe to pieces most of Bruce's ideas) and Linda's script ended up dumped on a dusty shelf.

And there the story might have ended, but for a script copy of his life and legend coming my way via a Hollywood contact. One glance through the mysterious pages was enough to convince me of its importance to the fact-thirsty fans of Bruce Lee. Therefore, coming up is what I believe to be the first ever review of *Bruce Lee His Life and Legend* - the film that never was!

It's unfortunate that no cast list comes with the script. Therefore I have no idea of who were to portray Bruce's family - and whether the original stars of his films were to take part in the re-enactment of the fight sequences from his various films. One strange thing is that the Little Dragon's parents have been dubbed Mr and Mrs Li - not Lee.

"Friends" of the Master have been given names like Jimmy, Louise and Cheng. There's no way of telling whether these are characterisations of Bruce's real life friends, or whether they are fictitious; only Linda or Robert Clouse could answer that, so final confirmation would be difficult to achieve.

I'm sure that by now, most readers of *KFM* have a pretty fair idea of the life story of Bruce Lee. Therefore for me to make comparisons between the details of his real life and those portrayed in the film would, for a large part, be a waste of time. A better way of presenting this rare find, I feel, is to try and give a visual description of what would have taken place, had the film been completed. I'll be making comments where necessary, but for the most part, I just want you sit back and enjoy the movie the most, if not all of us, are never like to meet up with - *Bruce Lee His Life and Legend*. It's 1940, and we see a touring Chinese opera company performing on stage. A woman in the window catches the attention of one the actors on stage who is dressed in traditional costume - with gruesome mask. She nods to him excitedly then runs away.

The opera finishes and the man rushes off stage to his dressing room - to meet his wife and newborn son. Someone reminds him that it is the year of the dragon - the father glances at the clock and realises that it's also the very hour of the dragon.

The movie jumps ahead to 1957; and we see the young Bruce Lee running down a busy Hong Kong street, darting in and out of three people with great agility. Arriving at a restaurant, he meets with his friends - plus his girlfriend Louise. Four youths start leering him from another table and one of them gesticulates insultingly. Accepting the challenge, Bruce throws himself into battle, knocking trays out of waiters' hands and generally upsetting the joint. Before long, the police arrive to break up the brawl and the young dragon finds himself dragged along to the police station.

He's questioned by an Inspector who ends up advising him to use his energies in a more constructive way. His moth-

er, who's also there, explains that he's a good dancer and that she'll see to it that his time will be taken up practicing for the championships.

The next scene shows six couples dancing away at the local Pavillion. Its finals night and eventually Bruce and Louise win. Unfortunately, things turn sour, for who should turn up but Jimmy - crawling on hands and knees. He tells Bruce how he got into a fight defending the young dragon's name - and points out the thug who hit him. "We can't fight in here says Bruce - there're too many police."

So the fight between Bruce and the thug, Robert Cheng, takes place on one of the hills, above Hong Kong. They stand opposite each other with a mass of car head lights blazing like torches to pierce the shadows. The action begins as soon it's obvious that Cheng's gang are the more skilled at fighting and before long, Bruce's men are eliminated. The young dragon, lying on the ground covered in mud and blood, sees Cheng looking down at him. He asks: "Who taught you this?" "Ip Man," came the answer. Suddenly, without warning Bruce lashes a leg at Cheng - which surprises him - and follows it through with a knee in the groin. "Never answer your enemy's questions," reminds Bruce, and as he staggers off into the night he asks Jimmy, "Who is this Ip Man?"

What follows next is a montage of the young dragon running through the streets of

Hong Kong until he almost collapses from exhaustion. It's a test, set by Ip Man - he's accepted Bruce into the school where he will learn the martial arts, not as a form of attack but to gain knowledge of self defence and total self control.

Another montage and this time its Bruce training, learning an art from its basics, slowly perfecting each and every move. Then we come to a famous story in Bruce's life. He's sitting on the steps of the school and, as the other pupils turn up, he explains that teacher is not well and class has been cancelled. Eventually, all his fellow students have gone home, and just Bruce is left to bask in Ip Man's great guidance. As we watch the young dragon working out, we see a definite improvement in grace and style.

As if to emphasise this change, we next fade up on Bruce walking past St John's English School. He's minding his own business and superficially looking at a rugby match when a red headed boy starts calling him a racial slur. The Little Dragon stares at the loudmouth with contempt, but the other boys join in and soon they've formed a circle around him. Red Head threatens, then lunges forward only to find that Bruce has stepped lightly to one side. Furious, he approaches again, but this time he's beaten by a threatened punch, followed by a real kick. In blind anger, the attacker lashes out this way and that, exhausting his energy as Bruce steps nimbly out of the way. Tired of the play-acting, the Little Dragon quickly and efficiently leads with swirling kicks and punches. The crowd politely make way as Bruce resumes his walk - leaving Red Head in a painful heap.

The Master sits in his sampan as it floats gently in Aberdeen Harbour. Staring into the water, he jabs at it - hardly a ripple forms. He smacks at it and a large splash sprays the air. He remembers the words of his teacher of how water was strong, yet soft, and how it always returned to its original form, even from the hardest blow. Bruce allows his mind to wander into a daydream as he sees himself as a great warrior.

Be back next month for part two of "The film that never was."

THE BRUCE LEE SOCIETY

Hello, fellow members of the Bruce Lee Society. Judging by the letters that have been piling in, it hardly needs me to tell you the sad, sad news. The British Board of Film Censors - the group of people who decide what's fit for us to see and what isn't - have finally brought *Enter the Dragon* and *Fist of Fury* into line with the rest of Bruce Lee's output by hacking out the nunchaku sequences! Intrigued as to why this should be happening so many years after the original release, we telephoned the Board's Mr Ferman to see what he had to say.

"Mr Ferman, we're approaching a decade of *Enter the Dragon* and *Fist of Fury*; why on earth chop them now?"

"*Enter the Dragon* and *Fist of Fury* are the only two films we've ever passed with chain stick sequences in as we didn't know what they were at the time! The films have now become standards; they go round time and again. Just like Douglas Fairbanks of the 20's and Errol Flynn of the 30's, Bruce Lee is the great action star of the 70's and his films will always be shown. The last time they went around, though, we had complaints about the

appearance of chain sticks among kids in playgrounds, football matches and so on."

"Of course for a good part it will be the action that people will remember. Therefore does it not worry you that you're often chopping out the main fight scenes?"

"It never amounts to much material; 3 or 4 minutes is the most we've ever cut from a Bruce Lee film."

"Why though, have nunchakus been singled out when just about all other conventional weapons are apparently okay?"

"The chain stick is easily available, and having made it, there is no other use. A knife, for instance, has many other uses. And you've got to ask, too, why this country is not alone in its concern. Japan, for instance, has banned them completely. In Canada, chain sticks simply aren't allowed to be carried around without a permit as they're considered an offensive weapon. I personally think France's attitude is best; they say they don't mind having the weapon in films because they're not going to allow it anywhere in society."

"I'm not in any position to dispute with you how many people have been caught using

nunchakus in an irresponsible way. However, it does seem to me that many of the films that pass the censor today are positively sickening in the effects they achieve. Don't you find this acceptance of what I call 'horror violence' far more worrying than anything Bruce Lee ever did? A good example, for instance, would be the slow motion, close-up of someone's brains being blown out that I saw recently."

"There are different kinds of violence. Some, like *The Deerstalker,* I agree is emotionally disturbing to watch. The problem with Bruce Lee films is that they're not emotionally disturbing to watch at all; they're bloody exciting and as I say, very easily imitated. What we've got to worry about is not the normal Bruce Lee fan; it's the abnormal Bruce Lee fan."

So there it is. It seems that emotionally disturbing violence is "okay", and that, as usual, the daft behaviour of the idiot few, is good enough excuse for the rest of us to miss out on what we love best. And as if all this isn't enough to worry about, try this for size. At present, there's a Williams Committee investigating for Parliament, amongst other things, the possibility of not allowing the private showing of unlicensed (i.e. uncensored) films. If that goes through in about a year's time, it would signal the end of the Bruce Lee Film Festival, at least as we know it. Stand by for a massive petition sometime in the future!

It's been several years now since we set the Bruce Lee Society subscription at £3.25 and unfortunately, the time is now set for a significant rise. As of April 1st the cost of a subscription will be £5.00 and although this may sound a lot, remember that we've been holding the price down while others have been increasing it as often as once a year.

If you want to beat the price rise, GET YOUR SUBCRIPTION IN NOW! £3.25's will be accepted up until the last day in March! The address to write is: 14 Rathbone Place, London W1P 1DE.

Thanks to *KFM*'s Bruce Sawford for interviewing Mr Ferman of the British Board of Film Censors. If you'd like to register your own protest, they're at 3 Soho Square, London W1. **PAM**

KICKBACK: THE LETTERS

Hello, its Jenny Lee here again with lots more of the readers' news and views. To begin with, though, an interesting slice of news from me. I expect you all remember the "daddy" Bruce Lee book of them all - *Bruce Lee - King of Kung Fu*. Well, one of its authors, Don Atyeo, is hot on the trail of producing his second Little Dragon epic. He tells me that it's likely to be named *The Bruce Lee Chronicles* and apparently there's some really hot, previously unknown, information lined up for it. If it turns out just half as good as the original, I can't wait!

MAKING INTRODUCTIONS

Dear Jenny,
I was reading recently about Ed Parker (who worked with Elvis Presley). He mentioned that he introduced Bruce and Dan Inosanto to the movies and he said that he got them lieu-jobs. He also held that Bruce was once "dumped" - or beaten - on a movie set by Gene LeBell, a Wrestler and Judo expert. I know anyone can be defeated, but I'd like to know what you think.
Karen, Newcastle

Dear Karen,
Ed Parker was of course the man who took the 8mm shots of Bruce at the Long Beach Tournament, and showed them to people who counted in the film industry. But although I suppose you could say that his action had a big effect on Bruce's subsequent career, I think it's overstepping for Ed to make the claim in exactly those words. I'm afraid I take these "so-and-so" beat Bruce Lee stories with a pinch of salt. There seem to be new ones arriving every week. I'm sure he was too professional to start real life punch-ups on the set.

TO RUSSIA WITH LOVE

Dear Jenny,
I thought I'd drop you a letter to let you know that I buy 15 copies of *KFM* every month - and send them to Mexico, Argentina, Japan, Brunei, Korea, Hong Kong, India, Thailand, the USA, Turkey, Canada, and now (after many months of trying to make a contact) Russia! I'll send details just as soon as I get my next letter from Nijenskaya, USSR.
Dave Langley, Runcorn, Cheshire

Dear Dave,
As there are a lot more countries to go, this could get expensive! Seriously, congratulations on helping spread the word in the best way possible.

CAUSE OF DEATH

Dear Jenny,
I cannot solve the secrets behind the death of Bruce Lee. But I don't believe that a headache pill would cause such a thing (as according to Roy Hollingsworth). According to my ideas, my searchings, the real reason for Bruce's death is being hidden or censored. Ask some questions yourselves and you may find the truth that lies underneath.
Ahmet Cruclar, Beykoz, Turkey

TRY A TOURNAMENT?

Dear Jenny,
Some time ago, my brother suggested my idea of a martial arts tournament, dedicated to Bruce Lee - one with all the trimmings of a real prestige tournament. Could it become a reality? I'm sure all the British governing bodies of martial arts would be glad to help.
Lee Rogers, Edinburgh, Scotland

Dear Lee,
I agree, the idea is a good one; I'm taking steps right now to test the reactions of those governing bodies.

WHERE'S THE SENSE?

Dear Jenny,
I recently saw *Enter the Dragon* at a club and although this may not seem strange to you, I'm only 13 years old. I can't understand why Bruce Lee films are "X" certificate. I've seen more upsetting and violent films on TV - for example *The Devil Rides Out*, *Legend of Hell House*, *Dracula* and many of the Hammer movies. Surely Bruce's films are harmless enough to be given an "AA" rating?
Graham Scott Taylor, Rossington, Doncaster

Dear Graham,
How utterly I agree with you. I suggest that you yourself let the Film Censorship Board know your feelings (the same goes for everyone else reading this). As you'll see from the Society page, the Board's latest action has made the situation ten times worse.

ANSWERS PLEASE

Dear Jenny,
Although I'm sure you will have already answered these questions a thousand times before; would you please do the honours one last time? Did Bruce receive serious abdominal injuries through knife wounds in the making of *The Big Boss*? Also, were there actors or stuntmen killed in the making of *Fist of Fury*? Lastly, keep up the brilliant work with *KFM*!
Don Quinn, Blackrock, Ireland

Dear Don,
Although Bruce sustained a number of "slight" and a couple of "not so slight" injuries while making his films - in keeping of course, with the dangerous nature of his work - there's no evidence that I've found of any abdominal knife wounds. Deaths during the making of Fist of Fury are also completely unsubstantiated.

KICKBACK QUICKIES

Richard Horsley, Hartlepool, Co. Cleveland - Glad your first view of the Master in action had such a great effect on you.

Glynn Darbyshire, Wickersley, S. Yorks - I'm just about fed up with all the talk about Li as well!

R. Stringer, Telford - I agree, those who break the law have no place in the martial arts.

Bruce, South Sheilds, Tyne & Wear - If you thought the last Convention could have been just that bit better, you'd better start booking right now for the next!

Michael Young, Richmond, Surrey - The record you heard was almost certainly *Dragon Power* - get the details from Satril Records, 444 Finchley Road, London NW2.

P. Nelligan, Deptford, London SE8 - The version of *Game of Death* that we show at the next Convention will be 35mm and uncensored!

John Haw, Lincoln - Bruce Lee died in Hong Kong, but he is presently burled in Seattle, USA.

Elvis Whetton, Streatham, London - Thanks for all the ideas - I must say I like the giant transfer.

Khalid Khan, Leeds, Lancs - Thanks for all the info on where to get things - I've passed it on to Pam for the next News Sheet.

Phillip Schimm, Atyenborough, Notts - Well done *Tiswas* for showing the *Enter the Dragon* scenes - even without much Bruce Lee!

Bryan Bath, Romford, Essex - Bruce for Madam Tussaud's? An interesting idea.

THE POSTER MAGAZINES - VOLUME TWO

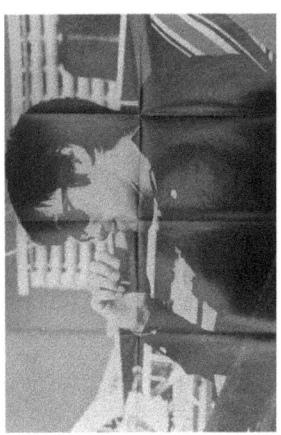

EDITORIAL

    Once again it's a great big Hi! to all you thousands upon thousands of *Kung-Fu Monthly* readers.
    And right off, I'm very happy to report that I'm devoting the whole of this month's feature space to the continuation of Linda Lee's amazing 'Film That Never Was.'
    If you read last month's edition then you'll know that this movie was meant to be the big one. To begin with, a great deal of money appeared to be behind it. Then all of a sudden - no more. I still can't tell you why that was, though believe me, we're investigating! Anyway, the main thing is what we can bring you is the final outline of the story, and a pretty interesting one it is too!
    Next up it's time to remind you that *KFM* and the Bruce Lee Society will once again be running Britain's only Official Convention - and as if you need reminding, it's on July 19th at the Kilburn State Theatre in London, Check it out in full by reading the big advertise-

ment this month, but do bear one thing in mind. I can definitely confirm that Ted Pollard (plus friend) win be attempting to re-stage the stupendous Lee/Norris confrontation from *The Way of the Dragon*. How well will he do? Sorry, that's a question only those there on the day can decide - but I bet my boots it'll be a major talking point for many months to come. I for one, won't be missing it! By the way, I hope all you readers of the *Sunday People* noticed our Ted on the centre spread of the May 4th edition - not a bad splash, eh? See you there on the day!

Felix Yen

Felix Yen
Editor-in-Chief

P.S. Late, late notice. Chuck Norris has been visiting Britain. Next month we expect to be bringing you our own, exclusive interview with the man who helped Bruce supply one of the greatest Kung Fu fights ever to be captured on movie film. Don't miss it!

THE FILM THAT NEVER WAS – PART TWO

To update, should you have missed last month's instalment, *KFM* reporter, Eddy Pumer, recently unearthed a fabulously rare script. In short, it was Linda Lee's own tribute to her husband but strangely the movie was never completed. Reasons have been put forward but none have ever been verified. Yet as was said last month, a great deal of time, effort and money had gone into the project - all apparently to no avail. The only tangible evidence that remains is the script itself, and that's where we resume this month; *KFM* reports the second and final segment of 'The Film That Never Was.'

Bruce's home life is becoming claustrophobic - at times he feels like kicking down the walls. His mother realises it won't be long before he's seeking his adventures elsewhere. But things aren't helped when a fortune teller indicates that much of his life will be filled with pain - and that many of his friends will live longer than he. The Little Dragon always remembers that omen.

The scene shifts to Bruce and his father talking. Mr Li is pleased to hear that his son is enjoying studying the martial arts - as any father is pleased when an offspring finds a path in life. He reaches to remove a paper butterfly from the end of his nose (the scene takes place after one of Mr Li's operatic performances) but Bruce does the job for him - with a sensational whirling kick. Amused, Mr Li asks how this skill will be put to use. "Maybe I'll teach," replies Bruce. Moving along, we see a version of the famous confrontation between Bruce's school and the Lin Po school - on top of the Yard Low building. Ip Man, who sees what's going on, screams at them to break it up. Tempers however are burning too fiercely and the police eventually have to intervene; everyone, including Ip Man ends up in jail!

Fed up with forever collecting her son from the police station, Mrs Li takes him to a nearby cafe and explains that both she and his father think it better he seek his fortune in the United States. He agrees, and promises he will not return until he's made something of himself. Mrs Li weeps.

Bruce's destination turns out to be Ruby Chow's restaurant and there we see Bruce washing dishes, while at the same time reading from a martial arts book that's propped up against the sink! He also spends all his free time exercising and the staff gradually grow more and more amazed at his speed and agility.

In time, they become interested in his art and he opens a small class where he teaches not only Kung Fu, but also the psychological and philosophical. One person in particular, Linda Emery, finds him particularly interesting. Soon we see Bruce arriving at Linda's house - he's there to meet her mother. The confrontation is a delight! Wearing a bright purple shirt and a strangely fitting suit, instead of bringing flowers, he humbly gives Linda a Kewpie Doll! And what does her mother get? Well, a bone-crunching handshake and the following compliment: "You know Mrs Emery, you've got the greatest legs of any woman your age I've ever seen!"

Another memorable episode is not long in appearing. Three men walk up to Bruce while he's training in the gym and they present him with a scroll that challenges him to a fight at their school. The reason for the challenge (for those who haven't heard the story before) is that the Little Dragon is allowing anyone to train at his school - thus in many eyes he's disgracing the art of Kung Fu. The catch is that, if Bruce loses, he has to close down his school.

Bruce demands the fight begin there and then and turns down their attempt to state rules. "You came here with an ultimatum - you made the challenge, so I'll make the rules. No holds barred - anything goes." It's hardly surprising that the Little Dragon ends up virtually taking them apart as they and the scroll disappear out the door.

We move on and as Linda gives birth to their first child, Bruce meanwhile takes the opportunity to appear in the Long Beach tournament. Two TV producers happen to be there, to take note of anything interesting. Over the public address come the words: "Chuck Norris versus Bob Wall, but before that here's a young man all the way from the Far East" - etc. etc. (in fact, as far as I know, Chuck and Bob were never present at this particular

tournament.)

Bruce steps up to the mike to explain the beneficial points of Kung Fu, when compared to Karate. "800 million Chinese can't be Wong." The audience like his dry humour. Pat Johnson moves into the picture, dressed in Karate uniform. Bruce explains that each time Johnson strikes him, he gains a point - and vice versa. After a couple of early points, Johnson hardly gets a look in and the judges lose count as the Little Dragon overwhelms with his retaliation.

The two producers see all this and are quite taken aback and eventually, they sign him up for *The Green Hornet* series. After showing one or two clips from the series, it slowly becomes obvious that Bruce is losing interest. He needs the money, but hates the endless round of parties he has to attend (we see him performing his famous coin trick) and trips to supermarkets where he has to sign autographs. Unfortunately the only other parts that ever seem to come his way are of the traditional 'chop chop' variety - which he refuses to accept.

By way of interest, he begins to give private lessons to such top Hollywood stars as James Coburn, Steve McQueen, James Garner, Elkie Summers and James Franciscus. It's not only that he likes their friendship, there's also the possibility of meeting other directors and producers.

The famous TV series, *Kung Fu* comes along, Bruce is keenly interested in going ahead in it and asks why they are so slow in getting started. "It's a new kind of fighting," explains his agent. "Yeah, about a thousand years old," replies Bruce,

Eventually they decide to go ahead, but the bad news is that Bruce's part is purely that of technical adviser - not the star. He runs home and proceeds to destroy the gym. Linda

hears what's going on, realising what the news must have been, rushes to the medicine cupboard for bandages and iodine. She finds Bruce leaning up against the wall, totally spent; she goes to him with tears in her eyes.

We cut to Bruce and James Coburn jogging down the street. James is trying to explain to him that TV is a kind of monster that chews you up in thirteen episodes, then leaves you for dead. And he says: "The western world isn't ready for an oriental star." "But I'm American," protests Bruce. "Yeah, but you've got funny eyes," replies Coburn.

They carry on running and James goes on to tell Bruce that now The Green Hornet series has become a smash hit in Hong Kong, he should quit America and seek his future back in the East. Coburn gets into the limousine that's waiting to take him back to the studio and Bruce says he'll think about it. That night, he and Linda make their decision.

It's a dramatic change of scene. Bruce has taken the advice and we see him raining lethal blows on twelve men. The fight ends in a bloody mess with the Little Dragon slumped across some steps. "Cut," shouts the director and the men jump up from the floor, all smiling and some applauding him.

But for Bruce, it's rather a lonely time. He misses the family (that now includes Shannon) and he's also missing the fresh meat and vegetables that he's used to eating. He writes Linda a letter telling her that the film, *The Big Boss*, is nearly completed and that he'll see her in Hong Kong in about a week.

Almost immediately, we're treated to the occasion of the premiere. The crowd's going wild, fists are being waved in the air and at the screen and as Bruce and Linda leave the theatre the two of them are mobbed. The chauffeur at the wheel of the Mercedes remarks that the Little Dragon is now King of Kong Kong.

Eager to see his old master again, they drive to Ip Man's school. Passing through the rows of young men working out Bruce makes his way to the office and knocks on the door. Entering, he sees a much older and wiser looking Ip Man - though still the same person who had taught him so much and who had put him on the road to success. Ip Man looks at the Little Dragon, smiles, and examining his one-time student who is now a supreme martial artist, says: "You are beautiful."

Time jumps ahead, and now we see Bruce at the premiere of his new epic, *Fist of Fury*. As before the crowd are going wild - especially at the line "We are not the sick men of Asia." On this occasion, however, as Bruce pulls away in the car he's rubbing his eyes. Worried, Linda asks him: "Are you okay?" "Just a little dizzy," he replies.

With his first two films hitting all-time highs in Hong Kong, Bruce is now a major star and Europe is at his fingertips. We see him running over the hills of Hong Kong until he reaches the cemetery where his father lies buried and explains over the grave how fruitful his life has become.

The Little Dragon is sketching out a fight sequence that he has in mind for his next movie - one that this time he wants to direct himself. The figures he draws dissolve into reality and all at once he is actually in combat with Chuck Norris. The sparring ends and they chat over the finer details; gradually Bruce begins to fantasise and, looking over the high walls, he sees Roman gladiators and great fighters before him. He battles with Kirk Douglas and Victor Mature as Caesar looks on. With a piercing scream, he jerks himself back to reality. "Who have you killed?" jokes Chuck who is holding a cup of coffee.

For Bruce, the flashback was almost for real. He explains of the lifetime gone and how he and Chuck may have been in combat for real - "You may have won," laughs Bruce. Chuck, looking a little more serious, replies: "You know something Bruce, I don't think so."

Later he meets up with some Italian film producers who explain that they'd like him to co-star in a film with Sophia Loren. Bruce is more than flattered but explains that he's just committed himself to a new Warner Brothers movie - to be entitled *Enter the Dragon*.

The film now turns its attention to some of those oft-mentioned comments that he made to reporters. We see him explaining to them that he doesn't recognise 'style' and that by the time a fighter has reached a required stance, he could well have been knocked

to the ground several times. Naturally these outrageous remarks draw him even more into the public eye and he's called on to explain them on a TV show.

The host has brought along three other martial artists for the programme - presumably to make the controversy even more interesting. However, hardly has he had time to ask Bruce about his thoughts on some of the classical styles of fighting when he is interrupted by the first guest - who springs to his feet and assumes a classical pose. The man challenges the other two to push him off balance. One of them pushes and pushes - to no avail; the other grapples every way he can - still to no effect. With a half smile, half smirk he calls on Bruce to try his luck: "Maybe the movie star wants to try." Reluctantly Bruce gets to his feet, faces the man, and with a lightning kick to the face sends him flying through the scenery. (In real life, it's believed that Bruce finished by saying to the host, "I don't push, I punch." He left the studio immediately.)

The location changes to the kitchen of their house. Linda shouts out to Bruce who is working in the gym to ask what he wants to eat. The exercise machine suddenly stops with a thud; she rushes into the practice room to find Bruce semi-conscious on the floor. The hospital report that follows reveals nothing wrong, with the added comment that he has the body of a man half his age.

Following the shock of his black-out, Bruce holds a business meeting. The offers come flooding in. Italy wants him for a million dollars, Run Run Shaw makes an offer unequalled by any other from Hong Kong. As Yang, his adviser, reads out the list, Bruce opens the window to let out the stench of cigar smoke and whisky. Each offer tops the one before until, finally, Bruce interrupts by taking a hold of the script for *Enter the Dragon* and tapping it whilst looking at them he says: "We have to make a picture that is more than Italian, more than Chinese." *Enter the Dragon* is under production and immediately we see a montage of clips from the underground cavern, the mirrored room and the tournament courts. Bruce is supervising the extras in the choreographed routines - showing total control of each situation.

The story continues with Bruce and Linda discussing what is to happen with their future. The Little Dragon is concerned about staying in Hong Kong, particularly from the point of view of the children. Linda feels that all will change once the film's been completed.

The director calls over to tell Bruce that he's ready to start shooting again. Standing before a grave in the catholic cemetery, he speaks his lines - but continually fluffs them. He holds his head. "You okay?" shouts the director.

Bruce explains that he's feeling dizzy. The scene dissolves into a further montage of Enter in production.

Bruce sits in the director's chair, relaxing with a cup of tea while waiting for the next scene to be set up. Suddenly he notices a young extra staring at him and with a feeling of resignation, he realises he's about to face another challenge.

"Forget it kid," warns Bruce. "You refuse?" asks the young man. Bruce explains that if he fights and wins, he'll be considered a bully, if he loses, it'll be the end of his reputation as a great martial artist and if he refuses to fight, he'll be called a coward.

By now of course a good sized crowd has appeared. The young challenger tells Bruce that he just wants to see how good he is but for the Little Dragon, the incident starts to strike a chord as he'd been just the same a few years back. Going along with it, Bruce puts down the mug of tea and gets ready for some action; the bout is foiled, however, by an assistant calling over to say that the set is ready. Bruce looks at the young fighter, smiles and says: "Now neither of us will ever know." It's believed, by the way, that in reality, the fight did take place and the youngster was knocked to the ground. There is no positive confirmation, however.

Enter the Dragon is finally completed and all concerned are delighted with the result. The final shots had taken place in a restaurant and the table is being cleared where Bruce and Linda, plus several reporters, are bringing their meeting to a close. The newsmen are amazed as the Little Dragon moves to pay the bill. The waiter meanwhile chips in that now he's become a star, presumably he'll be leaving his homeland. Linda reassures him that they'd always keep their house in Hong Kong.

Bruce reaches into his pocket and pulls out a pair of twisted old wire-framed glasses, held together by a paper clip; they've no lenses in them. "These were my reading glasses a few years ago. When I broke them, I was too poor at the time to get them fixed. I've kept them with me ever since to remind me where I came from, and how far." He and Linda get up to go and, deciding on a parting comment, he remarks to the reporters: "See you in the papers." They all laugh.

The two of them walk away down the street to the Mercedes. Word has obviously got around that the great man is in town for a good sized crowd has gathered and people are out on their balconies, waving and cheering. Bruce sees one man in particular shouting out his name. He smiles, lifts his thumb in the traditional Chinese 'A-Okay' gesture - and suddenly the picture freezes. A voice over tells us: "Four months after the completion of *Enter the Dragon*, Bruce Lee, at the age of 32, died. The film, his last, broke box office records in country after country and made him an international star of a magnitude that only he could have imagined or dared dream."

In Conclusion

Most fans will now be aware that a certain amount of 'poetic licence' has been used in the telling of this story. And, on the face of it, it could be argued too that the script-writer has attempted to fit a quart into a pint pot. Certainly, judging by the look of the script, there's very little 'flow' as the action hurtles from one incident to the next. It would however be unfair to pre-judge what might have been the result as after all, for most films, there's many a change between written line and final footage.

But even bearing all this in mind, I'm sure that, had Robert Clouse's interpretation of the Bruce Lee story been completed, it would have ended up the finest portrait of them all. Indeed, maybe now that the 'powers-that-be' can see there is a very real interest among fans for the project to be completed, they'll make the necessary moves to ensure that we get to see Linda Lee's 'Film That Never Was.'

THE BRUCE LEE SOCIETY

Pam Hadden invites you to JOIN THE BRUCE LEE SOCIETY.
For more than 4 years the *KFM* Bruce Lee Society has gone from strength to strength. Membership continues to rise, while public interest in the legend of the Master has never been greater. If you are not already a member, you really can't afford to wait a moment longer. Upon joining the society you will receive:

1. A first year kit, comprising of membership card, scroll biography and fact sheet, the Official Society Badge, action photos, and an autographed picture of Bruce Lee.
2. The famous 3-Monthly News Sheet send DIRECT to your home.
3. A regular Society page, right here in every edition of Kung-Fu Monthly.
4. All your enquiries answered by our tireless PAM HADDEN.
5. Competitions, Special offers, the Swop Shop, and lots, lots more...

All this for just £5.00 (Overseas rate £6.50)

KICKBACK: THE LETTERS

Hi there everyone! Well, It's that time of the year again - in other words, stand by for Britain's only official Bruce Lee Convention. Last year, we totally exceeded our expectations by attracting well over a thousand fans - this year, our Editor tells me that, as I write this, we've already sold a thousand tickets in advance. Remember that we really have to draw the line at 2,000 so don't hang around - book now or you may not get it! Lastly, thanks for sending in a particularly interesting batch of letters this month if only they'd give me two pages instead of one! Still, I've done all I can to pick out only the very best - so here we go!

RIP-OFF KING

Dear Jenny,
I think I have a film that beats all the rip-offs in *KFM* No.49; it's called *Enter the Game of Death* and the star of this rip-off is someone called Bruce Le (not Bruce Li). I haven't actually seen it yet, but I have seen *Fist of Fury* Part Three, starring Bruce Li, and my comment on this is that the film is okay, so are the fight scenes, and in fact, he's trying to act a bit better than in his last efforts.
Mick Palmer, Castle Vale, Birmingham

Dear Mick,
I can hardly believe it; Enter the Game of Death? I suppose next it'll be Way of the Fist of Fury or Enter the Big Boss! I think their lack of originality is pathetic. The trouble with Bruce Li, at least as it seems to me, is that just as one starts thinking that he's performing adequately, one look at a Bruce Lee film is enough to prove he's still light years behind.

TRIBUTE

Dear Jenny,
I've just received KFM No.54, and what a superb issue - the poster is fantastic. This year's Convention sounds terrific and I just can't wait. Screening the complete, uncensored Game of Death will be fantastic, plus the rest of the show, will make it out of this world. A lot of planning must go into these Conventions, and I realise how hard it must be for KFM staff to cope with the fans at the book stalls, etc. I must say a personal thank you to you all; without KFM, the good name of Bruce Lee would not be heard today. The magazine has a very deep and memorable place in my heart. Thank you and best wishes.
Mark Peters, Sutton, Surrey

Dear Mark,
What can I say - except thank you. It's letters like this that make everything worthwhile.

WHERE IS BRUCE?

Dear Jenny,
Can you please sort this out; where exactly is Bruce Lee buried? In one of my books it says at Seattle in the United States; in another it says first in Hong Kong, then to the United States, then finally flown to San Francisco. I am so confused! Also, has his wife, Linda, moved house yet?
Miss Sheena Little, Haves, Middlesex

Dear Sheena,
The answers are in fact very simple - despite the nonsense that has been written from time to time. Firstly, Bruce was not buried in Hong Kong to begin with - his body was flown more or less directly to America and to this day, his last resting place remains the Lakeview Cemetery in Seattle. Linda Lee has not moved house; she still live in Los Angeles.

BLOOD RISING

I have just looked at KFM No.53 and, apart from its usual ten out of ten standard, some of the contents got my blood level rising with excitement. Pam Hadden's trip to Hong Kong (where she met Robert Lee), the attendance figures for that Film Festival (I wouldn't have missed it for the world) - the figures just go to show that Bruce is more popular now than ever before. And now for the artery burster: Pam Hadden's idea of a statue of the Little Dragon has to be the best yet for keeping Bruce Lee's name and legend alive.
Jan Clark, Rotherham, S. Yorks

Dear Jan,
Final details on the statue are still in the pipeline but hopefully, we'll be announcing everything at the Convention.

LIFE SIZE?

Dear Jenny,
I'm sure many other fans would agree with me that a life size poster of our idol would be a great idea - perhaps an action shot. I hope you will be able to produce such a poster soon.
Reede Brown, Glenfield, Leicester

Dear Reede,
What a nice, unusual name! Actually we're ahead of you on the life size poster. Right now we're doing our very best to get one ready for the Convention. Thanks also for including the list of goodies that you have for sale; I've passed it on to Pam to see if she can include it in her next News Sheet.

PETITION

Dear Jenny,
How about starting an official petition to the BBC for their Bruce Lee tribute film (a letter from the BBC confirms its existence)?
Graham Ellis, Hinckley, Leicestershire

Dear Graham,
Yes, I think you're dead right - the time certainly has come for us to take some action. What we'll do is make a start at the Convention, then carry it on for a month or two afterwards.

KICKBACK QUICKIES

Mr G. Hawkes, Hullbridge, Essex - You ask about Flimsy discs - Well, they don't cost all that much to make although you have to order thousands to make it practical.
Mark Mest, Wythenshawe, Manchester - More scissoring and how dare they run a Bruce Lee film second string to a Bruce Li!
Thomas Leino, Strathclyde, Scotland - Thomas wants to know about any clubs/shops that sell books on Tae Kwon Do. Also, are there any Society members who are members of a Tae Kwon Do club? Write in to *KFM* with any details.
Mark Lucktaylor, Heckmondwike, West Yorks - Glad to hear that you're a lot happier with Bruce Li's *The Tiger Strikes again*. I still need some convincing!

Richard Horsley, Hartlepool, Cleveland - Actually, we never really picked up on the reader photo idea, mainly because the Society took over the scheme in its News Sheet. That said, the pictures you sent along look really great!

Kevin Taylor, Hartlepool, Co. Cleveland - Great to hear that you like the job we're doing. By the bye, if you want to see a bit more than those few minutes at the end of *Game of Death*, don't forget to come along to the Convention to see the complete, uncensored version.

Robert Bax, Halifax, Yorks - Thanks for the info on the video cassette you saw recently - sounds fantastic!

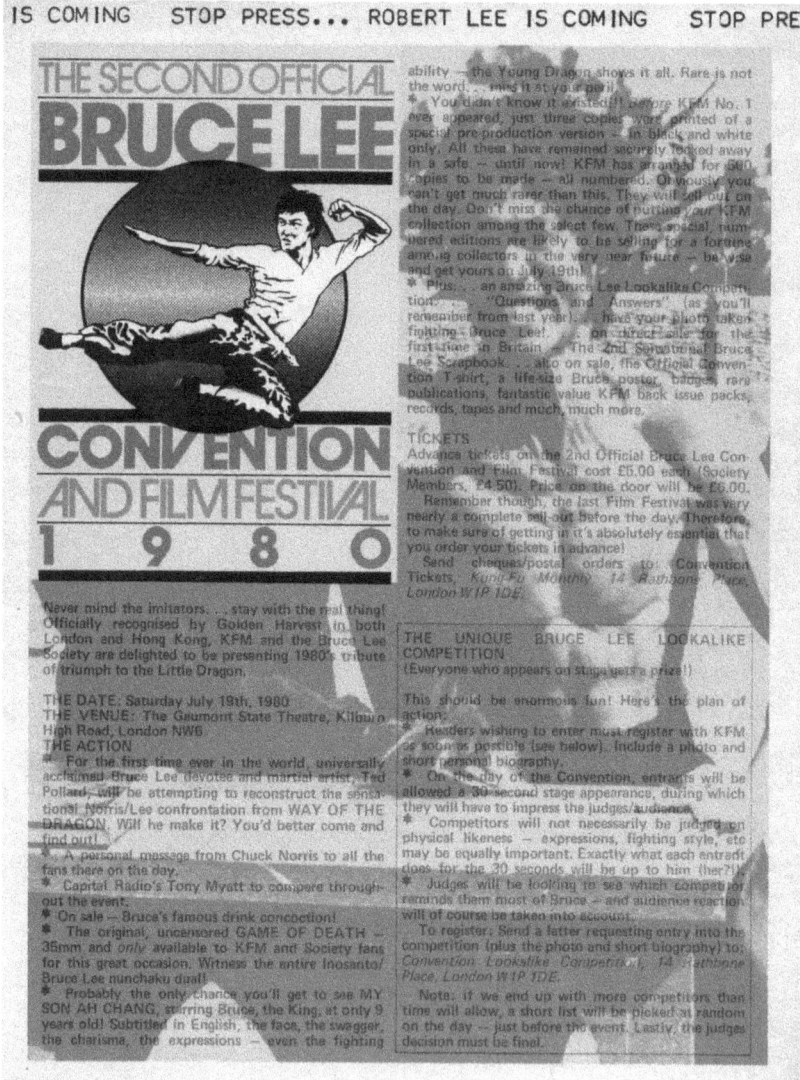

KUNG-FU MONTHLY

THE ARCHIVE SERIES
PUBLICATION DATES

THE POSTER MAGAZINES - VOLUME TWO

It is extremely difficult to put together a definitive list of publication dates for Kung-Fu Monthly. In the early days, the magazine was probably expected to fold in a very short space of time and therefore not many records were kept. That, combined with an ever-changing merry-go-round of staff and writers plus focus on newer publications does not help matters. It also does not help that the magazine was not a strict monthly publication despite its name suggesting so.

This list of publication dates has been compiled from several information sources including The History of Kung-Fu Monthly by Felix Dennis and the Kung-Fu Monthly magazines themselves, by utilising key dates of book releases, film releases, advertisement and conventions.

This list is not completely accurate and should only be viewed as a rough guide.

No. 1	Apr 1974	No. 34	Sep 1977	No. 67	May-Jun 1982
No. 2	May 1974	No. 35	Oct 1977	No. 68	Jul-Aug 1982
No. 3	Jun 1974	No. 36	Nov 1977	No. 69	Sep-Oct 1982
No. 4	Jul-Aug 1974	No. 37	Dec 1977	No. 70	Nov-Dec 1982
No. 5	Sep-Oct 1974	No. 38	Jan 1978	No. 71	Jan-Feb 1983
No. 6	Nov-Dec 1974	No. 39	Feb 1978	No. 72	Mar-Apr 1983
No. 7	Jan-Feb 1975	No. 40	Mar-Apr 1978	No. 73	May 1983
No. 8	Mar-Apr 1975	No. 41	May 1978	No. 74	Jun 1983
No. 9	May-Jun 1975	No. 42	Jun 1978	No. 75	Jul-Aug 1983
No. 10	July-Aug 1975	No. 43	Jul 1978	No. 76	Sep-Oct 1983
No. 11	Sep 1975	No. 44	Augt-Sep 1978	No. 77	Nov-Dec 1983
No. 12	Oct 1975	No. 45	Oct-Nov 1978	No. 78	Jan-Feb 1984
No. 13	Nov 1975	No. 46	Dec 1978-Jan 1979	No. 79	Mar-Apr 1984
No. 14	Dec 1975	No. 47	Feb-Mar 1979		
No. 15	Jan 1976	No. 48	Apr-May 1979		
No. 16	Feb 1976	No. 49	Jun-Jul 1979		
No. 17	Mar 1976	No. 50	Aug-Sep 1979		
No. 18	Apr 1976	No. 51	Oct-Nov 1979		
No. 19	May 1976	No. 52	Dec 1979-Jan 1980		
No. 20	Jun-Jul 1976	No. 53	Feb-Mar 1980		
No. 21	Aug 1976	No. 54	Apr-May 1980		
No. 22	Sep 1976	No. 55	Jun 1980		
No. 23	Oct 1976	No. 56	Jul-Aug 1980		
No. 24	Nov 1976	No. 57	Sep-Oct 1980		
No. 25	Dec 1976	No. 58	Nov-Dec 1980		
No. 26	Jan 1977	No. 59	Jan-Feb 1981		
No. 27	Feb 1977	No. 60	Mar-Apr 1981		
No. 28	Mar 1977	No. 61	May-Jun 1981		
No. 29	Apr 1977	No. 62	Jul-Aug 1981		
No. 30	May 1977	No. 63	Sep-Oct 1981		
No. 31	Jun 1977	No. 64	Nov-Dec 1981		
No. 32	Jul 1977	No. 65	Jan-Feb 1982		
No. 33	Aug 1977	No. 66	Mar-Apr 1982		

To view detailed information as to how this list was compiled, please scan the QR code below to go to the Kung-Fu Monthly Archive Series website where an updated version of this list will be displayed as more information becomes available.

KUNG-FU MONTHLY

THE ARCHIVE SERIES
MAGAZINE CREDITS

THE POSTER MAGAZINES - VOLUME TWO

KUNG-FU MONTHLY NO. 27 / COPYRIGHT 1975

Photo Credits: Golden Harvest Films, Cathay Films, Warner Bros., Peter Bennett, Rex Pictures

KUNG-FU MONTHLY NO. 28 / COPYRIGHT 1975

Photo Credits: Golden Harvest Films, Cathay Films, Warner Bros., Peter Bennett, Rex Pictures, Chester Maydole

KUNG-FU MONTHLY NO. 29 / COPYRIGHT 1977

Photo Credits: Golden Harvest Films, Cathay Films, Warner Bros., Peter Bennett, Rex Pictures

KUNG-FU MONTHLY NO. 30 / COPYRIGHT 1977

Photo Credits: Golden Harvest Films, Cathay Films, Warner Bros., Peter Bennett, Rex Pictures

KUNG-FU MONTHLY NO. 31 / COPYRIGHT 1977

Photo Credits: Golden Harvest Films, Cathay Films, Warner Bros., Peter Bennett

KUNG-FU MONTHLY NO. 32 / COPYRIGHT 1977

Photo Credits: Golden Harvest Films, Cathay Films, Warner Bros., Peter Bennett

KUNG-FU MONTHLY NO. 33 / COPYRIGHT 1977

No Credits Listed

THE KUNG-FU MONTHLY ARCHIVE SERIES

KUNG-FU MONTHLY NO. 34 / COPYRIGHT 1977

No Credits Listed

KUNG-FU MONTHLY NO. 35 / COPYRIGHT 1977

No Credits Listed

KUNG-FU MONTHLY NO. 36 / COPYRIGHT 1977

No Credits Listed

KUNG-FU MONTHLY NO. 37 / COPYRIGHT 1977

No Credits Listed

KUNG-FU MONTHLY NO. 38 / COPYRIGHT 1977

No Credits Listed

KUNG-FU MONTHLY NO. 39 / COPYRIGHT 1977

No Credits Listed

KUNG-FU MONTHLY NO. 40 / COPYRIGHT 1977

No Credits Listed

KUNG-FU MONTHLY NO. 41 / COPYRIGHT 1978

No Credits Listed

KUNG-FU MONTHLY NO. 42 / NO COPYRIGHT YEAR

No Credits Listed

KUNG-FU MONTHLY NO. 43 / NO COPYRIGHT YEAR

No Credits Listed

KUNG-FU MONTHLY NO. 44 / NO COPYRIGHT YEAR

No Credits Listed

KUNG-FU MONTHLY NO. 45 / NO COPYRIGHT YEAR

No Credits Listed

KUNG-FU MONTHLY NO. 46 / NO COPYRIGHT YEAR

No Credits Listed

KUNG-FU MONTHLY NO. 47 / NO COPYRIGHT YEAR

No Credits Listed

KUNG-FU MONTHLY NO. 48 / NO COPYRIGHT YEAR

No Credits Listed

KUNG-FU MONTHLY NO. 49 / NO COPYRIGHT YEAR

No Credits Listed

THE KUNG-FU MONTHLY ARCHIVE SERIES

KUNG-FU MONTHLY NO. 50 / NO COPYRIGHT YEAR

No Credits Listed

KUNG-FU MONTHLY NO. 51 / NO COPYRIGHT YEAR

No Credits Listed

KUNG-FU MONTHLY NO. 52 / NO COPYRIGHT YEAR

Design: Bill Bell

KUNG-FU MONTHLY NO. 53 / NO COPYRIGHT YEAR

No Credits Listed

KUNG-FU MONTHLY NO. 54 / NO COPYRIGHT YEAR

Design: Bill Bell

KUNG-FU MONTHLY NO. 55 / NO COPYRIGHT YEAR

Design: Bill Bell

ALL ISSUES PUBLISHED BY
H. BUNCH ASSOCIATES LTD

A HISTORY OF KUNG-FU MONTHLY

Writer & Primary Researcher
Carl Fox

BIBLIOGRAPHY

More Lives Than One: The Extraordinary Life of Felix Dennis
by Fergus Byrne (2015)

Felix Dennis Interview for Martial Arts Illustrated
by Peter Jagger (December 2011)

A Short History of Kung-Fu Monthly and The Bruce Lee Society
by Felix Dennis (1979)

The Secret Art of Bruce Lee
by the editors of Kung-Fu Monthly (1978)

The Wisdom of Bruce Lee
by Roger Hutchinson & Felix Dennis (2021)

The KFM Bruce Lee Society: A Retrospective Look at Bruce Lee Mania & The Kung Fu Craze of the 1970s
by Carl Fox (2021)

The Kung Fu Years
by BBC TV (1997)

Conversation with Dick Pountain
Conversation with Jeff Cummins
Conversation with Jonathon Green
Conversation with David Jenkins
Conversation with Bey Logan
Conversation with Colin James
Conversation with Don Atyeo
Conversation with Richards Adams
all by Carl Fox (2021/22)

SPECIAL THANKS

Richard Adams, Don Atyeo, Fergus Byrne, Jeff Cummins, Jonathon Green, Peter Jagger, Colin James, David Jenkins, Bey Logan, Tony Lundberg, Michael Nesbitt, John Overall, Dick Pountain, Matthew Robins, Bruce Sawford and Andrew Staton.

ALSO BY THE AUTHOR

THE K.F.M. BRUCE LEE SOCIETY

"BEAUTIFULLY CAPTURES THE HEART, SOUL, AND SPIRIT OF THE UNITED KINGDOM'S FLEDGLING BRUCE LEE FANBASE. UNDENIABLY COLLECTIBLE."

- BRUCE LEE REVIEW

"NOT JUST A COMPILATION OF NOSTALGIC NEWSLETTERS, BUT A BRITISH HISTORY GUIDE TO A PERIOD TIME WHEN WESTERN PEOPLE DISCOVERED THE UNIQUE TALENTS OF THE UNDISPUTED KING OF KUNG FU - BRUCE LEE."

- ANDREW J. STATON, BRITISH JUN FAN JOURNAL

"THANK YOU VERY MUCH FOR YOUR TIME AND EFFORT TO HONOUR PAM FOR HER GREAT WORK AND DEDICATION. I, TOGETHER WITH THE BRUCE LEE FANS WHO KNEW PAM SALUTE YOU!"

- ROBERT LEE

THE **KUNG-FU MONTHLY** BRUCE LEE SECRET SOCIETY BEGAN IN SEPTEMBER 1976, RUNNING FOR 30 ISSUES BEFORE IT'S FINAL ISSUE IN SEPTEMBER 1983. RUN BY THE FORMIDABLE PAM HADDEN, THE BRUCE LEE SECRET SOCIETY FUNCTIONED AS THE SOURCE OF INFORMATION FOR BRUCE LEE FANS IN THE UK AND LATER, THE REST OF THE WORLD. FOR THE FIRST TIME EVER, ALL 30 ISSUES HAVE BEEN PAINSTAKINGLY RE-EDITED AND RE-PRINTED IN THIS BOOK, ALONG WITH UPDATED NOTES AND RETROSPECTIVE STORIES BY THE PEOPLE MOST RESPONSIBLE FOR KEEPING BRUCE LEE'S MEMORY ALIVE - THE FANS.

AVAILABLE FROM **WWW.KUNGFUMONTHLY.UK & AMAZON**

THE WORLD FAMOUS MARKETPLACE

DON'T FORGET TO VISIT OUR WEBSITE FOR OTHER FANTASTIC ITEMS INCLUDING CLOTHING AND LIMITED EDITION SETS!

▶ BRUCE LEE KING OF KUNG FU

Written by Felix Dennis & Don Atyeo, Bruce Lee King of Kung Fu is the original and still one of the greatest books on Bruce Lee ever written. Packed with photos and essential information from the immediate year after Lee's tragic death, Bruce Lee King of Kung Fu provides the best of rock-solid backgrounds to the story of the man we all know and love.
170 PAGES

BUY ONLINE NOW!

amazon WHSmith Waterstones

OR VISIT OUR WEBSITE AT
WWW.KUNGFUMONTHLY.UK

KUNG-FU MONTHLY ▶ THE POSTER MAGAZINES

Volume One - No. 1 to 25, trade dummy plus an in-depth article on The History of Kung-Fu Monthly 1973 to 1979.
Volume Two - No. 26 to 55 plus interviews with former KFM staff.
Volume Three - No. 56 to 79, double-poster special edition issue plus an in-depth article on The History of Kung-Fu Monthly 1980 to 1984.
540-670 PAGES

▶ THE BOOK OF KUNG FU

The Book of Kung Fu was to be Kung-Fu Monthly's special annual issue, but was only published in 1974. Over one-hundred pages, many of them in colour, with a durable soft cover and scores of photographs, illustrations and articles. Don't miss this book! Bruce Lee, Angela Mao, David Carradine, Kung Fu Quiz, Comic Book and more - an incredible publication!
144 PAGES

THE SECRET ART OF ▶ BRUCE LEE

In 1976, the world took its first look at the now legendary Chester Maydole photographs. Arranged where possible, in 'fast-frame' action sequences, The Secret Art of Bruce Lee shows the founder of Jeet Kune Do, assisted by his friend and student Dan Inosanto, demonstrating the early development state of his art Jeet Kune Do during early days in Los Angeles.
110 PAGES

THE LOST KFM BOOK
FIRST TIME EVER IN THE UK!

◀ **THE WISDOM OF BRUCE LEE**

The Wisdom of Bruce Lee was to be one of the first books in the world to look at Bruce Lee's philosophy on life and martial arts. Mysteriously never released in the UK, The Wisdom of Bruce Lee is finally available to UK Bruce Lee fans after a wait of over forty years.
The full-length version includes a new introduction and interview with author Roger Hutchinson by Jun Fan Journal writer Andrew Staton, while the shorter abridged version is formatted in the style of the original Kung-Fu Monthly books.
70 PAGES / 170 PAGES

◀ **THE UNBEATABLE BRUCE LEE**

The Unbeatable Bruce Lee presents readers with a fighter's view of Bruce Lee the man and Bruce Lee the martial arts master. Beneath the sheer weight of known facts and figures that surround the tragically short life of Hong Kong's number one son, lies a strata of truth that only now is beginning to be picked.
112 PAGES

◀ **BRUCE LEE IN ACTION**

With Bruce Lee in Action, the Editors of Kung-Fu Monthly had compiled another fine addition to their library of Bruce Lee publications. Lavishly illustrated throughout with many previously unseen photographs at the time, this informative book investigates clearly and concisely, the birth and subsequent development of Lee's fighting style Jeet Kune Do, both on and off the screen.
106 PAGES

THE POWER OF ▶ BRUCE LEE

Bruce Lee was possibly the greatest exponent of the martial arts ever produced. The fact that he was a movie star often clouds his enormous contribution to the field. The Power of Bruce Lee explores many of his revolutionary methods of attack and defence, especially those relating to Jeet Kune Do, Lee's name for his own fighting system
110 PAGES

WHO KILLED ▶ BRUCE LEE?

Who Killed Bruce Lee? is a study of the pressures and the forces that, on the one hand were to elevate him to the highest plains of stardom and on the other, were to so tragically strike him down before his final fulfilment.
Who Killed Bruce Lee? was one of the first books to delve deep into the newspaper stories of Lee's early death.
108 PAGES

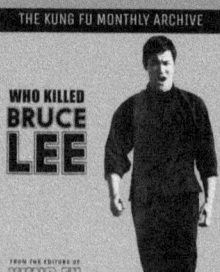

◀ THE GAME OF DEATH

This book combines two Kung-Fu Monthly special edition magazines released prior to Golden Harvest's 1978 film. Researched exclusively in Hong Kong, Kung-Fu Monthly reports on Lee's plot for Game of Death, the cast he intended to appear in the film, the scenes already filmed and Lee's hopes and expectations for the success of the project. Incredibly accurate for the time, this publication represents an important part of Bruce Lee fandom in the UK.
XXX PAGES

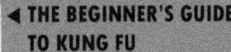

▶ THE BEGINNER'S GUIDE TO KUNG FU

Originally released in 1974, The Beginner's Guide to Kung Fu was the first martial arts book aimed primarily at the Kung Fu Craze generation. The graphic, easy to understand illustrations by Paul Simmons and the carefully conceived step by step instructions made this the perfect book for beginners who wished to take up Kung Fu.
XXX PAGES

▲ THE BRUCE LEE SCRAPBOOK

In 1974, Kung-Fu Monthly issued a Bruce Lee scrapbook in the form of a large A3 magazine, followed by a smaller A4 sized book in 1979. As part of the KFM Archive Series, both scrapbooks have been combined in a new chronological layout with brand new captions, location information and dates by Carl Fox and Jun Fan Journal writer Andrew Staton.
150 PAGES

THE KFM BRUCE LEE SOCIETY ▶

Long before the internet communities we know today, The Bruce Lee Society was the source of information in the United Kingdom for all things Bruce Lee. Now the history of the Bruce Lee Society is finally told in The Bruce Lee Society: A Retrospective Look at Bruce Lee Mania and the Kung Fu Craze of the 1970s. For the first time ever, all thirty issues of The Bruce Lee Society newsletters have been painstakingly re-edited and re-printed in this book, along with updated notes and retrospective stories by the people most responsible for keeping Bruce Lee's memory alive - the fans.
544 PAGES

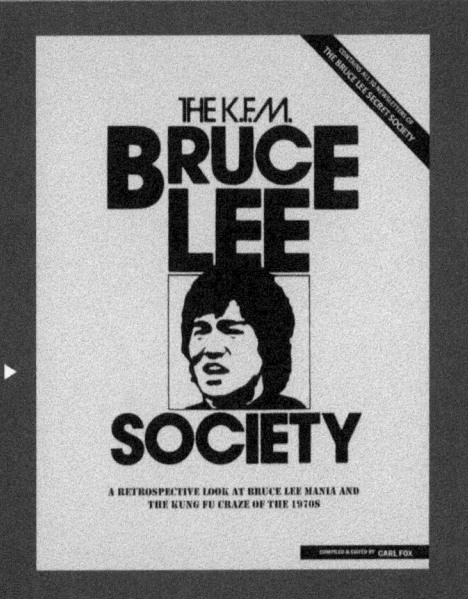

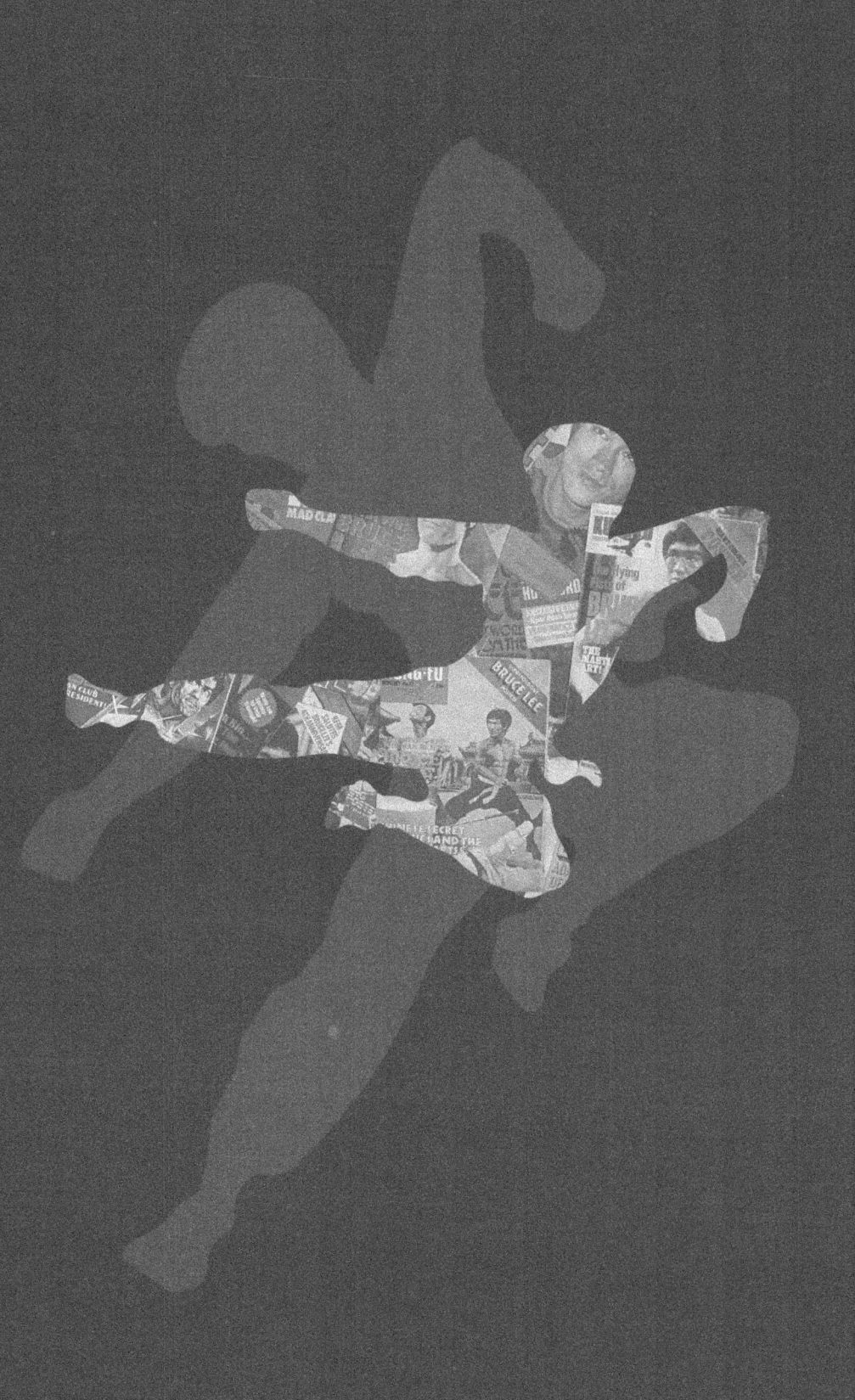

www.ingramcontent.com/pod-product-compliance
Lightning Source LLC
Chambersburg PA
CBHW041214130526
44590CB00061BA/4227